KAUFMAN FIELD GUIDE TO NATURE OF NEW ENGLAND

KENN KAUFMAN
AND
KIMBERLY KAUFMAN

with the collaboration of
ERIC R. EATON,
ERIC H. SNYDER,
KEN KEFFER,
AND JOHN SAWVEL

Illustrated with more than 2,000 images based on photos by the authors and other top photographers

HOUGHTON MIFFLIN HARCOURT
BOSTON NEW YORK
2012

www.hmhbooks.com

Library of Congress Cataloging-in-Publication Data is available.
ISBN 978-0-618-45697-0

Typefaces: Minion, Univers Condensed

Printed in China

SCP 10 9 8 7 6 5 4 3 2 1

CONTENTS

The main sections of this guide are marked with color tabs along the edges of the pages for quicker access.

Dedication

To Kenn, for making every day of my life
a celebration of love and discovery.
— Kimberly

To Kimberly, source of mystery and magic.
—Kenn

NATURAL NEW ENGLAND
A Note from Kenn Kaufman

The six states of New England, so rich in human history, are also abundantly blessed in terms of natural history. People who live there may take this natural treasure for granted or may sometimes fail to notice it, especially if they live in one of the region's larger cities. But everywhere in New England, even in the middle of those major cities, the diversity of living things is nothing short of astonishing.

Although I've never lived in New England, I visited for the first time at the age of 18 and have spent time there almost every year since. My early trips were all for birding, but before long, other things started to draw my attention: the wildflowers, the magnificent trees, the array of shells on the beach. As wonderful as the birds are, they are only part of the picture.

Once a person goes outdoors with senses attuned to nature, the sheer diversity of living things is both delightful and maddening, both reassuring and overwhelming. My wife Kimberly and I have discovered that over and over as we have explored New England at all seasons. If we try to look at everything in nature, we find so many things that we never get past the edge of the parking lot. If we go out determined to focus on only birds, inevitably we'll be distracted by some interesting flower or mushroom. If we go out with our day packs crammed with field guides to trees, ferns, and every other kind of plant, inevitably we'll run across some interesting frog or salamander, and we'll wish that we had the amphibians guide, too. I know that we will never get a firm grasp on the whole dizzying diversity of nature — there is just too much for a human lifetime, or a hundred lifetimes. But I also know that we will never be bored, always inspired.

This field guide is our attempt to share that inspiration with anyone fortunate enough to go outdoors in New England. I had coauthors on three previous Kaufman Field Guides, but it was a particular joy to work on this book with the person who shares my life and my last name. Kimberly and I met for the first time on a field trip, more than a decade ago, and discovered immediately that we shared the same kind of appreciation for everything in nature. That initial sense was affirmed countless times as we researched and compiled this book. Kim is currently executive director of the Black Swamp Bird Observatory, a midwestern organization with international reach, but before that she was their education director; one of her greatest skills is her ability to communicate the joys of nature to everyone. That ability illuminates every page of this book.

Despite the changes brought about in modern times, New England is still a wonderland of natural diversity, and every trip outdoors can be a magical treasure hunt. We hope that this guide will help you to launch your own explorations and discover your own treasures in nature.

HOW TO USE THIS BOOK

If you are already familiar with other books in the Kaufman Field Guides series, such as our guides to North American birds, butterflies, mammals, or insects, you should find it easy to pick up this volume and use it. But if you are new to the series or to field guides in general, a few words of introduction may be useful.

The plan of the book. It should be apparent that the guide is divided into sections, with each major section keyed to a different color tab along the edge of the pages, and this should make it easy to narrow down your choices when you're trying to identify something. If you see a squirrel, for example, you can turn immediately to the "Mammals" section. In some cases the boundaries between sections are vague, and we had to make arbitrary decisions — for example, is that a small shrub or a large wildflower? — so if in doubt, you may have to check more than one section. But most of the time, it should be easy to wind up in the right place.

Within each section, species are grouped by similarity. We arranged the wildflowers by color, but color is a poor way to classify most things. If you see a brown bird, for example, the color is not as important as noticing whether it's a duck, an owl, a hawk, a sparrow, or something else. So it's good to get in the habit of noticing shapes and markings of things, not just their colors. The introductory pages for many of the sections in this book include additional notes for ID of that particular group.

Range maps. For many groups of living things, we include range maps showing where each species is likely to be seen. It's always a good idea to glance at these to see what's expected in a given area. If you're in southern Connecticut, for example, you're unlikely to see a flower that's mapped as occurring only in Maine.

Regular map: darker shades of green indicate where the species is more common

Bird map: red for summer, blue for winter, purple for all seasons

Because many birds are migratory in New England and may be common at some seasons and absent at others, the color scheme for the birds' range maps is more complicated. It is explained in some detail on p. 186.

In the text, we often refer to the range of a species with a comment like "more common to the south" or "scarcer toward the west." In these cases, we are referring strictly to the occurrence in New England, although the point may also apply to the overall range of the species. In the interest of saving space, sometimes we say that a particular animal or plant is found "here," and that should be understood to mean "here in New England."

Scope of coverage. The number of species of living things in the New England states runs into the tens of thousands, and obviously we cannot begin to treat all of this variety in a compact field guide. Our intent has been to cover those things that people are most likely to notice, so we have exercised a bias toward the most conspicuous plants and animals. Of course, if you spend a lot of time exploring outdoors, you will find some things that are not in this guide. But this book should give you a good idea of what you are seeing the vast majority of the time.

We know many people who are strongly interested in a few aspects of nature but are at least mildly interested in everything else, and we hope that this guide will be useful for such people in a particular way — as a quick reference on those peripheral interests. If you are an expert botanist, for example, our treatment of plants may not tell you anything you don't already know, but the guide will still be handy for looking up turtles or bats or fish. If you are a keen birder, this guide may not have enough detail on birds to satisfy you, but you can carry it as a supplement to your favorite bird guide and use it to look up everything else.

Sizes. The size of a plant or animal is often a clue to its identity, but it's also a tricky thing to convey. This guide covers everything from whales and trees to tiny insects, and we try to give a general sense of the sizes of most things. For some small creatures, such as insects, we include a small silhouette of the actual size of one species on the page, an approach first used in our *Kaufman Field Guide to Butterflies* in 2003. For larger things, we generally give a measurement, either in the text or on the color plate.

Size is much more variable in some groups than in others. Considering trees, for example, the tallest specimens may be much larger than the average height. Fish may keep growing slowly throughout their lives, and anglers may occasionally pull up a fish that is much larger than average, even a record-sized individual. We have tried to convey the more typical or average sizes for most species, as a general guide to recognition, but you may run across individuals that are considerably larger or smaller than the measurements given in this book.

Names. Unless you've already studied some branch of natural history, you may be surprised to learn that not all species of living things have standardized or "official" names. Where standardized names do exist — for example, bird names recommended by the American Ornithologists' Union, or names on the official list of the Society for the Study of Amphibians and Reptiles — we have followed those authorities. In other cases, we've simply tried to use the names in most common usage. We follow most recent authorities in capitalizing the proper names of species. This helps provide clarity. For example, several kinds of trout may live in brooks, but if we write Brook Trout, we are referring to just one species. Many kinds of woodpeckers have red on the head, but if we write Red-headed Woodpecker, it's the name of a particular species.

GEOLOGY OF NEW ENGLAND

The foundation for everything in this region, literally, is the underlying structure of the earth's crust. Even though the basic bedrock is hidden from view in most areas — covered by soil and by entire habitats — it is still worthwhile to have an idea of what lies beneath the surface. This section presents a very brief overview of the history of New England's physical structure, followed by a guide to some of the most typical rocks and minerals of the region.

Coastal rocks at Hog Island, Maine

Geology section contributed by Eric H. Snyder

A QUICK GUIDE TO THE GEOLOGIC HISTORY OF NEW ENGLAND

The dominant landforms and rocks of New England were formed as a result of ongoing movements of Earth's outer crust over enormously long periods of time. The surface of the earth is a thin skin of brittle rock that is broken and fractured. It could be compared to the cracked shell of a hard-boiled egg. But unlike those pieces of eggshell, the pieces of the earth's outer crust — called tectonic plates — are continually sliding past one another, pulling apart, or colliding.

A little over one billion years ago,[*] as the first multicellular organisms began to appear on Earth, New England consisted of what is now the very western edge of Massachusetts, Vermont, and northern Maine. Since that time New England has grown as a result of tectonic plate collisions that occurred over millions of years. Each collision pushed up mountains, created volcanoes, or added land by scraping sediments off the surface of plates as they plunged beneath the North American plate.

The earliest event from which the effects still may be seen in New England was the Grenville collision, occurring 1.3–1.1 billion years ago. The heat and pressure from this collision process created a high mountain range of metamorphic rock. Remnants of these mountains remain as metamorphic gneisses throughout the Green Mountains of southern Vermont and the Berkshire Hills of western Massachusetts. Subsequently, 500 million years of minimal tectonic activity passed in New England as the mountains of the Grenville event slowly eroded.

About 650 million years ago, while most life was still microscopic, a rift opened along the New England coast and an ocean began to form in the depression between the two separating plates. While this ocean grew, New England was stable but largely covered by water. Being submerged allowed for the deposition and buildup of much sediment, which later formed into shales, sandstones, and limestones. Some of these rocks still remain as part of the Vermont Valley and Champlain Lowlands.

Approximately 450 million years ago, as the first green plants appeared on land, the crust movement changed and the newly formed ocean floor began to plunge beneath the North American plate. Lines of volcanic islands and dark muddy sediments scraped from the ocean crust compressed onto the side of North America. These deposits and many other rocks of New England were metamorphosed under the extreme heat and pressure of this impacting. The ocean continued closing and eventually, 375 million years ago, the European and African continents of the far shore collided with North America. Himalayan-scale mountains rose up and much of New England was faulted, folded, or metamorphosed again. The combining of all of these landmasses created the immense supercontinent called Pangaea.

As the age of dinosaurs began some 200 million years ago, the continents forming Pangaea began to separate along what is now the eastern shore of New England. This movement is still occurring as Europe and Africa slowly drift away from North America, allowing new ocean floor to form along a spreading fault in the center of the Atlantic Ocean.

Although often covered by soils, what generally remains in New England are bands of metamorphic and igneous rock trending southwest to northeast. Evidence of these bands can be seen in the bedrock map on the following page.

---

[*] *All dates are approximate and based on current scientific theory.*

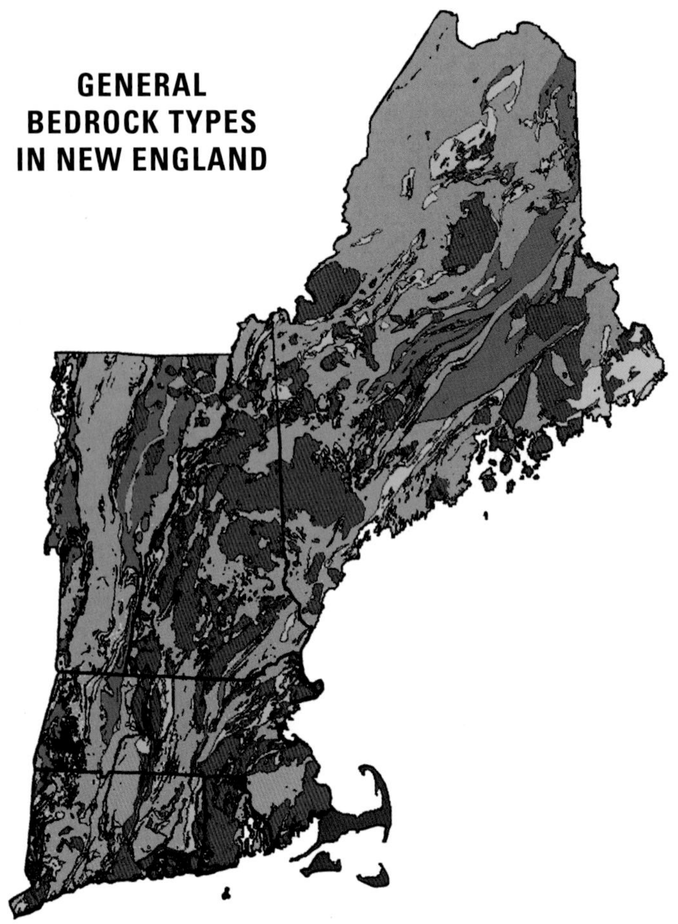

METAMORPHIC ROCKS

LIGHT IGNEOUS GRANITE ROCKS
DARK IGNEOUS (MAFIC) ROCKS

LIMESTONE-TYPE ROCKS
OTHER SEDIMENTARY ROCKS

LOOSE GLACIAL DEPOSITS

GLACIATION IN NEW ENGLAND

Although tectonic collisions created, folded, and changed the rocks of New England, a series of events that ended only 12,000 years ago has ultimately shaped our modern landscape.

For millennia, New England was covered by a slow-moving sheet of ice. More than a mile thick in most places, it scoured the landscape and left evidence of its presence across the entirety of New England. Sediments ranging from silt and clay to large boulders were incorporated into the ice and were borne southward. As the ice melted, these sediments were dropped along the way and were often piled along the southern limit of the ice. Today, these long ridges of mixed-size glacial sediments called moraines are found throughout New England. Some of the largest and most visible of these glacial deposits are Cape Cod, Nantucket Island, and Long Island.

Smaller land forms that remain from the glaciers are called drumlins. These are hills elongated in the direction of past ice flow, and many can be found throughout New England, with an especially great abundance in southern New Hampshire and eastern Massachusetts. Look for evidence of New England's icy past in the form of polished, scratched, or gouged surfaces on exposed bedrock. Striations, as these gouges are called, usually trend north to south, reflecting the dominant direction of ice flow.

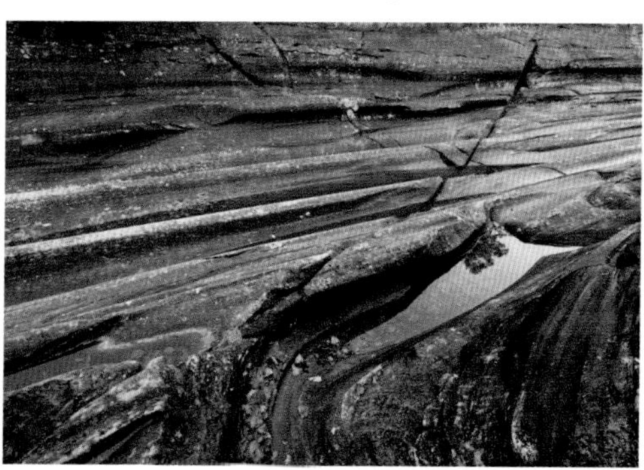

Striations or "glacial grooves" in bedrock

Large boulders that seem out of place with their surroundings are a common sight in New England, a reminder that the ice was fully capable of displacing rocks of almost any size by hundreds of miles. With this in mind, compare loose rocks with the local bedrock before using them to draw conclusions about local geologic history.

GUIDE TO ROCKS AND MINERALS

TIPS FOR CLASSIFYING AND IDENTIFYING ROCKS

With a little practice, rock identification is a fun way to learn geology and provide context to local natural systems. Rocks often fall along the broad spectrum between easily definable types, which can make identification difficult. To give yourself the best chance of identifying a rock, clean it thoroughly or break off a piece to obtain a fresh surface to study. Remember, some lichens, algae, and chemical weathering can change the color or texture of a rock surface, complicating identification. A small hand lens may be both fun and helpful when looking at rocks and their constituent minerals.

The source and context of a rock can help in both its identification and interpretation of local geologic history, so when possible, try to identify a rock from an outcropping of bedrock such as at a cliff or a road cut. As a result of glacial movements, weathering, and human activities, small rocks on the ground or a beach may not be representative of the underlying rocks of the region.

SOME COMMON MINERALS IN NEW ENGLAND ROCKS

Minerals are materials that have a distinct chemical composition and structure. They can be thought of as the ingredients that compose a rock. If you see a crystal alone or as part of a rock, you are looking at a mineral. Different rocks have different recipes based on what minerals are present, the proportions in which they occur, and how large the individual mineral crystals are. Mineral crystals are sometimes large and easy to see in a rock but are often too small to be seen with the naked eye.

Quartz often looks glassy and may come in many colors, including white, clear, and milky gray. When broken it does not break into sheets but will leave a curved surface. Quartz is very hard and often will remain after other minerals have been broken down and washed away. Most sand beaches are predominantly very small grains of quartz.

Some examples of quartz

Feldspar is a very common mineral, but it often breaks down into microscopic pieces to form the major ingredient in clays and other fine sediments. Feldspar comes in two major types. Orthoclase is usually pink or whitish gray and plagioclase is chalk white or yellowy gray.

Two examples of feldspar, with orthoclase on the left and plagioclase on the right

Mica, when present as small crystals, may give a rock a sparkling shimmer, while large crystals are fun to flake into very thin translucent sheets. Because of this property, large sheets of it were used for windows and viewing ports in furnaces and ovens. Mica comes in two major forms: biotite is dark olive green to black and muscovite is silvery white to clear.

Two examples of mica, with biotite on the left and muscovite on the right

Pyroxenes and Amphiboles can be difficult to distinguish in the field. Rarely found in sedimentary rocks, both may appear in igneous and metamorphic rocks, often found as long, slender, green or black crystals.

A GUIDE TO SOME COMMON ROCKS OF NEW ENGLAND

Rocks can be classified into three general types — igneous, metamorphic, or sedimentary — depending on how they were formed.

1. IGNEOUS ROCKS

All igneous rocks were once molten material that cooled and solidified. Rocks that cooled inside the earth usually have large mineral crystals that can be seen with the naked eye. This pattern occurs because magma inside the earth cools slowly, insulated by the rocks above it, giving the individual elements of the magma time to arrange and grow into crystals before they are locked in place. By contrast, volcanic rocks, which cool quickly on the earth's surface, often look more uniform in texture. A second major distinction of igneous rocks is whether they are light or dark in color. Light rocks are called felsic and contain more silica. These rocks make up most of the continental crust. The heavier and darker mafic rocks make up most of the ocean crust and contain more iron and magnesium. Igneous rocks usually have no banding or layering. This diagram may help you to visualize the four igneous rocks presented here according to color and mineral grain size.

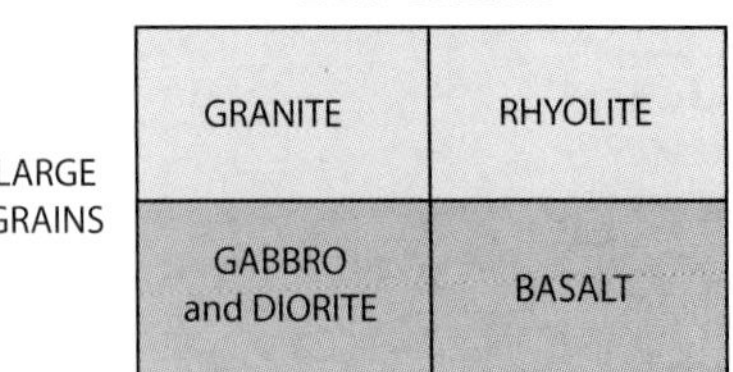

Granite

Granite usually has an overall light color, with crystal grains large enough to be seen without magnification. It may look whitish, pink, yellow, or gray and often will have specks of dark minerals throughout. Constituent minerals include quartz, feldspar, and mica. Granite is a common bedrock in New Hampshire, Rhode Island, scattered throughout Maine, north-central Vermont, eastern coastal Connecticut, and eastern Massachusetts except Cape Cod.

Rhyolite is often a gray, yellowish, or whitish rock and has very small crystals that often cannot be seen without magnification. Rhyolite is usually suggestive of volcanism and is similar in composition to granite but has cooled too quickly to allow the growth of large crystals. Rhyolite is very rare in New England.

Rhyolite

Gabbro

Gabbro and diorite are coarse-grained rocks that texturally may resemble granite but are dark (mafic) in color. They have almost no quartz but have high feldspar content. Gabbros have more pyroxenes, while diorite has more amphiboles.

Basalt is a fine-grained dark rock. Individual mineral crystals are usually too small to distinguish. Along with gabbro and diorite, basalt occurs as bedrock in eastern Connecticut, extending north past Boston. Pockets also occur in central Massachusetts, on the border between Vermont and New Hampshire, and in a number of locations in Maine including north central, the east coast, and a stretch from Portland to Augusta.

Basalt

2. METAMORPHIC ROCKS

These are the rocks that have been subjected to enough heat and pressure to transform their structure into a new type of rock. Any rock may be metamorphosed, and depending on the amount of heat and pressure, they will fall on a spectrum between low grade (little change) and high grade (highly changed). The lower-grade metamorphic rocks presented in this guide will generally have smaller grains and will break into sheets more easily than the higher-grade, larger-grained metamorphic rocks. Because of the tectonically active past of this region, metamorphic rocks are ubiquitous throughout New England. Locations with less metamorphic bedrock include Rhode Island and southeastern Massachusetts.

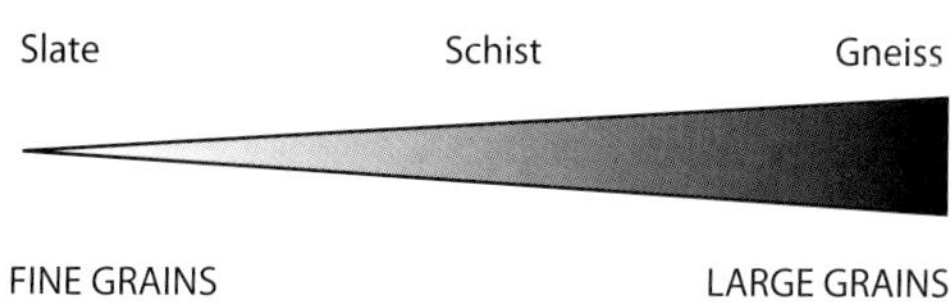

Slate is a low-grade metamorphic rock, generally gray to black, derived from shale or mudstone. Slate has a tendency to split into thin sheets. Individual minerals are generally not visible.

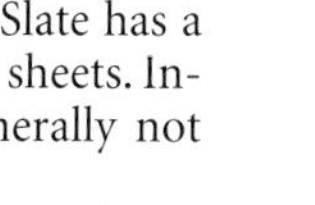

Slate

Schist is more highly metamorphosed than slate, allowing individual minerals to be seen. Schist will generally break into thick sheets, and flat minerals such as micas will be aligned with the rock structure. Schists come in many colors from light gray to almost black and are commonly derived from slates, sandstones, or fine-grained igneous rocks. Many schists will sparkle as a result of high mica content.

Schist

Gneiss

Gneiss (pronounced like "nice") is a highly metamorphosed rock that shows distinct banding of large crystals but usually will not break easily along the banding planes. With high enough heat and pressure gneiss may be formed from many different rocks of all categories and thus color varies widely. Gneisses will almost always contain feldspar, quartz, and biotite.

3. SEDIMENTARY ROCKS

Sedimentary rocks represent the dominant rock form covering the earth, although they are not as common in New England as in some regions. Sedimentary rocks can form when pieces of other rocks have been compacted into a new rock, or they may be chemically deposited out of a liquid. Look for sedimentary bedrocks in central Connecticut extending into Massachusetts, and eastern Rhode Island extending into Massachusetts. Grain size is a major factor in the classification of sedimentary rocks. The following diagram charts the relative grain sizes of the sedimentary rocks presented in this guide.

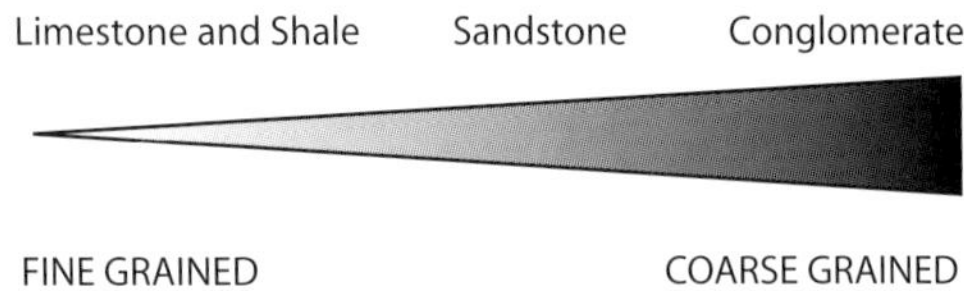

Shales are the most commonly exposed type of sedimentary rock and are very fine grained, often with a layered structure. They may come in many colors, including gray, red, and brown. Shales are the consolidated remains of ancient mud and clay deposits, which makes them a great place to look for fossils.

Shale

Sandstones are the solidified remains of beaches or other sand deposits and thus will likely have a gritty texture similar to sandpaper. Sandstones appear in a wide range of colors. Some banding may be present in these rocks, suggesting changes in the environment and/or the source of the sand as it was deposited.

Sandstone
(two examples)

Conglomerate

Conglomerates usually are mixtures of rounded chunks of rocks and minerals cemented together by a finer-grained material similar to sandstone or shale. These rocks form when streambeds, riverbeds, or pebble beaches become solidified.

Limestone is created when chemicals in water precipitate out and form a rock. Usually limestone is very fine grained, white or yellowish in color, and has the distinction that it will fizz when in contact with a dilute acid, such as vinegar. Shell fragments or the impressions of shells may often be found in limestone. Limestone and similar rocks may be found as bedrock in central Maine, eastern and western New Hampshire, and in some areas of western Massachusetts.

Limestone

Small fossils
in a base
of limestone

WEATHER AND CLIMATE

These two terms are related but different. "Weather" refers to the atmospheric conditions of the moment: things like temperature, humidity, wind speed and direction, cloud cover, and precipitation. Weather can change by the moment (and often does!). "Climate" represents the long-term average of weather conditions at all seasons at a particular location. Climate can change, too, but this usually happens very gradually, over long periods. To make the most of experiences with nature in New England, we need to be aware of both climate and weather.

Climate of a local area has a major impact on what plants and animals can live there.

As a part of climate, temperature can be measured in various ways, including normal maximum and minimum temperatures, average temperature by month or season, and average number of frost-free days per year. In general, temperatures in New England are colder toward the north and west, warmer toward the southeast. These maps show average temperatures for January and July (data from 1971 to 2000).

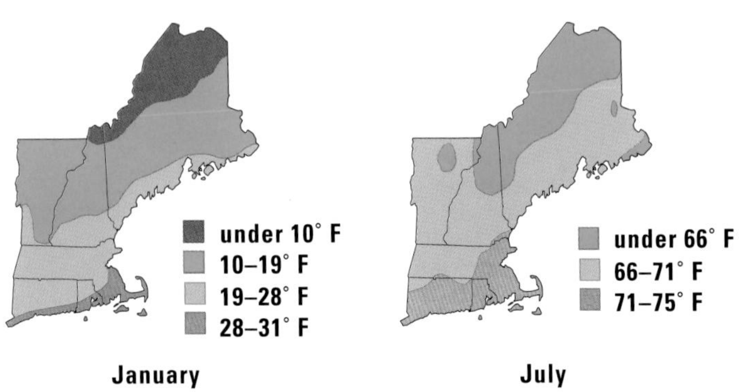

January

July

Aside from temperatures being colder toward the north and warmer toward the south, the ocean has a complex effect on readings near the coast. An additional point (one that doesn't show up well at the scale of these maps) is the way that temperature changes with elevation. As we go up in elevation, the air becomes cooler. The exact rate of change will vary, depending on other factors such as humidity and barometric pressure; but in general, the temperature will drop by between 3.3 and 5.4 degrees Fahrenheit for every 1,000 feet of climb. Thus, if we go to the highest point in New England — the top of Mount Washington, New Hampshire, at 6,288 feet above sea level — we could expect the air there to be about 17 to 28 degrees colder than in nearby lowland areas, which lie at only about 1,000 feet above sea level. Similar but less extreme changes in temperature can be expected in other mountainous areas of New England.

Weather affects everything we do outdoors. Despite the vast number of variables involved, science continues to give us better predictions of weather (and more ways to receive those predictions). It's sensible to take advantage of this and check the forecast before we head outside.

Earth's atmosphere is constantly in motion, like a giant, fluid machine of great complexity. The sun provides the energy to drive this machine. As air is heated by the sun in equatorial regions, it rises and begins flowing toward the poles; in polar regions the air cools, sinks, and begins flowing back toward the tropics. The rotation of the earth puts a spin on these simple air currents, turning them into prevailing westerly or easterly winds, depending on latitude. The water cycle — evaporation, condensation, precipitation — adds to the complexity. Warm air can hold more moisture than cold air, so water vapor will rise with warm air and then condense into clouds as it cools, eventually falling again as rain or snow.

At the latitude of New England, the major weather patterns generally move from west to east. Most changes in weather take place along fronts, which are the boundaries between masses of warm air and masses of cold air. Because cold air is denser than warm air, cold fronts tend to arrive with more force, often sweeping in rapidly from the north or west, while warm fronts may move in more gently from the southwest. The passage of a front almost always is marked by a change in wind direction.

Areas of high pressure and low pressure form along the boundaries between air masses, and these highs and lows bring their own distinctive weather. A high-pressure system is usually marked by fair weather, while a low may bring clouds and stormy weather. In the northern hemisphere, winds move in a clockwise direction around a high, counterclockwise around a low (as viewed from above). When a strong low-pressure area is positioned just east of the New England coast, this counterclockwise flow creates strong northeast winds, producing the classic "Nor'easter."

With the detailed weather information available today, naturalists and others who spend time outdoors can more easily see the connection between local weather and large-scale patterns.

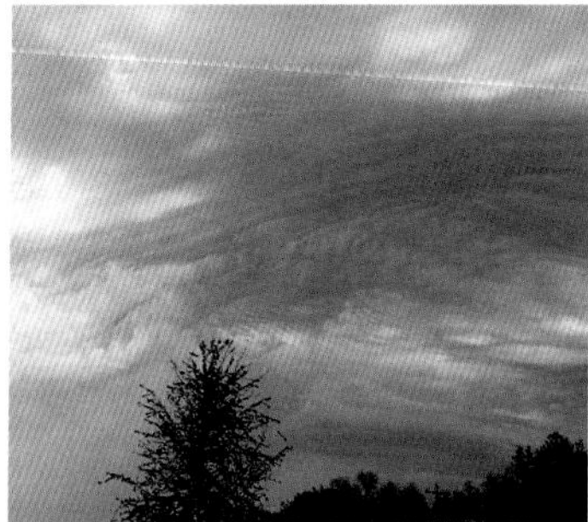

Intense swirling patterns in dark clouds can reflect dangerous storm conditions.

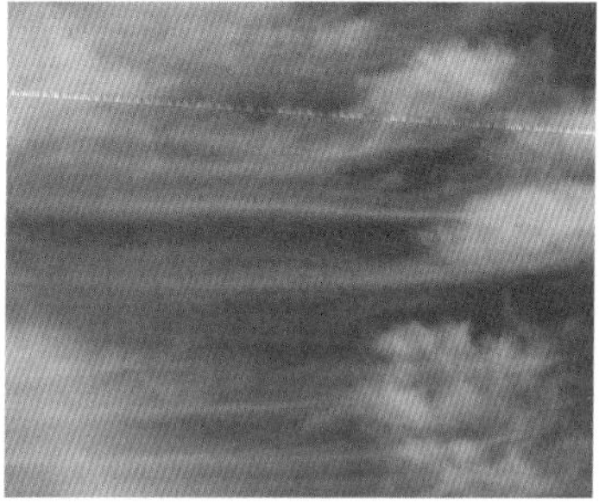

Cirrus clouds are thin, very high; may precede storms in winter but usually occur during fine weather in summer.

WONDERS OF THE NIGHT SKY

Most of this field guide is focused on small wonders near at hand in New England, so it might seem out of place to include a section on immense objects in the vastness of outer space. But campouts or night hikes in wilder parts of New England become more fascinating if we can recognize some of the stars and planets and know something about them.

For best viewing of the night sky, get as far away as you can from cities and other bright light sources on a clear night with low humidity. You'll be able to see more stars if the moon is not too bright, but ironically, it may be easier to begin learning about stars on the nights when you can't see quite so many: if the faint ones are out of sight, it can be simpler to make out patterns from the brighter stars that are still visible.

Constellations. These patterns of stars in the sky have been recognized by many cultures back to ancient times. Constellations are not "real" — these apparent groupings are not necessarily close to each other in space. For example, the brightest star in Lyra is 30 times closer to Earth than it is to some other stars in the same constellation. The stars just look close together when viewed from our vantage point. Still, these star patterns have their own beauty and importance. Small birds migrating at night use them for navigation, and for centuries human travelers did the same. Even if we don't often need them to find our way today, knowing constellations can add to our enjoyment of the night sky as it changes with the seasons.

Learning to recognize constellations. On the next eight pages we present a series of sky charts showing the relative positions of major constellations late in the evening — after dark but before midnight — in the middle of each season. As the earth rotates, stars appear to rise in the east and set in the west throughout the night. So if you stay out very late at night, you'll see constellations shown on the charts for other seasons.

A small, flat chart in a book can hardly represent the immense dome of the night sky. Our diagrams are mere caricatures of the real constellations, and it may take some practice to be able to make the translation from these little drawings to the patterns that you see in the sky. We suggest you start with some really distinctive constellations, such as Orion, Scorpius, or the Big Dipper, to see how their reality compares with the diagrams. Then work your way out to more obscure ones, using their locations relative to the ones that you already know.

Names of constellations and stars. Ancient civilizations looked at patterns of stars in the night sky, connected groups of stars with imaginary lines, and gave names and mythological meaning to the figures created in that way. Many of the names still in use today originated millennia ago in the Mediterranean world, which is why we still have constellations honoring Greek and Roman mythological characters. Today the names are standardized by the International Astronomical Union and are used to designate particular regions of the sky, not just the star groups themselves.

A few dozen bright stars have common names, such as Antares (in Scorpius) and Betelgeuse (in Orion), based on their ancient Greek or Arabic names. We label and discuss a few of these on pp. 30–35. In addition, however, thousands of stars are named in more formalized systems using either numbers or Greek letters and some version of the constellation names.

Brightness of stars. Some stars in the night sky look obviously brighter than others. This apparent brightness — caused by a combination of the star's actual properties and its distance from Earth — is referred to as the magnitude of the star. Over 2,000 years ago, the Greek astronomer Hipparchus classified stars into six groups, with the brightest in the first group and the faintest visible ones in the sixth. Modern instruments make it possible to measure magnitude with great precision. For example, Arcturus is magnitude –0.04, while Polaris (the North Star) is magnitude 2.0. The higher the number, the fainter the star. On our diagrams, we use larger spots for the brighter stars to give a general idea of how things look.

Stars vs. planets. Ancient stargazers, watching the heavens night after night, noticed that stars stayed in the same positions relative to each other but planets roamed across the sky, moving from one constellation to another over periods of months. If you look at the night sky only occasionally, it's harder to pick out the differences. We discuss all the visible planets on pp. 36–37, but for a rule of thumb, stars twinkle and planets don't! That sounds unscientific, but the reflected light from planets within our own solar system is less prone to being shifted by Earth's atmosphere than the points of light emanating from stars that are vastly farther away.

The Milky Way. On a clear night, with a good view of the sky and no distracting artificial light or moonlight, we can see a hazy, irregular band of brightness stretching all the way across the sky. This is our own galaxy, seen edge-on, from our position within it. Our galaxy is thought to be in the shape of a wide, flat spiral, containing a few hundred billion stars, and our sun is thought to be closer to the outer edge of the galaxy than to its center. Looking through the galaxy over the immense distances of space, these billions of stars seem to blend into a bright haze. We show the position of the Milky Way on the sky charts on the following pages, even though it won't be visible when viewing conditions are less than ideal.

Observing the night sky. A good astronomical telescope for viewing deep-space objects may have an astronomical price, but almost everything that we discuss in this field guide can be seen with the unaided eye on a clear night. Good binoculars will reveal even more, such as details on the surface of our moon, or the positions of the moons of Jupiter (see p. 37). A spotting scope purchased for birding or observing other wildlife can also be very useful for seeing details in the night sky. So don't assume that you need a giant telescope to make worthwhile observations.

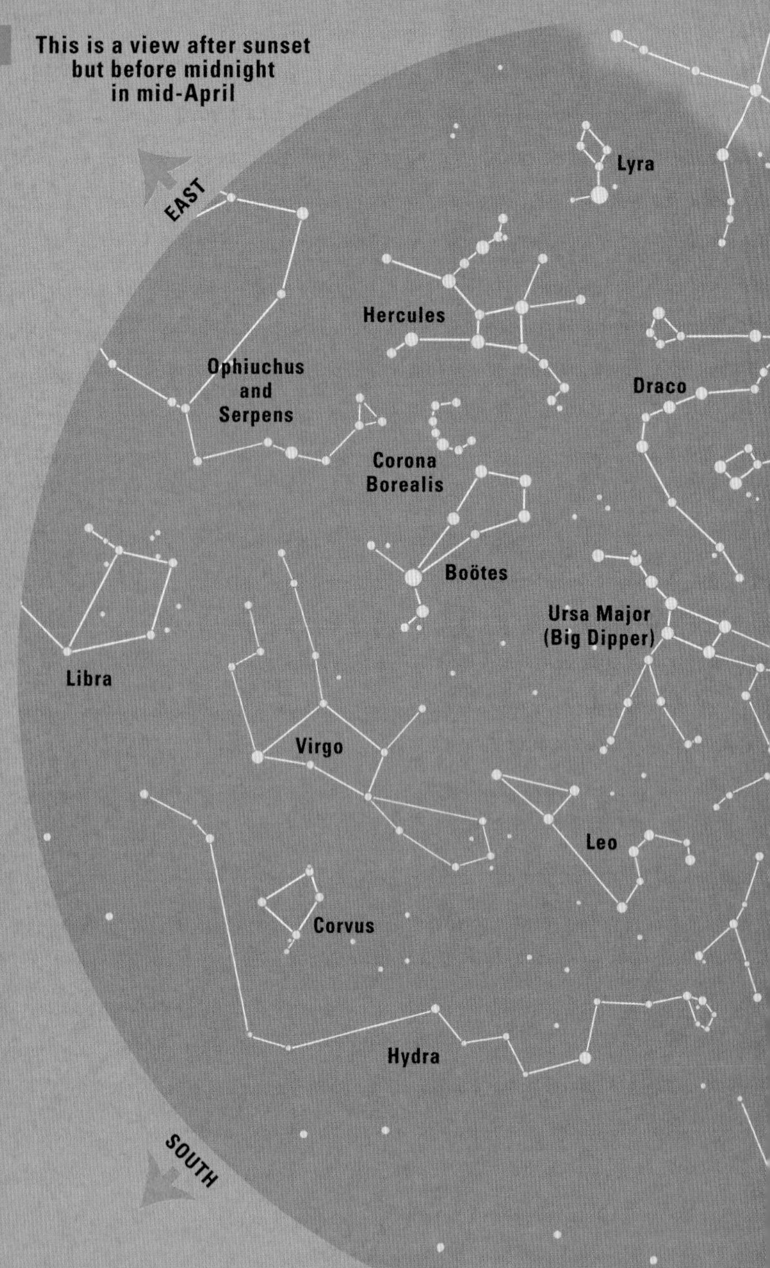
This is a view after sunset
but before midnight
in mid-April
EAST
SOUTH
Lyra
Hercules
Ophiuchus
and
Serpens
Draco
Corona
Borealis
Boötes
Ursa Major
(Big Dipper)
Libra
Virgo
Leo
Corvus
Hydra

SPRING CONSTELLATIONS

As seen over central New England

The pale band across the sky is the Milky Way

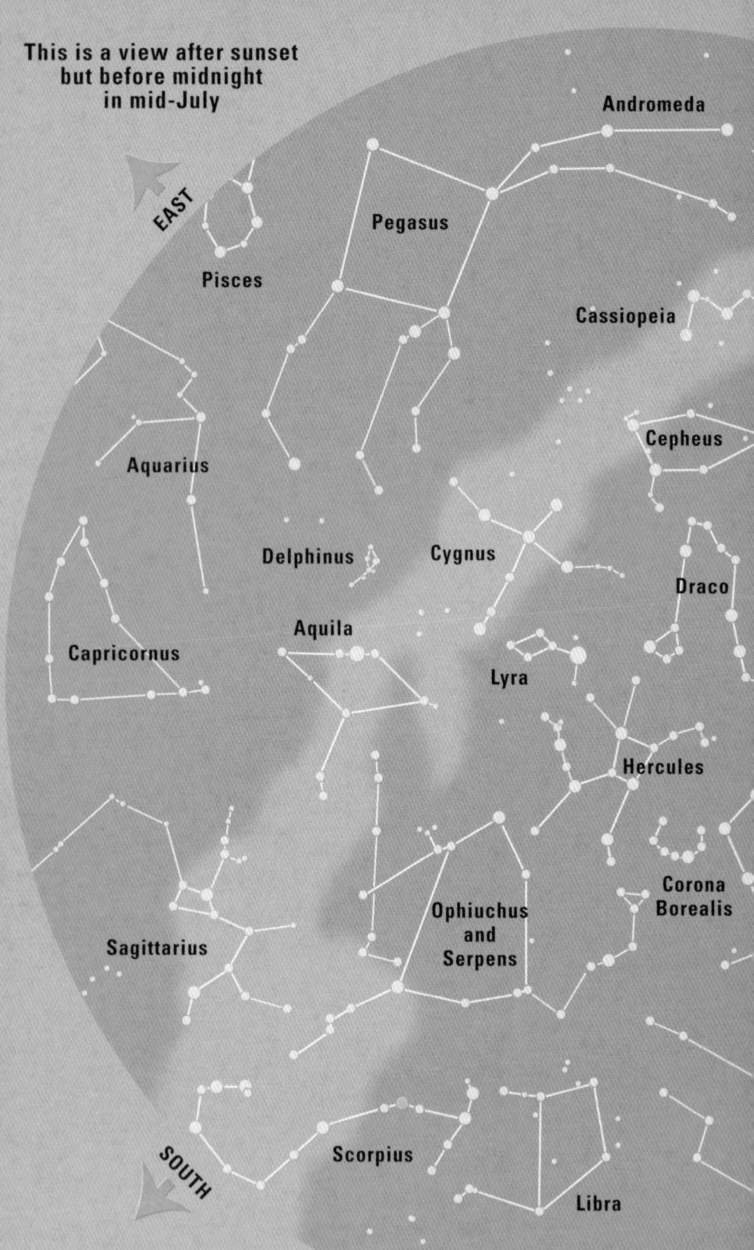
This is a view after sunset
but before midnight
in mid-July
EAST
SOUTH
Andromeda
Pegasus
Pisces
Cassiopeia
Aquarius
Cepheus
Delphinus
Cygnus
Draco
Capricornus
Aquila
Lyra
Hercules
Sagittarius
Ophiuchus
and
Serpens
Corona
Borealis
Scorpius
Libra

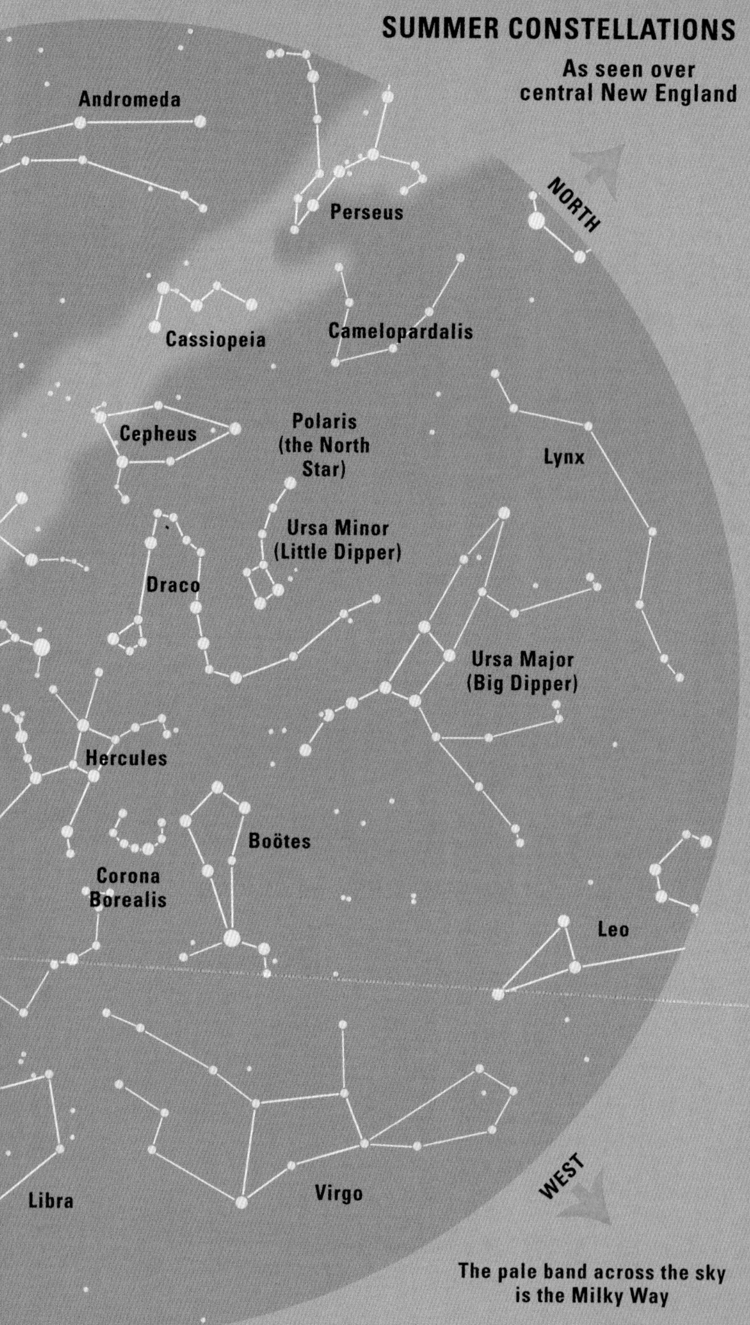
SUMMER CONSTELLATIONS
As seen over central New England
Andromeda
Perseus
NORTH
Cassiopeia
Camelopardalis
Cepheus
Polaris (the North Star)
Lynx
Ursa Minor (Little Dipper)
Draco
Ursa Major (Big Dipper)
Hercules
Boötes
Corona Borealis
Leo
Libra
Virgo
WEST
The pale band across the sky is the Milky Way

This is a view after sunset
but before midnight
in mid-January

EAST

Leo

Ursa Major
(Big Dipper)

Hydra

Cancer

Lynx

Canis
Minor

Gemini

Auriga

Monoceros

Orion

Canis
Major

Taurus

Lepus

Columba

Eridanus

SOUTH

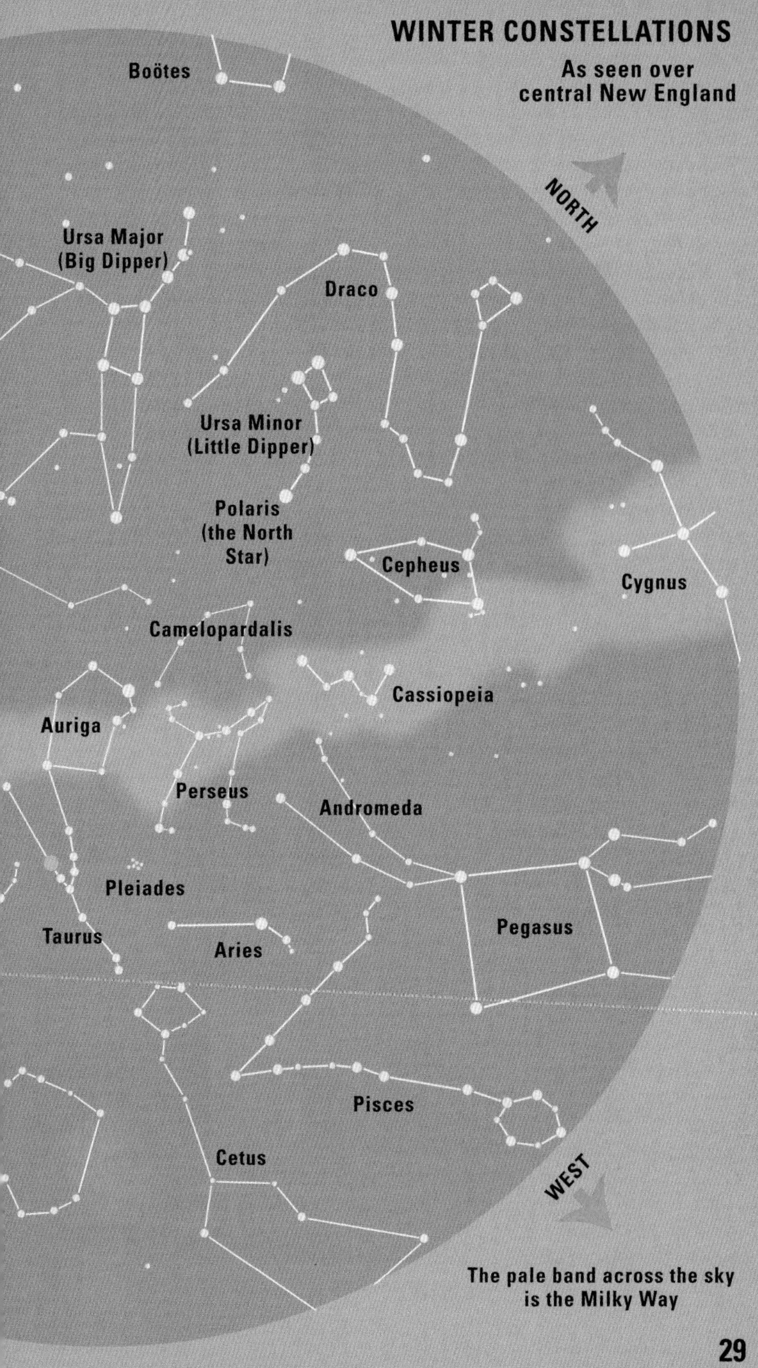
WINTER CONSTELLATIONS
As seen over central New England
NORTH
WEST
Boötes
Ursa Major (Big Dipper)
Draco
Ursa Minor (Little Dipper)
Polaris (the North Star)
Cepheus
Cygnus
Camelopardalis
Cassiopeia
Auriga
Perseus
Andromeda
Pleiades
Taurus
Aries
Pegasus
Pisces
Cetus
The pale band across the sky is the Milky Way

CONSTELLATIONS OF THE ZODIAC

The orbit of the moon around the earth, and the orbits of the earth and the other major planets around the sun, all lie on about the same plane. From our perspective on Earth, that means the sun, moon, and visible planets all seem to follow approximately the same path across the sky. More than 2,000 years ago, stargazers divided this path into 12 sections and named the major constellation in each, designating these as the signs of the zodiac. Periods of the year were identified by the position of the sun within the zodiac. For example, the sun was in Aquarius from about January 20 to February 18 (of course, Aquarius itself was not visible during that period, since it was in the sky during the daytime). Because of shifts in the earth's position in space, the sun now enters Aquarius almost a month later, but most astrological charts ignore the reality of the sky.

In ages past, astronomy (study of stars and other objects in space) and astrology (predicting the future based on stars) shared much of the same knowledge. Today astrology is a holdover of superstition from an earlier time. But the constellations of the zodiac are still worth recognizing.

Capricornus (the goat) contains no bright stars and is not conspicuous. Low in the south in summer and fall, it is most easily found by reference to other, more distinctive constellations. The same is true of **Aquarius** (the water bearer). **Pisces** (the fish) is visible during the first part of the night mainly in fall and winter. It may be found most readily by the oval of stars at the "head" of the fish and by its proximity to the "square" of the constellation Pegasus. **Aries** (the ram) is made up mainly of four stars, none very bright. **Taurus** (the bull), conspicuous during the early part of the night in fall and winter, is easily recognized by its sideways V anchored by the bright star Aldebaran. This star is so bright that its orange-red color can be seen. Associated with Taurus is the star cluster of the Pleiades, sometimes called the "seven sisters," although only six stars are visible to the naked eye; many more can be seen through binoculars or a telescope. **Gemini** (the twins), rising late at night in fall and easily located near Orion in winter and early spring, features the twin bright stars of Castor and Pollux. **Cancer** (the crab) is an inconspicuous group of relatively faint stars, most easily located by its position between Gemini and Leo. **Leo** (the lion), noticeable in spring and early summer, is known by its bright stars forming patterns of a sickle and a narrow triangle; at the base of the sickle is the bright star Regulus. **Virgo** (the virgin) extends over a large area of the sky, but most of its stars are fairly faint; its one bright star, Spica, seems isolated in the sky. Virgo is most easily located by its position below the diamond shape of Boötes in spring and summer. **Libra** (the scales) is another constellation without bright stars or a strong pattern, easiest to find in summer by its proximity to Scorpius. **Scorpius** (the scorpion), a dominant feature of the southern sky in summer, has a well-defined pattern — it almost suggests a scorpion! — and bright stars, featuring the reddish orange Antares. **Sagittarius** (the archer) is a sprawling constellation of summer, most easily located by its position near Scorpius. See the star charts on preceding pages for help in finding all of these constellations.

CONSTELLATIONS OF THE ZODIAC

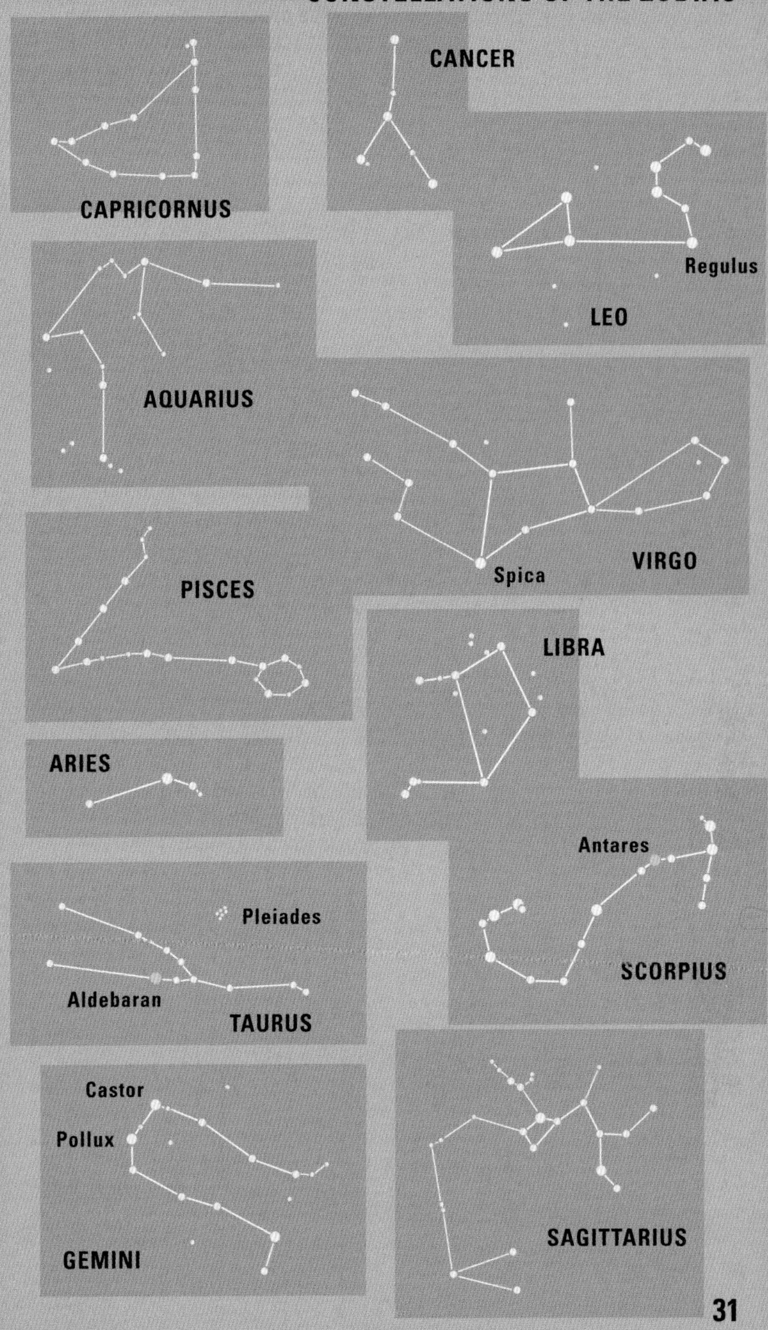

CONSTELLATIONS NEAR THE NORTH STAR

The earth's axis points almost directly at Polaris, the North Star. If you were standing at the North Pole and looking up, Polaris would be straight overhead. Because of this, as the earth spins on its axis, Polaris appears to stay in one place in the northern sky and all the other stars and constellations appear to rotate around it. From the latitude of New England, Polaris is always fairly high in the northern sky. Constellations close to it are visible on clear nights at all times of year, although their positions change during the course of each night and each season. So you can practice finding and recognizing these constellations all year.

Once you've learned a few constellations, you can find others by reference to them. Even though the constellations appear to move around the sky, their positions relative to each other remain the same. Study the star charts on pp. 22–29 to see relative positions. The Big Dipper is a good place to start, because it's easily recognized and because it has pointers to other prominent stars.

The **Big Dipper** is only part of Ursa Major, but it's better known than the constellation as a whole. If you take the two outer stars of the "dipper" portion and extend an imaginary line outward, this line will lead you almost directly to Polaris. By extending an imaginary line somewhat farther from the tip of the "handle," you'll come to Arcturus, the bright star at the base of Boötes (p. 34), a prominent constellation of spring and summer.

Ursa Major is the official name of the constellation that includes the Big Dipper. The name means "great bear," and apparently several different cultures in ancient times saw a bear in this star pattern, though seemingly a rather funky, long-tailed bear. The middle star of the "tail" (or "handle") appears to have a faint companion, another star that is really much farther away from us in space, visible only with sharp eyes (or optical help). **Ursa Minor** (the little bear) is better known as the Little Dipper. Two moderately bright stars form the outer edge of the "dipper," but the rest of the constellation is less noticeable, except for the "handle's" end at Polaris.

Cassiopeia (the queen) circles the North Star on roughly the opposite side from Ursa Major and Ursa Minor. Shaped like a distorted M or W, depending on position, it is easily recognized. Cassiopeia also lies in a relatively bright part of the Milky Way (see p. 21). **Cepheus** (the king) has a less distinctive pattern and is most easily picked out by its position between Cassiopeia and Draco (see the seasonal sky charts).

The long, straggling **Draco** (the dragon) starts off between Ursa Major and Ursa Minor, wraps around Ursa Minor, and then loops away from the North Star, with the "head" of the dragon out near Cygnus (see sky charts and p. 34). **Perseus** (the hero) circles the North Star opposite Ursa Minor and a little farther out than Cassiopeia. The Perseid meteor shower in August (see p. 37) appears to radiate from this constellation. **Auriga** (the charioteer), as usually depicted, includes one star that is shared by Taurus (p. 30). Auriga can be recognized by its proximity to Taurus and Perseus, and by its inclusion of Capella, the sixth-brightest star in the sky. Both Perseus and Auriga lie along the Milky Way.

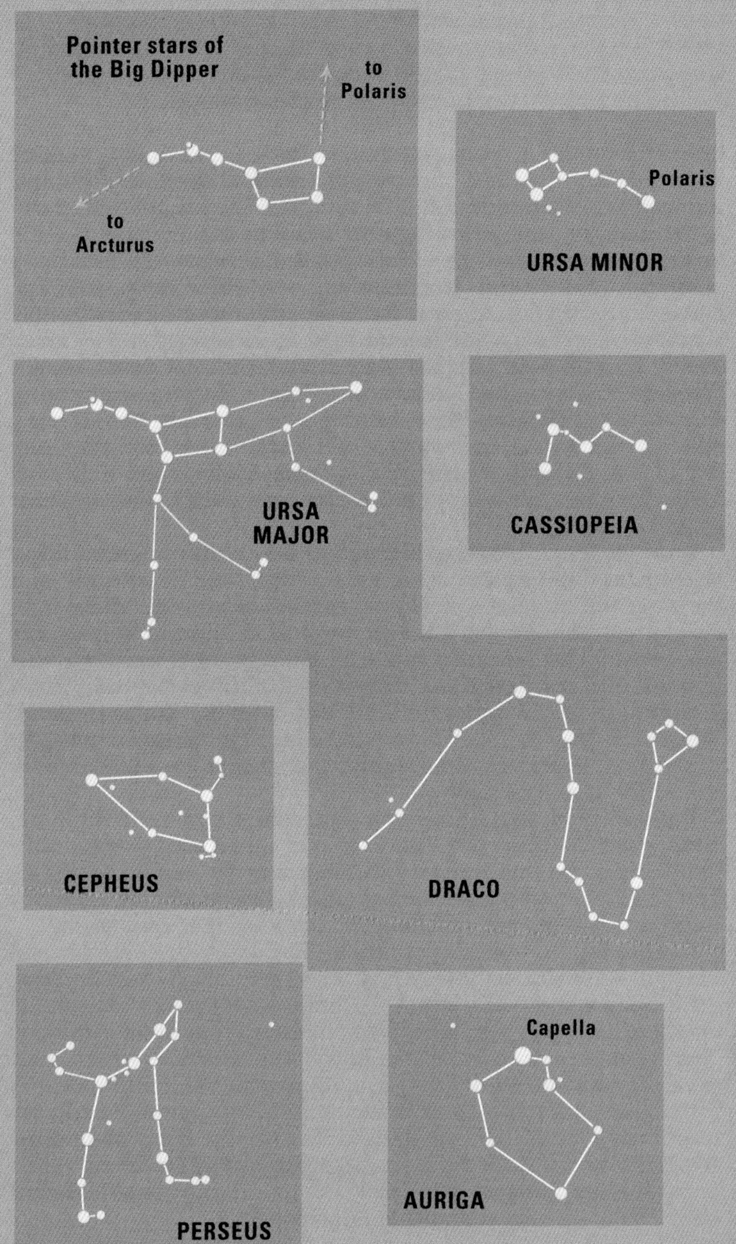
Pointer stars of
the Big Dipper
to
Polaris
to
Arcturus
Polaris
URSA MINOR
URSA
MAJOR
CASSIOPEIA
CEPHEUS
DRACO
PERSEUS
Capella
AURIGA

OTHER MAJOR CONSTELLATIONS

Here are a few other major or notable constellations. They're arranged here by the times of year at which they are at their most obvious in the late evening sky — after sunset but before midnight. Everything appears to move across the sky as the night progresses, and before dawn you'll see constellations that would seem typical of other seasons.

Late in the evening in spring and summer, follow the stars of the "handle" of the Big Dipper and then continue out in the same direction — the next very bright star you come to will be Arcturus. The fourth-brightest star in the entire sky, and with a distinctly yellowish cast, Arcturus is at the base of the narrow kite shape of the constellation **Boötes** (the herdsman), pronounced boh-oh-teez. Prominent high overhead in the summer sky, Boötes is a good reference point for finding other constellations. See the sky charts on pp. 22–29 to see how these line up in the sky. Just to the left of the kite shape of Boötes is a half-circle of stars marking **Corona Borealis** (the northern crown), and just to the left of that is the more widely spaced constellation of **Hercules.** The name of this star group, like those of many others, comes from the mythology of the Greeks, Romans, and other early civilizations. Although we can't go into details on this aspect of the stars in this field guide, astronomy can be a fine entry point to learning about ancient mythology.

Lyra (the lyre), a small constellation with an easily recognized shape, includes the fifth-brightest star in the sky, Vega. Near Hercules and near the "head" of Draco (see p. 32), Lyra is visible at various times of the night for much of the year, but it is high overhead in summer. So is **Cygnus** (the swan), which is unusual in actually having a shape suggesting what it's named for! Its brightest star, Deneb, is at the "tail" of the swan. Cygnus is located in a bright part of the Milky Way (see p. 21). Also in the Milky Way, not far from Cygnus, is **Aquila** (the eagle). This group is most easily picked out by three stars close together in a straight line with the center one, Altair, being very bright.

Pegasus (the winged horse) is most prominent high in the sky in fall, farther from the North Star than Cygnus or Cassiopeia. It is most easily recognized by the arrangement of stars known as the Great Square of Pegasus, although it isn't exactly a square and one of the four corners is now usually considered a part of the adjacent constellation of **Andromeda.**

Dominating the winter sky is **Orion** (the hunter), probably the most recognizable of all constellations. Two very bright stars in Orion are Betelgeuse (pronounced "bettle-jooz," not "beetle juice") at one "shoulder" of the figure and Rigel at one "foot." Below the straight line of stars of Orion's "belt" is an area known as the "sword," and with binoculars you can make out a blurry area here, a cloud of gas and dust called the Orion Nebula. Not far to the east of Orion is **Canis Minor** (the little dog), a small constellation most notable for its bright star Procyon. This is about the eighth-brightest star, but it is upstaged by Sirius, the single brightest star in the sky, nearby in **Canis Major** (the great dog). In mythology, naturally, Canis Major and Canis Minor were regarded as Orion's hunting dogs.

OTHER MAJOR CONSTELLATIONS

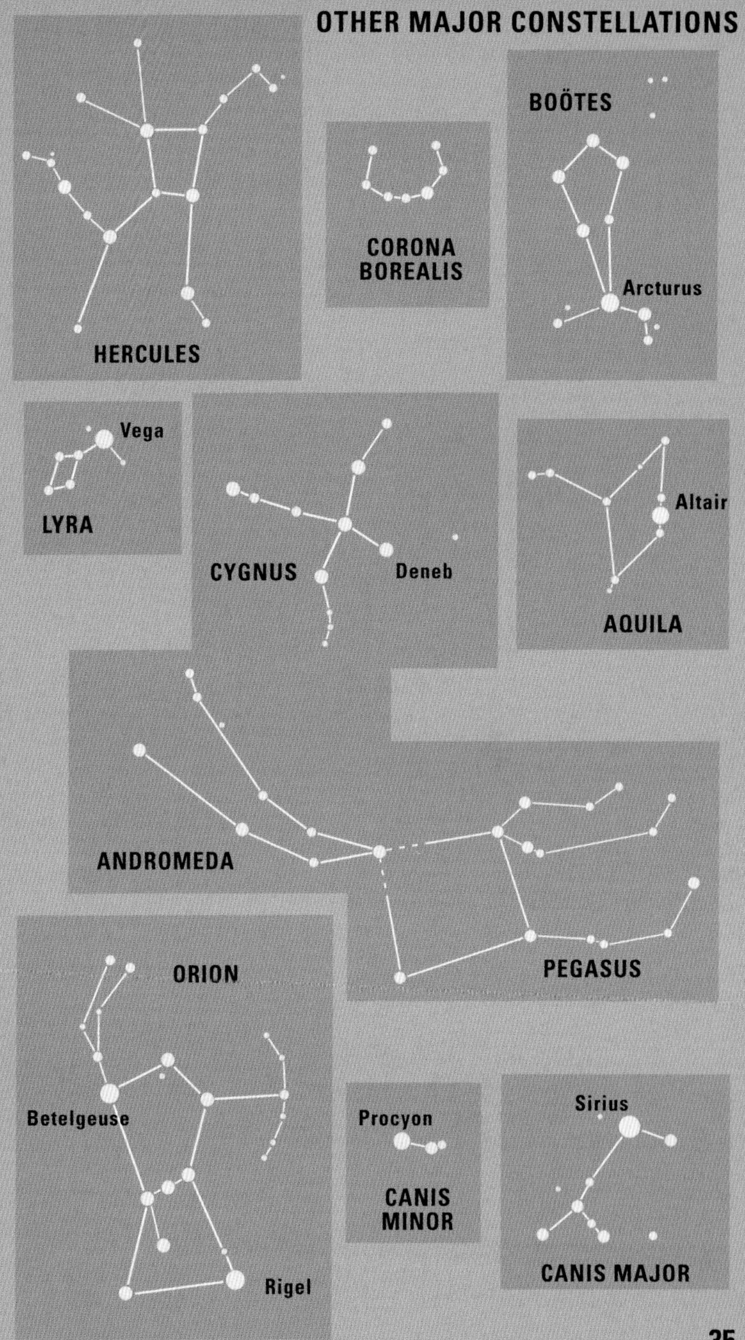

The preceding pages were devoted to stars and other objects in deep space. Here we treat objects inside our own solar system: the planets and other objects that revolve around our sun.

The moon. Our closest neighbor in space, averaging only about 239,000 miles from Earth. The period of time between successive full moons (about 29.5 days) is the basis for the system of months on our calendars, and the moon's gravity is a major cause of our oceanic tides.

Phases of the moon. As the moon orbits the earth, the same side of it always faces toward us. It appears to wax and wane depending on where it is situated, relative to us and to the sun. When the moon is opposite the sun, it rises as a full moon as the sun sets. Each night after that, the moon rises about 45 minutes later. By a week after the full moon, the moon is rising in the middle of the night and has waned to the phase called last quarter. The new moon is another week later, when the moon is between us and the sun and the side in shadow is toward us. After about another week, the moon is high in the southern sky at sunset and appears half full; this phase is called the first quarter. In about another week, the moon rises at sunset again and is full again, and the cycle repeats.

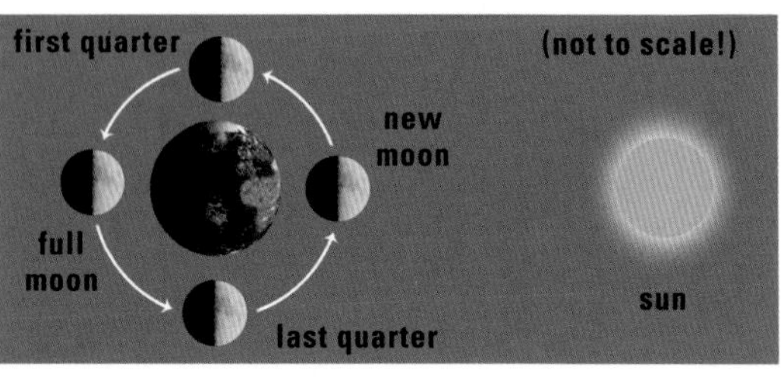

Eclipses. A partial or total eclipse of the moon (lunar eclipse) occurs at least twice per year, always during the full moon, when the moon is directly on the opposite side of the earth from the sun. The eclipse results when the moon passes partly or completely into the earth's shadow.

Eclipses of the sun (solar eclipses) occur about as often as lunar eclipses but are seen far less often from any one place. They are caused when the moon comes between the sun and the earth; but because the moon is so small and so close, relatively speaking, its shadow falls on only a small area of our planet. The area affected by a total eclipse follows a path only about 160 miles wide. By contrast, a lunar eclipse can be seen from anyplace where the moon is visible, as it is caused by a shadow falling on the moon itself.

The planets. Eight or nine planets orbit the sun, and five are close enough to us to be noticeable at times. All travel across the sky in the path of the zodiac, gradually changing position relative to the constellations. Some newspapers have astronomy columns that tell the current positions of the planets, or you can find their current positions by looking online.

Mercury is closest to the sun, so it is never visible except at twilight, close to the horizon just after sunset or just before sunrise. When it's visible it can be close to the magnitude of some of the brightest stars. It can't compare to **Venus,** however. Venus is the "morning star" or "evening star," but its reflected light is brighter than that of any actual star. The second planet out from the sun, Venus is usually visible low in the sky for only a few hours either after sunset or before sunrise.

The orbit of **Mars** is the next one out beyond Earth, about one and a half times as far from the sun as we are. Mars takes almost two of our years to make a complete orbit around the sun. It looks brightest when it is closest to us, that is, when the earth is between the sun and Mars. At such times the reddish color of Mars is quite obvious.

Between the orbits of Jupiter and Mars are hundreds (at least) of small objects called asteroids. Even the largest ones are almost never visible to the unaided eye, but debris from this zone may wind up here as meteors.

The orbit of **Jupiter** is about five times as far from the sun as Earth's. This is a huge planet, about 11 times the diameter of Earth. It has at least 16 moons, and four of these are large enough that they can be seen through binoculars — in fact, this is a good way to check the identity of a planet suspected to be Jupiter. With a small telescope we often can see horizontal bands of color or darker spots in Jupiter's dense atmosphere.

Saturn's orbit is more than nine times as far from the sun as ours, and this planet is more than nine times the size of Earth. Famous for its rings, which can be seen with a small telescope, Saturn also has at least 18 moons, but none of these is visible without serious magnification.

Meteors and meteor showers. When an object in space gets close enough to be pulled in by our gravity, and begins to fall toward Earth, friction against our atmosphere will heat it up to glow white-hot before it burns up completely and disappears. We see this as a spot of white streaking across the sky — a "falling star." Technically, it's a meteor (the rare one that reaches Earth's surface is called a meteorite). Most meteors are tiny fragments of asteroids or comets. When Earth passes through the trail of debris left by a comet, meteors streak across our sky at a rate of several per minute. These meteor showers occur at predictable seasons. Two notable ones are the Perseids in August and the Geminids in December. During these, the meteors fall from a particular part of the sky and seem to radiate from the constellations Perseus and Gemini, respectively, hence the names.

Comets. These mysterious objects are masses of rock and frozen gases with varied orbits around the sun. Most that we see have elliptical orbits, looping past the sun and then traveling far outside the solar system. The most famous comet, Halley's, comes past the sun once every 76 years and is expected back in 2061. The "tail" of a comet streams out directly away from the sun and consists of gases and dust melting from the comet and being pushed away by the sun's force. Only a few comets are bright enough to be visible to the unaided eye. In binoculars, a comet looks like a fuzzy star, with or without a "tail" pointing away from the sun.

HABITATS

New England is a region of remarkable variety and striking contrasts. In exploring this land, we might go from high atop Mount Katahdin in Maine to the sandy beaches of coastal Connecticut; from the fresh waters of Lake Champlain along Vermont's western border to salt marsh and rocky coast along the Atlantic Ocean; from peatlands, where water and land nearly become one, to hidden caves dotting the landscape. As we might expect, the varied landscapes here can boast a stunning diversity of living things, with every species finding its own unique niche.

View from atop Mt. Greylock, Massachusetts, in May

Habitats section contributed by Ken Keffer

A basic point for naturalists is that different animals and plants are found in different habitats and that these habitat associations are largely predictable. For example, in a meadow in Rhode Island we might see the same kinds of birds, butterflies, and flowers that we would see in a meadow in New Hampshire; but if we walk a hundred yards from that meadow into a forest, the birds, butterflies, and flowers will be mostly different. Learning about nature is not just a matter of recognizing individual species but also coming to understand how they fit together in habitats. Because all of the living things and other elements work together and interact in a functioning system, a habitat is often referred to by an alternate term, ecosystem, which has a similar meaning.

Often what we notice first about a habitat is the kind of plant growth there, so that makes a good place to start. Plant growth is affected by numerous conditions that work together or separately. These conditions can include soil type, precipitation, elevation, latitude, aspect (facing north or south, for example), and other factors. Plant communities are the associations of plant species that grow together based on these conditions.

Plant communities are not stagnant but can change as conditions change. After a disturbance, such as clear-cutting, fire, or a major storm, the plant community may change continuously for a period of many years, growing up from bare soil to whatever would be the climax community for that location. This process of plant community change is called ecological succession. As the habitat grows up, certain species get shaded out and replaced by other species of plants. The climax community (that is, the end of the succession, and the habitat type that would remain more or less stable over long periods) over much of New England is some forest type. Grasslands, if left undisturbed, will convert to shrublands. Similarly, under suitable conditions, shrublands will give way to forests. Historically, New England was dominated by forests, but a shifting mosaic of open grasslands also occurred.

Just as most plant species are not evenly distributed throughout the landscape, animal species also have habitat associations. Habitat is the basic requirement for animal survival. It is where an animal lives, and it can be defined by both living and physical components. The habitat basics for a particular creature include food, water, shelter, and space, but in a larger sense, the habitat is really the sum of the plants, soils, climatic conditions, winds, precipitation, and other environmental factors.

White-tailed Deer could be considered habitat generalists in New England, living in all kinds of forests as well as in fields, marsh edges, and even the edges of suburbia. However, the plants on which they graze and browse may be most abundant in areas with a mix of open meadows and forest edges.

Some animals have very distinctive habitat requirements and are found only in specific locations. Other animals are more generalists and can be found throughout New England. Many species of aquatic invertebrates, such as barnacles, oysters, and clams, live a sedentary life, anchored in place for most of their life cycle. For a Karner Blue Butterfly, year-round habitat might be found in an area no larger than a football field. A Downy Woodpecker can survive all year in a relatively small patch of urban forest. By contrast, other species of birds, especially the shorebirds and seabirds of coastal New England, are champions of migration that use habitats across much of the globe.

Animal habitats often closely mirror plant community associations, so we treat them together in this book. Depending on how precisely we define them, the number of different habitats in New England could run into the hundreds. For most naturalists, though, it is more useful to have a general idea of basic habitat types, so this section treats nine broad categories. The ecosystem types highlighted in this book represent both widespread habitats and those with very limited distributions.

ALPINE ZONE

As we climb in elevation, as a rule, the temperature drops. At the tops of New England's highest mountains, above treeline, we find the alpine zone. This is the harshest of landscapes, with low temperatures, long snowy winters, and winds whipping year-round. Short growing seasons and high drought stress can limit the diversity of plants. One might think of this as nearly an inhospitable habitat, but upon closer investigation we find that many species thrive here, all well adapted to these extreme environments. Plant life includes many short-stemmed dwarf species. These alpine plants hug the ground, both to be sheltered from the winds and to be able to capitalize on the earth's surface temperature. Sedges and lichen cling to life in the alpine zone, as do a number of invertebrate species, including butterflies that are more typical of the Arctic. New England alpine habitats are isolated mountaintop islands in the mountains of Vermont, New Hampshire, and Maine.

Krummholz is the name for the wind-whipped doughnut of short, twisted trees ringing the alpine zones of the northern New England states. While snow provides an insulating layer allowing for tree growth, the stunted trees are abraded by the winds, often exhibiting the characteristic flagged branches on the leeward sides of the tree trunks. Krummholz could be considered a transition between alpine habitat and the first of the forest types introduced next. It provides a summer home for a handful of bird species, most notably the rare Bicknell's Thrush.

FORESTS

New England is a land dominated by trees, and there are numerous forest cover types in the region.

Spruce-fir forests, requiring cool and damp conditions, are found in northern, central, and northern coastal Maine and above 2,600 feet in the mountains of New Hampshire and Vermont. Red Spruce and Balsam Fir are the most abundant tree species throughout much of the region. Black Spruce can be common in the cooler areas, especially in low-lying areas of damp soil, and White Spruce is characteristic of drier upland soils, often growing up in abandoned agricultural fields. A variety of hardwood trees can be found in these forests, including Red Maple, Paper Birch, Quaking and Bigtooth Aspen, and Mountain-ash. A thick understory and acidic soils can limit understory plants in coniferous forests, but they still provide important habitat for a range of animal life. Spruce Grouse survive winters nibbling on conifer needles. Cape May Warbler and Blackpoll Warbler breed here, while crossbills can inhabit these forests year-round, as long as the cone crops hold up. Canada Lynx and American Marten search out prey in these forests as well.

Northern hardwood–spruce forests are a transition forest type along mid to lower mountain slopes and in the southern reaches of northern New England. Hardwood species composition includes a mix of beech, birch, and Sugar Maple, while Red Spruce and Balsam Fir are replaced by Eastern Hemlock at lower elevations. Species like Ruffed Grouse, Wood Thrush, and Northern Long-eared Bat can be found here.

Deciduous forests, also known as hardwood forests or broadleaf forests, are iconic New England habitats. The tree species composition changes throughout the region, but one is never far from a hardwood forest.

Northern hardwood forests in their truest form include extensive stands of Sugar Maple, American Beech, and Yellow Birch. Habitat associates include Eastern Hemlock, Balsam Fir, Basswood, Black Cherry, and White Ash. Wetter areas include species like Red Maple, American Elm, Northern White-Cedar, and spruce. Northern hardwood forests cover parts of Maine, New Hampshire, Vermont, and the Berkshires in western Massachusetts. Habitat specialists include Red Bat, a species that roosts to mimic a tree leaf, as well as familiar species such as Black Bear.

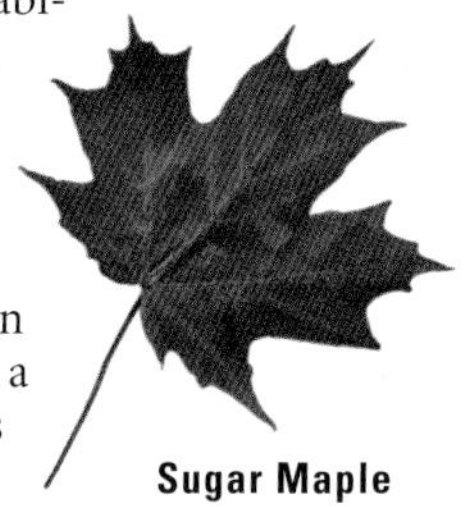

Sugar Maple

Transition hardwoods–White Pine forests have their core in central Massachusetts, southeastern New Hampshire, and bordering Maine, as well as along the Champlain and Connecticut River valleys. In addition to the dominant species of the northern hardwood forests, Eastern White Pines are found in pockets distributed throughout these woods, mostly on the drier sandier soils in central New England. Contrastingly, hemlocks add diversity among the moist, cool microclimates of the broadleaf forests, especially in the northern regions and along ravines and north-facing hillsides in the southern reaches of this forest type.

Central hardwood-hemlock–White Pine forests occur throughout southern New England and extend north to Maine along the coast. This region was formerly dominated by American Chestnut, but this species was decimated by Chestnut Blight a century ago. While Eastern White Pine can initially dominate abandoned agricultural fields, a mix of oaks, hickories, birches, and beech covers this landscape. Oak and hickory are particularly dominant in many southern New England forests. Many southern species of animals reach the northern extent of their range in these woods.

Pitch Pine–Scrub Oak has a limited distribution in New England, predominately along Cape Cod and in nearby areas of southeastern Massachusetts. This low-growing, scrubby habitat favors sandy, well-drained soils and may be maintained partly by repeated burning. Understory species can include Lowbush Blueberry and other shrubs in the heath family.

SHRUBLANDS

Appropriately enough, shrublands are dominated by shrubs. In New England these areas usually occur as a stage in succession, when an area is growing up following disturbance or management. Neglected farm fields and power line rights of way can be prime shrubland habitats. Blue-winged Warblers find shrublands suitable, as do Indigo Bunting and American Woodcock. The New England Cottontail survives in shrublands with thick understory. Moist shrublands are attractive to Black Racers.

GRASSLANDS

Although New England is a land of trees, nonforested habitats do add to the diversity of the region.

Historically, grasslands were found in a shifting mosaic following disturbances. Agricultural lands can imitate open grassland environments. During the summer growing season, hay and dairy fields can attract butterflies, songbirds, and Coyotes, while corn stubble fields feed wintering waterfowl and open-country birds like Horned Lark and Lapland Longspur. These agricultural fields are also home to various rodent species and their natural predators, such as Short-eared Owl, Red Fox, and Eastern Hognose Snake. Similarly, airports can replicate grassland conditions. Grasshopper Sparrows and Upland Sandpipers frequent airfields during the summer months, while Snowy Owls may move in during the winter.

FRESHWATER WETLANDS

Freshwater wetlands can occur in almost any other habitat type or can be unique standalone habitats.

Bogs and peatlands are characterized by spongy ground created by stagnant accumulations of water coupled with thick mats of vegetation. Sphagnum mosses, carnivorous pitcher-plants, heath, Northern White-Cedar, and American Larch are a few plant species that are adapted to these conditions of low nutrients and high acid content. Four-toed Salamanders are among the many distinctive species that depend on these habitats. In addition to supporting stunning species diversity, bogs and peatlands are important in carbon sequestration.

Freshwater marshes are open wetlands with saturated soil and standing water for much of the year and typically with no trees and few taller shrubs. They may form anyplace that is covered consistently with shallow water, such as along the margins of ponds or lakes, or along slow-moving rivers. Freshwater marshes host a distinctive set of plants, either rooted in shallow water or floating on the surface, including cattails, rushes, water-lilies, and certain grasses. Many marshes have been drained or degraded, but this is unfortunate, since this is an incredibly valuable habitat that supports an abundance of life both above and below the water's surface. Red-winged Blackbirds, Marsh Wrens, Common Muskrats, and various frogs and dragonflies are among the many creatures to be found here.

Water levels vary in marshes, and there is a gradual variation from very shallow marshes to damp meadows with no standing water. Damp meadows often have large stands of sedges, and they may support animals typical of either marshes or grasslands.

Red-winged Blackbird

Swamps are wetlands that occur in shrublands or forests. Shrub swamps can be dominated by any number of shrub species, including Buttonbush, Highbush Blueberry, Black Huckleberry, and many other shrubs. These can be in transition to forested swamps. Both deciduous and coniferous trees can dominate a swamp. In general, deciduous forest swamps, such as Red Maple swamps, have a richer shrub layer and a more open canopy, while coniferous swamps, such as Atlantic White-cedar swamps, are more acidic and support fewer amphibian species. While many animal species are restricted to certain swamp types, species like Bog Turtles and Eastern Ribbon Snakes can be found in numerous wetland habitats.

OPEN FRESH WATER

Streams and rivers are abundant throughout New England, defining many landscapes and affecting the condition of surrounding habitats. From headwaters in mountains and hills, small streams and brooks cascade downslope, eventually entering broad New England valleys as rivers. Ultimately these rivers empty into estuaries, blending with coastal salt waters. Cool mountain streams are home to stonefly and mayfly larvae, which feed Brook Trout and salamanders. Rivers connect uplands ecosystems with the sea, and some migratory fish like the Atlantic Sturgeon connect the ocean to the rivers.

Ponds and lakes dot New England, especially in the lowlands of more northern areas. These still bodies of water provide habitat for countless invertebrate species. They also are home to fish, including many species targeted by anglers. Ducks, geese, swans, and loons are pond and lake specialists, at least at certain times of year. By building dams across streams, American Beavers create their own ponds, and humans often do the same thing.

Vernal pools are ephemeral, often seasonal pools. They can be found in almost any other habitat type but often host a unique assemblage of species of their own. Most vernal pools in New England are filled with water during the spring, from snowmelt or spring rainfall or both, and then they gradually dry up by sometime in the summer. Certain amphibians, including Marbled Salamanders, may depend on vernal pools for reproduction and survival.

Marbled Salamander

COASTAL HABITATS

Estuaries occur at the mouths of rivers and streams, where fresh water drains into the ocean. Estuarine habitats are highly productive environments, although they are also highly susceptible to degradation, especially from pollution brought downstream.

Salt marshes, like estuaries, are highly productive ecosystems that are subject to twice daily tide cycles. Coupled with estuary waters, salt marshes are the nursery for the sea for numerous species, including many fish, mollusks, shrimp, and crabs. Salt marshes help protect land from storm surges of ocean waves, and they support many specialized species like American Bittern and Clapper Rail.

Tidal flats make up distinctive habitats in parts of New England. The shifting tides constantly alter the bifurcation between land and sea, and the littoral zone, also called the intertidal zone, is this area between high and low tide. Where the coastline slopes gradually into the sea, great tidal flats may be exposed at low tide. Various species of sandpipers and plovers work this interface, feeding on fiddler crabs, mollusks, and many marine invertebrates.

Fiddler Crab

Sandy beaches and associated sand dunes are more abundant in southern New England, along Long Island Sound, than they are farther north in New England. However, all coastal states of this region have at least a limited number of these distinctive habitats. Endangered Piping Plovers and other species of birds nest on the beach.

Rocky cliffs of northern New England and rocky coastal islands provide essential nesting habitats for several species of terns, Common Eider, and the classic Atlantic Puffin, as well as a diversity of life from barnacles to Harbor Seals. At low tide, these areas can highlight tide pool species like periwinkles, sea anemones, and sea stars.

OCEAN

Like the terrestrial habitats of New England, the Atlantic Ocean and coastal bays exhibit vast contrasts throughout the region. The broad distribution of ocean species is often temperature dependent, and Cape Cod delineates cool ocean conditions of the north from warmer southern ocean conditions. Bays and inlets provide shelter, allowing lobster to flourish. Shallow offshore banks help bring rich food sources of plankton (tiny, free-floating organisms) to the surface, where they form the base of the food chain, feeding everything from seabirds and fish to dolphins, porpoises, and whales.

Atlantic White-sided Dolphin

URBAN HABITATS

Human presence is felt throughout New England. Urban areas, from small villages to large cities, have a great impact on natural ecosystems. People continue to convert natural habitats into human-dominated landscapes at a rapid rate. While this conversion can have a negative consequence on plant communities and the animals that depend on them, some species do survive in the urban setting. Species such as Peregrine Falcons and Common Nighthawks may use rooftops as nesting platforms. Similarly, the Chimney Swift is now almost entirely dependent on human structures for nesting. Backyard gardens, especially when native plants are emphasized, can provide habitats for an entire suite of insects and small mammals. During spring and fall migration, any patch of green, including city parks, can provide stopover habitat for songbirds. Birds use these stopover sites to rest and refuel before continuing on their journeys.

WILDFLOWERS

With their beauty and variety, wildflowers are among the major delights of the New England landscape for more than half the year. Beginning with woodland flowers in early spring, continuing through the flower-filled meadows of summer, and finishing with the last asters and goldenrods of autumn, they provide an ever-changing palette of colors.

What is a wildflower? There is no universally accepted definition. In this guide we have used the term in a general way for any low-growing plant that has noticeable flowers for some part of the year. In some cases we had to make an arbitrary decision whether to include a particular species in this section or in the section "Small Shrubs, Vines, Groundcover," beginning on p. 134. If in doubt yourself about a borderline plant, check both sections.

New England has thousands of species of flowering plants (a broad term that includes grasses and trees, even if their flowers are not always obvious). Many of these can be identified at a glance, but some can be challenging even for experts. If you develop a serious interest in botany (the study of plants), you may find yourself using a magnifying glass or a microscope to look at fine details of flowers and memorizing dozens of technical terms. (The pursuit of botany can be rewarding and stimulating; indeed, Henry David Thoreau was an avid botanist, seeking out and identifying new plants even as he was writing the final revisions of *Walden.*) But for purposes of this guide, we will focus on recognizing wildflowers simply by their general appearance.

How this section is arranged. In a standard botany text all the plants are presented in taxonomic sequence, arranged by order, family, and genus, with related species close together. This isn't the most helpful approach for nonbotanists, however, since unrelated plants may look superficially similar, and related plants may look quite different from each other.

In this book we follow a simplified approach, grouping flowers by similarity, starting with their color.

Even within these color categories we had to make arbitrary choices; some flowers are on the borderline between white and yellow, and there's almost a smooth continuum from pink to pale purple to blue. Still, this breakdown should get you to the right area most of the time. And if you are colorblind, be aware that a great many flowers can be identified easily by their shape and structure; you'll just have to go through more pages to find the best match.

Parts of a flower. We avoid technical terms as much as possible in this guide, but some odd or interesting flowers are almost impossible to describe without mentioning some flower parts. For example, in some cases the flower itself is very small or petals are lacking, and what looks like showy petals may be sepals instead. In other cases, long stamens may be a notable feature of the flower. The very simplified diagram below shows some basic flower parts.

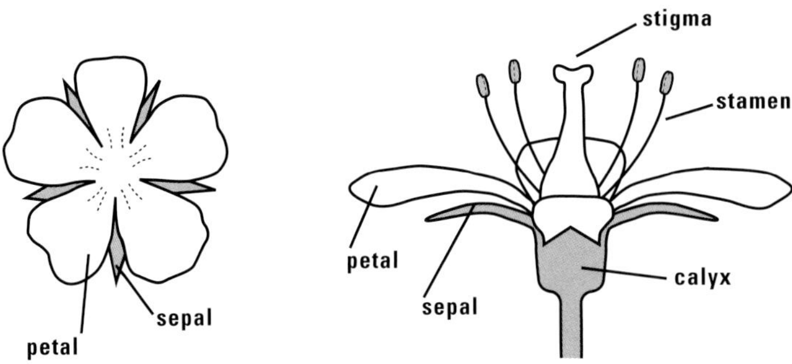

Aliens vs. natives. A shockingly high percentage of the most common and familiar wildflowers in New England are not native to North America at all. This is especially true in disturbed sites, such as roadsides and vacant lots. Many of the alien plants originated in parts of Europe where the overall climate is similar to ours. These plants had had many centuries to adapt to conditions of disturbance, such as farming or intensive livestock grazing. They had little difficulty in adapting to disturbed sites in the New World after their seeds were brought here, either by accident or by design. Our native plants, playing catch-up in such situations, often are crowded out altogether.

Of course we have included many of these introduced plants in this guide; after all, they represent the flowers that you are most likely to see in many areas. We do try to indicate which species are aliens, simply because the authors are always curious to know this about every plant!

Most alien plants do little harm. However, some serious problems are caused by invasive species, those with a tendency to move into natural or undisturbed habitats and crowd out the natives. Garlic Mustard (p. 56) and Purple Loosestrife (p. 80) are two examples of such troublesome invaders. In some places, conservationists are now having to invest considerable time and resources to control the invaders, a reminder that bringing in new species to a natural habitat is not something to be taken lightly.

WHITE WOODLAND FLOWERS

Wildflowers inside the forest are at their best in spring, before the trees are fully leafed out, while sunlight can still reach the forest floor. Here are some small but beautiful forest flowers, mostly blooming in spring.

STARFLOWER ***Trientalis borealis***

Common on the ground in all kinds of forest, blooming mainly in May, but recognized by its distinctive leaves later in the season. Primrose family (Primulaceae). ▸ Has 2 small white flowers, with 5 to 9 petals each, above a *single whorl* of *long, pointed leaves.*

CANADA VIOLET ***Viola canadensis***

More than 30 species of violets (family Violaceae) live in New England, including several with white flowers. This is one of the more distinctive ones. Common in rich woods in hilly areas, limestone soils. ▸ Leaves and 5-petaled flowers on *same* stems. Flower white with yellow at center, *purple tinge on back* of petals.

MITERWORT ***Mitella diphylla***

Blooms in spring in shady spots in rich woods. Saxifrage family (Saxifragaceae). ▸ Tiny white flowers (with delicate fringes when seen up close) grow along a single stem. Has large leaves at base like next species, but also distinctive *pair of leaves on stem.*

FOAMFLOWER ***Tiarella cordifolia***

Widespread and fairly common in spring in rich, damp woods. Saxifrage family. ▸ Flowers a little larger than those of Miterwort with much *longer stamens,* for a filmy or "foamy" look. Has large basal leaves but *lacks* the Miterwort's paired leaves on stem.

COMMON WOOD-SORREL ***Oxalis montana***

Common in damp woods. Unlike similar species here, blooms mainly in summer. Wood-sorrel family (Oxalidaceae). ▸ Has 5 white petals with pink veins. Leaves with 3 *heart-shaped* leaflets.

SPRING-BEAUTY ***Claytonia virginica***

Blooms in early spring in low, wet woods. Purslane family (Portulacaceae). ▸ Slender, standing 6–10" tall. Five white or pink petals with pink veins. A *pair of narrow leaves* halfway up stem.

CAROLINA SPRING-BEAUTY ***Claytonia caroliniana***

Despite the name, more widespread here than the preceding species, found in damp woods, edges, hilltops, blooming in early spring. Purslane family. ▸ Like the preceding, but the 2 leaves on the stem are much wider at the center.

CANADA MAYFLOWER ***Maianthemum canadense***

Small but numerous, often carpeting the ground in open woods. Blooms in late spring and early summer. Lily of the valley family (Convallariaceae). ▸ Tiny 4-parted flowers, followed by berries in late summer. *Two* glossy green leaves with heart-shaped bases.

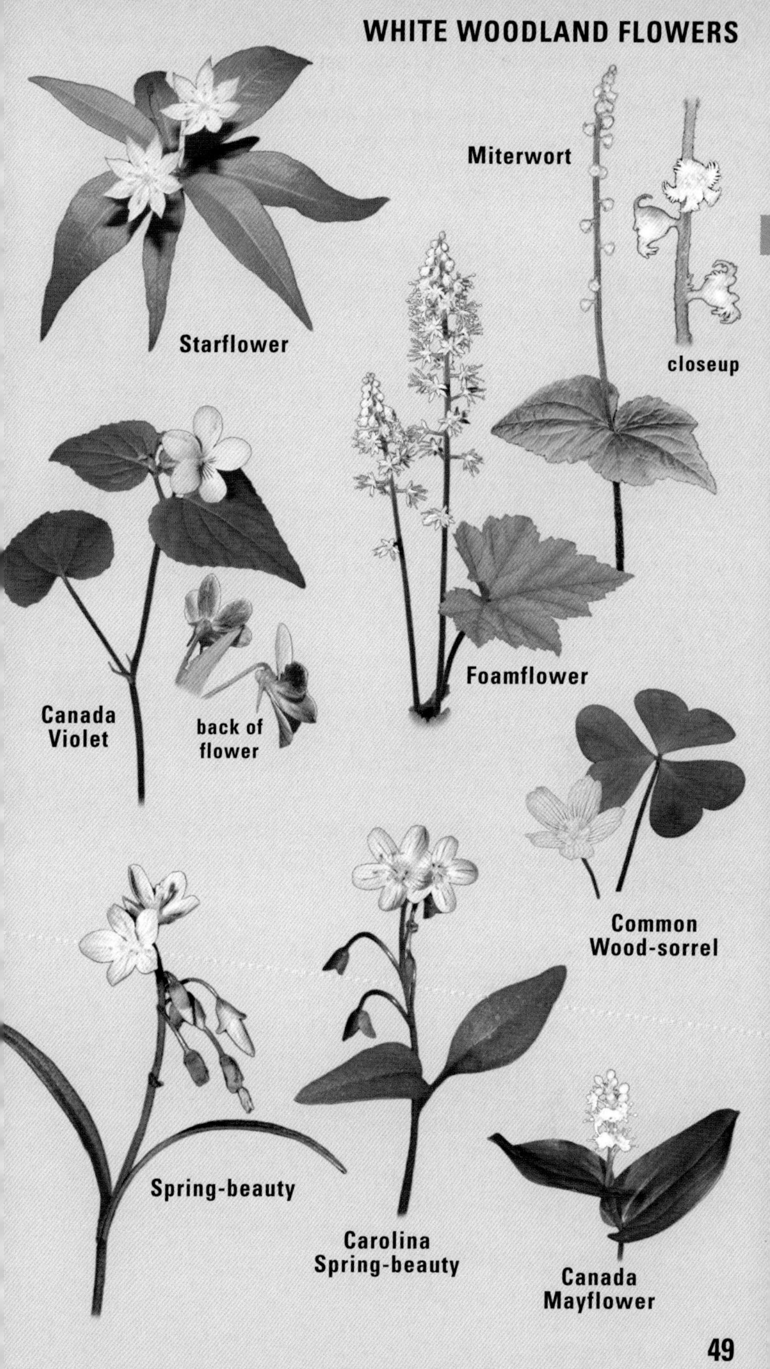
Starflower
Miterwort
closeup
Foamflower
Canada Violet
back of flower
Common Wood-sorrel
Spring-beauty
Carolina Spring-beauty
Canada Mayflower

Here are some more white flowers of spring and early summer.

WHITE TRILLIUM ***Trillium grandiflorum***

A beautiful sign of spring is the blooming of trilliums on the forest floor. This large-flowered species is mostly uncommon and local in damp, rich woods, especially in areas with limestone near the surface. Lily family (Liliaceae). ▶ Has 3 large, broad leaves, 3 *large* white petals (turning pink with age).

NODDING TRILLIUM ***Trillium cernuum***

Less conspicuous than the preceding but more widespread in New England, especially in damp, rich woods with thick, peaty soil. Lily family. ▶ The flower droops below the leaves; its 3 white petals (rarely pink) are strongly *curved back,* revealing bright *pink anthers* at the center.

BLOODROOT ***Sanguinaria canadensis***

In rich woods, this white flower appears just aboveground in early spring. Its single large leaf often grows up to surround the stem. The name comes from reddish orange juice that "bleeds" from a broken stem. Poppy family (Papaveraceae). ▶ Flower 1½" across, with 8–10 white petals and yellow center, on solitary stem. Single large, thick leaf has 3–9 lobes, long stalk.

DUTCHMAN'S-BREECHES ***Dicentra cucullaria***

To understand the whimsical name of this spring wildflower, take a close look: each bloom looks like a tiny pair of pantaloons turned upside down. Fairly common in rich woods. Fumitory family (Fumariaceae). ▶ In addition to the *unique flowers* drooping from a single stem, note the finely divided leaves.

SQUIRREL-CORN ***Dicentra canadensis***

Another spring bloomer with flowers dangling from a single stem. Mainly western New England. Fumitory family. ▶ Flowers roughly heart-shaped; leaves strongly divided, almost lacelike.

MAY-APPLE ***Podophyllum peltatum***

The nodding white flower in spring and the yellowish "apple" that develops in its place in summer are usually hidden by the huge leaves. Uncommon in open woods. Barberry family (Berberidaceae). ▶ *Gigantic, deeply lobed leaves,* the upper ones in pairs, with flower or fruit at the joint between the 2 stems.

BUNCHBERRY ***Cornus canadensis***

This unassuming little plant dots the forest floor, blooming from late spring to midsummer, showing small red fruits in late summer and fall. Dogwood family (Cornaceae). ▶ Actual flowers (tiny and greenish) are surrounded by 4 large, white, petallike bracts. Leaves are in whorls of 6.

White Trillium
Nodding Trillium
Bloodroot
Dutchman's-breeches
May-apple
Squirrel-corn
Bunchberry
flower detail

VIRGINIA STRAWBERRY ***Fragaria virginiana***

A fairly common small plant of woodland edges, fields, and roadsides, blooming mostly in May and June. Rose family (Rosaceae). ▶ Three coarsely toothed, rounded leaflets; white flowers on separate stem of equal height. **Wood Strawberry** *(F. vesca),* introduced from Europe, has more pointed leaves, taller flowers.

WOOD ANEMONE ***Anemone quinquefolia***

The actual flowers of anemones are tiny, but they are surrounded by showy, petallike white sepals (usually 5). This species blooms from spring to early summer in woods and clearings. Buttercup family (Ranunculaceae). ▶ Whorl of 3 leaves on stem, each deeply divided into 3–5 parts.

CANADA ANEMONE ***Anemone canadensis***

A taller anemone that blooms from spring to midsummer in meadows, woodland edges. Buttercup family. ▶ The deeply divided leaves are *stalkless,* clasping the flower stem.

GRASS-OF-PARNASSIUS ***Parnassia glauca***

Not a type of grass, despite the name, this flower graces damp meadows from midsummer into fall. Saxifrage family (Saxifragaceae). ▶ White petals are lined with greenish veins. Spade-shaped leaves at base of plant, and one on the flower stem itself.

ONE-FLOWERED WINTERGREEN ***Moneses uniflora***

(Not shown) This tiny flower blooms in summer in coniferous or mixed woods, bogs. Wintergreen family (Pyrolaceae). ▶ Single, nodding flower with 5 petals. Small, rounded leaves at base.

SPOTTED WINTERGREEN ***Chimaphila maculata***

The small, nodding flowers, often in pairs, are less noticeable than the sharply patterned leaves. Wintergreen family. ▶ Whorls of dark green leaves accented with *pale central stripe* and veins.

PARTRIDGEBERRY ***Mitchella repens***

A creeping, evergreen plant of the forest floor, sometimes forming solid mats, blooming in early summer. Madder family (Rubiaceae). ▶ Pairs of rounded leaves along stem, 2 white (or pink) flowers at end of stem, each with 4 hairy petals.

ENGLISH PLANTAIN ***Plantago lanceolata***

A common weed of roadsides, vacant lots. Plantain family (Plantaginaceae). ▶ Narrow leaves, short flower head. **Seaside Plantain** *(P. maritima)* is similar, grows in natural sites along coast.

COMMON PLANTAIN ***Plantago major***

Another common weed of open spots. Plantain family. ▶ Like the preceding, has tiny white flowers clustered in flower heads. On this species the flower heads are taller, leaves are much larger.

Virginia Strawberry
Wood Anemone
Canada Anemone
Spotted Wintergreen
Grass-of-Parnassus
Partridgeberry
English Plantain
Common Plantain

DISTINCTIVE OR ODD WHITE FLOWERS

Members of six families, with a wide variety of flower shapes, but all most notable for their distinctive structure.

INDIAN-PIPE ***Monotropa uniflora***

These ghostly plants have no chlorophyll; they grow in association with fungi that absorb nutrients from roots of other plants. Uncommon in understory of shady woods in summer. Indian-pipe family (Monotropaceae). ▶ Waxy, upright stems, white or pink, with flower at top (nodding at first, then upright).

WHITE TURTLEHEAD ***Chelone glabra***

An uncommon plant of wet meadows, streamsides, damp ground, blooming late summer to early fall. Figwort family (Scrophulariaceae). ▶ Flowers clustered at tip of stem, each with *odd shape* suggesting a turtle's head. Pairs of toothed leaves on stem.

HEDGE BINDWEED ***Calystegia sepium***

May grow as a trailing vine on the ground, or climbing over other plants or structures. Common in open areas, edges. Morning-glory family (Convolvulaceae). ▶ Large, trumpet-shaped flowers white or pink. Triangular leaves with *large, blunt* basal lobes.

FIELD BINDWEED ***Convolvulus arvensis***

Native to Eurasia, now common in New England, in roadsides, disturbed sites. Morning-glory family. ▶ Like Hedge Bindweed but with smaller flowers, leaves with smaller basal lobes.

FALSE SOLOMON'S-SEAL ***Maianthemum racemosum***

Common in the understory of deciduous woods. Lily family (Liliaceae). ▶ Large, oval-pointed leaves *arranged alternately* along stem, with *cluster of flowers at tip*. Creamy flowers in early summer, followed by berries (whitish, turning red) in late summer.

AMERICAN POKEWEED ***Phytolacca americana***

A large, coarse weed or small shrub (can be more than 6' tall), growing in fields, woodland edges, roadsides. **Note:** all parts of the mature plant, including the berries and roots, are poisonous. Pokeweed family (Phytolaccaceae). ▶ Reddish stems, large leaves. Whitish flowers in summer followed by purple-black fruits.

MOTH MULLEIN ***Verbascum blattaria***

Native to Eurasia, now common in fields and roadsides. Figwort family (Scrophulariaceae). ▶ Tall spike with 5-lobed flowers (white or yellow, with purple tinge); sparse triangular leaves.

BOUNCING BET ***Saponaria officinalis***

Native to Eurasia, now common in disturbed soils here, blooming in masses along roadsides in late summer. Pink family (Caryophyllaceae). ▶ Flowers white or pink, tubular, with 5 flaring petals notched at the tips. Leaves in pairs or whorls on stems.

Indian-pipe
White Turtlehead
Field Bindweed
Hedge Bindweed
unripe fruits
flower
American Pokeweed
False Solomon's-seal
Bouncing Bet
Moth Mullein

These flowers represent four different families.

WHITE CLOVER ***Trifolium repens***

Native to Eurasia and North Africa, this cheerful little weed now blooms throughout the warmer months all over North America in lawns, roadsides. Pea family (Fabaceae). ▶ Rounded, whitish flower head. Usually 3 leaflets, with pale mark on each.

(WHITE) SWEET CLOVER ***Melilotus officinalis***

Another Old World native, now common on our roadsides and vacant lots. Pea family. ▶ Small, pealike flowers in tall, narrow spikes; leaves with 3 leaflets. Also has a yellow form (p. 68).

GARLIC MUSTARD ***Alliaria petiolata***

This invasive alien is still spreading and can pose a serious threat. While most nonnative plants thrive on roadsides and other open sites, Garlic Mustard grows well in shade, and it can dominate the forest floor, crowding out natives. Mustard family (Brassicaceae). ▶ Tiny white flowers in spring surrounded by slender, erect pods. Leaves on stem triangular, basal leaves more rounded.

CUT-LEAVED TOOTHWORT ***Cardamine concatenata***

This native mustard species blooms in spring in the understory of damp, rich woods. Now considered endangered in Maine and New Hampshire. Mustard family. ▶ Small white flowers. Leaves in 3s, each divided into 3 *narrow, sharply toothed* sections.

TALL MEADOW-RUE ***Thalictrum pubescens***

Fairly common in wet meadows, streambanks, edges of damp woods, blooming mostly in mid- to late summer. Buttercup family (Ranunculaceae). ▶ May stand more than 6' tall. The flowers lack petals but have *showy, threadlike white stamens.* Leaves are divided into *leaflets in 3s,* most with 3 lobes.

EARLY MEADOW-RUE ***Thalictrum dioicum*** **(not shown)**

Blooms *much earlier* than preceding species, mostly in April and May, in rich, moist woods. Buttercup family. ▶ Smaller than Tall Meadow-rue, with *drooping* flower parts, more rounded leaves.

WHITE BANEBERRY ***Actaea pachypoda***

Fairly common in rich woods. Buttercup family. ▶ White flowers in late spring with long stamens. Leaves divided and sharply toothed. Most conspicuous for *white fruits with black spots* (like "dolls' eyes") on red stems, appearing in summer.

CATNIP ***Nepeta cataria***

Native to Europe, now widespread in New England, on roadsides, disturbed soil. Mint family (Lamiaceae). ▶ Dense cluster of white flowers with pink dots. Angular leaves growing on square stem. If in doubt, feed it to a cat and watch for the intoxicated reaction.

Sweet Clover
White Clover
Garlic Mustard
Cut-leaved Toothwort
Tall Meadow-rue
Catnip
White Baneberry

MASSES OF TINY WHITE FLOWERS

The first three species below are in the parsley family **(Apiaceae)**; the last four are in the daisy family **(Asteraceae)**.

QUEEN ANNE'S LACE ***Daucus carota***

Also called Wild Carrot; this is the ancestor of the familiar garden carrot. Native to Eurasia, but now widespread and often abundant in New England, forming masses in fields, roadsides, vacant lots. Blooms in summer and fall. ▶ Often stands 3' tall. Wide, flat-topped white flower head often has a *single dark purple flower* in the center. Leaves very finely and narrowly divided.

POISON HEMLOCK ***Conium maculatum***

Native to the Old World, this is the same hemlock that was used to execute Socrates in 399 BCE. It now grows widely in New England, mostly in disturbed sites. Caution: juices poisonous. ▶ Up to 6' tall, rangy with multiple branches, with clusters of small white flowers at top. Dark green stems often have purple spots. Finely divided leaves. Foul smell when foliage is crushed.

SPOTTED WATER-HEMLOCK ***Cicuta maculata***

Another highly poisonous plant, fairly common in wet meadows, swamps, marshes, blooming mainly in late summer. ▶ Clusters of small white flowers on *spreading* stalks. Green stem has *purple streaks*. Leaves divided into toothed leaflets.

YARROW ***Achillea millefolium***

An Old World plant, now abundant in roadsides and vacant lots of New England, blooming in summer. Leaves are sometimes boiled to make tea. ▶ Usually small (1–2' tall), with densely packed, flat-topped flower clusters. Leaves very finely dissected.

BONESET ***Eupatorium perfoliatum***

Common in late summer and fall around wet meadows, pond edges, swamps. ▶ Sometimes stands up to 5' tall. Clusters of tiny whitish flowers at top. The way the pairs of tooth-edged leaves *unite at the base* around the hairy stem is distinctive.

WHITE SNAKEROOT ***Ageratina altissima***

Locally common in understory and edges of rich woods. Poisonous, and its poisons can be transmitted to humans through the meat or milk of livestock that have eaten this plant. ▶ Masses of small white flowers in late summer and fall. Triangular or heart-shaped leaves, usually in pairs.

HORSEWEED ***Conyza canadensis***

A tall, rangy weed of fields, meadows, roadsides, blooming from late summer through fall. ▶ Up to 7' tall with abundant flower stalks on upper part of plant; white flowers open only narrowly. Numerous long, narrow leaves.

Queen Anne's Lace

Poison Hemlock

Spotted Water-hemlock

Yarrow

Boneset

White Snakeroot

Horseweed

WHITE DAISIES

The daisy family **(Asteraceae)** is also sometimes called the composite family because of the flower structure. What appears to be a single flower, even a small one, is usually a composite of multiple tiny flowers. These often take two forms: ray flowers around the edge (what we might call the petals) and central disk flowers. One of the largest families of flowering plants, with well over 250 species in New England.

OX-EYE DAISY ***Leucanthemum vulgare***

Native to the Old World, now very common and widespread here on roadsides, fields, blooming in summer. ► Classic daisy shape with white rays, yellow disk. Leaves narrow, lobed along edges.

MAYWEED ***Anthemis cotula***

Introduced from Europe, now common in open areas, blooming from summer to early fall. ► The small flower heads (not much more than 1" across) are attractive, but the finely divided foliage has a foul smell (alternate name is "Stinking Chamomile").

DAISY FLEABANE ***Erigeron annuus***

This adaptable native is common on roadsides, fields, blooming from spring to fall. ► Like a miniature of the preceding daisies, but with *dozens of very narrow white ray flowers* around yellow center. Wedge-shaped leaves are strongly toothed along edges.

PARASOL WHITETOP ***Doellingeria umbellata***

Also called Flat-topped White Aster. Common and widespread, blooming in August and September in damp meadows, woodland edges. ► Flower clusters fairly flat. Flowers with *few* white rays (2–15); yellow centers turn purplish later.

WHORLED WOOD ASTER ***Oclemena acuminata***

Fairly common in woodland edges and clearings, blooming in late summer and fall. ► The *large,* toothed leaves appear to be arranged in *spirals or whorls* around the stem. Rays narrow, white or purplish; center of flower often tinged pink.

CALICO ASTER ***Symphyotrichum lateriflorum***

Common in meadows, blooming from August to October. This and the 2 preceding species were formerly placed in the large genus *Aster.* ► Variable. Many small white flowers crowded on sprawling plant. Stems and flower disks may be tinged purple.

PEARLY EVERLASTING ***Anaphalis margaritacea***

Common in dry fields, thickets, woodland edges, blooming from midsummer to fall. ► Clusters of round flower heads, with whitish bracts around yellow centers, suggesting dried flowers. Very long, narrow leaves are tinged grayish.

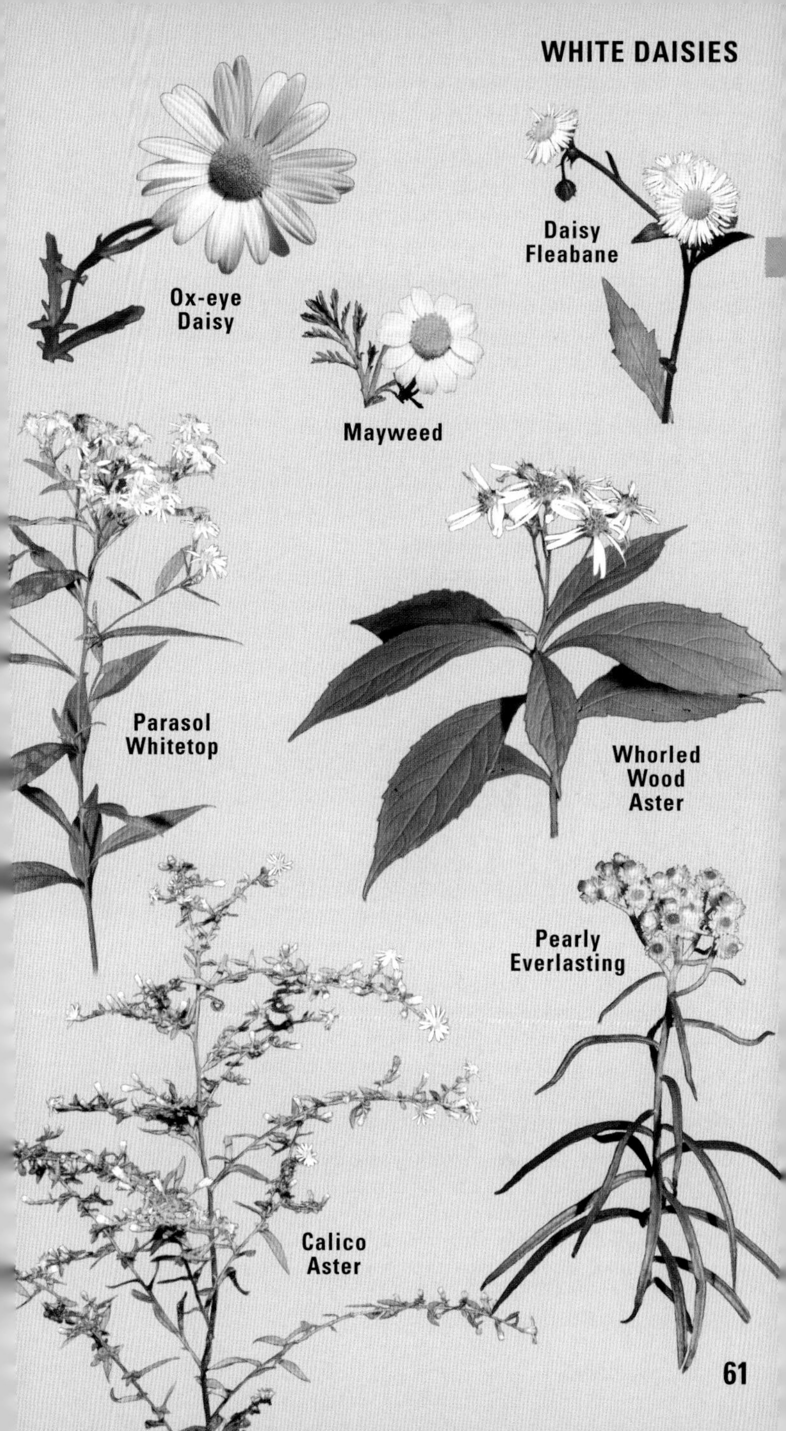
Ox-eye
Daisy
Mayweed
Daisy
Fleabane
Parasol
Whitetop
Whorled
Wood
Aster
Pearly
Everlasting
Calico
Aster

SOME DISTINCTIVE YELLOW FLOWERS

The first four species below are in the lily family **(Liliaceae)**, while the last four represent four separate families.

YELLOW TROUT-LILY ***Erythronium americanum***

A typical flower of early spring in understory and edges of damp deciduous woods. ▶ Drooping yellow to yellow-green flower. Two long, broad basal leaves, *mottled* with purplish brown.

YELLOW CLINTONIA ***Clintonia borealis***

Blooms in spring and early summer in cool, moist woods, edges of bogs. ▶ Yellow to yellow-green bell-shaped flowers, usually drooping, with long stamens. Flowers followed in summer by *dark blue berries.* Two or 3 long, broad basal leaves.

PERFOLIATE BELLWORT ***Uvularia perfoliata***

Fairly common in the understory of open woods, blooming mostly in May and June. ▶ Limp-looking, drooping yellow flower. More distinctive is the way the stem *passes through* the leaves.

CANADA LILY ***Lilium canadense***

Widespread but mostly uncommon in wet meadows, marshes, blooming in early summer. ▶ *Large, rich yellow* flower (varies to orange or red), with *spotted* interior. Whorls of leaves on stem.

YELLOW LADY'S-SLIPPER ***Cypripedium parviflorum***

Uncommon in swamps, bogs, wet woods. Threatened or endangered in some areas. Do not pick or dig up lady's-slippers; they have irritating hairs on stems, and they seldom survive transplanting. Orchid family (Orchidaceae). ▶ Yellow, *pouchlike* flower, large leaves. Varies in size and in color of twisted sepals.

YELLOW IRIS ***Iris pseudacorus***

Native to Europe, brought here as a garden plant, now commonly found growing wild in damp meadows, marshes. Iris family (Iridaceae). ▶ Distinctive iris shape, with broad drooping or arching petals and sepals, but *yellow,* not violet. Long, narrow leaves.

PALE JEWELWEED ***Impatiens pallida***

Uncommon in damp woods, especially in limestone areas, forming open thickets 3–5' tall. Ripe seedpods pop open explosively when handled. Touch-me-not family (Balsaminaceae). ▶ Like a pale yellow version of Spotted Jewelweed (p. 74). Short, puffy flowers dangle below large leaves.

DOWNY YELLOW VIOLET ***Viola pubescens***

More than 30 species of violets occur in this region. All are small plants of woods and meadows, and most bloom in spring or early summer. Flowers of many are violet or blue, but some are white or yellow. Violet family (Violaceae). ▶ The most widespread and common of our yellow violets. Variable, but usually has wide triangular or heart-shaped leaves.

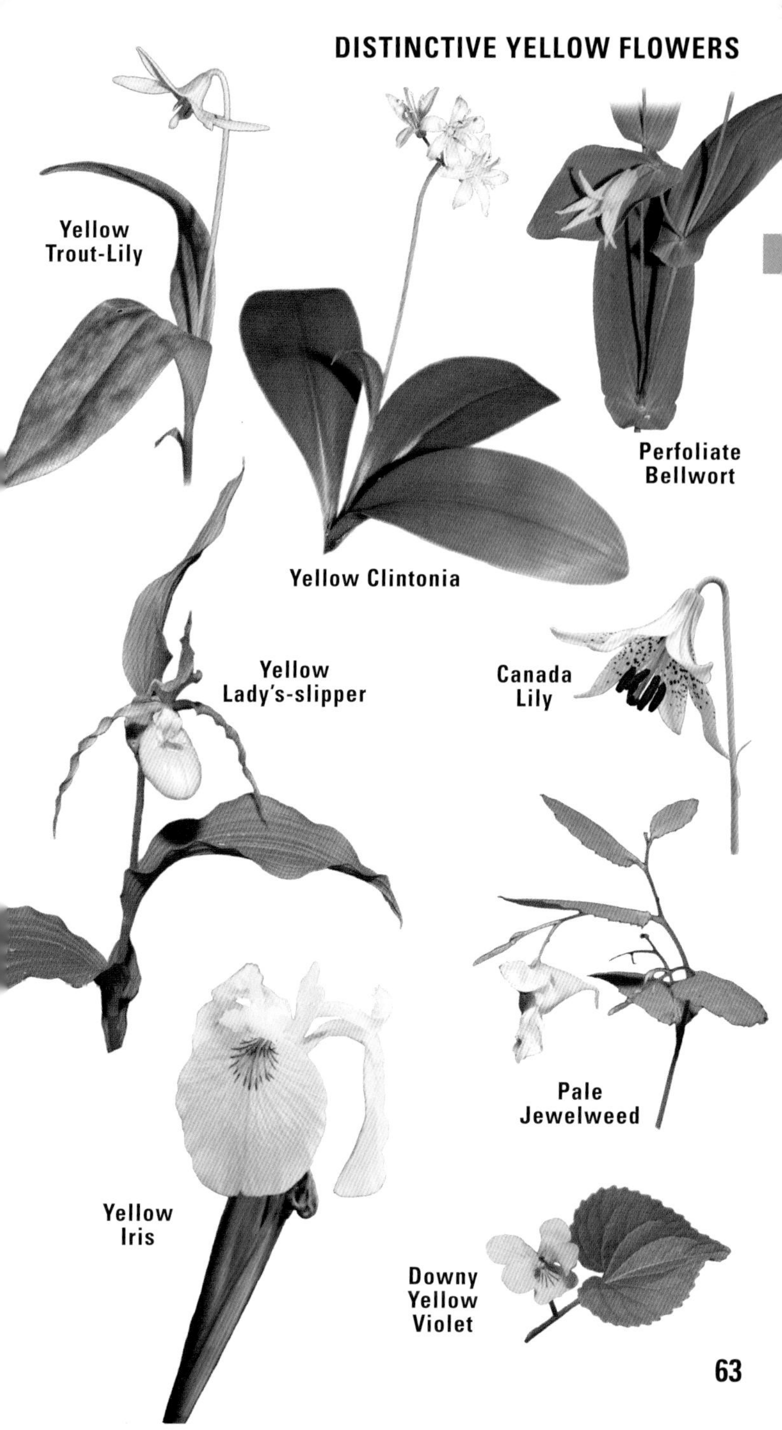
Yellow Trout-Lily
Yellow Clintonia
Perfoliate Bellwort
Yellow Lady's-slipper
Canada Lily
Pale Jewelweed
Yellow Iris
Downy Yellow Violet

DISTINCTIVE YELLOW FLOWERS

These include representatives of four families.

FLOWER-OF-AN-HOUR ***Hibiscus trionum***
Native to the Old World, now widespread in southern New England, in roadsides, fields. Mallow family (Malvaceae). ► Pale yellow to creamy flower has center marked with dark red-violet. The flower wilts quickly, hence the name. Leaves deeply divided, with narrow lobes.

YELLOW MARSH MARIGOLD ***Caltha palustris***
Along shallow, muddy streams, wooded swamps, marshes, and wet meadows, this bright flower blooms in spring (and occasionally in fall). Buttercup family (Ranunculaceae). ► 5–9 rich yellow sepals (looking like petals) surround a cluster of short stamens at center of flower. Leaves large, rounded or kidney-shaped.

TALL BUTTERCUP ***Ranunculus acris***
At least 25 species of typical buttercups are found in New England, including nearly 20 native ones, but this alien (introduced from Europe) is generally the most common and familiar. It blooms from late spring through summer in fields, roadsides, vacant lots. Buttercup family. ► Erect stem, standing 1–3' tall. Waxy yellow petals (usually 5) around cluster of short stamens. Leaves narrowly divided into 5–7 segments.

CELANDINE ***Chelidonium majus***
Native to Europe, now widespread in New England, in roadsides, damp fields, woodland edges. Blooms from spring through late summer. Poppy family (Papaveraceae). ► Flower has 4 rather frail-looking, pale yellow petals. Leaves large, deeply divided into lobes. Fine hairs on stems.

MOTH MULLEIN ***Verbascum blattaria***
Native to Eurasia, now common in New England, in fields and roadsides. Blooms from early summer into fall. Figwort family (Scrophulariaceae). ► Tall spike with 5-lobed yellow flowers, tinged with purple on the back. (Also occurs in a white form; see p. 54.) Narrow triangular leaves arranged sparsely on stem.

COMMON MULLEIN ***Verbascum thapsus***
This Old World plant is more notable for its distinctive structure than for its individual flowers. Common and widespread in roadsides, vacant lots, other disturbed sites, blooming in summer and early fall. Figwort family. ► Tall, clublike spike may grow to 6' tall. Large, woolly leaves appear as basal rosette in first summer, survive through winter, then send up tall flowering spike in second summer. Small 5-petaled flowers arranged on spike.

Flower-of-an-hour

Yellow Marsh Marigold

Tall Buttercup

Celandine

Moth Mullein

Common Mullein

YELLOW FLOWERS WITH FOUR OR FIVE PETALS

Their flowers may be superficially similar, but these plants represent four distinct families.

COMMON EVENING-PRIMROSE ***Oenothera biennis***

Evening-primroses (family Onagraceae), which are not closely related to the true primroses (see below), typically open in late afternoon and wilt the following day. This one is common and widespread in New England, in fields, roadsides. ▶ 4 broad yellow petals; small *cross-shaped stigma* at center of flower. Narrow leaves often look crowded on stem.

COMMON ST. JOHNSWORT ***Hypericum perforatum***

More than a dozen native species of St. Johnsworts are found in New England, but the most common and familiar species is this one, introduced from Europe. Widespread in fields, roadsides, disturbed soil. St. Johnswort family (Clusiaceae). ▶ Yellow flowers with 5 petals, cluster of long stamens at center. *Fine black dots* along edges of petals. Leaves in pairs.

COMMON CINQUEFOIL ***Potentilla simplex***

"Cinquefoil" means "5-leaved," an appropriate name for most members of this group. New England has more than a dozen cinquefoil species; this native is the most familiar, growing commonly in fields, woods, roadsides. Rose family (Rosaceae). ▶ Stems lie along the ground; 5-fingered leaves and 5-petaled yellow flowers rise from stems on separate stalks.

SULPHUR CINQUEFOIL ***Potentilla recta***

Native to Eurasia, this cinquefoil is now common throughout New England, in fields, roadsides. Rose family. ▶ Similar to Common Cinquefoil but stands erect (up to 2' tall), is densely hairy on stems and buds. Flowers tend to be a paler yellow, with petals notched at the tip. Leaflets relatively narrow. **Rough Cinquefoil** *(P. norvegica)*, another tall, hairy species, has 3 leaflets, not 5.

WHORLED LOOSESTRIFE ***Lysimachia quadrifolia***

An elegant, sparsely foliaged plant of woodland edges, thickets, marsh edges. Primrose family (Primulaceae). ▶ Stands 1–3' tall. Orderly and precise appearance, with leaves and small yellow flowers arranged in whorls of 4 (usually) around stem. Flowers have red dots near center.

MONEYWORT ***Lysimachia nummularia***

Also called Creeping Jenny. Native to the Old World, now widespread in New England, in disturbed wet meadows, woodland edges, roadsides near marshes. Primrose family. ▶ Stems trail along the ground, with pairs of round, shiny leaves (suggesting coins, hence the name "Moneywort") and with pairs of 5-petaled yellow flowers.

Common
Evening-
primrose
Common
St. Johnswort
Common Cinquefoil
Whorled
Loosestrife
Sulphur Cinquefoil
Moneywort

CLUSTERS OF SMALL YELLOW FLOWERS

Mostly small and mostly introduced, these represent five families.

BUTTER-AND-EGGS ***Linaria vulgaris***
Native to the Old World, this small but conspicuous plant is now common in New England, growing in clusters in fields, roadsides, vacant lots. Blooms in summer and fall. Figwort family (Scrophulariaceae). ▶ Usually about 1' tall, can be up to 3'. Top of spike crowded with creamy yellow flowers with orange "egg yolk" centers. Numerous narrow leaves crowded on stem.

BIRD'S-FOOT TREFOIL ***Lotus corniculatus***
Another alien species now found commonly here, especially in southern New England, blooming in summer and early fall. Pea family (Fabaceae). ▶ Clusters of small, bright yellow blooms with typical uneven shape of pea flowers. Small leaves arranged along trailing or upright stems, each with *5 leaflets.*

(YELLOW) SWEET CLOVER ***Melilotus officinalis***
Native to the Old World, now growing commonly on our roadsides, fields, vacant lots. Blooms from late spring through fall. Pea family. ▶ Small, pealike flowers in tall, narrow spikes; leaves with 3 leaflets. Also has a white form (p. 56), formerly treated as a separate species.

GOLDEN ALEXANDERS ***Zizia aurea***
A native North American spring flower, fairly common in edges of wet woods, meadows, roadsides. Blooms from April to June. Parsley family (Apiaceae). ▶ Top of plant with tiny golden flowers, separated into clusters on thin stalks. Complicated leaves are divided into 3 parts, each part with 3–7 leaflets.

CYPRESS SPURGE ***Euphorbia cyparissias***
Introduced from Europe, now very common on roadsides, vacant lots, other disturbed sites. Blooms from late spring through early fall. Spurge family (Euphorbiaceae). ▶ The flowers themselves are tiny, but they are framed by yellow-green bracts (may be tinged pink) that look like petals. Stems crowded with narrow, straight leaves that suggest pine needles.

COMMON TANSY ***Tanacetum vulgare***
Native to the Old World, now common in New England, in roadsides, disturbed soil. Blooms from midsummer through early fall. Daisy family (Asteraceae). ▶ *Strongly aromatic.* Flowers like fuzzy *yellow buttons;* leaves narrowly divided, fernlike.

PINEAPPLE-WEED ***Matricaria discoidea***
Another alien that thrives in disturbed sites such as vacant lots, roadsides. Daisy family. ▶ Small but distinctive, with *rounded* flower heads lacking rays, finely divided leaves. When crushed, foliage has a *smell of pineapple.*

Butter-
and-
eggs
Bird's-foot
Trefoil
(Yellow)
Sweet
Clover
Golden
Alexanders
Common
Tansy
Cypress
Spurge
Pineapple-
weed

DANDELIONS AND SIMILAR FLOWERS

These are all members of the daisy family (Asteraceae), most with flower heads consisting of clusters of short ray flowers. New England has many species similar to these; we illustrate some of the most common.

COMMON DANDELION ***Taraxacum officinale***

The familiar, cheerful weed of lawns and roadsides, introduced from Europe and now abundant here. The name has nothing to do with being dandy, but instead is based on the French "dent de lion," or lion's tooth, for the jagged leaf shape. ▶ Crowded flower head with bracts curved downward below it; milky sap in hollow stem; jagged leaves. Very similar **Red-seeded Dandelion** *(T. laevigatum)* has smaller flowers, red seeds, narrower leaf lobes.

COLTSFOOT ***Tussilago farfara***

Introduced from Europe, now widespread on roadsides, vacant lots, blooming in spring. ▶ Flower like dandelion but with *scaly leaves* along *thick* stalk. *Large leaves* appear later than flowers.

MEADOW HAWKWEED ***Hieracium caespitosum***

Another European import, now common on roadsides, blooming in summer. ▶ Leaves (with rounded edges) only at *base* of flower stalk; whole plant covered with prickly hairs. Aside from color, very similar to Orange Hawkweed (p. 74).

CANADA HAWKWEED ***Hieracium canadense***

A native species, common in woodland edges and meadows as well as disturbed sites. Blooms in late summer. ▶ May grow to 3' or taller. Stemless, toothed leaves *climb* the flower stalk.

SOW-THISTLE ***Sonchus*** **sp.**

Three species of sow-thistles, all native to the Old World, grow on New England roadsides, vacant lots, and other disturbed sites. They bloom in mid- to late summer. ▶ Flowers like dandelion, but *long* leaves on flower stalk have *spiny edges.*

YELLOW GOAT'S-BEARD ***Tragopogon lamottei***

Another plant from Europe, now common on roadsides, blooming in summer and early fall. Flowers close by midday. ▶ Long, thin, grasslike leaves clasp the smooth stem.

GOLDEN RAGWORT ***Packera aurea*** **(not shown)**

Common in wet woods and swamp edges, blooming in late spring and summer. ▶ Cluster of small blooms at top of stem, each with orange-yellow center, sparse pale yellow rays. Leaves along stalk finely divided, those at base of plant larger, *heart-shaped.*

ROUNDLEAF RAGWORT ***Packera obovata***

Fairly common in rich woods, especially in limestone areas, blooming in spring and early summer. ▶ Similar to Golden Ragwort but basal leaves *oval-shaped,* with long, tapering bases.

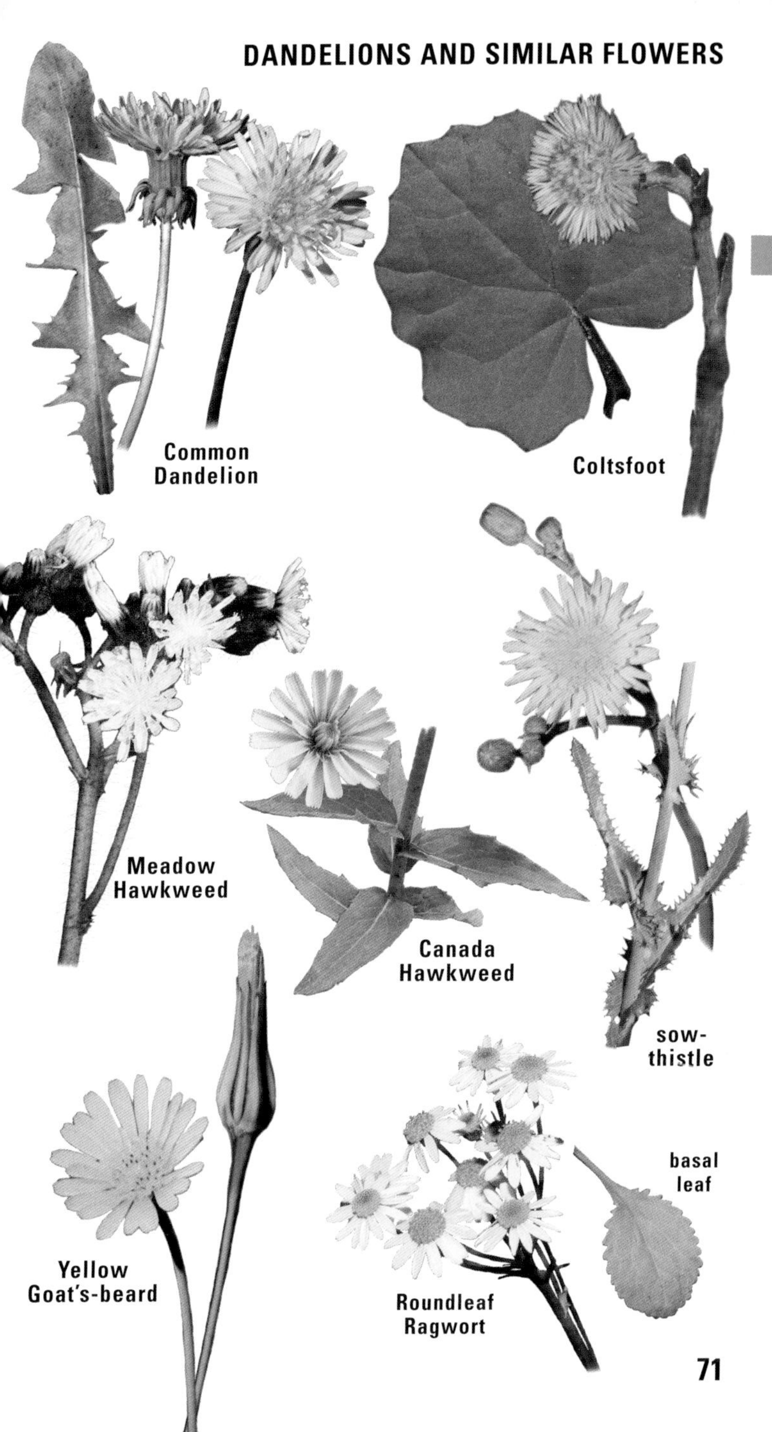
Common
Dandelion
Coltsfoot
Meadow
Hawkweed
Canada
Hawkweed
sow-
thistle
Yellow
Goat's-beard
Roundleaf
Ragwort
basal
leaf

GOLDENRODS AND SUNFLOWERS

Despite the seemingly different structure of the goldenrods, they (like all the others on this page) belong to the daisy family **(Asteraceae)**.

ROUGH-STEMMED GOLDENROD ***Solidago rugosa***

Goldenrods provide masses of rich color across fields and along edges of woods all over New England from late summer through fall. They are sometimes blamed for outbreaks of hay fever, but these seasonal allergies are more likely to be caused by ragweeds (p. 92), which bloom at about the same time and are much less conspicuous. New England has at least 2 dozen species of goldenrods, most of which are difficult to distinguish, so we recommend just calling most of them "goldenrod, sp." ▸ Goldenrods in general have masses of tiny yellow flowers, each with 1–25 rays (usually about 5–12), depending on species. The stems are usually very leafy. This common species has very rough or hairy stems, leaves with toothed edges and often a wrinkled appearance.

SEASIDE GOLDENROD ***Solidago sempervirens***

One of the more distinctive goldenrods is this coastal species. Common in dunes, marsh edges, coastal rocks, often very close to salt water. ▸ *Smooth-edged* leaves *thick*, tough, interspersed with flowers at top of plant.

BLACK-EYED SUSAN ***Rudbeckia hirta***

New England has dozens of species of flowers of the general sunflower type, daisylike with yellow rays. This is one of the most common, in fields, roadsides, woodland edges, blooming in summer and fall. ▸ The *hairy stem* has a *single* flower at the top, with *dark brown center* and 10–20 rays.

GREEN-HEADED CONEFLOWER ***Rudbeckia laciniata***

Fairly common in wet woods, swamps, edges of marshes, blooming in late summer and early fall. ▸ May stand 3–10' tall. Flower has raised *greenish knob* at center, 6–10 swept-back, *drooping* yellow rays. Leaves *strongly divided* into 3–7 narrow sections.

WOODLAND SUNFLOWER ***Helianthus divaricatus***

Common and widespread in southern New England, in dry woods, open thickets. Blooms from midsummer through fall. ▸ May stand 2–6' tall. Center of flower flat, yellow. Leaves (in pairs on smooth stem) have very short stalks, rough or hairy texture.

COMMON SNEEZEWEED ***Helenium autumnale***

Fairly common in southwestern New England, in damp meadows, streambanks. Blooms in late summer and fall. ▸ Distinctive structure, with *ball-shaped* yellow center, short petals *swept back* and *scalloped* at the tips. Leaves extend as winged flanges down along stem.

Rough-
stemmed
Goldenrod

Seaside
Goldenrod

Black-
eyed
Susan

Green-headed
Coneflower

Woodland Sunflower

Common
Sneezeweed

ORANGE AND RED FLOWERS

Only a few wildflowers are truly orange or deep red. The orange ones in this book are all on this page, while red flowers (as well as the many that lean toward pinkish red) continue on pages following this one.

SPOTTED JEWELWEED ***Impatiens capensis***

Common in undergrowth of wet woods, blooming in late summer. A member of the touch-me-not family (Balsaminaceae), so called because ripe seedpods pop explosively when touched, a neat trick to show beginners. ► May form thickets 3–5' tall. *Pale orange* flowers with darker spots *dangle* below leaves.

BUTTERFLY-WEED ***Asclepias tuberosa***

Our only orange milkweed, fairly common in dry open fields, sandy places, blooming in summer. True to its name, this is a popular nectar source for butterflies. Milkweed family (Asclepiadaceae). ► Small but complicated 5-parted orange flowers are clustered at top of stem 10–20" tall.

ORANGE HAWKWEED ***Hieracium aurantiacum***

Native to Europe but now common over most of New England in open fields, roadsides, blooming in summer. Aster family (Asteraceae). ► The hairy stem is topped with dandelion-like flowers, crowded with short rays. Many yellow flowers are similar but this is the only orange one. Smooth-edged leaves at base of plant.

COLUMBINE ***Aquilegia canadensis***

A spot of bright color in shady woods of spring, usually found along rocky ledges, hillsides. Buttercup family (Ranunculaceae). ► Bright red, *nodding* flower has yellow center and 5 *long, curved red spurs.* Leaves are strongly 3-parted.

TURK'S-CAP LILY ***Lilium superbum***

A striking native lily, mostly uncommon in southern New England in wet meadows, clearings in damp woods. Blooms in late summer. Lily family (Liliaceae). ► *Nodding* flowers have swept-back petals, dark spots, greenish star-shaped pattern in center.

WOOD LILY ***Lilium philadelphicum***

Another beautiful native, fairly widespread in dry woods, clearings, meadows. Blooms in summer. Lily family. ► Flowers are bright orange to red-orange and heavily spotted, and *face upward.* Leaves arranged in whorls around stem.

ORANGE DAY-LILY ***Hemerocallis fulva***

Native to Eurasia, a garden plant that often spreads into waste ground, vacant lots, marsh edges. May form masses of color along ditches in midsummer. Day-lily family (Hemerocallidaceae). ► Large, milky-orange flowers *face upward,* are *unspotted.* Long, pointed leaves rising from base.

TRUMPET-CREEPER ***Campsis radicans***

Showy flowers on climbing vine. See p. 140.

seedpod
Spotted Jewelweed
Butterfly-weed
Orange Hawkweed
Columbine
Turk's-cap Lily
Wood Lily
Orange Day-lily

TRILLIUMS, ORCHIDS, AND OTHERS

Trilliums are in the lily family **(Liliaceae)**. The next five species below are in the orchid family **(Orchidaceae)**; New England has more than 50 orchid species, but many are small, inconspicuous, or rare. Fringed Polygala suggests an orchid but belongs to the milkwort family **(Polygalaceae)**.

RED TRILLIUM (WAKEROBIN) ***Trillium erectum***

Another name for this spring flower is "Stinking Benjamin." Its foul-smelling blooms attract flies that act as pollinators. Fairly common in rich woods. ► Three *dark red* petals (sometimes pink, white, etc.) above three *large*, rounded leaves.

PAINTED TRILLIUM ***Trillium undulatum***

An uncommon but striking spring flower of moist woods and bogs. ► Three narrow, wavy-edged, white petals, with a *blaze of red* at the base, rising on a slender stem above three large leaves.

PINK LADY'S-SLIPPER ***Cypripedium acaule***

This orchid is also called moccasin-flower. Mostly uncommon and local in woods with acid soil. Do not pick or dig up lady's-slippers: they rarely survive transplanting, and glandular hairs on stem may cause severe rash. ► Large, pink, *pouchlike* flower on single stem; 2 large, smooth-edged leaves at base.

SHOWY LADY'S-SLIPPER ***Cypripedium reginae***

Our tallest native orchid. Local and uncommon in swampy woods, threatened by overpicking. ► Unmistakable. White sepals and petals contrast with pink pouch; leaves along thick stem.

SHOWY ORCHIS ***Galearis spectabilis***

This striking orchid, uncommon and local, blooms in late spring and early summer in rich woods. ► Sharply *bicolored* flowers feature a pinkish purple hood (lateral petals and sepals) and bright white spur. Two large, smooth-edged leaves rise from the base.

ROSE POGONIA ***Pogonia ophioglossoides***

In wet meadows, bogs, and swamps, this orchid blooms from early to midsummer. ► Single flower and leaf on slender stem, with pink petals rising above prominently *fringed lip*.

GRASS-PINK ***Calopogon tuberosus***

Another summer-blooming orchid of bogs, peat meadows, marshes, swamps. ► The crested lip (marked with yellow) is held *above* the other petals. Several flowers on a stem.

FRINGED POLYGALA (GAYWINGS) ***Polygala paucifolia***

This orchidlike little flower blooms in the shade in damp, rich woods during late spring and early summer. ► Fringed lip at tip of tubular pink blooms. Flaring sepals ("wings") on either side of flower. Leaves may stay green in winter.

Red Trillium
Painted Trillium
Pink Lady's-slipper
Showy Orchis
Showy Lady's-slipper
Rose Pogonia
Grass-pink
Fringed Polygala

SWAMP ROSE MALLOW ***Hibiscus moscheutos***

In marshes, especially near the coast, the huge blooms of this tall plant are eye-catching in late summer and early fall. Mallow family (Malvaceae). ▶ Flowers up to 6" wide, usually pink, with column of yellow stamens at center. Leaves whitish underneath.

COMMON MILKWEED ***Asclepias syriaca***

Broken stems release milky juice, hence the name. Chemicals in the plants confer protection on insects able to eat them, such as larvae of Monarchs (p. 312) and some orange-and-black beetles and bugs. This species is common in fields and roadsides. Milkweed family (Asclepiadaceae). ▶ *Round* clusters of distinctively shaped, purple-pink flowers *interspersed* with thick, smooth-edged leaves. Large, bumpy seedpods develop in late summer.

SWAMP MILKWEED ***Asclepias incarnata***

A common species of wetter habitats, such as damp fields, marshes, swamps. Milkweed family. ▶ Small clusters of pink flowers at *top* of plant. Narrow, pointed leaves.

CARDINAL-FLOWER ***Lobelia cardinalis***

A stunning plant of wet woods, swamps, streambanks, blooming in late summer. Bellflower family (Campanulaceae). ▶ Spikes of *scarlet* flowers with lobed petals. Leaves with toothed edges.

DEPTFORD PINK ***Dianthus armeria***

Introduced from Europe, now common in fields and roadsides, blooming in summer. Pink family (Caryophyllaceae). ▶ *Small* flowers, 5 pink petals with *white spots.* Leaves *very narrow.*

RED CLOVER ***Trifolium pratense***

Another Old World species, now common on open ground here, blooming spring to fall. Pea family (Fabaceae). ▶ Round, purple-rose flowers; often pale chevrons on leaves.

WILD GERANIUM ***Geranium maculatum***

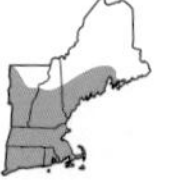

Common in open woods and edges, blooming in spring and early summer. Geranium family (Geraniaceae). ▶ *Deeply divided,* 5-parted leaves. Five wide pink petals.

NORTHERN PITCHER-PLANT ***Sarracenia purpurea***

This bizarre carnivorous plant has open, pitcher-shaped leaves, usually half-filled with water. Stiff downward-pointing hairs on the inner surfaces help to trap insects, directing them down to the water, where they are digested. Widespread but uncommon in bogs, swamps. Pitcher-plant family (Sarraceniaceae). ▶ Best recognized by unique leaves. Flowers are nodding, dark red, developing in late spring and summer on separate stalks.

Swamp Rose Mallow
Common Milkweed
Cardinal-flower
Swamp Milkweed
Deptford Pink
Red Clover
Wild Geranium
Northern Pitcher-plant

PURPLE LOOSESTRIFE ***Lythrum salicaria***

Masses of loosestrife paint the marshes in summer and early fall, but this beauty comes with a price: this nonnative invader crowds out open water and native plants necessary to wildlife. Loosestrife family (Lythraceae). ▶ Dense, narrow spike of small 6-petaled flowers. Leaves in pairs or 3s.

FIREWEED ***Chamerion angustifolium***

Named for its tendency to colonize land that has been cleared by fire or other disturbance. Common, especially toward the north, blooming in summer and early fall. Evening-primrose family (Onagraceae). ▶ Erect spike (2–7' tall) with *4-petaled,* bright pink flowers. Narrow leaves may be paler on underside.

STEEPLEBUSH ***Spiraea tomentosa***

Fairly common in meadows, overgrown fields, blooming from midsummer into fall. Rose family (Rosaceae). ▶ Tiny, 5-petaled pink flowers packed tightly in a *steeple-shaped* cluster. Stem and undersides of leaves *densely fuzzy.* Shrubby, stands up to 4' tall.

DAME'S ROCKET ***Hesperis matronalis***

This alien species is now locally common in New England, forming masses of color on roadsides. Blooms late spring to midsummer. Mustard family (Brassicaceae). ▶ Flowers with 4 petals, may be pink, white, or purple; multiple colors may grow in same patch. Narrow pods follow flowers. Leaves tooth-edged.

CROWN-VETCH ***Securigera varia***

Native to the Old World, this creeping plant has been planted here for erosion control. Now common in roadsides, disturbed sites. Pea family (Fabaceae). ▶ Roundish head of small *bicolored* flowers (pink and white). Many pairs of small leaflets.

MOTHERWORT ***Leonurus cardiaca***

Native to the Old World, now widespread here, in roadsides, vacant lots. Foliage can cause skin irritation for some people. Mint family (Lamiaceae). ▶ Pairs of *wedge-shaped* leaves on stem, with clusters of pink flowers at leaf bases.

WILD BERGAMOT ***Monarda fistulosa***

Fairly common in woodland edges, thickets, blooming in late summer. Mint family. ▶ Rounded flower head crowded with pale lavender-pink flowers, each a narrow spiky tube. Stem (*square* in cross-section) has pairs of tooth-edged leaves.

SEA-LAVENDER ***Limonium carolinianum***

A small plant of coastal marshes, noticeable as a haze of lavender in late summer. Leadwort family (Plumbaginaceae). ▶ Narrow, branching stems, with tiny flowers. Larger basal leaves.

Purple
Loosestrife
Fireweed
Steeplebush
Dame's
Rocket
Crown-
vetch
Motherwort
Wild
Bergamot
Sea-lavender

Teasels (family **Dipsacaceae**) are native to the Old World. One species thrives in New England, and other introduced forms might be found. All the other plants on this page are in the daisy family **(Asteraceae)**.

TEASEL ***Dipsacus fullonum***

Fairly common in disturbed sites such as overgrown fields, roadsides, blooming from midsummer to fall. ► Most noticeable for structure, with prickly oval flower head on tall stalk (up to 6'). In bloom, tiny pink flowers coat its surface, but dried head remains distinctive through winter. Large, paired leaves meet at stem.

BULL THISTLE ***Cirsium vulgare***

New England has several native thistles, but the 2 most familiar species are both Old World imports. This one is common in fields, roadsides, blooming from midsummer into fall. ► Usually 1–3 *large* flower heads, with *yellow-tipped spines* on bracts below bloom. Spiny stem; spiny leaves extend as "wings" down stem.

CANADA THISTLE ***Cirsium arvense***

Despite the common name, native to Europe. Very common in open areas, blooming in late summer. ► Smaller, *much more numerous* flowers than Bull Thistle; mostly *smooth* stem.

NEW ENGLAND BLAZING-STAR ***Liatris scariosa***

Uncommon in dry woodland edges, sandy areas, blooming in early fall. Considered endangered in New Hampshire and Rhode Island, threatened or of concern elsewhere. ► Tufted, frayed flowers look somewhat thistlelike, but plant structure differs, with blooms and narrow leaves arranged on spike 1–3' tall.

GREAT BURDOCK ***Arctium lappa***

Burdocks, introduced from Europe, are now common here in roadsides, disturbed land. ► Large, globular flower heads on long stalks; very large basal leaves. **Common Burdock** *(A. minus)* has very short flower stalks, flowers less than 1" across.

SPOTTED KNAPWEED ***Centaurea stoebe***

Another European import, now common in roadsides and fields, blooming in summer. ► Flower heads have a *stringy* look, may be pink or white; black tips on lower bracts. Narrowly lobed leaves.

SPOTTED JOE-PYE-WEED ***Eupatoriadelphus maculatus***

Fairly common in wet meadows, blooming midsummer into fall. ► Flat-topped cluster of tiny pink flowers. Stem *spotted* purple. Leaves in whorls of 4 or 5. Compare to ironweed (p. 90).

SALTMARSH FLEABANE ***Pluchea odorata***

Common in coastal marshes, blooming in August and September. ► Rather *flat* clusters of stiff, brushlike pink flowers, without spreading rays. Strong-smelling. Leaves have toothed edges.

winter
Teasel
Canada Thistle
Bull Thistle
New England Blazing-star
Spotted Knapweed
Spotted Joe-Pye-weed
Great Burdock
Saltmarsh Fleabane

Many plants on the preceding few pages have flowers that could be called either lavender or pink, but with this page we begin to address those that are more toward the blue end of the spectrum.

BLUE FLAG IRIS ***Iris versicolor***

Suggesting the common iris of gardens, this native is common throughout New England in marshes, pond edges. Blooms spring to midsummer. Iris family (Iridaceae). ▶ Complex flower, with 3 rising petals, 3 broad, drooping sepals showing *veined pattern.* Leaves long and broad, rising from the base. Stands 2–3' tall.

BLUE-EYED GRASSES ***Sisyrinchium* sp.**

Despite the group name, these are members of the iris family. Half a dozen species of blue-eyed grasses occur in New England, all fairly similar, growing in marshes, wet meadows, fields. Most bloom from late spring to midsummer. ▶ Slender and delicate, usually less than 2' tall. Flowers with 6 petals, blue-violet (white in one species) with *yellow* centers.

VIRGINIA SPIDERWORT ***Tradescantia virginiana***

Usually somewhat uncommon but widespread, in edges of deciduous woodlands, thickets, meadows, roadsides. Spiderwort family (Commelinaceae). ▶ Slender, upright plant with cluster of *3-petaled* purple flowers at top; leaves long, slender, pointed.

ASIATIC DAYFLOWER ***Commelina communis***

As the name implies, this sprawling weed is not native here but is becoming common in roadsides, vacant lots, other disturbed areas. Spiderwort family. ▶ *Uneven* shape, with 2 larger violet-blue petals, 1 smaller white one. Wider leaves than Spiderwort.

GREAT LOBELIA ***Lobelia siphilitica***

Uncommon but striking is this flower of wet woods and swamps. Blooms in late summer and early fall. Bellflower family (Campanulaceae). ▶ Complex flower, bell-shaped with 2 narrow petals above, 3 wider ones below. White stripes on lower violet-blue petals. Pointed leaves on stem. Stands 1–3' tall.

HAREBELL ***Campanula rotundifolia***

Widespread around rocky slopes, hilltops, ledges, often in limestone areas, blooming in summer. Bellflower family. ▶ Stems and leaves very narrow; flowers droop. Has round basal leaves at first, but these soon wither.

GREATER FRINGED GENTIAN ***Gentianopsis crinita***

A beautiful, fall-blooming flower of wet meadows, edges of wet woods, stream margins. Gentian family (Gentianaceae). ▶ The blue-violet, tubular flower spreads out at the top into 4 *fringed* petals. Pairs of leaves along stem. Stands 1–3' tall.

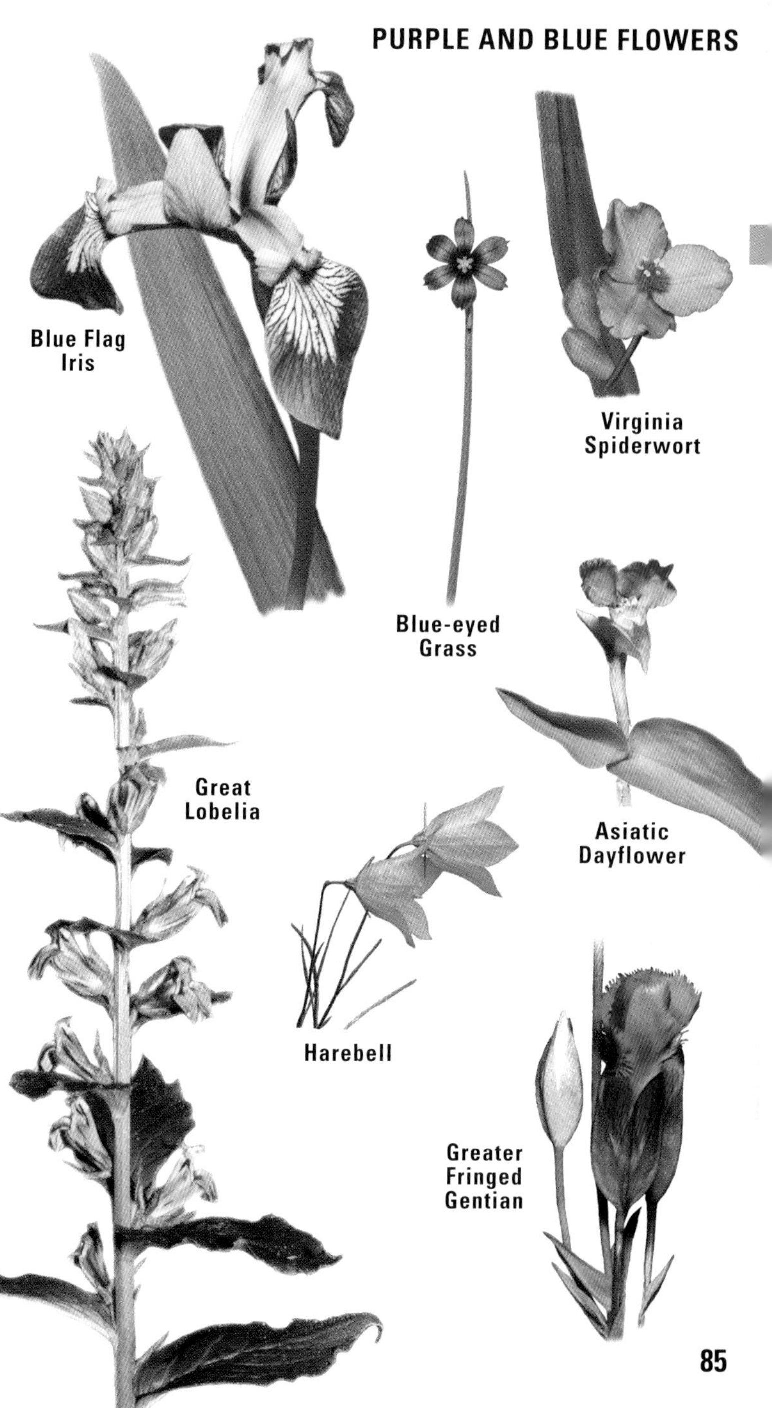

Blue Flag Iris

Virginia Spiderwort

Blue-eyed Grass

Great Lobelia

Asiatic Dayflower

Harebell

Greater Fringed Gentian

WILD LUPINE ***Lupinus perennis***

Common in dry fields, open woods, especially on sandy soil, blooming from May to July. Pea family (Fabaceae). ► Small blue-violet blooms, with uneven shape of pea flowers, arranged on a spike up to 2' tall. Compound leaves with 7–11 *radiating leaflets.* Note: cultivated varieties of lupines are often found growing wild in disturbed sites, such as roadsides, and they outnumber the native species in some areas. They are often larger (up to 4' tall), with denser flower heads, and with 12 or more leaflets per leaf; their flowers vary in color (can be pink or white).

COW VETCH ***Vicia cracca (not shown)***

Vetches are sprawling or trailing plants, mostly growing in overgrown fields, woodland edges. All of the common ones in New England (more than half a dozen species) are native to the Old World, including this and the next species. Cow Vetch blooms from late spring through summer. Pea family. ► Blue-violet flowers densely packed along *one side* of stem. Leaves with 8–12 pairs of small leaflets and with tendril at end.

HAIRY VETCH ***Vicia villosa***

Another nonnative vetch, common in fields and disturbed sites, blooming from late spring to fall. Pea family. ► Similar to Cow Vetch but usually with *bicolored* flowers (blue-violet and white). Somewhat more hairy, and with fewer leaflets (6–8 pairs).

BITTERSWEET NIGHTSHADE ***Solanum dulcamara***

Introduced from Europe, this may grow as a low plant or as a climbing vine in thickets, overgrown fields. Blooms from late spring to early fall. Nightshade family (Solanaceae). ► The small flowers have 5 pale violet petals bent back away from the protruding yellow center. Leaves with small "ears" at bases.

PURPLE AVENS ***Geum rivale***

Locally common in swamps, wet meadows, blooming in late spring and summer. Rose family (Rosaceae). ► *Nodding* flowers at top of tall stem; yellowish petals are mostly hidden by conspicuous *purple* sepals. Leaves on stem are moderately small and 3-parted; basal leaves usually much larger and wider.

PICKERELWEED ***Pontederia cordata***

In marshes and shallow ponds, these plants form solid patches, blooming in summer and fall. Water-hyacinth family (Pontederiaceae). ► Spikes of blue-violet flowers up to 4' tall; large leaves, roughly arrowhead-shaped. Blooms of Purple Loosestrife (p. 80) are smaller, more reddish purple. Compare leaves to those of Broad-leaved Arrowhead (p. 94).

Wild
Lupine
Hairy
Vetch
Purple
Avens
basal
leaf
Bittersweet
Nightshade
Pickerelweed

TRUE FORGET-ME-NOT ***Myosotis scorpioides***

A small plant of wet places, such as along the edges of ponds and slow-moving streams, blooming from late spring to fall. Borage family (Boraginaceae). ▶ *Small* 5-petaled flowers are sky blue with yellow centers. They grow along spreading, curving stems that uncoil as the flowers bloom.

AZURE BLUETS ***Houstonia caerulea***

These tiny flowers can be conspicuous for their sheer numbers, forming a haze of pale dots in grassy places during spring and early summer. Madder family (Rubiaceae). ▶ Very small flowers (less than ½" across) with 4 petals; pale blue to whitish, with yellow at center. Leaves mostly at base of plant.

COMMON BLUE VIOLET ***Viola sororia***

New England has more than 30 species of violets, small plants of woods and meadows, most blooming in spring or early summer. A few have white or yellow blooms, but violet-blue is the color for most; the many species are separated mainly by leaf shape and by fine details of the flowers. This is one of the most common of the blue species. Violet family (Violaceae). ▶ Has 5 petals, the lowest larger and strongly veined. Heart-shaped leaves.

HENBIT ***Lamium amplexicaule***

Native to the Old World but now widespread here. Individual plants are small, but they may carpet large areas of vacant lots, disturbed sites. Mint family (Lamiaceae). ▶ Small pinkish to purple flowers rise from leaf bases. Leaves rounded, with scalloped edges, upper ones *clasping* the square stem.

GROUND-IVY ***Glechoma hederacea***

Another alien species that establishes well on lawns, vacant lots, roadsides. Mint family. ▶ Small purple flowers rise from leaf bases; leaves rounded, with scalloped edges. Suggests Henbit, but all leaves have stalks, not clasping the stem.

MARSH SKULLCAP ***Scutellaria galericulata***

Widespread and fairly common in marshes, swamps, wet meadows, blooming summer to early fall. Mint family. ▶ Stands 1–3' tall. Pairs of leaves, with slightly toothed edges and very short stalks, on square stem. Blue-violet flowers grow from leaf bases.

VIRGINIA WATERLEAF ***Hydrophyllum virginianum***

Locally common in understory of rich, deciduous woods, especially in wet places, blooming from late spring through summer. Waterleaf family (Hydrophyllaceae). ▶ Flowers pale purple to whitish, with very long stamens creating a fringed look. Leaves large, with 5–7 toothed lobes, and often with a mottled look.

True Forget-me-not

Common Blue Violet

Azure Bluets

Henbit

Ground-ivy

Marsh Skullcap

Virginia Waterleaf

These are all in the daisy family **(Asteraceae).**

NEW ENGLAND ASTER ***Symphyotrichum novae-angliae***
New England has some 3 dozen species of asters, the majority of which have blue to violet flowers and bloom in late summer or fall. They add a beautiful touch of early fall color to fields and woodland edges throughout this region. Until recently they were all placed in the genus *Aster,* which was easy to remember, but recently almost all have been reclassified into other genera. Identifying all of these asters can be a challenge, but this is one of the more common and distinctive ones. ► Large and colorful, standing 2–7' tall, with many flowers, each flower having 40 or more rays. Flowers usually blue-violet, sometimes pink or white. Bases of leaves clasp the hairy stem.

STIFF ASTER ***Ionactis linariifolius***
Another widespread and fairly distinctive aster, this one grows mainly in drier sites, including fields, woodland edges, roadsides with sandy or rocky soil. Like most of the other asters, it blooms in fall. ► Pale blue-violet rays around yellow centers of flowers, as on many other asters. *Stiff stems,* often with many growing close together; leaves *very narrow* and stiff.

TALL BLUE LETTUCE ***Lactuca biennis***
Fairly common in damp woodland edges, thickets, clearings, blooming from midsummer to fall. ► Somewhat similar to asters but with many small flowers crowded at top of plant (flowers usually pale blue, sometimes white or yellow). Very large, *coarsely toothed* leaves. May stand up to 15' tall. Other species of blue lettuces in New England are shorter, with smaller leaves.

NEW YORK IRONWEED ***Vernonia noveboracensis***
Fairly common in southern New England in wet meadows, edges of ponds and streams, rank thickets, blooming in late summer and early fall. ► May stand 3–7' tall. Top of plant crowded with clusters of magenta flowers. Numerous long, narrow, stalkless leaves on stem. Compare to Spotted Joe-pye-weed (p. 82).

CHICORY ***Cichorium intybus***
Introduced from Europe, this beautiful weed is now widespread and abundant in North America, growing in all types of open fields, roadsides, thickets, and woodland edges, and blooming through most of the summer and fall. ► Pale blue flowers (rarely pink or white) grow along the stiff stem. Petals roughly squared off and *fringed* at the tips. Lobed, coarsely toothed leaves, growing mainly at base of plant.

Stiff Aster

New England Aster

Tall Blue Lettuce

New York Ironweed

Chicory

SOME ODD GREEN AND BROWN FLOWERS

JACK-IN-THE-PULPIT ***Arisaema triphyllum***

A treasure of the spring woods is this fascinating plant, found blooming from April to June in swamps, bogs, forests. Arum family (Araceae). ► Flowers are tiny, hidden within the structure of the "pulpit" where the preacher, or "Jack" (the spadix), stands under the curved canopy. One or two large, 3-parted leaves.

SKUNK CABBAGE ***Symplocarpus foetidus***

In wooded swamps and along shallow forest streams, the huge leaves of this plant (foul-smelling when crushed) are conspicuous in summer. Before the leaves develop, in early spring, the odd flower is more eye-catching. Arum family. ► Structure enclosing flower may be green to brown, heavily mottled.

WILD GINGER ***Asarum canadense***

Locally common in rich deciduous woods, blooming in spring. Pipevine family (Aristolochiaceae). ► The small, reddish brown flower is less noticeable than the large, *heart-shaped* leaves.

STINGING NETTLE ***Urtica dioica***

Native to the Old World, this weed is now unfortunately widespread and fairly common in New England, in woods, roadsides, thickets. The plant is covered with painfully effective stinging hairs. Nettle family (Urticaceae). ► Leaves in pairs, heart-shaped with toothed edges. Sprays of tiny greenish flowers at leaf bases.

COMMON RAGWEED ***Ambrosia artemisiifolia***

Widespread and common, this native has successfully adapted to roadsides and other disturbed sites. Ragweed pollen causes hay fever for many. Daisy family (Asteraceae). ► *Finely divided* leaves. Spikes of tiny yellow-green flowers in late summer and fall.

GREAT RAGWEED ***Ambrosia trifida***

Another adaptable native now found widely on roadsides and vacant lots. Daisy family. ► Much larger than Common Ragweed (up to 15' tall) with large, *3-pointed leaves.*

MARSH-ELDER ***Iva frutescens***

This tall, shrubby plant grows along the upper margins of salt marshes, just above normal high tide, blooming in late summer and fall. Daisy family. ► Up to 10' tall. *Thick* leaves grow in opposite pairs. Small, nodding green flowers among upper leaves.

COCKLEBUR ***Xanthium strumarium***

Widespread in roadsides, farms, vacant lots, sandy places. Daisy family. ► The tiny, greenish male flowers are hardly noticeable, but the female flowers develop into burs that are a little too noticeable when they hitch a ride in our socks or shoelaces. Large leaves, often with reddish stalks.

Skunk Cabbage
Jack-in-the-pulpit
Stinging Nettle
Wild Ginger
Great Ragweed
Marsh-elder
Common Ragweed
Cocklebur

SOME FLOWERS OF PONDS AND MARSHES

FRAGRANT WATER-LILY ***Nymphaea odorata***
Common and widespread on ponds, open marshes, and other still waters, blooming in summer and early fall. Water-lily family (Nymphaeaceae). ▶ The large floating leaves (lily pads) may be turned up at edges, exposing purple tinge to underside. Flowers up to 5" across, white with numerous tapering petals.

YELLOW WATER-LILY ***Nuphar lutea***
Another common plant of marshes, slow-flowing rivers, blooming from spring to fall. Water-lily family. ▶ Large floating leaves (lily pads). The odd *globular* flower (actually yellow sepals concealing the flower) does not open up fully.

AMERICAN LOTUS ***Nelumbo lutea***
Local and uncommon in calm, shallow waters of southern New England, conspicuous where it occurs. Lotus-lily family (Nelumbonaceae). ▶ Suggests a water-lily, but most of the huge leaves are held above the water, with fewer floating on the surface. Huge, pale yellow flowers (up to 9" across) with raised disk in center.

WATER ARUM ***Calla palustris***
This odd plant is widespread in bogs, edges of ponds. Arum family (Araceae). ▶ Bloom is a yellow spike of tiny flowers, with backdrop of single white spathe. Large, heart-shaped leaves.

BROAD-LEAVED ARROWHEAD ***Sagittaria latifolia***
Arrowheads grow in shallow water of ponds and marshes. New England has several species; this one is usually most common. Water-plantain family (Alismataceae). ▶ Arrowhead-shaped leaves of variable width. 3-petaled white flowers in groups of 3.

BROAD-LEAVED CATTAIL ***Typha latifolia***
Familiar plants forming solid patches in marshes, ponds, ditches. Cattail family (Typhaceae). ▶ Upright, bladelike leaves. Stem with brown "sausage" of pistillate flowers, and briefly with pale staminate flowers just above. **Narrow-leaved Cattail** *(T. angustifolia)* has thinner leaves, *gap* between dark and pale flowers.

BUR-REED ***Sparganium* sp.**
Often common in marshes and ponds. New England has 7 species in this group. Bur-reed family (Sparganiaceae). ▶ Long, narrow leaves, angled stems. Flowers form green, burlike balls.

UMBRELLA SEDGE ***Cyperus* sp.**
New England has about 20 species of sedges in this group. Not all are aquatic; some grow in dry, sandy places, fields, roadsides. Sedge family (Cyperaceae). ▶ Variable in appearance, but with 3-sided stem, flowers in form of clusters of spikelets.

Fragrant Water-lily
Yellow Water-lily
American Lotus
Water Arum
bur-reed
Broad-leaved Cattail
Broad-leaved Arrowhead
umbrella sedge

TREES AND LARGE SHRUBS

It goes without saying that trees are the most obvious of New England's natural attractions and are among the most important natural resources. The timber and forest products industry has played a leading role in the region's economy in the past and continues to be significant. Tourists now flock to parts of New England annually to witness the brilliant display of fall colors. Of course, we don't need such economic reasons in order to appreciate the beauty of trees and to understand their importance in defining the natural regions of New England. And trees become even easier to appreciate if we know what kinds we're seeing.

What's a tree? This might seem like a silly question — every four-year-old knows a tree on sight. But in fact, there is no universally accepted definition of a tree. In particular, there's no consensus on the difference between a small tree and a large shrub.

Some definitions suggest that a tree has a single trunk and stands more than 15 (or more than 20) feet tall, while a shrub has multiple trunks and is shorter. But there are many borderline cases that could be considered either small trees or large shrubs, so we have combined them in this section. Some distinctive small shrubs are included in the section after this one, but we have placed a few here because they are so clearly similar to related trees (for example, Creeping Juniper is included here with other junipers). If in doubt, check in both sections.

Native, naturalized, and planted trees. In this guide, we include most of the native trees that you are likely to see in New England. However, hundreds of other kinds of trees grow in this region as well — species from other parts of the world that have been planted here and cultivated varieties that don't look quite like anything in nature. We can't include all of these possibilities in a compact field guide, of course. So in city parks, gardens, and residential areas, you probably will see some trees that look like nothing in this guide.

Most of these exotic trees do not establish themselves here, because they are not well adapted to local conditions, but there are exceptions. For example, Ailanthus is native to Asia, but this adaptable tree is often found growing wild in disturbed sites in southern New England. Such plants are said to be naturalized. We have tried to include those naturalized trees that you are most likely to see.

Identifying trees is a valuable exercise for anyone with an interest in any aspect of nature. Habitat types are often defined by the common trees there. An oak-hickory forest is likely to have a different mix of wildlife and wildflowers than a maple forest, for example, and recognizing the basic trees is an important first step. Here are some things to consider:

Leaf shape is an obvious point, but be sure that you're looking at the whole leaf! Some trees have compound leaves, with multiple leaflets attached to one central stalk. If you're not sure whether you're looking at a whole leaf or at one leaflet of a compound leaf, check its base. Where a leaf stalk attaches to a twig, typically there is a small bud and a small structure called a stipule. Where a leaflet attaches to a central stalk, there's no bud or stipule. With a little practice, it's easy to tell the difference.

simple leaf of Common Witch-Hazel

compound leaf of Bitternut Hickory, with nine leaflets

There is often a lot of variation in leaf shape, even on the same tree, so it's important to look at several leaves on a tree to get an accurate idea of shape. Leaf size also varies, and leaves may be larger on young saplings or on branches in the shade.

On coniferous trees, the leaves are modified into needles or scales. It's still important to note their shape, their length, their number, and how they're attached to the twigs.

Bark pattern makes a few trees instantly recognizeable — sycamores, for example. On most it is not quite so distinctive, but it's always worth noticing, and it often helps to distinguish among similar species.

Flowers of trees are often small, inconspicuous, and short-lived. There are exceptions; some trees have large, showy flowers, drawing attention and making them quickly identifiable, even from a distance. We have tried to illustrate or at least mention the tree flowers that you are likely to notice.

Fruits of trees can be very useful for identifying them, especially for some trees after they lose their leaves in fall. It's important to remember that botanists define the word "fruit" more broadly than what we find in the produce section at the grocery store. The fruit is the structure that encloses the seed, and depending on the type of tree, a non-botanist might call it a fruit, a berry, a cone, a nut, a winged seed, or something else.

fruits of oaks, known as acorns, don't fit the popular image of "fruit"

PINES

are separated from our other evergreens by having their needles arranged in *clusters* of 2–5. Along with the hemlocks, firs, and spruces on the next page, they make up the pine family **(Pinaceae).** To identify pines, note the number of needles per cluster, the length and color of the needles, bark color and texture, and shape of the cones.

EASTERN WHITE PINE ***Pinus strobus***

When the Pilgrims landed, forests of White Pine covered much of the northeast, some of the trees standing 200' tall. The superior wood of this tree became very important in the economy of the colonies, and almost all the virgin forest was logged; but this is still a very common tree in New England forests, and some older specimens are again attaining impressive size. ▶ Up close, recognized by *slender* needles, 2–4" long and 5 to a cluster (our other pines have 2 or 3). Cones *long and thin.* At a distance, note the elegant shape, with branches arranged in widely spaced whorls.

RED PINE ***Pinus resinosa***

Fairly common on upland sites in northern New England, often found with Eastern White Pine although usually less numerous. Also known as Norway Pine but for no good reason, as it is native to only Canada and the U.S. ▶ Needles 4–6" long, in clusters of 2, rather brittle: if bent, they may snap cleanly, rather than bending like most pine needles. Trunk bark usually tinged reddish.

PITCH PINE ***Pinus rigida***

Thrives on sandy and gravelly soils in southern New England; common on Cape Cod. ▶ Stout needles 3–5" long, in *clusters of 3.* Cones egg-shaped; old cones stay attached and may accumulate on trees. Trunk bark is dark gray and brown, deeply furrowed.

JACK PINE ***Pinus banksiana***

Usually a small tree growing on poor soil. Cones remain closed for years, opening after fires, allowing this tree to colonize burned areas. ▶ *Needles short,* only 1–1½" long, in clusters of 2. Cones usually *curved.* Many old cones may accumulate on trees.

SCOTCH PINE ***Pinus sylvestris***

Native across Europe and northern Asia, commonly used as an ornamental in New England and sometimes found growing in the wild. ▶ Needles mostly 1½–3" long, in clusters of 2, tinged blue-green. Trunk bark reddish brown to gray; on older trees, upper trunk looks *orange.*

AUSTRIAN PINE ***Pinus nigra***

Another Old World species popularly used in plantings, sometimes growing in the wild, especially in Massachusetts. ▶ Needles dark green, 3–6" long, in clusters of 2. Cones 2–3" long, with tiny prickles at tips of scales. Trunk bark gray, often with yellow tinge. Red Pine (see above) has brittle needles, lacks cone prickles, and usually has reddish tinge to bark.

Eastern White Pine
Red Pine
Pitch Pine
Jack Pine
Scotch Pine
Austrian Pine

Spruces, firs, and hemlocks are in the pine family with the true pines on the previous page; the yew family is distinct **(Taxaceae).**

BLACK SPRUCE ***Picea mariana***

Abundant farther north, in solid stands over large areas of the subarctic. More local in New England, mainly in bogs, subalpine areas. ▶ Spruces have short, roughly 4-sided needles, densely packed around the twigs. The needles leave short stubs when they fall, so bare twigs are rough. At a distance, spruces look steeple-shaped. This species is known by needles less than ½" long, cones only about 1" long, many old cones remaining on trees.

RED SPRUCE ***Picea rubens***

Fairly common in hillside woods, well-drained soils. ▶ Like Black Spruce but needles at least ½" long and *yellow-green;* cones more than 1" long, falling soon after they mature.

WHITE SPRUCE ***Picea glauca***

A tree of the far north; locally common in New England, in damp, rich woods, or in stunted form in high mountains. ▶ Like other spruces but needles distinctly *blue-green with a whitish bloom* and mostly more than ½" long. Cones 1–2" long and falling soon after they mature. Foliage has unpleasant odor when crushed.

COLORADO BLUE SPRUCE ***Picea pungens*** **(not shown)**

Commonly planted as an ornamental, sometimes found growing in the wild. ▶ Suggests White Spruce but needles even more distinctly *blue*-green, mature cones longer than 2", crushed foliage *lacks* unpleasant odor.

NORWAY SPRUCE ***Picea abies***

Another popular ornamental, often found growing in wild or semiwild situations. ▶ Dark green needles more than ½" long; *drooping* twigs. Best known by *very long cones,* usually more than 4" long.

BALSAM FIR ***Abies balsamea***

A northern tree with aromatic foliage, making it popular for use in wreaths and pillows and as a Christmas tree. ▶ Differs from spruces in having *flatter,* blunt needles, curved upward on the twigs. Short cones stand *upright* on upper branches.

EASTERN HEMLOCK ***Tsuga canadensis***

A typical tree of cool, shady forests, especially in hilly or rocky terrain. ▶ *Flattened* needles ½" long, dark green above with narrow whitish lines on underside. Needles grow in flat sprays along the sides of twigs. Cones very small, dangling from twigs.

CANADA YEW ***Taxus canadensis***

An evergreen shrub, not a tree, growing 3–6' tall in undergrowth of forest. ▶ Flat, pointed needles are dark green above, pale green below. *Red, berrylike fruits* appear in late summer.

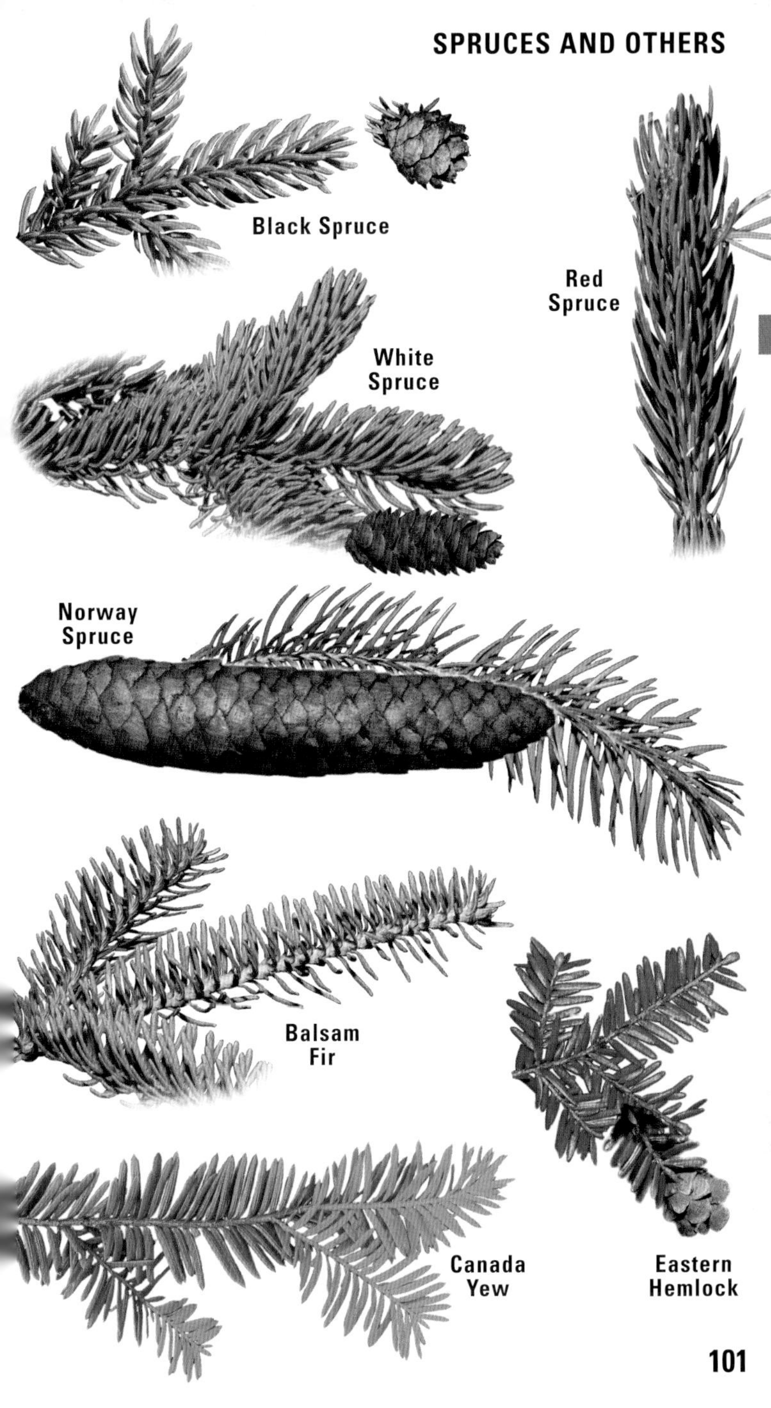
Black Spruce
Red Spruce
White Spruce
Norway Spruce
Balsam Fir
Canada Yew
Eastern Hemlock

JUNIPERS, CEDARS, LARCHES

The first five species below, with tiny, scalelike, evergreen leaves arranged on feathery sprays, belong to the cypress family **(Cupressaceae)**. The Tamarack is classified in the pine family **(Pinaceae)** along with most of the plants on the two preceding spreads.

EASTERN REDCEDAR ***Juniperus virginiana***

Common in southern New England, usually in open woodland, overgrown fields, dry areas. The blue "berries" (actually small cones with a fleshy covering) are popular with many birds. ▶ Usually a medium-sized, columnar tree, but can grow in shrubby form. Feathery evergreen foliage, mostly scalelike but with some elongated, sharper needles. Bark is dry, shredding in thin strips.

COMMON JUNIPER ***Juniperus communis*** **(not shown)**

Generally growing as a shrub in New England, only occasionally reaching the size of a small tree. Fairly common in pastures, woodland edges, dry rocky places. ▶ Suggests a shrubby Eastern Redcedar but foliage has more *elongated* needles, *whitened* on one side and arranged in whorls of 3.

CREEPING JUNIPER ***Juniperus horizontalis*** **(not shown)**

Probably never reaches tree size, but included here since it looks recognizably similar to other junipers. Uncommon, scattered, on rocky or sandy soils. ▶ Similar to Common Juniper but rarely over 3' tall. Needles greenish or whitish, but *not* bicolored.

NORTHERN WHITE-CEDAR ***Thuja occidentalis***

Widespread but mostly uncommon in New England, in swamps and forest. ▶ Medium-tall evergreen with very *flattened*, feathery foliage. Trunk bark with fibrous pattern, grayish to reddish brown. Cones are small, with only a few scales.

ATLANTIC WHITE-CEDAR ***Chamaecyparis thyoides***

Localized, mostly in swamps near the coast. ▶ A medium-tall tree, similar to Northern White-Cedar but with foliage not so strongly flattened. Cones slightly larger and with a fleshy covering. Trunk bark reddish brown, with orderly ridges.

TAMARACK (AMERICAN LARCH) ***Larix laricina***

An "evergreen" that loses its leaves in winter. Grows mostly in very wet places: bogs, swamps, edges of ponds. ▶ Needles short (about ½" long), flexible, pale green, growing in tufts on short spur twigs. Needles turn yellow and then fall off in autumn. Recognized in winter by spindly shape, orange-brown "dead" look. Cones very small, ½" long. **European Larch** *(Larix decidua)*, planted as an ornamental and sometimes found growing wild, has longer needles and cones (over 1" long).

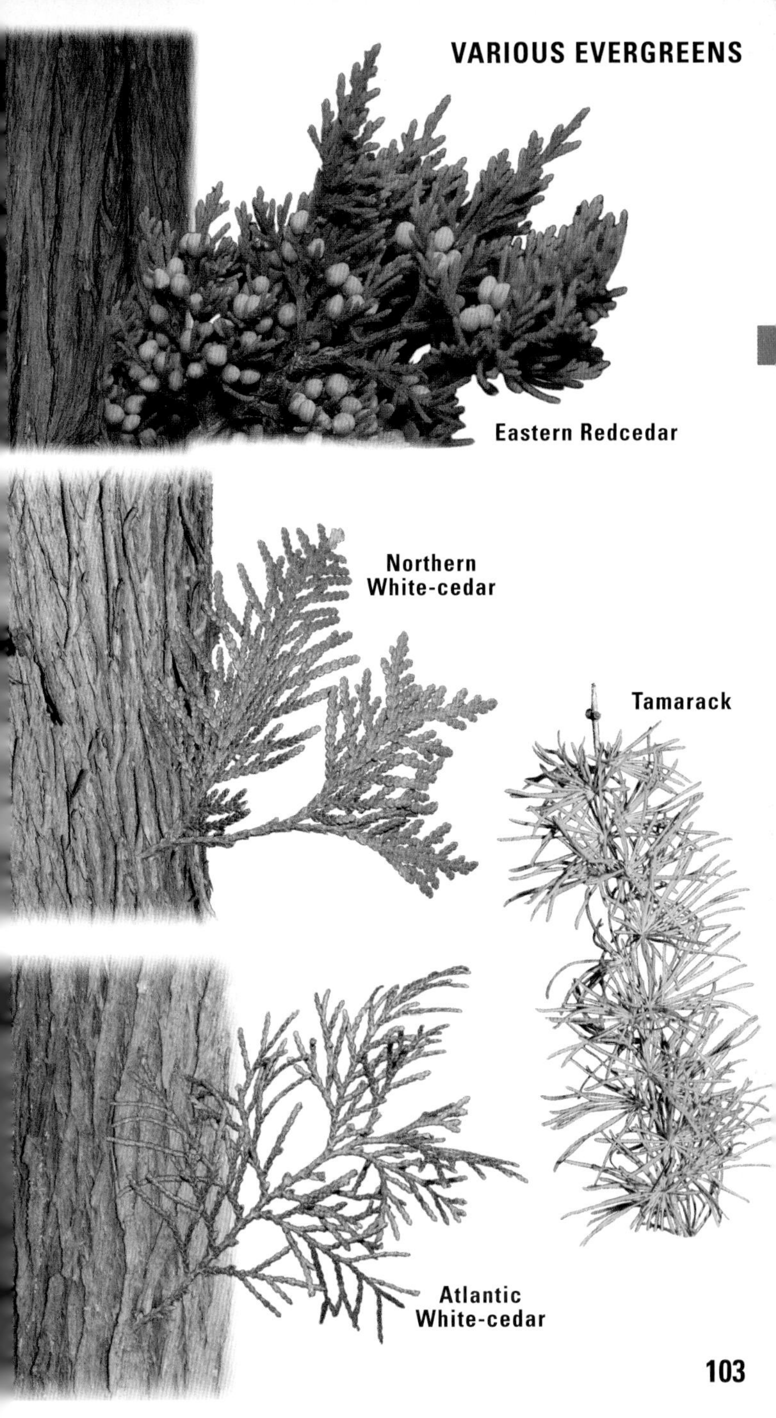
Eastern Redcedar
Northern White-cedar
Tamarack
Atlantic White-cedar

MAPLES

(family **Aceraceae**) have great economic importance to New England as the source for the sap used in producing maple syrup — a process the colonists learned from Native Americans. The beautiful wood of maples is popular for making furniture, and these trees are stars in the foliage display that draws thousands of tourists every fall. Maples are our only trees with opposite, lobed leaves. Their distinctive fruit, called samaras or keys, are winged seeds that spiral to the ground like tiny helicopters.

SUGAR MAPLE ***Acer saccharum***

Popular among "sweet-tooths," Sugar Maple is the main source for sap used to produce maple syrup and sugar. Also prized by those seeking fall colors for its stunning, multicolored foliage in autumn. ▶ Large tree with dense, rounded crown. **Black Maple** *(A. nigrum)*, local in New England, is similar but often has darker bark and leaves. Its leaf edges are *wavy and drooping*.

SILVER MAPLE ***Acer saccharinum***

Rapidly growing, popular shade tree. Short-lived. Brittle branches break easily during storms. Bark and wood contain tannins used by the pioneers to make ink and dyes. ▶ Medium to large tree with short trunk and wide-spreading crown. Leaves pale green above, *silvery white* below. Broken twigs may have an unpleasant odor. Fall color pale yellow.

RED MAPLE ***Acer rubrum***

A rapid grower frequently found in swamps. Often the first tree to kick off the dazzling fall color display for which New England is famous. ▶ Medium sized, slender, with upright branches forming a somewhat narrow crown. Flowers, fruit, leafstalks, and fall foliage *red*. Broken twigs do not have an unpleasant odor.

STRIPED MAPLE ***Acer pensylvanicum***

A small tree or large shrub with *green*, white-striped bark. Important winter food source for many animals, including Ruffed Grouse and Moose. Sometimes called "moosewood." ▶ Bright *green bark* with *whitish stripes* and bright *yellow flowers* are the most distinctive features. Twigs smooth. Fall color yellow.

EASTERN MOUNTAIN MAPLE ***Acer spicatum***

This small tree or shrub is almost always found in the company of Striped Maple. Hardy and adapted to shade, it sometimes forms fairly dense thickets. ▶ Similar to Striped Maple. Best separated by its dark bark (*without* white stripes), smaller leaves, and velvety twigs. Fall color bright red or orange.

NORWAY MAPLE ***Acer platanoides***

Introduced species, native to Europe. Popularly planted as a "street tree" for its resistance to pollutants. Rapidly expanding its range. ▶ Resembles Sugar Maple, but leaves usually larger, darker, shaped like Sycamore leaves. When snapped, leafstalks produce *milky juice*. Fall color bright yellow.

Sugar Maple
bark
fruit
fall color
Black Maple
fall color
bark
underside of leaf
Silver Maple
Red Maple
fruit
Eastern Mountain Maple
flower
fruit
bark
Striped Maple
Norway Maple

belong to the beech family **(Fagaceae).** Various oaks are among the dominant trees in many forest types in North America, and their acorns are important food for many kinds of wildlife. The species in our area are generally divided into two groups, red oaks (below) and white oaks (p. 108). Red oaks have pointed bristly tips on the leaf lobes, and their acorns take two years to mature. White oaks lack the bristles, and their acorns develop and mature within one growing season. Within each of these groups, there are frequent hybrids, so some oaks seen in the wild will not be a perfect match for any one species. The first four oaks below become tall trees, commonly standing more than 70 feet tall, but Bear Oak is always a shrub and rarely exceeds 15 feet.

NORTHERN RED OAK ***Quercus rubra***

A common forest tree, our most widespread oak. ▶ Leaves with sharp-pointed lobes, only moderately divided, dull green above. Acorns with only a *shallow, flat cap.* Fall leaves red to brown; bark dark, furrowed, often with silvery raised ridges. Compare to next species. Scarlet and Pin Oaks have leaves more deeply divided.

EASTERN BLACK OAK ***Quercus velutina***

Common in southern New England, often in areas with relatively dry or sandy soil. ▶ Very similar to Northern Red Oak; may be difficult to separate without some comparative experience. Leaves tend to be thicker, glossier, and darker green above. Scratching a twig may reveal *orange or yellow-orange inner bark.* Acorns distinctive, with deep *bowl-shaped cap* with hairy or fringed edges. Fall leaves brown to dull red; trunk bark dark, furrowed.

SCARLET OAK ***Quercus coccinea***

Named for its contribution to fall color, this oak is common in southern New England, especially on dry slopes and ridges and poor, sandy soils. ▶ Leaves *deeply divided* between sharp-pointed lobes. Acorn cap bowl-shaped and deep, but relatively smooth. Fall leaves bright scarlet; trunk bark dark, narrowly furrowed.

PIN OAK ***Quercus palustris***

Similar to Scarlet Oak but more restricted in range, typically found in wet forest, swamps. ▶ Leaves like those of Scarlet Oak, but shape of tree different, with lower branches sloping down, trunk with many short spur or "pin" branches. Acorn cap is shallow and thin. Fall leaves scarlet, trunk bark dark.

BEAR (SCRUB) OAK ***Quercus ilicifolia***

A small tree or shrub that forms dense thickets in poor, sandy or rocky soil, cleared areas. ▶ Relatively *small* leaves (2–4" long) with a few pointed lobes, only shallowly divided. Small acorns with deep fringed cap. Fall leaves yellowish brown to dull red, turning pale brown and often remaining attached in winter.

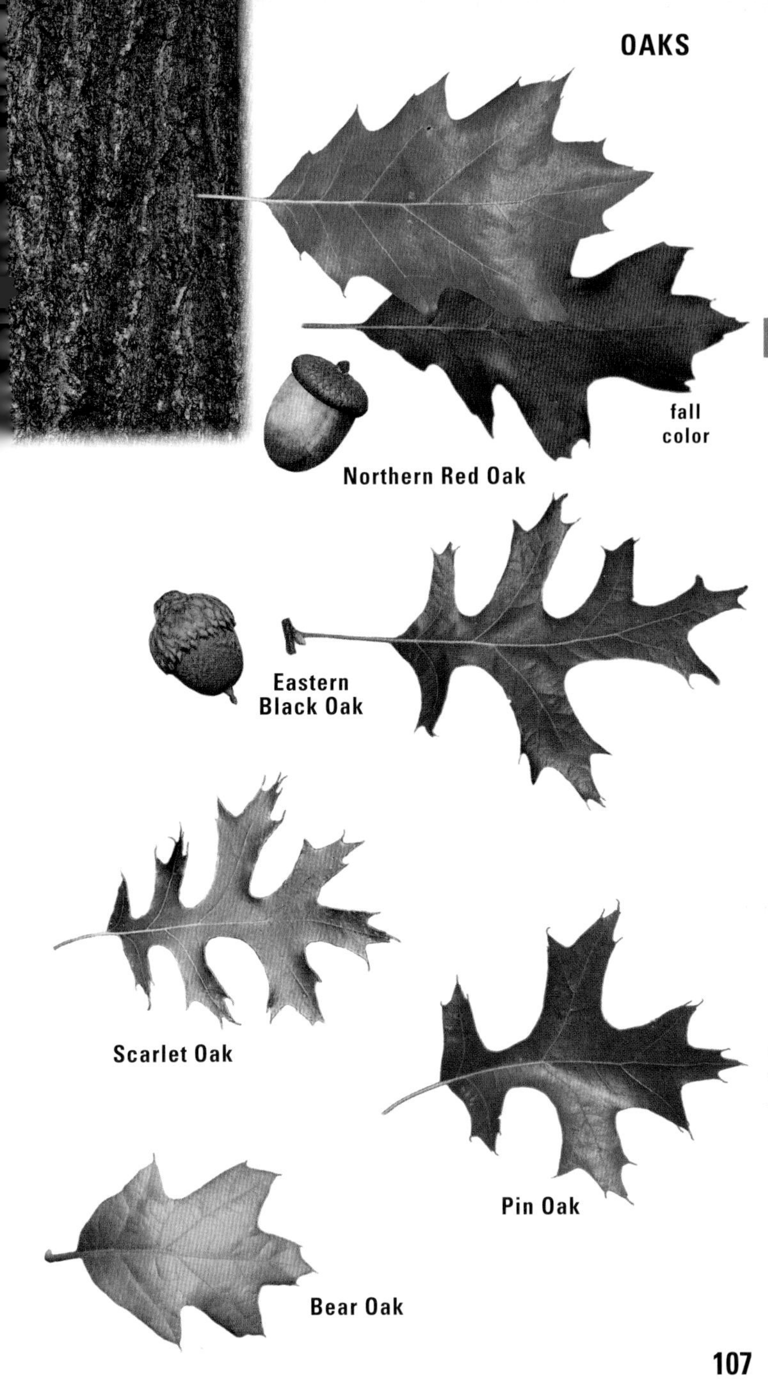
fall
color
Northern Red Oak
Eastern
Black Oak
Scarlet Oak
Pin Oak
Bear Oak

These belong to the "white oak" group described on p. 106.

EASTERN WHITE OAK ***Quercus alba***

A grand forest tree, widespread in New England, often common. White Oaks may live for centuries and may grow to great size, often more than 100' tall. Timber from this tree was favored for ship-building in early America. ▶ Leaves with distinctive shape, *deeply divided* with *rounded lobes.* Acorn with shallow cap. Fall leaves brown to red; trunk bark *pale gray,* with shallow furrows.

BUR OAK ***Quercus macrocarpa***

Uncommon and local in New England, usually in bottomland areas with rich soil. ▶ Distinctive leaves *deeply divided at center,* with rounded lobes, broad tip. Acorn with deep, *fringed cap.* Fall leaves yellow to brown; trunk bark gray, deeply furrowed.

SWAMP OAK ***Quercus bicolor***

Fairly common along streams, floodplains, swamps. ▶ Wavy-edged leaves have 4–9 pairs of *shallow, rounded lobes* and are somewhat whitened on underside. Acorns have *long stalks* (1–3"). Fall leaves brown to red; trunk bark fairly light *gray.*

CHESTNUT OAK ***Quercus montana***

Found mainly on upland sites with rocky or sandy soil, most common on dry ridges. ▶ Wavy-edged leaves have 8–16 pairs of *small, shallow, rounded lobes* (or rounded teeth). Acorn cap bowl-shaped. Fall leaves yellow; trunk bark *dark, deeply ridged.*

CHINKAPIN OAK ***Quercus muehlenbergii***

Local, uncommon, mostly on limestone outcroppings or lowland woods. ▶ Leaves have *pointed* teeth or small lobes, 8–15 pairs. Deep, bowl-shaped acorn cap. Fall leaves red to brown; trunk bark gray, not deeply furrowed.

DWARF CHINKAPIN OAK ***Quercus prinoides***

Grows mostly as a shrub less than 10' tall in open barrens on sandy or rocky soil. ▶ Leaf shape like Chinkapin Oak, but smaller, with *fewer lobes* (5–9 pairs, usually 7 or fewer). Typically grows as a multitrunked shrub, not a single-trunked tree.

POST OAK ***Quercus stellata***

This small oak (usually less than 50' tall) grows locally in southern New England, mostly on dry uplands. ▶ Thick leaves with outer 3 lobes forming a *wide cross.* Bowl-shaped acorn cap.

ENGLISH OAK ***Quercus robur***

Popular as an ornamental, this elegant oak from the Old World now grows in the wild in parts of New England, especially near the coast. ▶ Leaves resemble those of Eastern White Oak but smaller, more compact, with *rounded lobes* at base. Acorns have *long stalks;* trunk bark is dark.

Eastern White Oak

Bur Oak

Swamp Oak

Chestnut Oak

Chinkapin Oak

Dwarf Chinkapin Oak

English Oak

Post Oak

BEECH, ELMS, AND OTHERS

Beech and chestnut, along with the oaks, belong to the beech family **(Fagaceae).** Hackberries, formerly classified with elms, are now placed in the hemp family **(Cannabaceae)**; elms make up the **Ulmaceae.** Tupelos, related to dogwoods, are usually placed in a distinct family, **Nyssaceae.**

AMERICAN BEECH ***Fagus grandifolia***

This tall, stately tree is widespread and common, a dominant part of many forests. ▶ *Smooth, pale gray* trunk bark. Long leaves, toothed along edges, turn yellow in fall but may persist on tree into winter. Distinctive *long* buds. Edible nuts, developing in fall, are enclosed in spiky husks that open when mature.

AMERICAN CHESTNUT ***Castanea dentata***

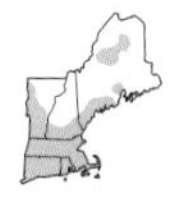

Before about 1900, this was one of the most important large trees in forests of southern New England; it was practically wiped out by a fungal disease introduced early in the 20th century. Shoots still sprout from stumps of former forest giants, but large specimens are now rare. ▶ Narrow, tooth-edged leaves, longer than those of American Beech; shorter buds, deeply furrowed bark.

NORTHERN HACKBERRY ***Celtis occidentalis***

A fairly common forest tree in southern New England. ▶ Often best recognized by rough, bumpy, gray bark. Pointed, tooth-edged leaves usually have uneven bases. Small, dull red fruits appear in fall, look shriveled when dry, persist on tree through winter.

AMERICAN ELM ***Ulmus americana***

Formerly a common shade tree and forest tree, until most large specimens were killed by Dutch elm disease. Small individuals are still widespread. ▶ Leaves have coarse teeth along edge, short stalks, usually *uneven* bases. Small, flat fruits hang on *long* stalks. Bark gray, with network of furrows and flat ridges.

SLIPPERY ELM ***Ulmus rubra***

Fairly common as a small to medium-sized tree in forest edges, streamsides. The name "slippery," referring to inner bark, belies the very rough texture of the leaves. ▶ Similar to American Elm (which sometimes has rough leaves) but fruits have *short* stalks.

SIBERIAN ELM ***Ulmus pumila*** **(not shown)**

Resistant to Dutch elm disease, this Asian elm is widely planted and now grows wild in southern New England. ▶ *Small* leaves, very short stalks on fruits. Sometimes called "Chinese Elm," but that name applies to another species, *U. parvifolia*, known by its small leaves and *orange-patched* bark.

BLACK TUPELO ***Nyssa sylvatica***

Also called Black Gum or Sourgum. Fairly common along rivers, wet woods, swamp edges. ▶ Bark of mature trees with strongly "checkered" look. Leaves shiny, dark green, with mostly smooth edges; turn bright red in fall. Small blue-black fruits in fall.

American
Beech
long buds
upperside and
underside of leaf
American Chestnut
Northern
Hackberry
American Elm
Slippery Elm
Black
Tupelo

TREES WITH DISTINCTIVE LEAVES

Easily recognized but unrelated, belonging to five different families.

SASSAFRAS ***Sassafras albidum***

Usually a medium-sized to large tree, sometimes shrubby. Oil from roots and root bark used in the making of soaps, perfumes, candy, tea, and root beer. Large quantities of root bark were shipped to Europe by early colonists who believed it a tonic for all medical ailments. Laurel family (Lauraceae). ▶ *Twigs green.* Leaves variable even on same branches, often *mitten-shaped,* with *pleasant aroma* when crushed. *Greenish yellow flowers* clustered at end of drooping stems. Fall leaves yellow, orange, or red.

TULIPTREE ***Liriodendron tulipifera***

Mostly southern, widely planted as an ornamental. One of the tallest and most massive eastern hardwoods and an important source of wood used in making furniture and toys. Magnolia family (Magnoliaceae). ▶ Named for *tulip-shaped flowers* borne in late spring and early summer. *Uniquely shaped leaves* dangle on slender stems. Fall leaves bright yellow.

EASTERN SYCAMORE ***Platanus occidentalis***

Generally considered the most massive tree in the eastern U.S. Often found along streams in southern New England, also planted as an ornamental. Hollows in trunks provide important shelter for wildlife. Plane-tree family (Platanaceae). ▶ The *pale, peeling, splotchy, multicolored bark* is distinctive, as are the large leaves with 3–5 broad lobes and the *ball-shaped brown fruits,* dangling on long stems. European and Oriental sycamores, often planted in parks, have 2 or more fruits per stem, not just 1.

AMERICAN BASSWOOD ***Tilia americana***

A large, rapidly growing tree, often having 2 or more trunks. Frequently planted for shade. Its flowers are a preferred nectar source for honeybees, thus its nickname of "Bee-Tree." Wildlife eat seeds and twigs. The soft, lightweight wood is popular among carvers and furniture makers. A member of the Linden family (Tiliaceae). ▶ Leaves *roughly heart-shaped* with *coarsely jagged edges,* on long slender leaf stems. Fragrant yellowish white flowers; small fruits hang below leafy wings (see illustration). Four nonnative relatives are sometimes planted here.

NORTHERN CATALPA ***Catalpa speciosa***

Native to the midwest, but widely planted in New England. The highly distinctive leaves, flowers, and pods make this a favorite among naturalists who are struggling to learn to identify trees. A member of the Bignonia family (Bignoniaceae). ▶ *Very large, heart-shaped, long-pointed leaves,* with unpleasant odor when crushed. Lovely white flower clusters blanket the tree in late spring and early summer. Slender *pods* may reach 24" long. Two other similar species of catalpas are sometimes planted in New England.

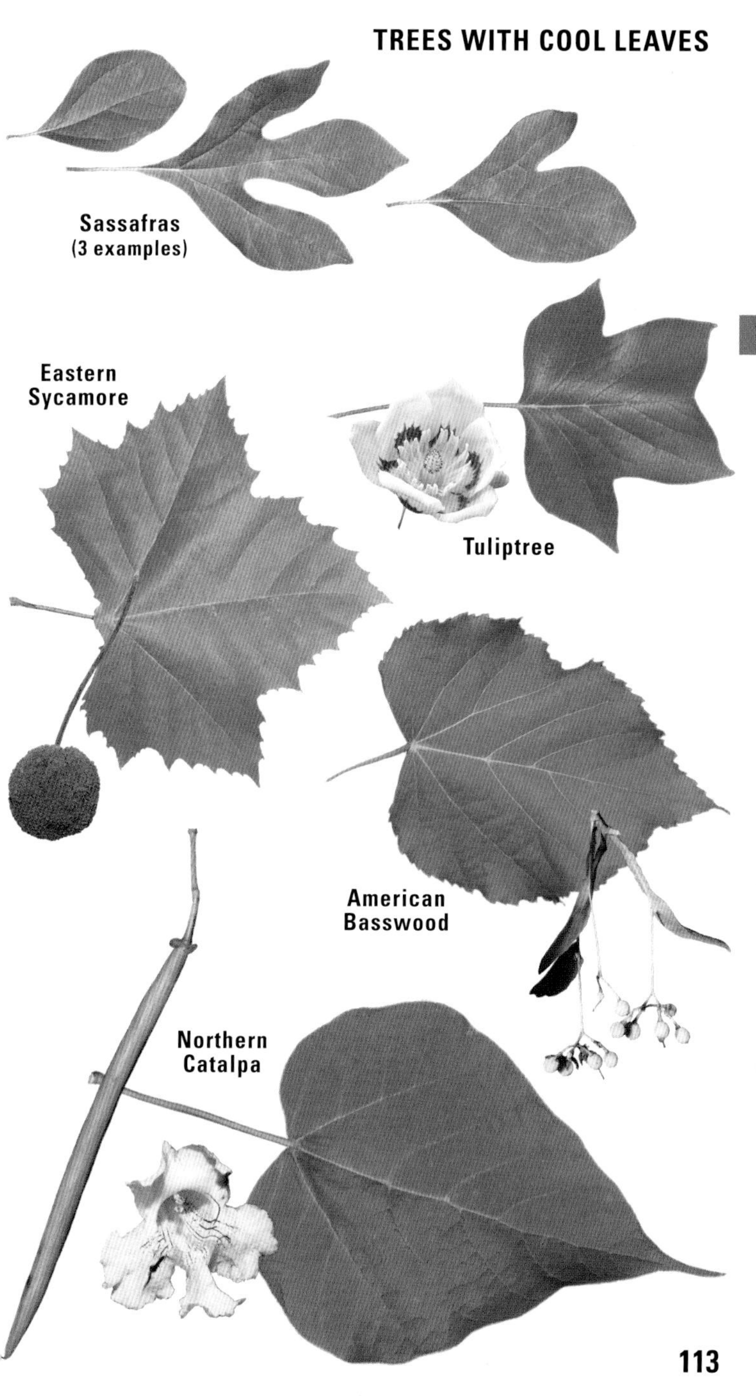
Sassafras
(3 examples)
Eastern
Sycamore
Tuliptree
American
Basswood
Northern
Catalpa

HICKORIES, WALNUTS, AND HORSECHESTNUT

Hickories and walnuts are two major groups in the family **Juglandaceae.** Both groups have compound leaves and large nuts; hickories generally have fewer leaflets per leaf, and the husks of their nuts split open when mature. Horsechestnut is now placed in the family **Sapindaceae.**

SHAGBARK HICKORY ***Carya ovata***

Common in southern New England, in forest of upland areas, relatively dry sites. ► Usually 5 (sometimes 7) *large* leaflets on each leaf, with the terminal leaflet often largest (more than 5" long). Named for the very "shaggy" bark, with loose strips peeling away from trunk. A large tree, up to 100' or taller.

MOCKERNUT HICKORY ***Carya tomentosa***

Locally common in southern New England, growing in woods and field edges, mostly on well-drained soils. ► Large leaves like those of Shagbark, but usually with 7–9 leaflets, *fuzzy* on the undersides and on leaf stalk. Bark tightly furrowed, *not* shaggy.

PIGNUT HICKORY ***Carya glabra***

A tall tree of forests, especially areas of rich soil on relatively dry sites. ► Usually 5 (or less often 7) leaflets, typically narrower and more uniform in size than those of Shagbark. Bark pale gray, tightly ridged or sometimes slightly shaggy.

BITTERNUT HICKORY ***Carya cordiformis***

Widespread in woods. Named for the bitter taste of its nuts, usually avoided even by animals. ► Note the *yellow* buds. Usually 7–11 leaflets, variable in shape. Bark tightly ridged.

BLACK WALNUT ***Juglans nigra***

A sturdy tree of open forests and edges. Prized for high-quality wood and veneer; the ripe nuts are popular with squirrels and other animals. ► Each leaf with numerous narrow leaflets (up to 20 or more), the terminal leaflet often small or lacking. Round green fruits in fall turn dark brown; nuts are blackish brown and wrinkled. Trunk bark is dark brown with rough furrows.

BUTTERNUT ***Juglans cinerea*** **(not shown)**

Formerly common in woods, riversides. Now disappearing because of an introduced fungal disease, butternut canker. ► Similar to Black Walnut but leaflets often broader, terminal leaflet present, bark with wider, *pale gray* ridges. The similar **Japanese Walnut** *(Juglans ailantifolia),* sometimes found growing wild in New England, usually has leaflets more blunt-tipped.

HORSECHESTNUT ***Aesculus hippocastanum***

A tall, stately tree imported from Europe, sometimes found growing in the wild. ► Big palmate leaves (often more than a foot across), with 7–9 wedge-shaped leaflets. Spikes of white flowers in spring. Related to the buckeyes, native farther south in the U.S., which usually have 5 leaflets.

Shagbark
Hickory
Mockernut
Hickory
Pignut
Hickory
Bitternut
Hickory
Black
Walnut
Horsechestnut

ASPENS AND POPLARS (genus *Populus*) make up a distinctive group within the willow family **(Salicaceae)**. They are fast-growing and short-lived trees, often forming extensive groves on cleared or burned areas. Woodpeckers frequently excavate holes in the relatively soft wood of dead limbs and trunks, so groves of these trees may be magnets for cavity-nesting birds. Although not related, their bark patterns and leaf shapes can suggest the birches; see p. 118. Birch leaves tend to have more veins, and their double-toothed edges give them a more jagged look.

QUAKING ASPEN ***Populus tremuloides***

A common and beautiful tree of northern forest. It gets its name because the leaf stalks are so flattened that the leaves quake and tremble in any breeze. Groves of Quaking Aspen may consist of many trunks arising from a single root system. ▶ Leaves are rounded, with very fine teeth along edges; leaf stalks are *very long* and flattened. Bark is smooth and pale, with dark scars, darker and rougher on old trees. Leaves turn bright yellow in fall.

BIGTOOTH ASPEN ***Populus grandidentata***

Common and widespread, generally found as single trees in dry woods, not growing in extensive groves. ▶ Similar to Quaking Aspen, with pale bark and long leaf stalks, but leaves have *large, rounded teeth* along edge. Leaves emerge relatively late in spring.

EASTERN COTTONWOOD ***Populus deltoides***

A tall tree of the midwest, more local in New England, mostly along rivers and lakes. ▶ Leaves are large, triangular, turning bright yellow in fall. Develops into a large tree with massive limbs; trunk bark is pale and smooth at first, but turns dark gray and deeply ridged on mature trees. Hanging clusters of green fruits in spring release seeds floating in cottony down in early summer.

BALSAM POPLAR ***Populus balsamifera***

Common in northern woods, especially along edges of streams and clearings. ▶ Leaves more narrow and elongated than those of aspens, dark green above and paler below. Leaf stalks usually *not* flattened. Bark is smooth and grayish green on young trees, turning darker gray and ridged when mature.

LOMBARDY POPLAR ***Populus nigra*** **(not shown)**

Native to the Old World, this form — a cultivar of the Black Poplar — is widely used in landscaping. ▶ Has very wide, triangular leaves, but most easily recognized by the tree's *tall, narrow, columnar shape.*

WHITE POPLAR ***Populus alba***

Another Old World tree, widely planted and often growing wild in roadsides, disturbed areas. ▶ Leaves dark green above and whitish below. Twigs and leaf stalks whitish, bark usually pale with dark scars. Quite variable in New England, with many cultivars and hybrids found.

distant trunk

Quaking Aspen

Bigtooth Aspen

Eastern Cottonwood

Balsam Poplar

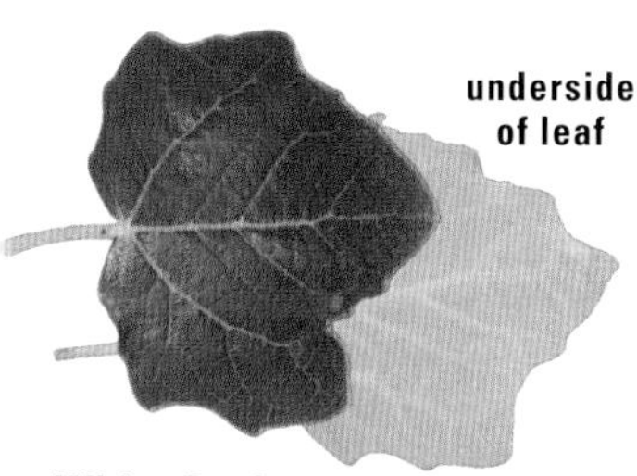

underside of leaf

White Poplar

BIRCHES

As useful as they are beautiful, birches (family **Betulaceae**) are among our most prized and valued native trees. Historic accounts of Native Americans and pioneers reflect a myriad of uses and a deep reverence for these trees. Today birches are favorites for landscape design and are of great commercial value as well, widely used for lumber and in the manufacture of furniture. Winter reveals a conspicuous feature — dangling clusters of flowers called catkins. These catkins open in spring to release pollen and will then develop into conelike fruits with winged nutlets. The unusual peeling bark of some birches should never be pulled from the live tree, as it is replaced with an unattractive black scar that never heals. This family also includes the alders and others (p.120).

PAPER BIRCH ***Betula papyrifera***

Among the most beautiful of our native trees. Creamy white bark peels back in curling strips to reveal an inner bark of bronzy apricot. Best known for its use in the building of birch bark canoes; modern uses for wood include toothpicks, clothespins, broom handles, and toys. ▸ Distinctive *bark* is best field mark. *Oval leaves* usually with 5–9 veins on each side. Branches *drooping*, cones thin-stalked and dangling, 1¾". Fall color light yellow.

GRAY BIRCH ***Betula populifolia***

A small tree. Often forms clumps growing from a single root source, trunks leaning slightly outward. ▸ Chalky white, smooth bark with many dark horizontal lines; *black chevron* marks the trunk under base of each branch. Long, triangular leaf shape; warty glands cover reddish brown twigs. Cones short-stalked and dangling, 1". Fall color pale yellow. See Quaking Aspen (p. 116).

YELLOW BIRCH ***Betula alleghaniensis***

Legendary in the past for its great size, although few today attain the towering heights recorded historically. Valued for its lightweight yet incredibly strong wood, the Yellow Birch supplies most of the birch wood harvested for commercial use. ▸ Trunk bark has a *distinct yellowish cast.* Most leaves with 9–11 veins on each side. Cones nearly stalkless, upright, 1" long. Leaves and twigs give off a *slight scent of wintergreen* when crushed. Fall color bright yellow. Young trees resemble Sweet Birch but are distinguished by the greenish brown, hairy twigs.

SWEET BIRCH ***Betula lenta***

The sweetness of this birch is expressed in a strong aroma of wintergreen in crushed twigs and leaves. Used historically to produce oil of wintergreen to flavor medicines and candy. Birch beer is also made from the sap. ▸ Separated from other birches by the *deep reddish black bark* that in mature trees is covered with scaly plates. *Elliptical* leaves are often notched at the base, most with 9–11 veins on each side. Twigs are dark brown and hairless. Cones nearly stalkless, upright, 1". Fall color bright yellow.

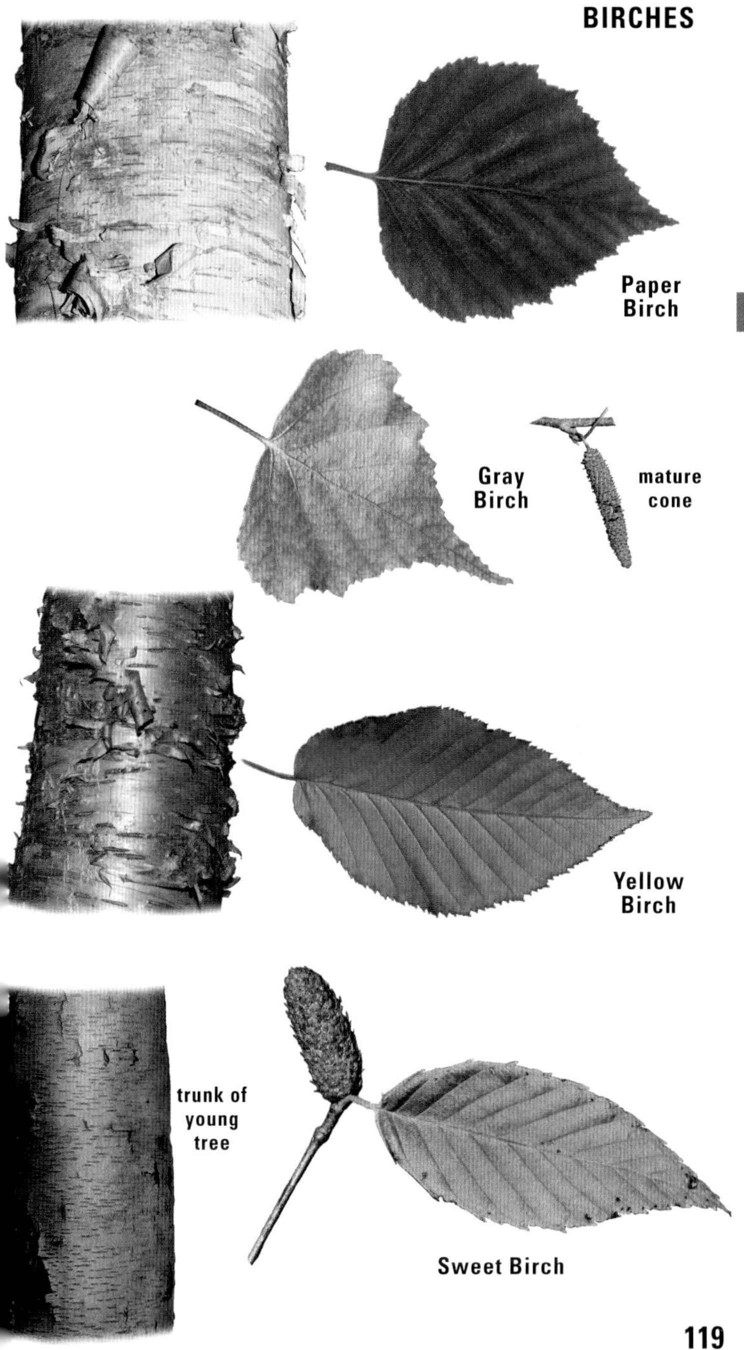
Paper
Birch
Gray
Birch
mature
cone
Yellow
Birch
trunk of
young
tree
Sweet Birch

ALDERS AND OTHERS

The plants below are all shrubs or small trees in the birch family. Alders make up a distinctive group; low and dense, they usually have multiple trunks. Thickets of alders along streams or ponds represent an important habitat, especially in the north. Species of alders are best identified by leaf shape, bark, and sometimes details of their small, woody "cones."

SPECKLED ALDER ***Alnus incana***
The most widespread alder in New England, common along edges of streams, swamps, beaver ponds. ► Oval leaves have variable shape at base, jaggedly double-toothed edges. Bark is heavily marked with narrow, pale, horizontal lines (or "speckles").

SMOOTH ALDER ***Alnus serrulata***
Common in southern New England, in damp soil and waterside situations. ► Like Speckled Alder but leaves wedge-shaped at base and finely toothed on edges. Bark gray, few or no pale "speckles."

GREEN ALDER ***Alnus viridis***
Typically a shrub with multiple trunks, often growing in rocky areas near water. ► Leaves finely toothed like those of Smooth Alder, but not so wedge-shaped at base. Bark has scattered pale spots. Woody "cones" have longer stems than on other alders.

EUROPEAN ALDER ***Alnus glutinosa***
Native to Europe, often planted here and sometimes found growing wild. ► Unlike other alders, often reaches tree size. Relatively large leaves usually indented or double-rounded at tip.

AMERICAN HORNBEAM ***Carpinus caroliniana***
Fairly common in southern New England woods. ► Usually grows as a small tree. Leaves are pointed and double-toothed, but more distinctive are the *smooth, gray, bulging* trunk, with its "muscular" look, and the fruits, dangling clusters of papery bracts.

EASTERN HOPHORNBEAM ***Ostrya virginiana***
Widespread and fairly common in deciduous woods. ► Leaves similar to those of American Hornbeam, but trunk bark is very different: except on the youngest trees, brown with a scaly or shaggy look. Fruits are inflated, papery capsules.

BEAKED HAZELNUT ***Corylus cornuta***
Usually seen growing as a large shrub along the edges of woods, streams, cleared areas. ► Wide oval leaves with jagged teeth along edges; nuts enclosed in a husk extended into a "beak."

AMERICAN HAZELNUT ***Corylus americana*** **(not shown)**
Another large shrub, fairly common in southern New England along streams, woodland edges, roadsides. ► Similar to Beaked Hazelnut, but the husk around the nut is not "beaked."

Speckled Alder
Green Alder
Smooth Alder
European Alder
American Hornbeam
Beaked Hazelnut
Eastern Hophornbeam
unripe fruit

DOGWOODS AND OTHER SMALL TREES

Members of the dogwood family **(Cornaceae)** are mostly shrubs or small trees (though one's a wildflower — see p. 50). The veins of their leaves are distinctively curved. Serviceberries are in the rose family **(Rosaceae),** Buttonbush is in the madder family **(Rubiaceae),** and Sweet Pepperbush is our only member of the **Clethraceae.**

FLOWERING DOGWOOD *Cornus florida*

A small tree, common in the woods of southern New England, also widely planted. ▸ Best known by showy white "flowers" (actually 4 bracts, notched at tips, around small green flowers) in spring. Twigs often purple or green. Smooth-edged or wavy-edged leaves turn deep red in fall. Clusters of red berries in fall.

ALTERNATE-LEAF DOGWOOD *Cornus alternifolia*

A small tree, widespread in lower story of woods. ▸ As the name suggests, the leaves are arranged alternately on twigs (other dogwoods have leaves opposite). White flowers in flat-topped sprays develop into purple-black berries by late summer.

GRAY DOGWOOD *Cornus racemosa*

A large shrub, common in southern New England, forming thickets on roadsides, old fields. ▸ Tiny white flowers (in late spring) and small whitish berries (in late summer and fall) are arranged in conical spikes and have *red* stalks.

RED OSIER DOGWOOD *Cornus sericea*

A large shrub of swamps and stream edges, often forming dense thickets. ▸ Twigs noticeably *red* in winter, greenish to dull red at other seasons. Flat-topped clusters of tiny white flowers in late spring, small whitish berries in early fall.

DOWNY SERVICEBERRY *Amelanchier arborea*

Also known as Juneberry, shadbush, and shadblow, this shrub or small tree is conspicuous in the forest understory when it bursts into white blooms in early spring — around the time that shad are ascending tidal rivers near the coast. ▸ Flowers have 5 long, narrow petals. Pointed leaves with finely toothed edges. A close relative, **Smooth Serviceberry** *(A. laevis)*, is very similar.

BUTTONBUSH *Cephalanthus occidentalis*

A common shrub or small tree of pond edges, often forming thickets or "buttonbush swamps" in standing water. ▸ Best recognized in summer by the ball-shaped flower heads atop long, thin stalks. Variable long-oval leaves.

SWEET PEPPERBUSH *Clethra alnifolia*

Another common shrub of swamps and pond edges. ▸ Tiny white flowers in tall upright spikes in late summer and early fall; dried remains can be seen through the following spring. Leaves wider and more obviously toothed on outer half.

Flowering
Dogwood
Alternate-leaf
Dogwood
Red Osier Dogwood
Gray
Dogwood
Downy
Serviceberry
Buttonbush
Sweet
Pepperbush

SUMACS AND OTHERS

These all have compound leaves composed of multiple leaflets. Sumacs are in the cashew family **(Anacardiaceae),** elderberries are currently classified in the **Adoxaceae,** and bladdernut is in the **Staphyleaceae.** Boxelder, despite its odd leaf shape, is a maple (family **Sapindaceae**).

STAGHORN SUMAC ***Rhus typhina***

Sumacs are large shrubs or small trees that form thickets along roadsides, woodland edges. Typical sumacs are recognized in winter by their persistent spires of red fruits, eaten by birds mainly in late winter, after other wild fruits become scarce. Their clusters of greenish flowers in early summer are less conspicuous. Leaves turn bright scarlet in fall. Staghorn is the most prevalent sumac in New England. ▶ Leaves up to 2' long with many toothed leaflets (up to 31); twigs, leaf stalks, and fruits densely *hairy.*

SMOOTH SUMAC ***Rhus glabra*** **(not shown)**

Common, but not as widespread as Staghorn Sumac. ▶ Similar to Staghorn, but twigs are *smooth,* not hairy. Usually not as tall. These two sumacs may hybridize, producing intermediates.

WINGED SUMAC ***Rhus copallina***

Common, forming thickets on roadsides, edges of dry woods, sandy areas. ▶ Similar to the preceding two sumacs, but the very *shiny,* smooth-edged leaflets are *joined by "wings"* along the midrib of the leaf. Blooms later in the season, in late summer.

POISON SUMAC ***Toxicodendron vernix*** **(not shown)**

This dangerous shrub or small tree is widespread in New England but usually uncommon, in wooded swamps, streamsides. Contact with any part of the plant (or with smoke produced by burning it) can cause severe skin reactions. ▶ Leaflets (7–15 per leaf) more oval than those of other sumacs, usually shiny, often with reddish leaf stalks. Fruits *white,* in dangling clusters.

COMMON ELDERBERRY ***Sambucus canadensis***

A shrub or small tree that forms thickets in open areas. ▶ Leaves have 5–11 leaflets. *Purplish black fruits* in late summer follow flat-topped sprays of white flowers in early summer.

AMERICAN BLADDERNUT ***Staphylea trifolia***

A shrub or small tree that often grows in dense thickets in shady places. ▶ Has 3 dark green leaflets. White flowers in spring, followed by *inflated, papery fruits* from late summer through fall.

BOXELDER (ASHLEAF MAPLE) ***Acer negundo***

Locally common in wet woods, swamps, streamsides, usually growing as a small to medium-sized tree. ▶ Leaves with 3, 5, or sometimes 7 leaflets, often *uneven* in size and shape. Young twigs often pale green. Paired seeds similar to those of other maples (see p. 104).

SUMACS AND OTHERS

TREES WITH COMPOUND LEAVES

Although all the trees on this page have similar leaf structure (large compound leaves, with leaflets arranged along a central leaf stalk), they belong to four different families.

BLACK LOCUST ***Robinia pseudoacacia***

Native to areas farther south and west, Black Locust is widely planted in New England and often grows wild in open places. Its white blooms are conspicuous along roadsides in late spring. Pea family (Fabaceae). ► Leaves with multiple *oval* leaflets. *Pairs* of *small thorns* near leaf bases. Clusters of hanging white flowers in May and June. Bark on mature trees dark, deeply ridged.

HONEY LOCUST ***Gleditsia triacanthos***

Another tree from farther west, now fairly common in this region. Pea family. ► Leaflets narrower than on Black Locust, but more easily recognized by impressive *large thorns* on twigs, branches, trunk. Flowers (in spring) greenish, inconspicuous.

WHITE ASH ***Fraxinus americana***

The most numerous and widespread of the native ash species in New England, in upland woods, well-drained soil. (All ashes here may soon be threatened by Emerald Ash Borer, a small green beetle from Asia, now spreading this way from the midwest.) Olive family (Oleaceae). ► Usually 7 leaflets, with or without toothed edges, often pale (to whitish) on underside. Winged seeds in summer. Fall foliage varies, yellow to brownish red. Very similar species: **Green Ash** *(F. pennsylvanica)* often grows on wetter sites, fall foliage mostly yellow. **Black Ash** *(F. nigra)* usually has 9 leaflets, grows in swampy sites.

AMERICAN MOUNTAIN-ASH ***Sorbus americana***

A small tree, fairly common in forest edges, open woods. Flat-topped clusters of bright fruits persist from fall into winter and are popular with many birds. Rose family (Rosaceae). ► Leaves have *long-pointed* leaflets with toothed edges. Flat clusters of white flowers in early summer; red-orange fruits develop in early fall. Similar species: **European Mountain-ash** *(S. aucuparia)* has shorter leaflets with more rounded tips. **Showy Mountain-ash** *(S. decora)* also has shorter leaflets and usually grows as a shrub. Compare to Elderberry and others (p. 124).

AILANTHUS (TREE-OF-HEAVEN) ***Ailanthus altissima***

Native to Asia but widely planted in North America, commonly found growing wild in heavily disturbed sites around cities, roadsides. Quassia family (Simaroubaceae). ► The *huge leaves* may be more than 2' long and may have more than 40 leaflets, each smooth-edged except for angular teeth near the base. Inconspicuous greenish flowers in late spring are followed by clusters of dry, hanging fruits in fall.

Black Locust

spring blooms

major thorn

Honey Locust

seeds

White Ash

fruits

flowers

American Mountain-ash

Ailanthus

fruits

Willows (family **Salicaceae**) are found worldwide, often growing at the edge of water, or in damp, open habitats such as meadow or tundra. New England has more than 30 species. Most of our willows have multiple trunks and narrow leaves; most grow as shrubs, not as trees; and most are hard to identify. Hollies (family **Aquifoliaceae**) are represented in New England by six native species and many cultivated varieties. The witch-hazel family **(Hamamelidaceae)** has one common species here, and the Hoptree belongs to the rue family **(Rutaceae).**

BLACK WILLOW ***Salix nigra***

Of the native willows in New England, only this one regularly grows to respectable tree size. Fairly common along riverbanks, edges of swamps, other wet habitats. ▶ Long, narrow leaves with toothed edges. Bark of mature trunks very dark, deeply ridged.

WEEPING WILLOW ***Salix* sp.**

The original Weeping Willow was native to China, but cultivated forms and hybrids are now commonly planted around the world. May grow wild at the edge of water, and may reach large tree size, especially in the southern part of our region. ▶ All forms and hybrids marked by strongly "weeping" or drooping shape.

LARGE PUSSY-WILLOW ***Salix discolor***

This large shrub is noticeable only in spring, when the male flowers, opening on the bare twigs, are covered with long, soft, grayish whitish hairs, suggesting a kitten's paw. ▶ Leaves somewhat wider than on many other willows.

AMERICAN HOLLY ***Ilex opaca***

This small tree is most noticeable in winter, with its evergreen foliage and red berries. Most common in the understory of open woods on sandy soil. ▶ Stiff, *evergreen* leaves are shiny dark green above, usually with *sharp points* along edges. Cultivated forms of **English Holly** *(I. aquifolia)* may be very similar.

COMMON WINTERBERRY HOLLY ***Ilex verticillata***

A shrubby holly with deciduous leaves, growing in wet woods, swamps, edges of ponds. ▶ Leaves *dull green* with toothed edges, not large points. Red berries in fall and winter.

AMERICAN WITCH-HAZEL ***Hamamelis virginiana***

A common large shrub or small tree of woodland understory. Branches were once used as "divining rods" for locating water underground. ▶ Large, rounded leaves with wavy teeth along edge, *lopsided base.* Wispy yellow flowers appear in fall.

COMMON HOPTREE ***Ptelea trifoliata***

An uncommon small tree of woods and roadsides. ▶ Leaves have 3 smooth-edged leaflets (sometimes is confused with Poison Ivy, p. 140). Distinctive papery fruits in fall and winter.

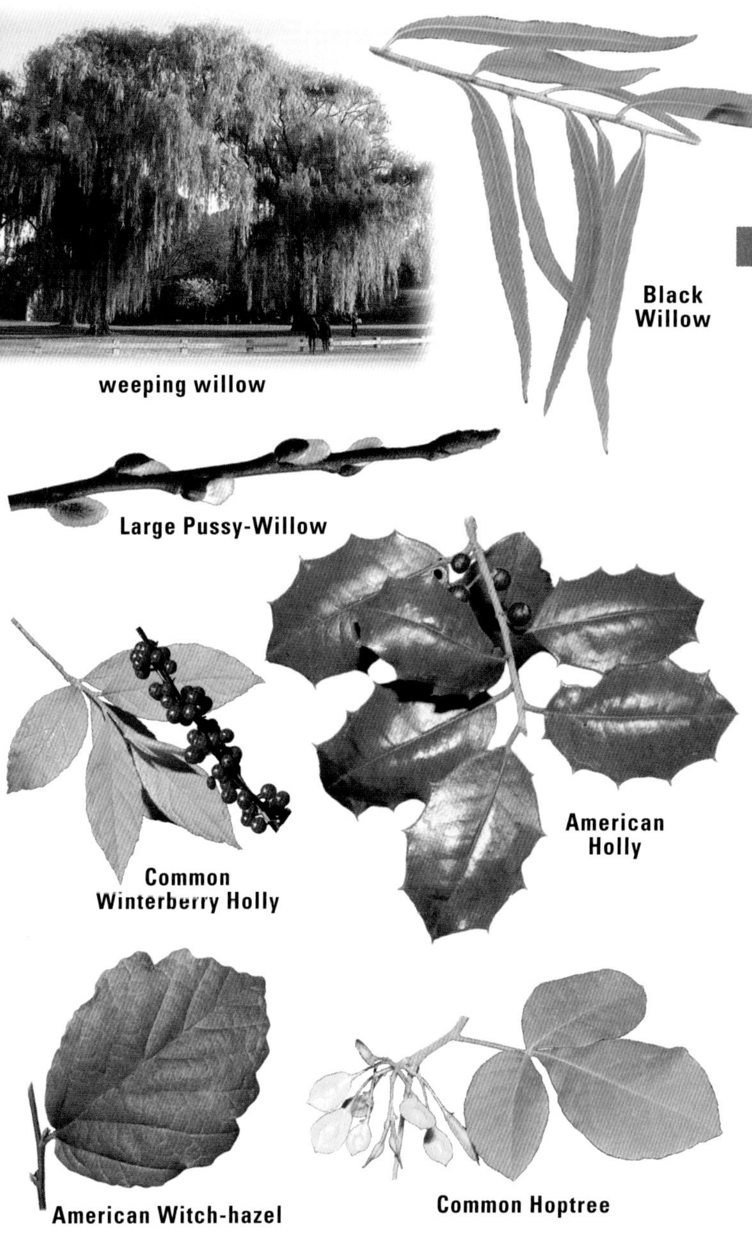

weeping willow
Black Willow
Large Pussy-Willow
Common Winterberry Holly
American Holly
American Witch-hazel
Common Hoptree

VARIOUS FRUITING TREES

Cherries, hawthorns, apples, and crab-apples belong to the rose family **(Rosaceae).** All bloom in spring, with beautiful five-petaled flowers (usually white, sometimes pink); most produce good-sized fruit in fall. Mulberries (family **Moraceae**) have inconspicuous flowers and produce tight clusters of juicy, berrylike fruits.

BLACK CHERRY ***Prunus serotina***

Most cherries are small trees, but this one attains considerable height, sometimes more than 60' tall. Fairly common in open woods, woodland edges, fields. ▶ Leaves are narrowly pointed, with finely toothed edges. Bark of young trees and small branches may be smooth, grayish to reddish, with small horizontal whitish lines; mature trunks have dark, rough bark, often with horizonal pale lines. Fruit (late summer) dark red to blackish.

HAWTHORNS ***Crataegus* sp.**

Hawthorns, as a group, are widespread and fairly common in New England, in woods, edges, overgrown fields. Classification of the genus *Crataegus* is very complicated and controversial. According to different experts, the number of species of hawthorns in New England could be as few as a dozen or as many as several hundred! Unless you are a very serious botanist, it's best to leave these debates to the professionals, simply call them all hawthorns, and enjoy them for their beauty and variety. ▶ Usually with *long, sharp spines.* Leaf shape varies by species, but often with roughly toothed edges. Fruits are usually small (less than 1") and rounded, red to yellow, ripe in late summer or fall.

APPLE / CRAB-APPLE SPECIES ***Malus* sp.**

No apples or crab-apples are native to New England, but many are cultivated here. Some have become naturalized in the wild. ▶ The familiar domestic apple, now often growing wild, has oval leaves and large fruit. Crab-apples typically have smaller fruit, less than 2" in diameter; leaf shape may be similar or more varied.

WHITE MULBERRY ***Morus alba***

Native to Asia, this small tree was introduced to New England in the 1700s by the British, in a failed attempt to establish a silk industry (silkworms, a type of moth caterpillar, feed on its leaves). Now widespread in open areas, roadsides. ▶ Leaves *smooth* and shiny, quite variable in shape, even on the same tree: oval, coarsely toothed, often *deeply indented.* Fruits usually whitish to red.

RED MULBERRY ***Morus rubra***

This native mulberry is less numerous and widespread here than the introduced White Mulberry. ▶ Leaves variable in shape like those of White Mulberry, but usually with *rough, sandpapery surface.* Fruits vary from dark red to blackish.

Black Cherry

hawthorn

crab-
apple

Red Mulberry

White
Mulberry

INVASIVE SMALL TREES AND SHRUBS

When a species of plant is brought to New England from another part of the world, if it happens to be well adapted to local soil and climate, it may become a troublesome invasive. Far from its original home, it may be free of the specific insects, diseases, and other limiting factors that normally would keep it in check; so it may spread aggressively into local habitats, crowding out native plants. The shrubs and small trees on this page all are recognized as problems in parts of New England. Most have fruits eaten by birds, which then may disperse the seeds over long distances.

EUROPEAN BUCKTHORN ***Rhamnus cathartica***
Native to Eurasia and North Africa, this small tree is found in all New England states. It may form dense thickets, shading out other plants. Buckthorn family (Rhamnaceae). ▸ Relatively small leaves (2" long or less) with finely toothed edges. Leaf veins often appear *indented,* and curve toward leaf tip. Blackish, berrylike fruits in fall may persist into winter.

GLOSSY BUCKTHORN ***Frangula alnus*** **(not shown)**
Another native of Eurasia and North Africa, almost as widespread in New England as the preceding species. Buckthorn family. ▸ Similar to European Buckthorn, but leaves have *smooth* edges.

AUTUMN OLIVE ***Elaeagnus umbellata***
Native to eastern Asia, this large shrub now occurs in all New England states. It is numerous in many open situations, such as roadsides and old fields. Oleaster family (Elaeagnaceae). ▸ Smooth-edged leaves may be somewhat whitish on underside. Tubular, creamy white flowers in late spring are followed by clusters of orange to reddish fruits in late summer.

ORIENTAL BITTERSWEET ***Celastrus orbiculatus***
Native to eastern Asia, this is actually a vine, but usually seen growing over and choking out shrubs or small trees. Recorded in all New England states. Staff-tree family (Celastraceae). ▸ Small greenish flowers along stems in late spring, followed by bicolored red and orange-yellow fruits in fall.

MULTIFLORA ROSE ***Rosa multiflora***
Native to Asia, now widespread here, often forming dense, impenetrable thickets. Rose family (Rosaceae). ▸ Small, toothed leaflets, thorny stems. Masses of white flowers in late spring, red fruits in late summer.

JAPANESE BARBERRY ***Berberis thunbergii***
Now widespread in New England except for northernmost areas. May form dense thickets. Barberry family (Berberidaceae). ▸ Small leaves and thorns along stems, masses of creamy flowers in late spring, red fruits in fall.

JAPANESE HONEYSUCKLE ***Lonicera japonica***
Grows as a vine, but forms dense shrubby thickets. Honeysuckle family (Caprifoliaceae). ▸ Dense foliage, evergreen in warmer climates. Pairs of fragrant, creamy flowers in spring and summer. Small black berries in fall. Other invasive honeysuckles occur here, including **Tatarian Honeysuckle** *(L. tatarica),* which has pairs of red berries in late summer.

European Buckthorn
Autumn Olive
Oriental Bittersweet
Multiflora Rose
Japanese Barberry
Japanese Honeysuckle

SHRUBS

Most of these are smaller shrubs with relatively inconspicuous flowers. The first five species below, like the last three on the preceding page, are in the heath family **(Ericaceae)**; Northern Bayberry and Sweet-fern belong to the bayberry family **(Myricaceae)**.

HIGHBUSH BLUEBERRY ***Vaccinium corymbosum***

A good-sized shrub of swamps, fields, woodland edges. Blooms in May and June. ▸ Stands 3–10' tall, sometimes taller. Flowers are small, bell-shaped, white or pink. Leaves more than 2" long. Edible, dark blue berries ripen in summer.

LOWBUSH BLUEBERRY ***Vaccinium angustifolium***

Widespread and common in woodland edges, clearings. Where glacial deposits have left sandy plains, as in eastern Maine, these plants dominate treeless "blueberry barrens," and the berries are commercially harvested. ▸ Usually stands less than 2' tall. Clusters of tiny white or pinkish bell-shaped flowers in May and June. Leaves small, finely toothed. Edible blue berries in late summer.

LARGE CRANBERRY ***Vaccinium macrocarpon***

A low-growing, evergreen shrub of lake margins and bogs. In many places where they grow in bogs, cranberries are now cultivated and harvested. ▸ Usually about 1' tall. *Nodding* flowers with 4 *curved-back petals* and orange-red centers, blooming in summer. Edible, dark red berries ripen in fall.

BEARBERRY ***Arctostaphylos uva-ursi***

A low, trailing shrub or groundcover, usually a few inches tall, growing in rocky or sandy areas. ▸ Small, thick, evergreen leaves with tapered bases and rounded tips. Reddish bark on branches. Clusters of tiny, nodding, bell-shaped flowers, white or pale pink, in spring; red berries develop later.

LABRADOR-TEA ***Ledum groenlandicum***

A small evergreen shrub of bogs, pond edges, moist alpine areas, blooming in spring and early summer. ▸ Long, narrow leaves have *edges rolled under, brown fuzz* on undersides. Small white flowers with 5 petals. Leaves are fragrant when crushed.

NORTHERN BAYBERRY ***Morella pensylvanica***

Can be more than 20' tall, but more typically a shrub of about 6', forming thickets in sandy areas near the coast. ▸ Narrow, oblong leaves. Best known by clusters of small, waxy, silver-blue berries all along stems from late summer through winter.

SWEET-FERN ***Comptonia peregrina***

An odd little shrub, seldom more than 3' tall, noticeable mainly for its distinctive leaves. Common in woodland edges, roadsides, disturbed soil. ▸ Long, thin leaves have rounded lobes along edges, suggesting some true ferns (pp. 148–152).

Highbush
Blueberry
Lowbush
Blueberry
Bearberry
Large Cranberry
Labrador-
tea
Northern
Bayberry
Sweet-fern

Some of these could be considered borderline cases and called either large shrubs or small trees. Spicebush is classified in the laurel family **(Lauraceae),** while viburnums are members of the honeysuckle family **(Caprifoliaceae).**

NORTHERN SPICEBUSH ***Lindera benzoin***

Grows as a large, rounded shrub. Fairly common in southern New England, in swamps and wet woods. ► Usually less than 10' tall. Smooth-edged leaves. Bark of twigs and branches tinged green. Blooms in April and May, with tiny yellow flowers clustered along twigs; develops red, oval-shaped berries in summer. As the name suggests, the plant often has a spicy fragrance.

MAPLE-LEAF VIBURNUM ***Viburnum acerifolium***

Generally grows as a low shrub in the understory and edges of deciduous woods. Blooms are conspicuous from late spring to midsummer. ► Usually less than 5' tall. Unlike other viburnums, leaves usually *3-lobed* and somewhat *maplelike;* some variations have leaves unlobed or nearly so. Round clusters of tiny white flowers are followed later in the season by clusters of small, shiny black berries.

ARROWWOOD VIBURNUM ***Viburnum dentatum***

A variable shrub or small tree of swamps, wet woods, edges. Native Americans reportedly used the strong, straight young shoots of this plant to make arrow shafts. ► Usually less than 8' tall, sometimes taller. Variations on this species have the leaves longer or wider, fuzzy or smooth on the underside, but always *strongly toothed* along the edges, and heavily veined. Upright clusters of tiny white flowers in spring and early summer; clusters of dark blue berries in late summer.

HOBBLEBUSH ***Viburnum lantanoides***

Common in northern New England, mostly in coniferous and mixed forest. May grow as a sprawling, spreading shrub, with new shoots taking hold around existing plants. ► Usually less than 8' tall. Pairs of large leaves (7–9" long) with finely toothed edges. Blooms in May and June, in clusters with large white outer flowers and tiny central ones. Small red to black berries in summer.

NANNYBERRY ***Viburnum lentago***

Larger than other viburnums treated here, reaching small tree size. Common in western and northern New England, in woods, fields, pond edges, more local elsewhere. ► Sometimes more than 20' tall. Pairs of small leaves (2–4" long) with finely toothed edges. Blooms in May and June, clusters of tiny white flowers. Clusters of blue-black berries on red stems later in the season.

Spicebush
Maple-leaf Viburnum
Arrowwood Viburnum
Hobblebush
Nannyberry

VINES

A loose category of plants. In general, vines have flexible stems and cannot grow upright without support; they may trail along the ground or climb up over other plants or other objects, reaching great heights. Some vines have fast-growing, slender tendrils to help hold them in place.

TRUMPET-CREEPER ***Campsis radicans***
Native just a little farther south, this vine is often planted in southern New England, and sometimes grows wild here. Its spectacular blooms in summer and fall are very popular with hummingbirds. In sheltered spots, it may live for years and achieve great size. Trumpet-creeper family (Bignoniaceae). ▶ Known by its clusters of showy orange-red flowers, each shaped like a flaring trumpet more than 2" long. Leaves with 7–11 toothed leaflets.

TRUMPET HONEYSUCKLE ***Lonicera sempervirens***
Locally common in southern New England, in woodlands, edges, and thickets, blooming from May to September. Honeysuckle family (Caprifoliaceae). ▶ Flowers are shorter and much narrower than those of Trumpet-creeper and grow in whorls at the ends of stems. Oval leaves have smooth edges and grow in pairs; upper ones often *joined* around stem.

WILD GRAPE ***Vitis* sp.**
At least 3 species of wild grapes are common in southern New England, less common toward the north. Depending on situation, they may trail over low thickets or climb high on trees. Grape family (Vitaceae). ▶ Leaf shape varies among (and within) species, but generally broad, with heart-shaped base. Clusters of small, greenish flowers in late spring and early summer, followed by clusters of grapes in late summer and fall.

VIRGINIA CREEPER ***Parthenocissus quinquefolia***
A common vine, often scaling the trunks of tall trees or covering masonry walls, aided by naturally adhesive pads on its tendrils. Grape family. ▶ Distinctive leaves with 5 toothed leaflets, turning brilliant scarlet in fall. *Note:* a very similar vine, *P. vitaceae,* differs mainly in lacking sticky pads on tendrils, and thus is less able to climb walls. The map at right includes both species.

POISON IVY ***Toxicodendron radicans***
An important plant to recognize: contact with any part of the plant causes severe skin rashes in most people. Common and widespread in woods and fields, and may grow as a groundcover or a climbing vine, sometimes reaching great heights on trees. Cashew family (Anacardiaceae). ▶ Has 3 pointed leaflets, with glossy surface and often somewhat uneven shape. Dark green leaves turn brilliant scarlet in fall. Tiny greenish flowers in spring, white berries in fall. *Note:* New England plants might be 2 species, differing in minor details.

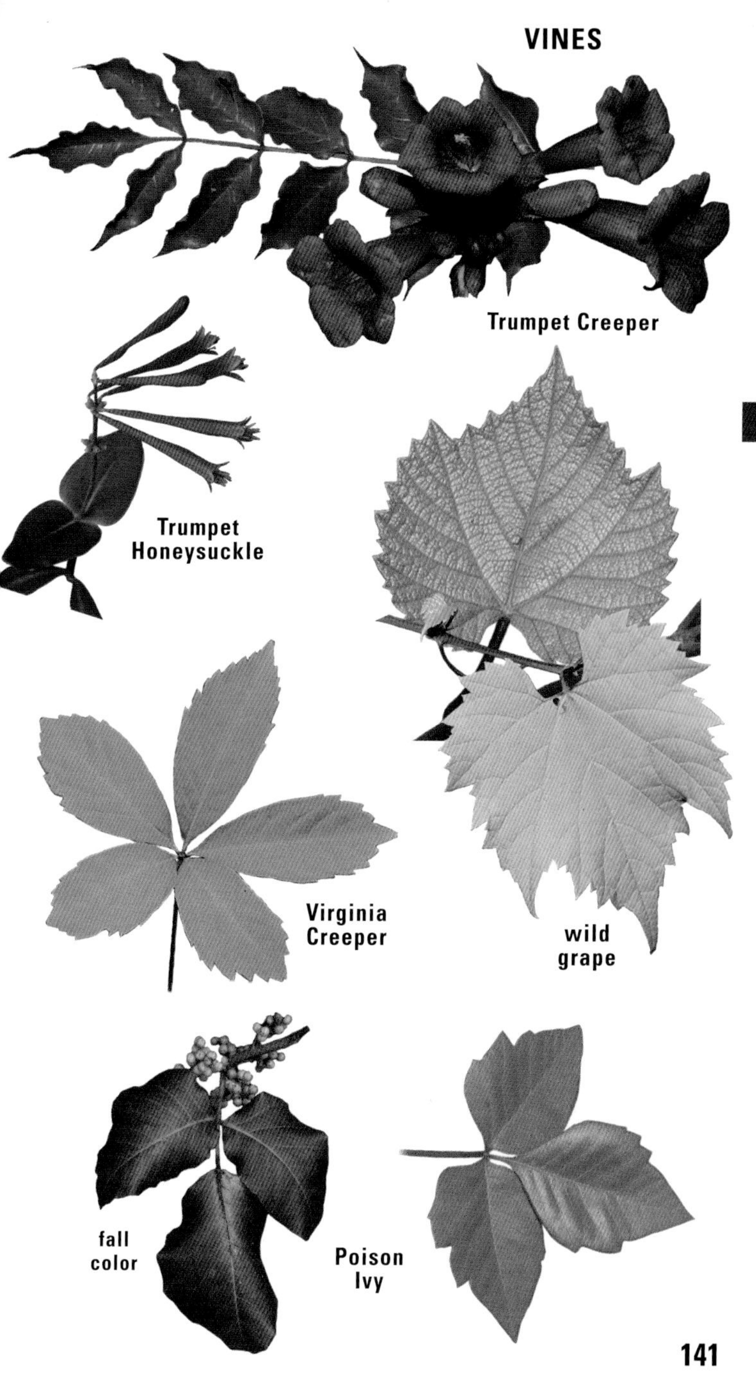
Trumpet Creeper
Trumpet Honeysuckle
Virginia Creeper
wild grape
fall color
Poison Ivy

These may be lower and less conspicuous than the vines on p. 140.

WILD CUCUMBER ***Echinocystis lobata***

This vine is common in a variety of situations, from streambanks and swamps to thickets and roadsides. Gourd family (Cucurbitaceae). ▸ Leaves somewhat *maplelike*, usually with 5 pointed lobes, long stalks. Many 3-forked tendrils along the stems. Blooms in late summer, small 6-petaled white flowers. The inedible fruit (or "cucumber") is fleshy and green, covered with small spikes.

ONE-SEEDED BUR-CUCUMBER ***Sicyos angulatus***

Fairly common in southern New England, in riversides, woodland edges, thickets. Gourd family. ▸ Large leaves with 3–5 lobes, often broader and rounder than those of Wild Cucumber. Clusters of small, 5-petaled, whitish flowers in late summer. Clusters of small green fruits, each one almond-shaped with sparse spines, during the fall.

ROUND-LEAVED GREENBRIER ***Smilax rotundifolia***

Greenbriers are thorny, twining vines, sprawling over low growth rather than climbing high. This species is common and widespread in southern New England, in woodland edges, thickets, roadsides. Greenbrier family (Smilacaceae). ▸ Leaves rounded, green above and below. Clusters of small greenish flowers in late spring and early summer, small blue-black berries later.

CAT GREENBRIER ***Smilax glauca***

A thorny vine like the preceding, this species is more limited to open habitats and sandy soils in southern New England. Greenbrier family. ▸ Similar to Round-leaved Greenbrier, but leaves are strongly *whitened* on undersides.

GROUNDNUT ***Apios americana***

Widespread and common, this slender vine grows over shrubs in woodland edges, thickets, fields, roadsides, blooming in summer. Pea family (Fabaceae). ▸ Leaves with 5–7 *pointed* leaflets. Clusters of fragrant, dark, reddish brown to maroon flowers.

BEACH PEA ***Lathyrus japonicus***

A sprawling vine, mostly growing along the ground and carpeting large areas, widespread and common on beaches and dunes near the coast; also found locally along Lake Champlain. Blooms in summer. Pea family. ▸ Variable leaves with broad, blunt-tipped leaflets, growing either in pairs or alternating. Showy purple to pink flowers with typical pea shape.

fruit
Wild Cucumber
fruits
One-seeded Bur-cucumber
leaf underside
Round-leaved Greenbrier
leaf underside
Cat Greenbrier
Beach Pea
Groundnut

GROUNDCOVER

In natural habitats in New England, we don't commonly see a lot of bare soil. Of course there are exceptions, such as areas of the forest floor in early spring or open sand dunes at any season; but in most cases, bare soil soon comes to be colonized and covered up by plants that take advantage of the opportunity.

We use the term "groundcover" in a very general way, to apply to some small plant types that do just that. A few of the very small shrubs in the current chapter might have been included here. The term also could include some of the mosses and other primitive plants in the next section, beginning on p. 146.

American Beachgrass *(Ammophila breviligulata)*

Grasses are abundant and diverse, but they are largely ignored by most people. In fact, many people are surprised to learn that New England has well over 200 species of true grasses, as well as hundreds of species in other families of grasslike plants (see sedges and rushes on next page).

The true grasses (family Poaceae) are classified as flowering plants. This may come as a surprise, since hardly any of them have structures that would be recognized as flowers by the average person. The reason? Showy flowers function to attract pollinators, such as insects or hummingbirds, but grasses are pollinated by the wind. They produce large amounts of lightweight pollen that becomes airborne easily. Therefore, grass flowers simply need to be raised above the level of the surrounding leaves to catch the wind.

Flowers of Redtop Panicgrass *(Panicum rigidulum)*

The cultivation of grass has been of pivotal importance to human civilization — not just for lawns and golf courses, but for food: wheat, corn, and rice, as well as other grains such as rye and barley, all belong to the grass family.

Sedges (family Cyperaceae) go largely unnoticed by the general public, but they are remarkably diverse. No fewer than 275 species of sedges are known for New England, including about 170 currently classified in a single genus, *Carex!* Needless to say, indentifying most of these to species is a job for a botanical superhero. Even recognizing them as sedges can be a challenge, but the stems of sedges are very often *triangular* in cross-section, while stems of grasses are usually flat or round. Although there are exceptions, the majority of sedges grow in low spots where the soil is at least partly damp, and many are quite restricted to particular types of wetland habitats.

This solid stand of *Carex* sedges would be easy to pass off as mere grass without a close look.

Rushes (family Juncaceae) also look very grasslike, and like sedges, they are also typically found in damp or wet habitats. Their stems are usually round, sometimes flat, unlike the triangular stems of sedges. A naturalist ditty states that "Sedges have edges, while rushes are round" — it doesn't always work that way, but it's an easy way to remember the usual pattern. About 40 species of rushes occur in New England.

Other low-growing plants come from many different families. Many plants that we have included as wildflowers (pp. 46–95) may be recognized by their leaf shapes before and after their periods of bloom. A number of mosses and other primitive plants (see next page) also could qualify. Then there are plants that are simply hard to categorize, such as glasswort (genus *Salicornia*), a member of the goosefoot family (Chenopodiaceae) growing on salt flats next to tidal areas.

Glasswort growing on flats next to salt marsh

As we had mentioned earlier, even some low shrubs could be thought of as groundcovers. For example, see the compact mat of Bearberry in the photo at right. (For a detailed look at this plant, see the treatment on p. 136.) At times when such plants are not in bloom or in fruit, they could be almost impossible to figure out unless you already know them from their more distinctive states at other seasons.

Bearberry in August

The three sections before this focused on flowering plants, grouped loosely by their overall size and structure: Wildflowers (pp. 46–95), trees and large shrubs (pp. 96–133), and small shrubs, vines, and groundcover (pp. 134–145). In this chapter we treat the nonflowering plants: those that produce no flowers, fruits, or seeds, instead reproducing with tiny spores. These are considered to be the most primitive plants. (Indeed, the fossil record suggests that plants recognizeably similar to today's ferns and clubmosses thrived on Earth more than 300 million years ago.) In this section we also treat fungi and lichens, which look rather like plants but are considered to represent something else altogether.

Ferns make up a conspicuous element in the understory of forests, swamps, stream edges, and clearings. New England has roughly 75 species of ferns, and some of them are very common.

A few of our ferns are evergreen, but most die back during the winter. They are sustained through the cold months by a horizontal stem, called the *rhizome,* which often grows just below the surface of the soil and which bears both the roots and the aboveground parts of the fern. In spring, when the fronds begin to grow, they first appear as shoots with coiled tops, called *fiddleheads.* These uncoil as they grow, eventually forming the full-grown fronds.

In this guide we have avoided almost all technical terms, but even in our simplified treatment, it's worthwhile to note that we use the word *blade* for the leafy part of the frond, while the latter term applies to the whole growth aboveground. We mostly use the term *leaflet,* not leaf, for smaller sections of the blade. We refer to the central stem of the frond simply as the stem, but botanical texts will distinguish between the lower part of the stem, below the leafy part, called the *stipe,* and the leaf-bearing upper part of the stem, called the *rachis.*

Another notable distinction is between fertile fronds, which bear spores, and sterile fronds, which do not. In some ferns, the difference is extreme (see Cinnamon Fern, p. 150). In others the difference is much more subtle, and most or all fronds may be fertile.

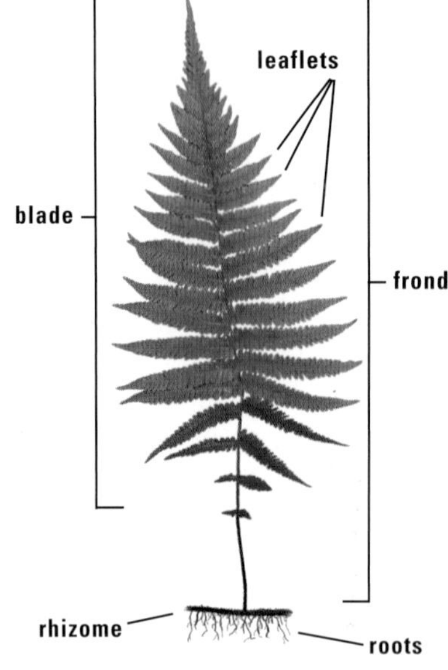

Simplified diagram of the parts of a fern

The spores from which ferns reproduce are microscopic in size, but in a typical fern these spores are gathered in tiny natural cases called *sporangia.* On many of our common ferns, these sporangia in turn are aggregated in clusters called *sori.* By turning over the fronds of many ferns, you can easily see the sori, which appear as brown or tan dots arranged in regular patterns on the undersides of the leaflets. When the spores are ripe, the sporangia pop open and disperse them to drift on the breeze.

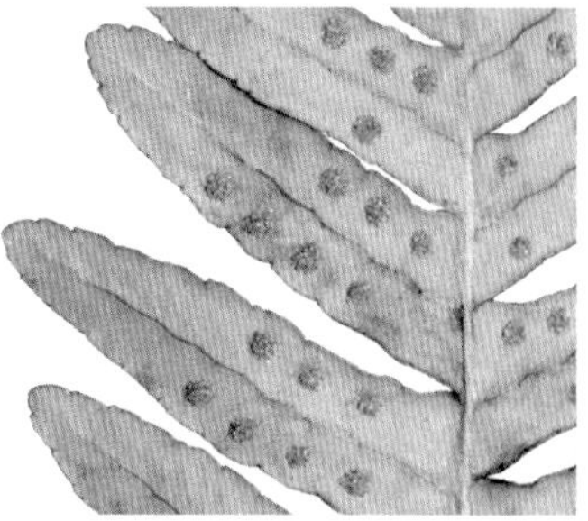

Detail: sori on underside of leaflets of Common Polypody

Other primitive plants include some that are more or less related to the ferns, such as horsetails, clubmosses, and spikemosses. Not related to ferns, but also considered primitive, are the true mosses and the algae. These groups are discussed briefly on p. 154.

Fungi are included in this chapter only for convenience. There was a time when all living things were divided into two groups, the animal kingdom and the plant kingdom, and under that system fungi did appear more plantlike. But science has moved far beyond such a simple classification system, and fungi are now regarded as a distinct group. Unlike plants, they do not perform photosynthesis (using the sun's energy to convert carbon dioxide into nutrition) so they must get their food from other living (or formerly living) things. Many fungi are tiny or obscure, and in this guide we cover only a handful of the most obvious forms: mushrooms.

Lichens are among the most remarkable of all living things. Each lichen actually has a double identity: it consists of a fungus and a colony of tiny algae (either green algae or cyanobacteria) living together in cooperation. In this arrangement, the algae uses photosynthesis to supply nutrition, while the fungus absorbs nutrients and moisture from the surface on which the lichen is growing (usually rock, dirt, or tree bark). The fungus appears to be dominant in establishing the type of lichen that is produced, since in some cases the fungus may associate with various types of algae. As a rule, the species of fungus involved in creating lichens are found only in these associations and do not occur independently in nature.

Scientists still differ in their interpretations of the relationship between fungi and algae in lichens: is it mutually beneficial, or is it at least partly parasitic? Regardless of the answer, it seems to be a successful approach to life, as there are many thousands of species of lichens.

Despite their noticeable differences in shape, ferns on this page are all regarded as belonging to one family, the wood ferns **(Dryopteridaceae).**

NORTHERN LADY FERN ***Athyrium filix-femina***

Common throughout New England in various habitats, including rich woods, swamps, meadows. ▶ Grows in circular clumps, fronds up to 3' tall. Broad leaf blades taper to a pointed tip and taper slightly toward the base. Very finely divided, *lacy or feathery look,* with toothed edges to smallest leaflets. Compare to Hay-scented Fern (p. 150). New York Fern (p. 152) is somewhat similar, but its smallest leaflets are not finely toothed.

COMMON OAK FERN ***Gymnocarpium dryopteris***

A small fern, fairly common in a variety of woodland types, but mainly in cool, shady conditions. Often near rocks or rocky slopes. ▶ Leaf blade looks broadly triangular and divided into 3 major parts, with the lower 2 simpler and larger. Compare to Broad Beech Fern (p. 152).

CHRISTMAS FERN ***Polystichum acrostichoides***

Widespread and common in forest, especially around damp, rocky hillsides. Named for the fact that some fronds stay green throughout the winter. ▶ Grows in circular clumps, with some fronds more than 2' long. Leaves thick, leathery, dark green. Each leaflet has a distinctive *bump* at the base (has been likened to the toe on a Christmas stocking).

OSTRICH FERN ***Matteuccia struthiopteris***

Uncommon but distinctive, a large fern of swamps, stream margins, and wet woods. ▶ Grows in clumps, with arching fronds that may be more than 4' long. The broad leaf blades, with their long, graceful, finely divided leaflets, may suggest the shape of ostrich plumes. Shorter, stiffer fertile fronds appear in late summer and may persist through winter.

SENSITIVE FERN ***Onoclea sensibilis***

A widespread, common fern with a distinctive appearance. Often found growing in dense colonies along the edges of wet woods, swamps, marshes, in either sunlight or shade. Called "sensitive" because the green fronds will turn brown and wither at the first frost in fall, unlike some ferns that are evergreen. ▶ Tall sterile fronds (up to 3' long) have distinctive structure. Broad segments of leaf blade are *broadly connected* along the central stem, for a very different shape from most ferns. Fertile fronds, produced in late summer and persisting into winter, are much shorter, densely compact, and brown when mature.

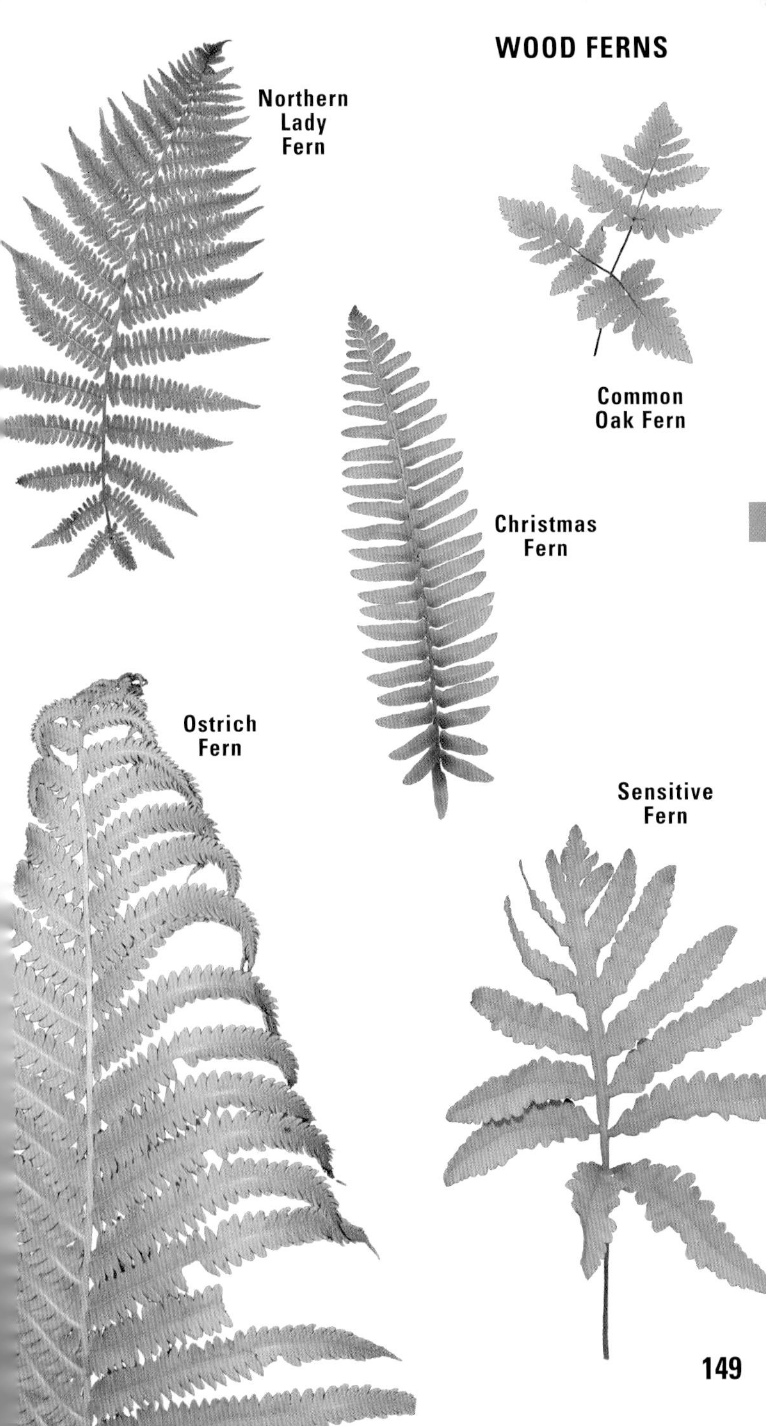
Northern Lady Fern
Common Oak Fern
Christmas Fern
Ostrich Fern
Sensitive Fern

COMMON AND DISTINCTIVE FERNS

These are five large, distinctive, widespread ferns that are found almost throughout New England. The first two species below, despite their differences in appearance, both belong to the family **Dennstaedtiaceae.** The last three species are our only members of the so-called flowering fern family, **Osmundaceae.**

BRACKEN ***Pteridium aquilinum***

A large, coarse fern, often common in dry woodlands, clearings, disturbed sites, and areas of poor soil. In such places it may form solid colonies. ► Best recognized by overall structure: the tall central stem (can be more than 3' tall) has broad, *3-parted* blade at the top, reflexed back to lie almost horizontally.

HAY-SCENTED FERN ***Dennstaedtia punctilobula***

Common and widespread, forming solid patches in clearings in areas of dry forest. Usually grows best in sunlight or partial shade. ► From the rhizome (underground runner), single blades may rise more than 2' tall. Each blade tapers to a fine point and is noticeably soft and finely divided into small lobes, giving a feathery or lacy impression. Especially in late summer, the fronds give off a smell like a freshly cut hayfield, hence the name.

ROYAL FERN ***Osmunda regalis***

This regal species may stand more than 5' tall. Widely distributed around the world, it is fairly common throughout New England, in wet woods, swamps, and pond edges. ► Looks recognizeably fernlike at a distance, but up close its leaf structure is distinctive, with numerous *small, oval leaflets,* suggesting a member of the pea family. Fertile fronds are topped with dense clusters of spore-bearing structures.

CINNAMON FERN ***Osmundastrum cinnamomeum***

Another distincive fern of wide distribution on several continents, common throughout New England in wet woods, swamps, and edges of marshes. ► Grows in clumps, with the sterile fronds sometimes standing up to 5' tall, broadly tapering toward the tip. Fertile fronds appear first in spring (and wither by midsummer), green at first but then turning bright cinnamon-brown, usually standing less than 2' tall.

INTERRUPTED FERN ***Osmunda claytoniana***

Common throughout New England in woodland edges, meadows, edges of swamps and marshes. ► Grows in clumps, with the fertile fronds standing as much as 5' tall, the sterile fronds shorter and more curved. The fertile fronds are *"interrupted" in the middle* by clusters of spore-bearing structures. Leaflets below the "interruption" are smaller and more widely spaced.

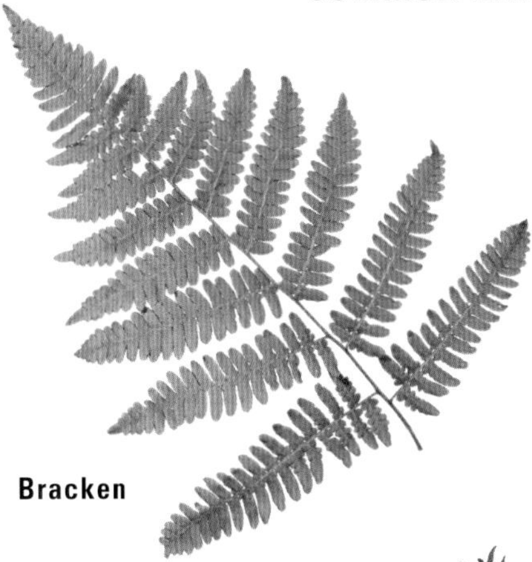

Bracken

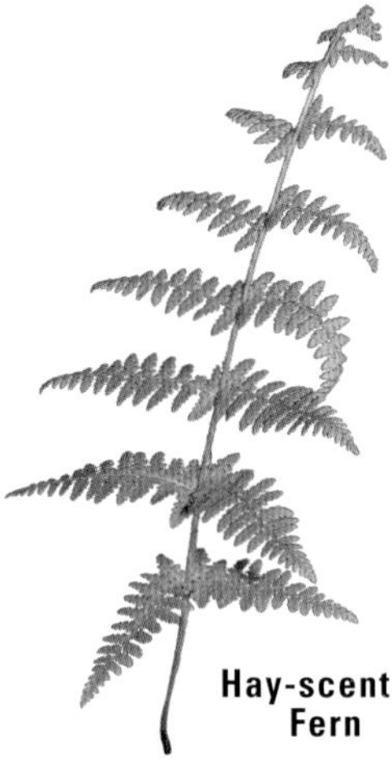

Hay-scented Fern

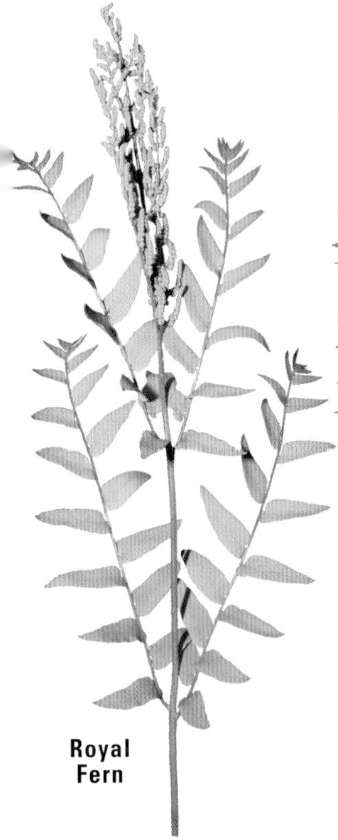

Royal Fern

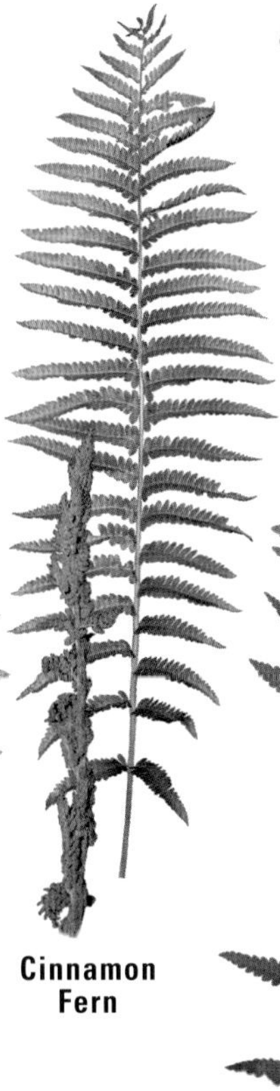

Cinnamon Fern

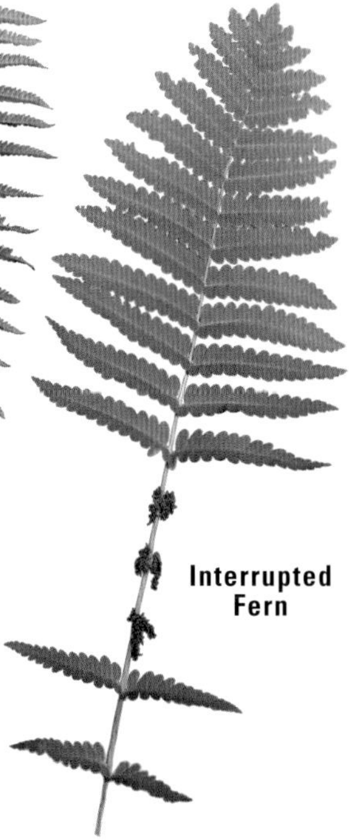

Interrupted Fern

FERNS

These four ferns belong to three separate families.

NORTHERN MAIDENHAIR FERN ***Adiantum pedatum***

Widespread and common in moist woodlands (mainly deciduous), often on shaded, rocky slopes, especially in limestone areas. Maidenhair fern family (Pteridaceae). ▸ Usually less than 2' tall, with a graceful and somewhat delicate appearance. Upright stems are shiny *blackish* or dark reddish brown, with a horizontally arranged, fan-shaped blade, bearing numerous small, *distinctively shaped* leaflets.

COMMON POLYPODY ***Polypodium virginianum***

Also called Rock Polypody. This evergreen fern brightens up the dark woods in winter and early spring. It grows commonly on rocks and cliffs, especially close to water, in cool, shady spots. Also sometimes grows on old logs or stumps. Polypody family (Polypodiaceae). ▸ The thick, dark green blades, which can be more than a foot long, have simple, straplike leaflets along the sides, shorter toward the end, tapering to a pointed tip.

NEW YORK FERN ***Thelypteris noveboracensis***

Common in the understory of rich woods, either deciduous or mixed, especially near streams. It may form dense colonies in patches where some sunlight reaches the ground. Marsh fern family (Thelypteridaceae). ▸ Fronds may be up to 2' tall. The leaf blade is *tapered at both ends* — that is, the side leaflets are longest at the middle, and become shorter toward the pointed tip and also toward the base. On two similar species, **Marsh Fern** *(T. palustris)* and **Massachusetts Fern** *(T. simulata),* the leaflets toward the base are only slightly shorter, so the leaf blade does not appear to taper strongly toward the base. Compare also to Hay-scented Fern (p. 150).

BROAD BEECH FERN ***Phegopteris hexagonoptera***

Fairly common, especially in southern New England, in rich, deciduous or mixed woods. Marsh fern family. ▸ Usually stands less than 18" tall. The leaf blade is often wider than long, in a *broadly triangular* shape. "Wings" along the central stem connect the leaflets. **Narrow Beech Fern** *(P. connectilis),* also widespread in New England, including more northerly woods, is not so broadly triangular in overall shape.

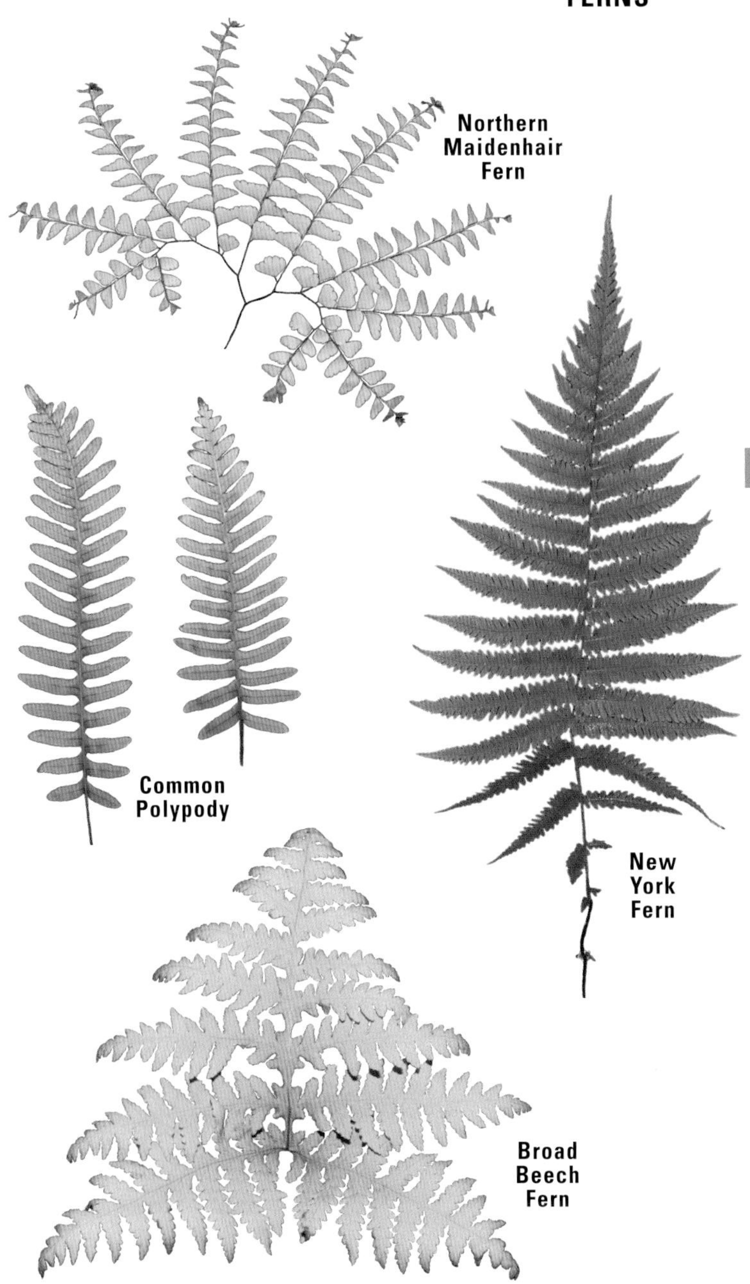
Northern Maidenhair Fern
Common Polypody
New York Fern
Broad Beech Fern

FERN RELATIVES AND OTHER PRIMITIVE PLANTS

The first three groups below are distantly related to the ferns, and like the ferns, they reproduce from spores, not seeds. The spore-bearing parts of the plants may be obvious on some of these, appearing like small "cones" or "seedheads," while on others the spore capsules look scarcely different from the rest of the plant.

Horsetails (family Equisetaceae) include about 8 species in New England, all in the genus *Equisetum.* They are all low plants with thin, round, upright stems having thickened nodes. When these nodes are bare, a patch of horsetail may suggest a stand of tiny bamboo stems; often, however, whorls of thin, horizontal branches are attached at the nodes. Tiny silica particles give the plants a rough texture, and at one time they were used for scouring pots and pans, hence the alternate name of scouring rush. Horsetails are found growing in many kinds of situations, from woodland interior to open meadows and marshes, and from gravel to muddy spots, but they tend to be in wetter spots, or in places where water is not far below the surface.

Clubmosses and firmosses (family Lycopodiaceae) are mostly small, low-growing plants of damp places on the forest floor. Many species are evergreen, and they suggest the appearance of tiny evergreen trees, as suggested by some of their alternate names such as ground pine or running pine. In general they have very small, short leaves, with a very symmetrical arrangement on the stems. New England has about 17 species.

Spikemosses (family Selaginellaceae) are mostly tropical plants, and New England has only 3 or 4 species (all in the genus *Selaginella).* Superficially they may look similar to the true mosses, but a close look with a magnifying glass will show that their tiny leaves have veins, while the true mosses lack veins altogether. Spikemosses are small, creeping plants growing on rock or on damp soil.

True mosses (division Bryophyta) differ from all the plants that we have treated up to this point. All of them, from spikemosses to dandelions to oak trees, are classified as *vascular plants:* that is, they have a vascular or circulatory system for transporting water and minerals through the plant. Mosses are *nonvascular plants.* Because they lack veins for circulation, they generally grow in damp environments where moisture will be available to the whole plant.

Most true mosses are difficult to identify, but some are very important. For example, sphagnum moss (peat moss) is a dominant element in many bogs in the north woods, forming a dense, spongy foundation and acidifying its surroundings.

Algae represent an ongoing challenge to human attempts to classify all living things. Many scientists now say that it would not be accurate to refer to algae as plants at all. In our region, tiny green algae often develop in fresh water, but the largest and most conspicuous algae are various kinds of "seaweeds," which we cover briefly on p. 386.

SOME PRIMITIVE PLANTS
(not all shown at same scale)

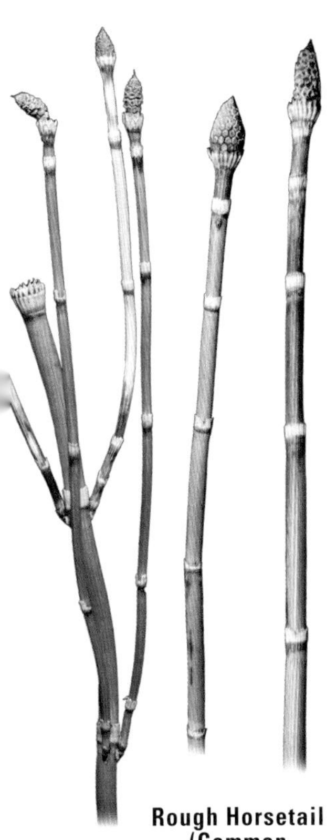

Rough Horsetail (Common Scouring Rush)

Shining Clubmoss

sphagnum moss

spikemoss

The things that we think of as mushrooms are the visible parts of fungi that may have existed for years within the soil or within the dead wood of a log, stump, or tree. The mushroom itself is a fruiting body, putting out spores that will produce future generations.

Many people are interested in mushrooms for culinary reasons. While some mushrooms are quite tasty, some are quite deadly, and you will need much more detail on identification than we can provide here before you can even think about finding the edible ones.

MEADOW MUSHROOM ***Agaricus campestris***
Widespread and common in pastures, meadows, large lawns. Clusters or "fairy rings" of these mushrooms often appear after rains, especially in mid- to late summer. Field mushroom family (Agaricaceae). ► White cap, 2–4" in diameter; hemispherical in shape at first, becoming flatter as the mushroom matures. Stem mostly white, surrounded by a single ragged ring. Gills on underside of cap vary from pale red to dark brown.

GIANT PUFFBALL ***Calvatia gigantea***
Widely distributed in meadows and open woodlands, full-grown Giant Puffballs draw attention for their sheer size. They are most frequent in late summer and early fall. Puffball family (Lycoperdaceae). ► Bloated and irregularly puffy, can be more than 20" across. No obvious stem; anchored to ground by short, rootlike extension. All white outside at first, later turning tan or brown and cracking open to release spores.

KING BOLETE ***Boletus edulis***
Fairly common in summer and fall in woodlands, either coniferous or mixed. Bolete family (Boletaceae). ► Can be 4–8" across and can stand 7" tall. Cap is rounded, and varies from reddish brown to yellowish brown. Stem is very thick, and its surface has a fibrous appearance.

DESTROYING ANGEL ***Amanita bisporigera (A. virosa)***
Beautiful but deadly, this is among the *most poisonous* of mushrooms. It is fairly common on the ground in the interior and edges of deciduous forest. Amanita family (Amanitaceae). ► Can stand 6" tall, with cap 2–5" across. Bright white overall, including gills and smooth cap.

FLY AGARIC ***Amanita muscaria***
Common and widespread in woods, meadows, pastures, this is another poisonous species. Amanita family. ► Can stand 6" tall, with cap 3–7" across. Cap rounded at first but becoming flatter, *brightly colored* above, yellow to red with whitish patches. Gills and stem whitish.

GOLDEN CHANTARELLE ***Cantharellus cibarius***
Chantarelles are fairly common on the ground in woodlands during late summer. Chantarelle family (Cantharellaceae). ► Rather small, 2–3" tall and 2–4" across. *Bright yellow* to yellow-orange overall. Cap is rounded at first but soon becomes depressed at center or even trumpet-shaped. Gills *extend well down* onto stem.

Meadow Mushroom

Giant Puffball

King Bolete

Destroying Angel

Fly Agaric

Golden Chantarelle

MUSHROOMS

These are more varied in shape than the mushrooms on p. 156. New England has many hundreds of species of mushrooms, so we can treat only a small representative sample.

ARTIST'S FUNGUS ***Ganoderma applanatum***

This is an example of a bracket or shelf fungus, growing as a horizontal "shelf" on a living or dead tree, stump, or log. This one is named for the fact that its white underside will bruise to brown, making it possible to draw or write on that surface with a pointed stick. Family Ganodermataceae. ► Can be more than 18" wide, although usually smaller. Upperside gray to brown, with concentric rings or furrows. Underside white until bruised.

BIRCH POLYPORE ***Piptoporus betulinus***

Commonly seen on trunks or logs of dead birches, sometimes on living birches. Family Fomitopsidaceae. ► Variable in size, can be up to 9" wide and extending out from tree by up to 6". The cap is rounded to somewhat flattened, with the outer edges rolled under; whitish to pale gray at first, becoming brownish. Habitat (birch) is a good identification clue.

CHICKEN MUSHROOM ***Laetiporus sulphureus***

Also called "chicken of the woods." Common in forest, growing on oaks and other deciduous trees, or sometimes on conifers. Family Polyporaceae. ► Usually grows as a cluster of fan-shaped, flat, overlapping shelves, attached directly to wood. Bright yellow to orange, with yellow underside.

EARTHSTAR ***Geastrum* sp.**

Several species of earthstar mushrooms are found in woodlands in New England in summer and early fall. Earthstar family (Geastraceae). ► An earthstar is tough to recognize at first, when it appears as smooth, oval ball 1–2" wide. At maturity the outer skin splits open to form a "star" surrounding the round spore case at the center.

OYSTER MUSHROOM ***Pleurotus ostreatus***

Common in forested areas, growing on stumps and logs, and sometimes on standing trees. Tricholoma family (Tricholomataceae). ► Caps are 2–8" across and variable in shape, flat to funnel-shaped, but usually with wavy edges. Whitish to pale brown or gray-brown.

CORAL FUNGUS

A category for several unrelated mushrooms, some of which are common in New England woods. They represent several families, including Clavulinaceae and Ramariaceae. ► Variable. Some look like stands of coral, others suggest antlers or fingers, in whitish, pink, yellow, or brown.

MOREL ***Morchella* sp.**

Many mushrooms are typical of summer or fall, but morels appear mainly in spring. They are fairly common and widespread in forests and orchards, including recently burned areas. Morel family (Morchellaceae). ► Morels can stand up to 6–8" tall, and are known by the "honeycomb" structure of the fruiting head.

Artist's Fungus

Chicken Mushroom

Birch Polypore

Oyster Mushroom

Earthstar

Coral Mushroom

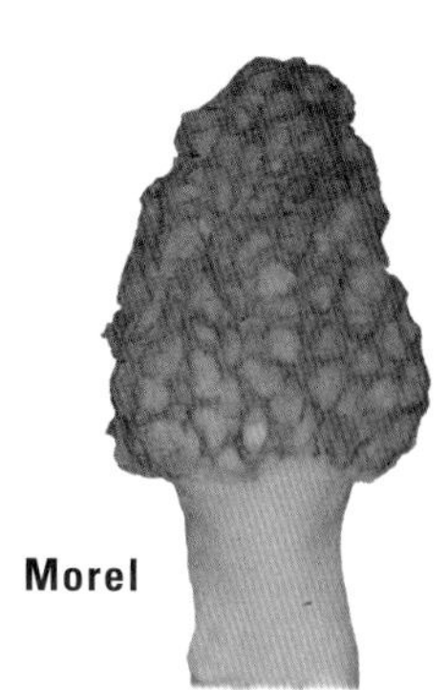

Morel

LICHENS

As described on p. 147, lichens are remarkable dual organisms. Each one consists of a specific kind of fungus growing in intimate association with an algae or cyanobacteria. There are so many thousands of kinds of lichens that we can present only a few examples here.

Lichens typically grow on rocks, soil, or tree bark. Most are very slow-growing, but they may live for years, or even for centuries. They are found in a wide variety of situations, from the extreme cold of the polar regions to extreme tropical heat, so it might seem that they are very tough. Unfortunately, it turns out that many are quite sensitive to air pollution, and lichens have practically disappeared from some heavily industrialized regions.

The classification of lichens is complex. The species name given to each lichen is that of the fungus involved in the relationship. Identifying the various lichens to family is thus not particularly useful for anyone who is not a specialist on these organisms. For purposes of field observers and naturalists, it may be more helpful to classify them by overall structure.

Some types are referred to as **crustose lichens,** because they seem to grow like a crust on their substrate. One widespread example of crustose lichen is the **Map Lichen** *(Rhizocarpon geographicum).* Its neat pattern of yellow-green patches with black outlines might suggest the apperarance of a map. It grows on rocks, especially in mountainous regions.

Foliose lichens are so called because parts of their structure appear leaf-like (suggesting foliage). Sometimes the classification seems arbitrary; for example, **sunburst lichens** (genus *Xanthoria*) seem crustlike in the center and only slightly leaflike around the edges, but they are considered foliose. On the other hand, **dog lichens** (genus *Peltigera*) are more convincingly leaflike, peeling away from the rock or soil on which they grow.

Some of the most interesting and distinctive forms are found among the **fruticose lichens.** Widespread and common is the **British Soldier Lichen** *(Cladonia cristatella),* which grows on the ground or on wood in forest clearings. Its tiny gray-green stalks are capped with bright red fruiting bodies. Even more numerous is **Reindeer Lichen** *(Cladina rangiferina),* sometimes (incorrectly) called "reindeer moss." Common in northern New England and abundant farther north, forming great masses on the tundra, this lichen is actually a major food source for caribou.

Common in the forests of northern New England is **Usnea lichen** (genus *Usnea*), commonly called "old man's beard" or "treemoss." In healthy forests away from sources of air pollution, great masses of Usnea hang from the branches of trees. It looks very much like Spanish moss, which is common in the southeastern U.S., but it is totally unrelated.

LICHENS
(not all shown at same scale)

Map Lichen

sunburst lichen

dog lichen

British Soldier Lichen

Usnea lichen

Reindeer Lichen

MAMMALS

The most numerous mammals in New England are humans, of course, but many species of wild mammals live here as well. A varied lot, they include land mammals from mice to moose, as well as the bats that take to the air, moles that live underground, and whales and dolphins that live at sea. All mammals in New England (and throughout North America) are warm-blooded creatures that give birth to live young.

Some New England mammals are easy to observe: squirrels are frequent visitors to backyard bird feeders, White-tailed Deer are numerous in some areas, and Woodchucks may be seen along roadsides in open country. But seeing most mammals requires some effort or luck.

To seek nocturnal mammals, try driving slowly on rural roads at night or walking quietly with a flashlight on a deserted road or trail. In either situation, you will spot many mammals first by their *eyeshine.* Many species that are active in the dark have an additional reflective layer, the *tapetum lucidum,* at the back of the retina. Light reflected from this layer may be seen at a great distance, but in order for you to see it, your own eyes must be lined up with the source of the light. This occurs more or less automatically when you are driving, as you will be looking along the beam of the headlights. With a flashlight, try holding it up next to your head at the level of your eyes, or use a headlamp. You may spot creatures at a surprising distance: not only mammals, but also night birds such as Whip-poor-wills, and even the eyeshine of spiders! Check to see if your local nature center offers night hikes, as these can be fine opportunities for learning.

You can sometimes spot marine mammals from coastal headlands, but for the best chances of seeing them, try one of the whale-watching trips offered from several New England ports. The waters of Stellwagen Bank, off Massachusetts, are particularly good for seeing Humpback Whales, Bottlenose Dolphins, and others. You can see Harbor Seals and Gray Seals on small nearshore islands and sandbars from Cape Cod north to Maine.

Often we see signs of wild mammals even if we don't see the actual animals. Beaver lodges and dams are distinctive, and Muskrat lodges are often visible in shallow marshes. The alert naturalist often can see squirrel nests in trees, the ridges and mounds left by tunneling moles, and the burrow entrances of Woodchucks and other ground-nesting mammals. And of course, tracks (see next page) can tell us not only what kinds of mammals have been present, but a little about what they have been doing.

Safety issues: A few New England mammals are large enough to be potentially dangerous, although common sense will usually be sufficient to prevent problems. Mother bears with cubs or moose with calves should be avoided, of course, and male moose or even deer can be belligerent in mating season. It is generally a bad idea to feed animals such as bears or coyotes, as these may become dangerous once they learn to associate humans with food. A mammal such as a fox, skunk, or bat that is behaving strangely and approaching humans, or allowing close approach, might have rabies. Such animals should be avoided and reported to local law enforcement or wildlife authorities.

Tracks of some mammal species are more likely to be observed than the animals themselves. Freshly fallen snow or fresh mud around ponds and streams may reveal the recent history of creatures that have passed by unseen. Identifying animal tracks is a rewarding pursuit in itself, and for those who want to know more, we recommend *A Field Guide to Animal Tracks* in the Peterson series, or *Tracking and the Art of Seeing* by Paul Rezendes. A few sample tracks (not all to scale) are shown below.

Eastern Cottontail: hind feet (up to 3" long) land in front of the front feet. Furry feet make tracks look soft-edged.

Virginia Opossum: notice the splayed "thumb." Hind track can be more than 2" wide.

Northern Raccoon: five long toes usually show on each track. Hind foot up to 3" long.

American Beaver: huge, webbed hind foot can be up to 6" long.

hind
foot

Black Bear: hind track about 7" long.

Bobcat: front track about 2" long. Claws usually do not show in track.

Red Fox: front track about 2.5" long. Dog tracks can be similar.

Striped Skunk: front track about 1.5" long, with long claws.

White-tailed Deer: track about 2.5" long.

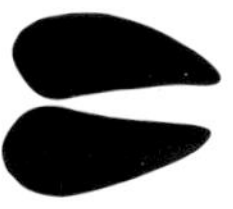

Moose: track about 5" long.

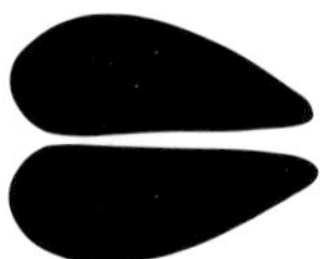

RABBITS, OPOSSUM, AND WOODCHUCK

Rabbits and hares (family **Leporidae**) are prolific vegetarians with big ears. Besides those shown here, European Rabbits have been released on islands near Boston, Black-tailed Jackrabbits on Nantucket.

EASTERN COTTONTAIL ***Sylvilagus floridanus***

Common elsewhere in the eastern U.S. but not native to New England, this adaptable cottontail was introduced and is now common in open country, farms, marshes, even suburbs. The breeding season lasts from March to September; a female may have 4 litters per year in New England. ► Shades of brown and gray, with rusty legs and pale feet, and a round, puffy tail, conspicuously white below. Sometimes has white spot on forehead.

NEW ENGLAND COTTONTAIL ***Sylvilagus transitionalis***

Formerly widespread in New England, now local and scarce. Status not well known because of confusion with introduced Eastern Cottontail, but the New England Cottontail seems to be more shy and secretive, living in areas with dense cover, and seems less able to adapt to changes in the landscape. ► Almost identical to Eastern Cottontail, not safely identified, but tends to have shorter ears with blackish edging, often a *black spot on forehead* (where Eastern Cottontail sometimes has a white spot).

SNOWSHOE HARE ***Lepus americanus***

Named for its huge hind feet, this hare is well equipped for traveling across the surface of snow. It lives mainly in northern forests, hiding in thickets by day and foraging at night. ► Mostly brown in summer (with white or brown feet), *all white* in winter. (Some feral pet rabbits can be all-white also.) In summer, separated from cottontails by smaller tail, *much larger hind feet.*

VIRGINIA OPOSSUM ***Didelphis virginiana***

North America's only marsupial, a group of mammals in which young are born tiny and complete their development in a pouch on the mother's body. Opossums are rather slow-moving omnivores. If threatened, may play dead ("playing 'possum"). Can wrap prehensile tail around branch and hang that way, unlike any other New England mammal. ► Distinctive appearance, rather ratlike but much larger, with *whitish face* and naked tail.

WOODCHUCK ***Marmota monax***

The only eastern species of marmot, a group of very large ground squirrels (related to animals on p. 166). Also known as the "groundhog," and famed for its supposed forecasting abilities on February 2. Woodchucks are common in open country, feeding on many low plants (including those in gardens!) and digging deep burrows. ► Heavy-bodied, with short legs and short, bushy tail. Nothing else in New England is similar.

New England Cottontail
L 16″

Eastern Cottontail
L 17″

summer

Snowshoe Hare
L 18″

winter

Virginia Opossum
L 26″

Woodchuck
L 22″

CHIPMUNK AND SQUIRRELS

(family **Sciuridae**) include some of our most familiar mammals.

EASTERN CHIPMUNK ***Tamias striatus***

An active little ground squirrel, common in deciduous and mixed forest but also found in shady suburbs. Spends most of its time on the ground, especially in areas with many rocks and logs, and digs extensive burrows underground, but can also climb trees fairly well. It feeds on nuts, seeds, berries, snails, and other items, storing food in underground chambers and surviving on this food during the winter rather than hibernating. Its voice includes birdlike chips and clucks. ▶ Unmistakable in New England, although other chipmunks and striped squirrels occur elsewhere.

EASTERN GRAY SQUIRREL ***Sciurus carolinensis***

The familiar squirrel of mixed woods and city parks, a frequent raider of backyard bird feeders. Spends most of its time in trees, building globular nests of leaves and twigs among the branches or in hollows in the trunk. Feeds on nuts, seeds, berries, and sometimes birds' eggs or insects. Active at all seasons but may stay in its nest for days during bad winter weather. ▶ Usually mostly gray with a brownish tinge, but a more blackish color form is common in some areas.

RED SQUIRREL ***Tamiasciurus hudsonicus***

Widespread and common in coniferous and mixed forest, this noisy, active little squirrel is most numerous in spruce forest of northern New England. Has a varied diet like other squirrels but feeds heavily on evergreen cones. Harvests unripe cones in summer, storing them for later use; hoards are usually in tree hollows or other natural shelters but may be in sheds or attics. ▶ Smaller and redder than Eastern Gray Squirrel, with more obvious white eye-ring. Blackish line on side is more apparent in summer.

SOUTHERN FLYING SQUIRREL ***Glaucomys volans***

Common in deciduous forest and even suburbs, these wide-eyed gnomes are often overlooked because they are active mostly at night. They are really gliders, not fliers. Launching from a high branch, the squirrel spread-eagles itself in the air, spreading a flap of loose skin that stretches from the foreleg to the hindleg on each side and using its broad flat tail as a rudder, and may glide more than 200'. Usually glides from tree to tree, spending little time on ground. ▶ Recognized by small size, loose skin on sides, flat tail, and large-eyed expression. Compare to next species.

NORTHERN FLYING SQUIRREL ***Glaucomys sabrinus***

Our two species of flying squirrels overlap widely in New England, but this one is usually in evergreen forests. ▶ Very similar to Southern Flying Squirrel, but averaging larger. Its tail tends to be darker toward the tip. Habitat may be a clue.

Eastern Chipmunk
L 10″

Eastern Gray Squirrel
L 19″

Red Squirrel
L 12″

Southern Flying Squirrel
L 10″

Northern Flying Squirrel
L 12″

MEDIUM-SIZED MAMMALS

These are roughly similar in size but belong to five different families.

NORTHERN RACCOON ***Procyon lotor***

Adaptable and tough, this "masked bandit" lives almost anyplace it can find trees and fresh water, even around suburbs and city parks. An omnivore, eating fruits, nuts, and any small creatures it can catch on land or in water, plus items scavenged from trash cans. Uses its front paws like hands to manipulate items and may appear to be "washing" its food. Our only member of the family Procyonidae. ▸ Overall color varies: gray to dark brown to tan. Black face mask set off by white; tail ringed dark and light.

STRIPED SKUNK ***Mephitis mephitis***

Famed for its smelly defense. Glands near the tail can shoot a foul spray up to 15'. Active mostly at night, feeding on insects, small animals, eggs, refuse. A skunk acting oddly may have rabies and should be avoided for multiple reasons! ▸ Unmistakable, New England's only member of the skunk family (Mephitidae). Pattern varies, tail with more or less white, stripes broad or narrow.

NORTH AMERICAN PORCUPINE ***Erethizon dorsatum***

This slow-moving vegetarian (of the family Erethizontidae) can make surprisingly quick moves if threatened, spinning about and lashing out with its quill-covered tail. The hollow quills come loose easily from the porcupine, but barbs at the tip make them much harder to remove from the predator or other creature on the receiving end. Climbs well, feeds on buds, leaves, bark, nuts, some fruits. ▸ Unmistakable, our only animal with spiny armor.

COMMON MUSKRAT ***Ondatra zibethicus***

Although they do belong to the rat family (Muridae), muskrats have fully adapted to an aquatic lifestyle, swimming and diving well. They build lodges like those of beavers but made of cattails, not sticks, or nest in burrows in streambanks. ▸ Distinctly smaller than beaver with a narrow, ratlike tail. Swims with top of head, back, and sometimes part of tail showing above water.

AMERICAN BEAVER ***Castor canadensis***

Our largest rodent and the most impressive landscape architect among our wild animals, the beaver reshapes its surroundings by cutting down trees, building lodges and dams, creating ponds. Dams and lodges are made of sticks and mud; along rivers, beavers may nest in burrows in banks instead. Disappeared from much of New England after heavy trapping but has recovered, now considered a pest in some areas where its activities may flood roads or yards. Feeds on green plants in summer, bark in winter. Slaps water with tail when alarmed. Family Castoridae. ▸ Recognized by large size, blocky head, and especially the wide, flattened tail. Swims with only upper part of head above water.

Northern Raccoon L 30″

young skunks

Striped Skunk L 27″

North American Porcupine L 28″

Common Muskrat L 20″

beaver lodge

American Beaver L 40″

(family **Mustelidae**) are all active predators. All have scent glands near the tail and may use the musky odor to mark their territories.

NORTHERN RIVER OTTER ***Lontra canadensis***

This powerful swimmer can dive deep and swim underwater for minutes at a time, catching fish, frogs, and other aquatic prey. Otters are often seen in family groups, and lucky observers may get to watch them sliding down muddy or snowy riverbanks into the water. ► Large and long-bodied, with thick-based tail, short legs, broad head. Mostly brown above, paler below.

AMERICAN MINK ***Mustela vison***

Usually living around marshes, lakes, or rivers, this large weasel does much of its hunting in water in summer, on land in winter. Active mostly at dusk and at night, it hunts small to medium-sized mammals, such as Muskrats, as well as birds, frogs, and other creatures. Its den may be in a burrow in a riverbank or in an old Muskrat house. ► Mostly smooth dark brown. Larger, darker, and more uniform than Long-tailed Weasel, smaller and more slender than Fisher.

LONG-TAILED WEASEL ***Mustela frenata***

This agile predator lives in various habitats, often near water, but usually goes unnoticed as it slips through the undergrowth. Hunts small mammals such as mice or young rabbits, also birds, eggs, insects, even carrion. ► In summer, brown above and creamy, yellowish, or brownish below. In New England, usually molts to whitish fur for winter. Always has black tail tip. Tail looks almost as long as body, or more than half of combined head-body length. As in other weasels, male is larger than female.

ERMINE ***Mustela erminea***

Uncommon in woods, fields, thickets, this small weasel is elusive and seldom observed. Active day and night at all seasons, it feeds on rodents and other small creatures. Summer is its mating season, but young are not born until the following spring. ► Brown above and white below in summer, white in winter, always with extensive black tail tip. Tail distinctly shorter than body, black for up to one-third of its length.

FISHER ***Martes pennanti***

An uncommon forest animal, expanding its range in New England. Despite the name, feeds mostly on small mammals and birds, not fish. This is one of the few predators that can tackle porcupines, deftly flipping them over to get at their unprotected bellies. ► Distinctive shape with muscular body, furry tail, small head. Dark brown all over. **American Marten** *(Martes americana)*, not shown, rare in northern New England, is smaller (mink-sized), paler brown, with orange-buff throat and chest.

Northern
River Otter
L 40″
American Mink
L 23″
Long-tailed Weasel
L 15″
winter
summer
winter
summer
Ermine
L 11″
Fisher
L 39″

WILD DOGS AND CATS

Domestic dogs and housecats, allowed to run loose, do tremendous damage to wildlife. However, our native dogs (family **Canidae**) and cats (family **Felidae**) play essential roles in natural habitats.

RED FOX ***Vulpes vulpes***

This adaptable canine is undoubtedly more numerous in New England today than when the Pilgrims landed, and its current population is partly descended from foxes brought from Europe in the late 1700s. It thrives in open woods, farmland, even some cities, hunting a variety of smaller animals, also eating berries, carrion. Den is usually in a burrow on a hill. Litters, averaging 5 pups, are born in spring, cared for by female until fall. ► Usually mostly reddish brown, with *white tail tip,* black on lower legs and feet. Some color variants show extensive black or gray.

GRAY FOX ***Urocyon cinereoargenteus***

More of an omnivore than other wild dogs, the Gray Fox eats fruits and grass as well as rodents, birds, insects, etc. This is our only canine that regularly climbs trees. Most common in brushy woods, avoiding open farmland. ► Mostly gray with rusty trim, white on face and throat; tail has black stripe on top and *black tip.* Red Fox can be partly gray, but has white tail tip, blackish feet.

COYOTE ***Canis latrans***

Native to the west, the Coyote spread over most of the continent during the last two centuries as larger predators were eliminated. It is now common in some New England habitats. Coyotes communicate with yips and howls, often heard at night. ► Mostly grizzled gray with rusty tinges. Larger than foxes, with longer legs, longer snout. Some large dogs are similar; they usually run with the tail up, while Coyotes run with the tail down. The Gray Wolf, which might stray into northern New England, is larger, with broader snout, bigger feet, tail held straight out while running.

BOBCAT ***Lynx rufus***

This wily cat is seldom seen but fairly common in parts of New England, especially in woods with rocky ledges, where it may sleep in its den by day. Often hunts rabbits but will take a variety of other prey, sometimes even small deer. ► Bigger than housecat. *Short tail* is black-tipped on top, *white below.* Black bars on legs, black stripes on face ruff, back of ears black with large white spot.

CANADIAN LYNX ***Lynx canadensis***

Formerly thought to be a missing lynx, but recent searches have turned up fair numbers in northwestern Maine, possibly a few in New Hampshire. This northern cat has large furry feet, allowing it to run across the surface of snow in pursuit of Snowshoe Hares, one of its main prey species. ► Like Bobcat but slightly larger, with *all-black tip* on very short tail, longer tufts on ears.

variation

Red Fox
L 38″

Gray Fox
L 38″

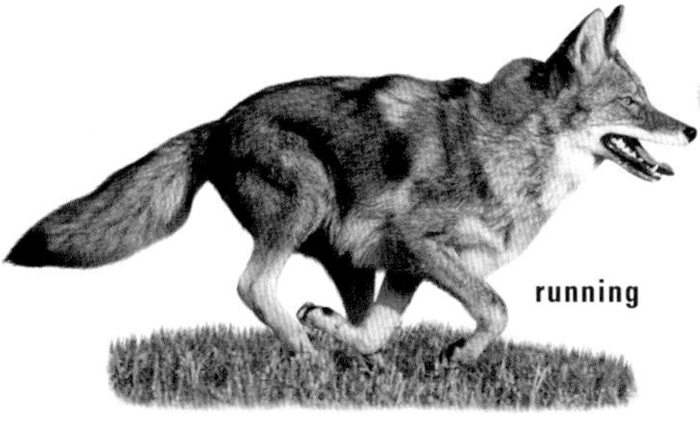

Coyote
L 45″

running

Bobcat
L 32″

kittens

Canadian Lynx
L 35″

The three largest species of wild animals on land in New England today.

BLACK BEAR ***Ursus americanus***

After disappearing from southern New England in past centuries, bears have rebounded in numbers and are now found even around towns. These animals feed mostly on fruits, nuts, roots, and other plant material, plus grubs, carrion, and small animals. They are usually no threat to humans, but bears that are fed may become dangerous. If you encounter a bear while hiking alone, the best advice is to back away slowly, but not to run. Bears in New England usually den up and sleep from late fall to spring; cubs are born in the den in midwinter. Family Ursidae. ► Unmistakable. Black Bears in the west may be brown or gray, but those in the east are usually black with tan muzzles.

WHITE-TAILED DEER ***Odocoileus virginianus***

White-tails are undoubtedly more numerous in New England today than when the Pilgrims landed, with the opening up of the forest and the great reduction in numbers of natural predators. In some areas, deer are now so numerous that they can damage forest by wiping out the understory. They are browsers and grazers, feeding on a wide variety of grasses, leaves, twigs, nuts, fruits, fungi, and sometimes garden plants. Males (bucks) grow antlers each year, starting in spring and growing them through the summer. The soft velvet covering of the antlers is shed in fall, and the bucks use their bare antlers in posturing and jousting with other males for dominance, competing for females. Fawns (usually 2) are born in spring or summer. For about their first 4 weeks, fawns lie motionless on the ground when the mother is away foraging; later they follow her, and may stay with her for more than a year. Family Cervidae. ► Overall color more reddish brown in summer, grayer in winter. Elk and Caribou formerly occurred in New England, but no similar species live there today.

MOOSE ***Alces alces***

Our most impressive land animal, a member of the deer family but bigger than a horse. Common in areas of forests, meadows, and lakes. Does much of its foraging in water in summer, feeding on many aquatic plants as well as the leaves and twigs of willow, aspen, and other plants. Adults may consume up to 45 pounds of forage in a day. Males shed their antlers in late winter and regrow them during the spring and summer, using them for posturing and actual fights over females in fall, the mating season. Calves are born in late spring. Females with calves, and males during the fall rut, are best viewed from a safe distance. ► Males (much larger than females) have wide, flat antlers for most of the year. Females are separated from White-tailed Deer (and from various farm animals) by large size, shoulder hump, long head.

female with cubs

Black Bear
L 6′

White-tailed Deer
L 6′

doe with fawn

moose cow with calf

Moose
L 9′

bull moose

HOUSE MOUSE ***Mus musculus***
Native to the Old World, probably associated with humans for more than 3,000 years, this mouse now lives with us worldwide. ▶ A mouse found indoors in citites or suburbs is probably this species. Plainer than any native mouse, dusty grayish all over, without any sharp contrasts.

WHITE-FOOTED DEERMOUSE ***Peromyscus leucopus***

Common in forest and fields of southern New England, active at night in all seasons. Feeds on seeds, berries, insects, shoots. Builds domed nest, sometimes on top of old bird nest. ▶ Brown above, white below, with big ears, big eyes, long tail, whitish feet.

NORTH AMERICAN DEERMOUSE ***Peromyscus maniculatus***

Widespread and common, especially in forests of western and northern New England. ▶ Similar to White-footed Deermouse, tail more furred and more strongly 2-toned, belly brighter white.

MEADOW JUMPING MOUSE ***Zapus hudsonius***

If startled in fields or open woods, this mouse may reveal its identity by leaping away. In a separate family (Dipodidae) from others on this page (all in Muridae). Unlike them, it hibernates in winter. ▶ Strongly tricolored pattern (white belly, buff sides, dark back), jumping habits. **Woodland Jumping Mouse** *(Napaeozapus insignis),* not shown, is more orange and has a white tail tip.

MEADOW VOLE ***Microtus pennsylvanicus***

Abundant in fields, marshes, woods, making runways in grass and often leaving little piles of grass cuttings. Prolific females can give birth to a new litter every 3 weeks. Many predators rely on Meadow Voles as staples of their menu. ▶ Short tail, short snout, inconspicuous ears. Brown above, pale gray below.

SOUTHERN BOG LEMMING ***Synaptomys cooperi***

Active at night in forests and fields as well as bogs. Makes runways through grass; feeds mostly on grasses, sedges. ▶ Very dark brown with big head, small ears, shorter tail than Meadow Vole.

SOUTHERN RED-BACKED VOLE ***Clethrionomys gapperi***

Fairly common in damp forest, meadows, bogs, especially around fallen logs. This and the preceding are "southern" only by comparison to related rodents in the far north. ▶ Medium-length tail, large head. Larger ears than Meadow Vole, more colorful; contrasting stripe down back usually reddish, sometimes gray.

BROWN RAT (NORWAY RAT) ***Rattus norvegicus***
Two rats from the Old World are established in North America, but only this one is common as far north as New England, mostly around cities and farms. ▶ Large, with scaly tail, a bit shorter than head/body length. **House Rat** *(Rattus rattus),* not shown, formerly lived in some New England cities but is mostly eradicated. It averages darker, with distinctly longer tail.

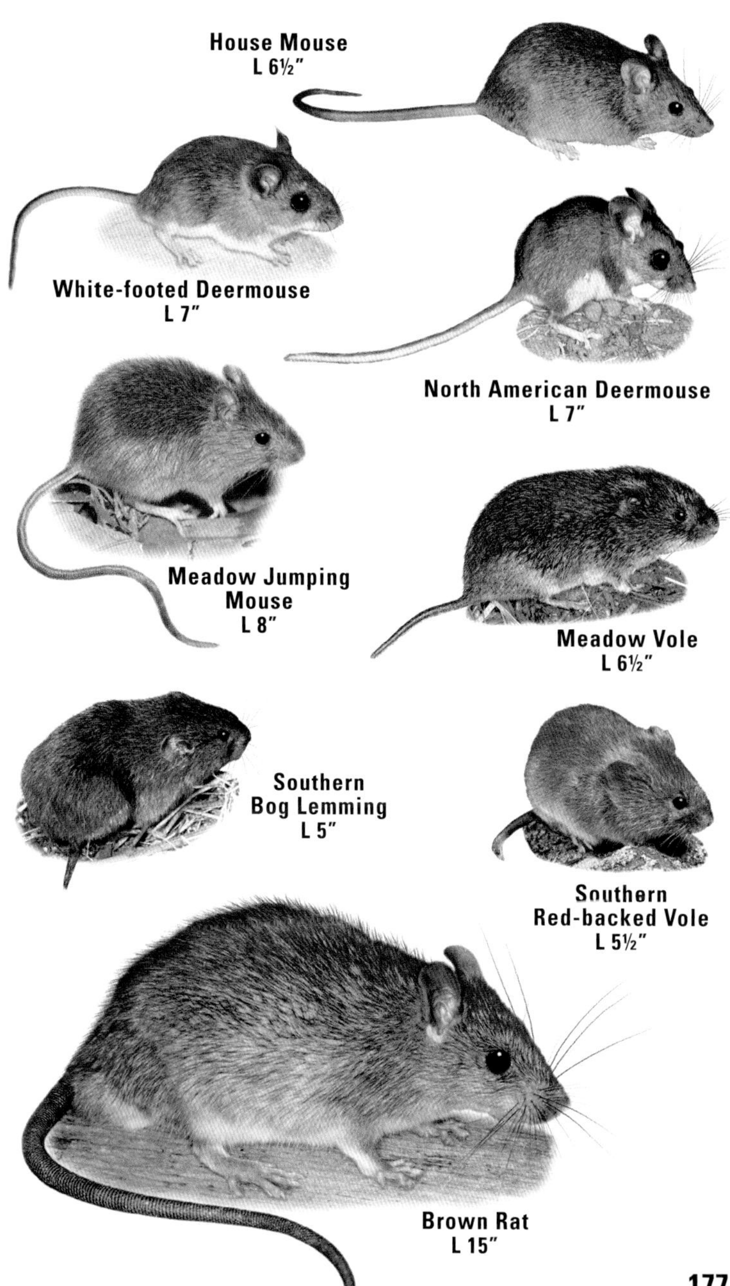

House Mouse
L 6½″

White-footed Deermouse
L 7″

North American Deermouse
L 7″

Meadow Jumping Mouse
L 8″

Meadow Vole
L 6½″

Southern Bog Lemming
L 5″

Southern Red-backed Vole
L 5½″

Brown Rat
L 15″

MOLES AND SHREWS

are sometimes mistaken for rodents, but they belong to a separate order, the Insectivora. Moles (family **Talpidae**) are well adapted for life underground, with small eyes covered by a thin layer of skin, no external ear openings, and soft flexible fur that allows them to move forward or backward in their tunnels without friction. They use their large, flat front feet to dig rapidly through the soil, searching for the grubs, various other insects, and earthworms that they eat. Their tunnelling activities aerate the soil and could be considered helpful to those gardeners who can tolerate the visual effect of their tunnel ridges and molehills. Most moles tend to be solitary except when mating or raising young. Shrews (family **Soricidae**) are frenetic little predators, dashing about constantly in search of small prey. They eat mostly insects, earthworms, and other invertebrates but will also eat small fish, amphibians, even mice. At least half a dozen species occur in New England, but most are rarely seen.

EASTERN MOLE ***Scalopus aquaticus***

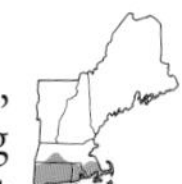

Fairly common in southern New England but not often seen, usually detected by the prominent ridges left by its tunneling near the surface. Digs deeper in cold weather and to make nest for raising young. ► Broad feet and partly bare snout like other moles. Fur mostly blackish brown. Tail is *short and hairless.*

HAIRY-TAILED MOLE ***Parascalops breweri***

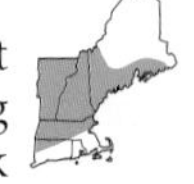

Lives in loose soil under forests and fields. Active day and night and may come out on surface at night. Ridges left by tunneling may be less obvious than those of Eastern Mole. ► Mostly dark gray to blackish, with short but *heavily furred tail.*

STAR-NOSED MOLE ***Condylura cristata***

Active year-round in very wet habitats, this bizarre "spaghetti-faced" mole burrows through mud or snow and may have tunnels leading into the water, where it swims well. The 11 pairs of protuberances on the snout are very sensitive and may even be able to detect prey underwater by electrical impulses. ► Best recognized by *ring of short "tentacles" on snout.* Tail longer than in other moles and moderately hairy.

WATER SHREW ***Sorex palustris***

Uncommon at water's edge, mainly on fast-flowing streams bordered with dense cover. Swims and dives well and can run for short distance across water's surface, thanks to air trapped by hairs on large hind feet. ► Like a hyperactive mouse with small ears, pointed snout. Larger and more aquatic than most shrews.

NORTHERN SHORT-TAILED SHREW ***Blarina brevicauda***

Common in woods and meadows, more often seen than most shrews. Active all year, makes shallow burrows in soil or under snow. Poisonous saliva may help it subdue prey. ► *Broader snout, shorter tail,* larger size than most shrews.

emerging from tunnel using broad front feet

Eastern Mole
L 6″

Hairy-tailed Mole
L 6½″

Star-nosed Mole
L 7″

Water Shrew
L 6″

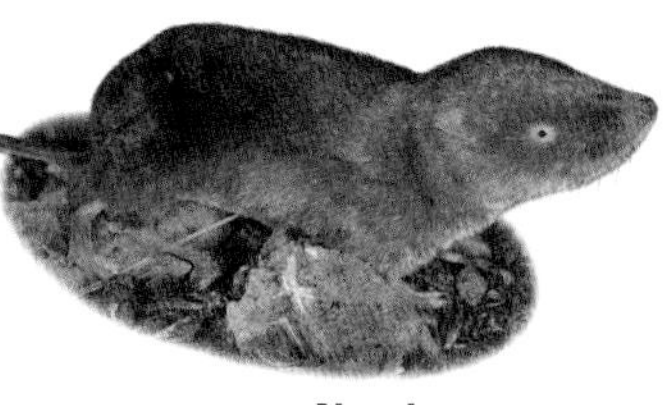

Northern Short-tailed Shrew
L 5″

BATS

(order **Chiroptera**) were once feared and persecuted by the superstitious, but today they have many admirers. The only mammals that can truly fly ("flying" squirrels are really gliders), bats have elongated bones of the fingers and outer arm, connected by a membrane of skin and tissue. Bats can navigate in darkness using echolocation, giving high-pitched calls and detecting obstacles by the echoes that bounce back. Bats roost during the day by hanging upside down in caves, buildings, or other shelters. Identifying bats in flight is difficult, although size offers some clues. Sizes given here are the length of the head, body, and tail combined; distance from wingtip to wingtip is distinctly larger. **Note:** since 2006, more than a million hibernating bats in North America have been killed by a mysterious, fungus-based ailment called white-nose syndrome, which now has been documented at numerous sites in western New England.

LITTLE BROWN MYOTIS ***Myotis lucifugus***

The most common New England bat, although numbers in some areas are being decimated by white-nose syndrome. Daytime roosts and maternity colonies are often in barns or other buildings, while winter roosts are often in caves or mine shafts. ▶ Very small, pale brown, with conspicuously *darker ears* and face.

EASTERN PIPISTRELLE ***Pipistrellus subflavus***

A tiny bat, usually seen in slow, erratic flight at dusk. Small numbers roost in buildings, caves, or hollow trees in summer; larger concentrations hibernate in damp caves in winter. ▶ Very small, buffy to gray-brown, with *ears and face pale,* not dark.

BIG BROWN BAT ***Eptesicus fuscus***

Widespread and common in various habitats, roosting in buildings, hollow trees, under bridges. Diet includes many beetles. May become active on abnormally warm winter days. ▶ Mostly brown, with rounded blackish ears and blackish face.

EASTERN RED BAT ***Lasiurus borealis***

Fairly common in summer in forest edges, roosting among foliage by day. Most migrate south in fall, may be seen migrating along coast. ▶ Male washed with pale orange-red, female more brown, frosted grayish, with orange-red head.

HOARY BAT ***Lasiurus cinereus***

An uncommon summer visitor to New England, usually seen singly. Fast and direct in flight. ▶ Large, with brown fur tipped with white for a hoary or frosted look. Fur around face is contrastingly *yellow.* Whitish spots on folded wings.

SILVER-HAIRED BAT ***Lasionycteris noctivagans***

A migratory species, apparently present in New England mainly in summer. Most may migrate to hibernating sites farther south for winter. Forages in slow flight, often low over ground or water. ▶ Dark overall with *silver tips on hairs,* especially when young.

Little Brown Myotis
L 3½"

Eastern
Pipistrelle
L 3¼"

Big Brown Bat
L 4¼"

Eastern
Red Bat
L 4½"

Hoary
Bat
L 4¾"

Silver-
haired
Bat
L 4"

SEALS, PORPOISE, AND DOLPHINS

Seals are related to carnivores such as bears and cats, while dolphins, porpoises, and whales are related to deer and other hoofed mammals.

HARBOR SEAL ***Phoca vitulina***
The common seal of New England waters, often seen resting on offshore rocks or sandbars with head and tail both raised in "banana" posture. Feeds on fish and other creatures and can stay underwater for 30 minutes. ▶ Color and pattern variable. *Short, blunt snout* with V-shaped nostrils.

GRAY SEAL ***Halichoerus grypus***
Less numerous than Harbor Seal but increasing, especially around Cape Cod region. Feeds on fish. ▶ Averages larger than Harbor Seal, with distinctly *longer snout.* Nostrils look parallel when viewed from front.

HARBOR PORPOISE ***Phocoena phocoena***
The only true porpoise on the East Coast, usually in shallow waters close to shore. Tends to be inconspicuous, not approaching boats as dolphins will. ▶ Small and plain, with dark line angling back from corner of mouth. Dorsal (back) fin is relatively *small and triangular.*

BOTTLENOSE DOLPHIN ***Tursiops truncatus***
Famed as a star of marine life shows, and the most numerous dolphin off the New England coast. Usually travels in small groups; will approach boats to ride bow wave. ▶ Mostly gray, with curved dorsal fin, short "beak."

SHORT-BEAKED COMMON DOLPHIN ***Delphinus delphis***
A very fast swimmer, fairly common far off the New England coast, sometimes seen in groups of hundreds. ▶ Pattern of *"hourglass" or shallow* × on side is distinctive; yellow or buff section of pattern may look gray at sea.

ATLANTIC WHITE-SIDED DOLPHIN ***Lagenorhynchus acutus***
Sometimes seen in large groups offshore and may associate with whales. Feeds on squid and small fish. ▶ Strong contrasting pattern, with white and *yellow* flank patches. Yellow is hard to see under some conditions.

WHITE-BEAKED DOLPHIN ***Lagenorhynchus albirostris***
These striking dolphins may associate with whales well offshore or with White-sided Dolphins. ▶ Variable in pattern, but has larger dorsal fin than most dolphins, no yellow flank patches. "Beak" may be dusky, not white.

RISSO'S DOLPHIN ***Grampus griseus***
Groups of these large dolphins are sometimes seen far offshore in New England waters. ▶ Blunt-headed compared to preceding dolphins. Size and shape more like Pilot Whale, but usually *paler,* with *higher dorsal fin.*

LONG-FINNED PILOT WHALE ***Globicephala melas***
These big dolphins travel in tight pods. Mariners once thought that one individual would guide or "pilot" the group. Usually farther offshore in winter and spring, closer to land in spring and summer, and large numbers will occasionally be grounded on beaches. ▶ *Blunt, bulbous head;* blackish overall color; low, curved dorsal fin.

SEALS AND DOLPHINS

mother and pup

Harbor Seal
L 5½′

Gray Seal
L 7′

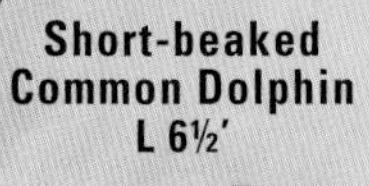

Harbor Porpoise
L 5′

Bottlenose Dolphin
L 8½′

Short-beaked Common Dolphin
L 6½′

Atlantic White-sided Dolphin
L 8′

White-beaked Dolphin
L 8′

Risso's Dolphin
L 11′

Long-finned Pilot Whale
L 17′

Their numbers were reduced by commercial whaling in the past, but these huge mammals still are seen in New England waters, especially over Stellwagen Bank off Massachusetts. Those shown here are all baleen whales: instead of teeth, their mouths are lined with narrow hardened strips called baleen. The whales feed by lunging into schools of tiny fish or crustaceans, taking in great mouthfuls of water, then straining out their prey by forcing the water out through the gaps between baleen strips. Whales are often first spotted by the "spout" or "blow," an exhalation of steamy breath through the blowholes on top of their heads.

HUMPBACK WHALE ***Megaptera novaeangliae***
The whales seen most often off New England, Humpbacks summer in our waters, wintering in the Caribbean where their young are born. Very active, often lunging partway out of water (breaching) and falling back with a mighty splash. Usually raises tail flukes when diving. Patterns on undersides of flukes are distinctive; researchers can recognize and keep track of individuals by these patterns. ► *Very long* flippers are *mostly white.* Also note low dorsal (back) fin, bumps on head, stout-bodied shape.

NORTHERN RIGHT WHALE ***Eubalaena glacialis***
An endangered species, and its name reflects the reason: whalers considered it the "right" whale to kill because it was rich in oil and it floated when dead. Small numbers still live off the New England coast. ► Stout, blackish, with *no dorsal (back) fin.* Head often has roughened areas covered with pale parasites called cyamids (whale lice). Blow is divided, in a V shape.

NORTHERN MINKE WHALE ***Balaenoptera acutorostrata***
This small whale is still fairly common over the continental shelf in New England waters. ► Relatively small, with a distinctly pointed snout. Usually has a *white patch on top of the flipper.* Dorsal (back) fin is set rather far forward compared to the next three species.

SEI WHALE ***Balaenoptera borealis***
Sei Whales (pronounced like "sigh") are rare and unpredictable visitors in our waters. ► Lacks obvious field marks. Large and dark, more streamlined than Humpback or Right Whales. Dorsal fin often more prominent than on Fin Whale, and lacks the asymmetrical pattern of that species.

FIN WHALE ***Balaenoptera physalus***
The second-largest animal on Earth and the largest one expected in New England waters, seen regularly offshore. A fast swimmer, able to reach 25 miles per hour. ► Diagnostic but not easy to see is the *lopsided coloring of the jaw,* white on the animal's right side, dark on the left. Shows a faint pale chevron behind the eye. Huge and dark overall, with dorsal fin set far back.

BLUE WHALE ***Balaenoptera musculus***
A rare visitor to New England waters, this is the largest animal ever known, surpassing the largest dinosaurs in size. Commercial whaling almost drove this magnificent creature to extinction. ► Known by its enormous size and pale *blue-gray color* with lighter mottling.

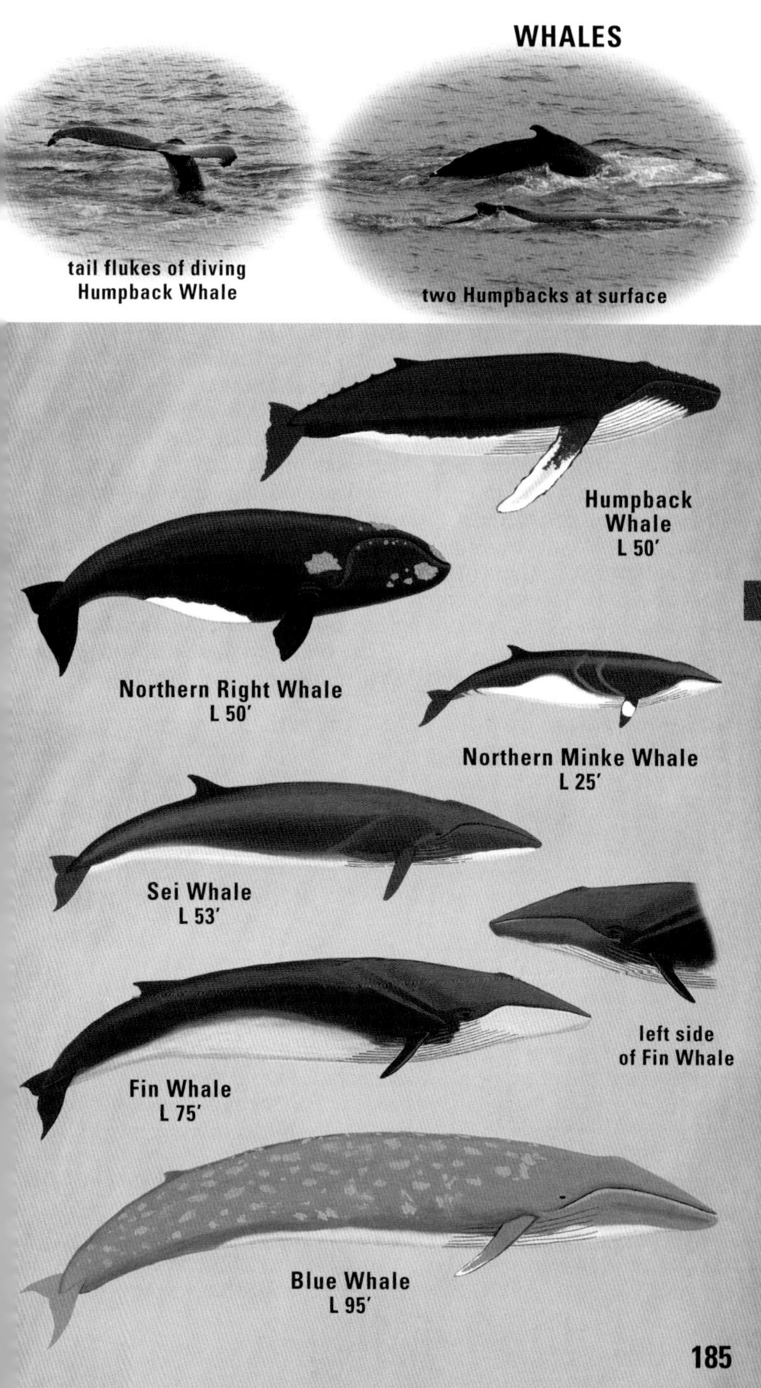
tail flukes of diving
Humpback Whale
two Humpbacks at surface
Humpback
Whale
L 50′
Northern Right Whale
L 50′
Northern Minke Whale
L 25′
Sei Whale
L 53′
left side
of Fin Whale
Fin Whale
L 75′
Blue Whale
L 95′

BIRDS

(class Aves) are the most noticeable wildlife in New England, and bird watching, or birding, is tremendously popular here. Well over 450 species of birds have been recorded in these states, although many of those have been rare visitors from other regions — or even from other continents! This section treats all the birds you are likely to see, but if you become seriously interested in birding, you will want to carry a more comprehensive guide such as the *Kaufman Field Guide to Birds of North America.*

New England birdlife changes with the seasons. Some species live here year-round, but more are seasonal visitors. Many species, especially songbirds that feed mainly on insects, arrive here in spring to spend the summer with us, building nests and raising young before they leave in the fall; they may spend the winter in the southern U.S. or in the tropics. Other birds, especially hardy seed-eaters and waterfowl, arrive here in fall from much farther north and spend the winter with us. And many species nest farther north and spend the winter far to the south of us, migrating through New England only in spring and fall. The arrivals and departures and passage of all these species create much of the excitement of birding.

Because birds move around so much, their range maps have to convey more information. These maps can help you identify birds by telling you what to expect. For example, Chipping Sparrow and American Tree Sparrow are both common in New England, but not in the same season: Chipping in summer, Tree in winter. We use colors on these maps to indicate different seasons and different levels of abundance, as shown below:

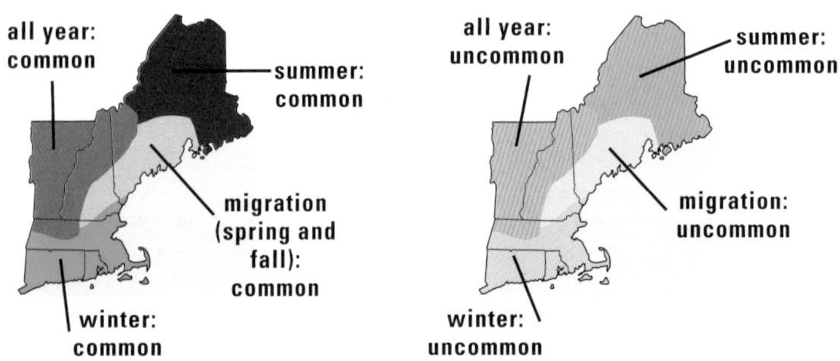

While this may seem like a lot of colors, there are really only three to remember: red (a hot color) for summer, blue (a cold color) for winter, and gray for migration. Red plus blue makes purple for birds found year-round, and for all colors, paler shades mean that the birds are less common.

Binoculars can make birds easier to identify and enjoy. It's good to try binoculars before buying, by visiting a nature center or wild bird store that carries several models. Check for a sharp, bright image, good close focusing (we often want to look at birds that are fairly close), and comfortable fit for your hands and eyes. Good optics are expensive but well worth it.

Finding birds is a skill that increases with practice, but a major part is just being alert, watching and listening for bird activity. Visiting different habitats, and visiting them in different seasons, will help you find more different bird species. In spring and summer, birds may be much easier to find early in the morning when they are actively foraging and singing, but in cold weather, time of day is less important.

Feeding birds is a wonderful way to bring them in for close observation. By placing feeders in strategic locations, you can turn your ordinary windows into windows on bird life! While traveling in search of birds adds to the sense of adventure, enjoying them from the comfort of your own home is, perhaps, the ultimate way to begin to study birds and their behavior.

Bird feeding has become a multibillion-dollar industry. A plethora of different types of bird feeders are available, and wild bird feeding supplies can be found in an ever widening range of markets. No matter which types of feeders you select, you should keep them filled — and clean! It is also very important to keep your cats indoors at all times, but this is especially important if you plan to entice wild birds to your yard.

Identifying birds is always rewarding but sometimes challenging. When you see an unfamiliar bird, try to see as much detail on it as possible before you reach for the field guide. For starters, try to place it in the right general group. A bird's color is usually less important than its shape and behavior. House Sparrow and Great Horned Owl are both brown, but their shapes and actions are very different! In particular, the shape of a bird's bill is often a good clue to its identity. Study the bill shapes on birds on various pages in the following section and you'll see what we mean.

A bird's size is a good clue, although it can be hard to judge sizes accurately in the wild. In this book, sizes are indicated in inches, giving the total length of each bird from the tip of its bill to the end of its tail. These are average figures for each species. It's most effective to compare an unknown bird to the size of a familiar one: for example, to say that a given bird was about the size of a crow, or a little smaller than a robin.

With practice, you'll learn to look for *field marks:* distinctive markings that are often referred to as "the trademarks of nature." Look for markings on the bird's *face,* such as an eye-ring, whisker marks, or an eyebrow stripe. If the face is totally plain, without any obvious markings, that could be considered a field mark as well. The *wings* may show prominent wing bars or a patch of contrasting color, or they may be plain. Many birds have some white in the tail, most obvious when the bird flies; this may consist of white outer edges or corners, or spots partly concealed halfway up the tail. Many birds are paler below than above; the pale underparts may be plain or may be marked with lengthwise streaks, crosswise bars, round spots, or some other pattern. In all cases, the more details you can notice, the better chance you have of identifying the bird. And the more birds you can identify, the more satisfying your birding will become.

DABBLING DUCKS

Among the ducks, geese, and swans (family **Anatidae**), dabblers are the familiar ducks of ponds and marshes, dipping their heads or upending in the shallows. Only the females incubate eggs or care for the young.

MALLARD ***Anas platyrhynchos***
Abundant and widespread in the wild, also often living in a semi-wild state on city park ponds. ▶ Male with white neck ring, curled feathers above tail. Female mottled brown, with orange and black on bill. ♪ **Voice:** thin whistles, noisy quacks.

AMERICAN BLACK DUCK ***Anas rubripes***
Still common, but declining, perhaps being replaced by Mallard. Favors woodland ponds, salt marshes. ▶ Like a *darker version* of female Mallard, but male has *yellow bill.* Hybrids with Mallard (green patches on head) are often seen. ♪ **Voice:** like Mallard's.

NORTHERN PINTAIL ***Anas acuta***
An elegant duck of open marshes, mostly a migrant here. ▶ Slim with long neck and tail. Male gray with white neck stripe, brown head. Female brown with gray bill. ♪ **Voice:** whistles, quacks.

GADWALL ***Anas strepera***
Regular migrant, scarcer at other seasons, in marshy ponds. ▶ Looks plain at a distance; male gray with *black stern.* Female brown with gray and orange bill. ♪ **Voice:** short *ghenk.*

GREEN-WINGED TEAL ***Anas crecca***
Our smallest dabbler. In flight, flocks look fast, twisting in the air. ▶ Male has dark head, gray body; female brown with gray bill. Both very small, with yellow "tail-light." ♪ **Voice:** squeaky *chyerk.*

BLUE-WINGED TEAL ***Anas discors***
Common migrant in marshy ponds, local in summer, mostly gone in winter. ▶ Spring male has *white face crescent,* white spot near tail. Females and many fall males brown with paler face. *Blue wing patch* shows mostly in flight. ♪ **Voice:** peeps, quacks.

NORTHERN SHOVELER ***Anas clypeata***
Swims in shallows with head low, bill half submerged, straining the muddy waters for food. ▶ *Long wide bill* diagnostic. Male has green head, white chest, rusty belly. ♪ **Voice:** low *thook-thook.*

AMERICAN WIGEON ***Anas americana***
Fairly common migrant, especially in fall. Some winter on open ponds. ▶ Pinkish body, gray head; male with green eye patch, *white crown stripe.* Male **Eurasian Wigeon** *(A. penelope),* a rare visitor, has rusty head, gray sides. ♪ **Voice:** shrill 3-note whistle.

"PARK POND DUCKS"
An almost endless variety of plumages may be seen on the tame ducks on park ponds, most of which are descended from the Mallard.

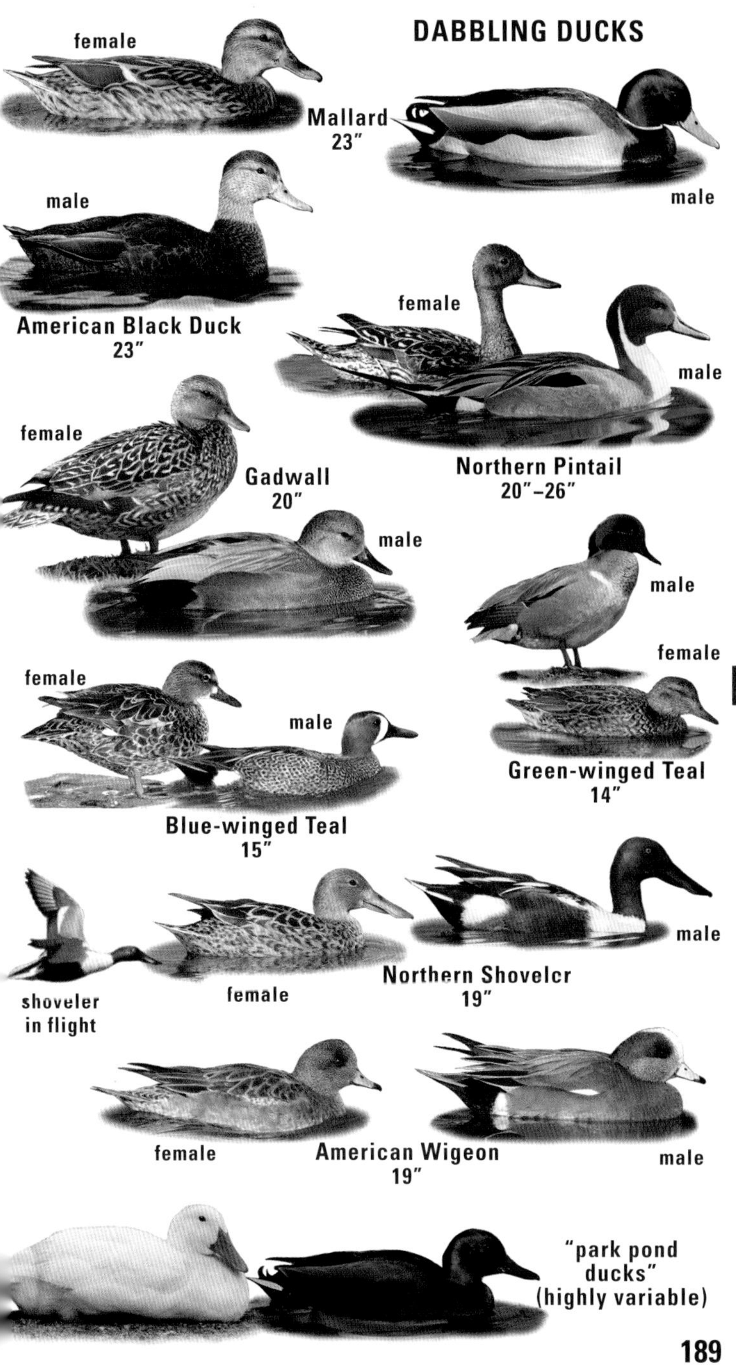
DABBLING DUCKS
female
Mallard
23″
male
male
American Black Duck
23″
female
male
Northern Pintail
20″–26″
female
Gadwall
20″
male
male
female
Green-winged Teal
14″
female
male
Blue-winged Teal
15″
male
shoveler
in flight
female
Northern Shovelcr
19″
female
American Wigeon
19″
male
"park pond
ducks"
(highly variable)

WOOD DUCK AND DIVING DUCKS

Wood Ducks are dabblers, like those on p. 188. The others here seek their food by diving and swimming underwater. These divers are awkward on land and must patter across the water to take flight.

WOOD DUCK ***Aix sponsa***

A beautiful dabbling duck of wooded swamps, ponds, rivers. Lays its eggs in a tree cavity, often quite high, or in a nest box placed near water. ▶ Ornate male unmistakable at most seasons. Female duller, with white eye patch. ♪ **Voice**: shrill *oowheak!* in flight.

HOODED MERGANSER ***Lophodytes cucullatus***

Unlike most ducks, mergansers eat fish (mainly very small ones). Hooded Merganser favors woodland ponds but also appears on open bays. Nests in tree cavities or in Wood Duck boxes. ▶ Male's crest may be raised or lowered. Female has shaggy dark head.

RED-BREASTED MERGANSER ***Mergus serrator***

Usually seen on coastal bays in winter, in small flocks just offshore. ▶ Male has shaggy green head, contrasting white collar, red bill. Female with dull brown head fading to whitish throat.

COMMON MERGANSER ***Mergus merganser***

Often on lakes and large rivers, also on coast in winter. Nests in large tree cavities. ▶ Striking male mostly white with green head, red bill. Female with rusty head, sharply defined white throat.

COMMON GOLDENEYE ***Bucephala clangula***

Nests around northern lakes and rivers, common in winter on coastal bays. Wings make whistling sound in flight. ▶ Male with round white spot on black head; female gray, with chocolate-brown head. Male **Barrow's Goldeneye** *(B. islandica)*, a scarce winter visitor, has blacker back, *crescent* spot in front of eye.

RUDDY DUCK ***Oxyura jamaicensis***

An odd little duck, resting in flocks on lakes and bays, its stiff tail feathers often pointed up. ▶ Male has *white cheeks, dark cap;* blue bill and rusty body in summer. Female has dark cheek stripe.

BUFFLEHEAD ***Bucephala albeola***

Our tiniest diving duck, usually seen in small flocks on deep lakes and bays. ▶ Male has white "scarf" on black head; looks mostly white at a distance. Female gray, with white central face spot.

LONG-TAILED DUCK ***Clangula hyemalis***

Nests in Arctic, winters in flocks offshore. ▶ Mostly pale in winter, male with strong pattern and long tail. In flight, wings solidly dark. ♪ **Voice**: musical *yow-owdle-ow,* often heard from flocks.

HARLEQUIN DUCK ***Histrionicus histrionicus***

Scarce in winter on coast, mostly along rocky shorelines, jetties. ▶ Clown-patterned male unmistakable. Female small, dark, with white face spots.

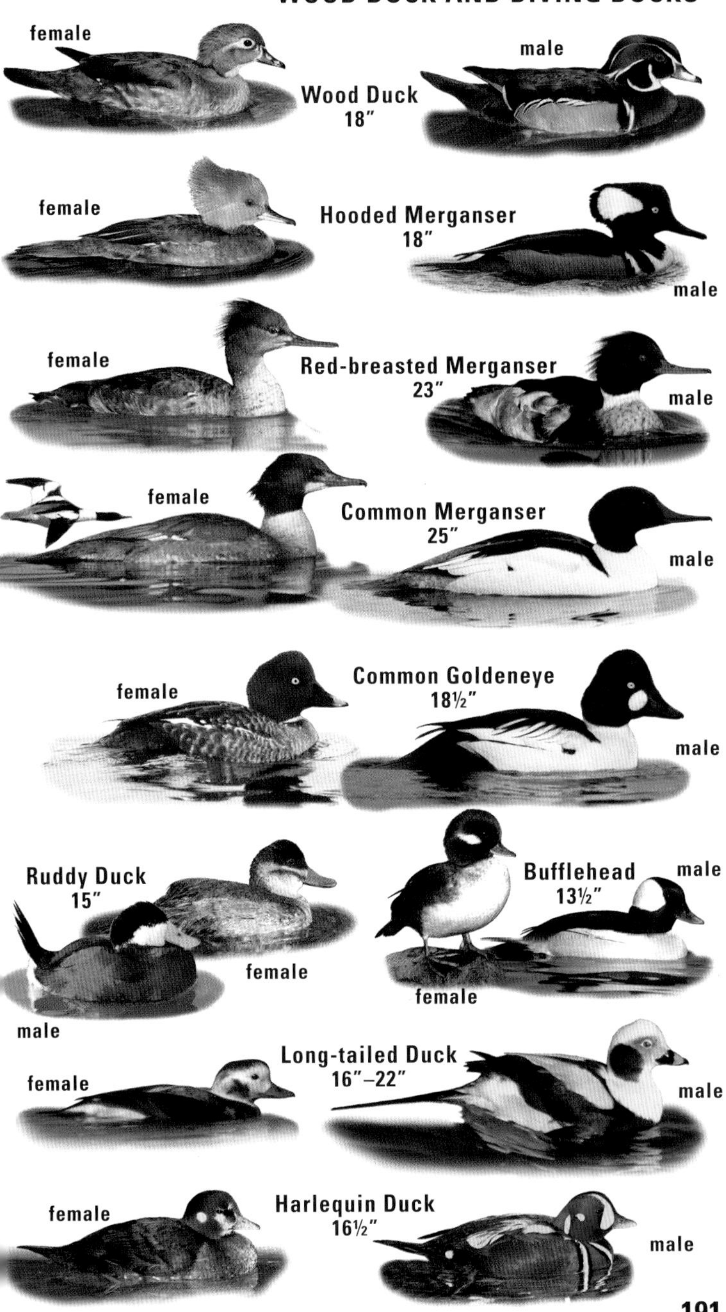
female
male
Wood Duck
18″
female
Hooded Merganser
18″
male
female
Red-breasted Merganser
23″
male
female
Common Merganser
25″
male
female
Common Goldeneye
18½″
male
Ruddy Duck
15″
female
male
Bufflehead
13½″
male
female
Long-tailed Duck
16″–22″
female
male
female
Harlequin Duck
16½″
male

DIVING DUCKS

The first five below are seen regularly on lakes and ponds as well as coastal bays, while the rest are usually on salt water in New England.

GREATER SCAUP ***Aythya marila***

Common in migration and winter along coast, also on large lakes. ▶ Scaup are black at both ends and white in the middle. This species has rounder head (glossed green in males), bigger bill.

LESSER SCAUP ***Aythya affinis***

Found in same habitats as Greater Scaup but usually less common here. ▶ Very much like Greater Scaup but has more *peaked* head (with *purple* gloss in males), slightly grayer sides.

RING-NECKED DUCK ***Aythya collaris***

Found on woodland ponds more often than most divers. ▶ Neck ring is faint, but *ring on bill* is obvious. Male has white slash between black chest, gray sides. Female has peaked head, eye-ring.

CANVASBACK ***Aythya valisineria***

Common in winter on some southern New England bays. ▶ *Long sloping profile* is distinctive. Male has *white back,* black chest, rusty head. Female has pale tan head and chest, gray body.

REDHEAD ***Aythya americana***

Usually uncommon here. Unlike most diving ducks, often on shallow waters, dabbling and tipping up to feed. ▶ Male *gray* with *rounded rusty head.* Female very plain, slight ring on bill.

SURF SCOTER ***Melanitta perspicillata***

Scoters are big dark sea ducks, usually seen offshore. Large flocks may migrate along coast. ▶ Male ("skunkhead coot") has white head patches, bright bill. Female has long bill, pale face patches.

WHITE-WINGED SCOTER ***Melanitta fusca***

Migrates along coast, and abundant offshore in winter, especially in Nantucket Sound. ▶ Large, long-billed, dark, with small white eye spot in male. *White wing patch* is visible mainly in flight.

BLACK SCOTER ***Melanitta americana***

Common offshore, sometimes on lakes in migration. ▶ Adult male all black, with *orange bill knob.* Female dark, with bicolored head. Compare to Ruddy Duck (p. 190).

COMMON EIDER ***Somateria mollissima***

A big, bulky duck, seen in flocks along coast or offshore. Females use soft down to line nests, among rocks near beach. ▶ Unmistakable adult males often outnumbered by females and young, which are brown with long heads, heavily barred pattern.

KING EIDER ***Somateria spectabilis***

Rare in winter, with Common Eider flocks. ▶ Adult male distinctive. Female resembles Common but has shorter bill, scalloped pattern on sides.

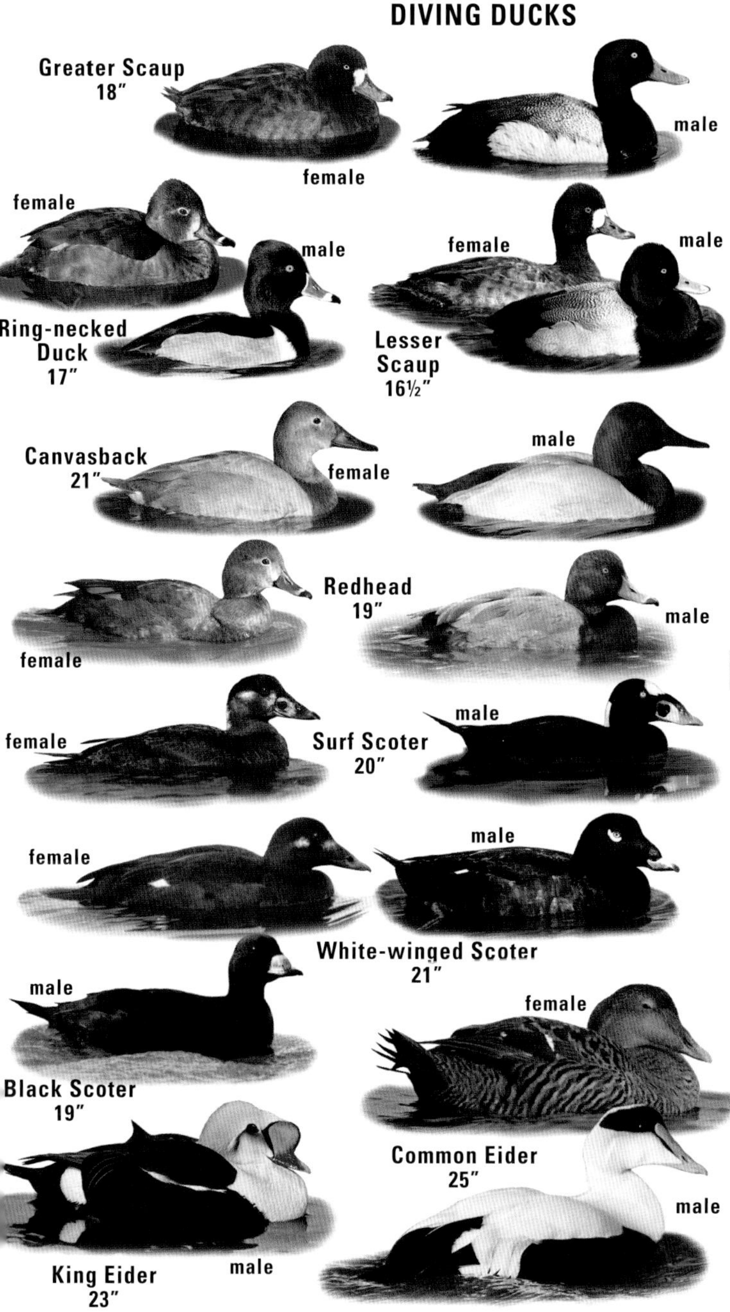
Greater Scaup
18″
female
male
female
male
Ring-necked
Duck
17″
female
male
Lesser
Scaup
16½″
Canvasback
21″
female
male
Redhead
19″
female
male
female
Surf Scoter
20″
male
female
male
White-winged Scoter
21″
male
Black Scoter
19″
female
Common Eider
25″
male
King Eider
23″
male

Geese and swans are related to ducks (pp. 188–193). Loons (family **Gaviidae**) and cormorants (family **Phalacrocoracidae**), unrelated but sometimes mistaken for each other, are expert swimmers and divers.

BRANT ***Branta bernicla***

Nesting in the Arctic, this goose can be very common along our coast during migration and winter. ► Black *chest,* neck, and head, *small* white neck spot, pale belly. ♪ **Voice:** hoarse, low honking.

CANADA GOOSE ***Branta canadensis***

Formerly just a migrant from nesting grounds in Canada, their flocks in V-formation arriving in late fall as visitors from the wilderness. Introduced populations are now common all year in New England, even in city parks. ► Black head and neck with *white chin strap, pale chest,* brown body. ♪ **Voice:** deep honking.

SNOW GOOSE ***Chen caerulescens***

Another Arctic nester, passing through our region in migration, especially in April. Rare in winter. ► White with *black wingtips,* pinkish orange bill. Dark morph ("Blue Goose"), rare in New England, has blue-gray body, white head. ♪ **Voice:** nasal *owk-owk.*

MUTE SWAN ***Cygnus olor***

Native to Europe. Beautiful but sometimes damaging to native habitats in New England. ► Huge, all white, with black knob on *orange bill.* Young bird has pinkish gray bill. The native **Tundra Swan** *(C. columbianus),* a rare migrant here, has a black bill.

COMMON LOON ***Gavia immer***

A beautiful summer bird of northern lakes, migrating and wintering along coast. ► Striking in adult summer plumage. Fall and winter birds (and summering young birds) gray above, white below, with patterned neck. ♪ **Voice:** wild yodeling, often at night.

RED-THROATED LOON ***Gavia stellata***

Nests in the Arctic, very common migrant along our coast, with some wintering. ► Smaller and plainer than Common Loon with *thin, upturned bill.* Usually paler face in fall/winter plumage.

DOUBLE-CRESTED CORMORANT ***Phalacrocorax auritus***

Very common in summer and migration seasons, especially along coast. Nests in colonies, with bulky stick nests in trees or on ground, mainly on islands. Migrates along coast in flocks, sometimes in V-formation. ► Adult dull black with orange throat pouch. Young browner, paler below, often whitish on neck.

GREAT CORMORANT ***Phalacrocorax carbo*** **(not shown)**

Maine islands in summer, widespread on coast in winter, when it outnumbers the Double-crested Cormorant. ► Bulkier than Double-crested. Adult has *white* on throat; also white flank patch in spring. Young has *dark neck, white belly.*

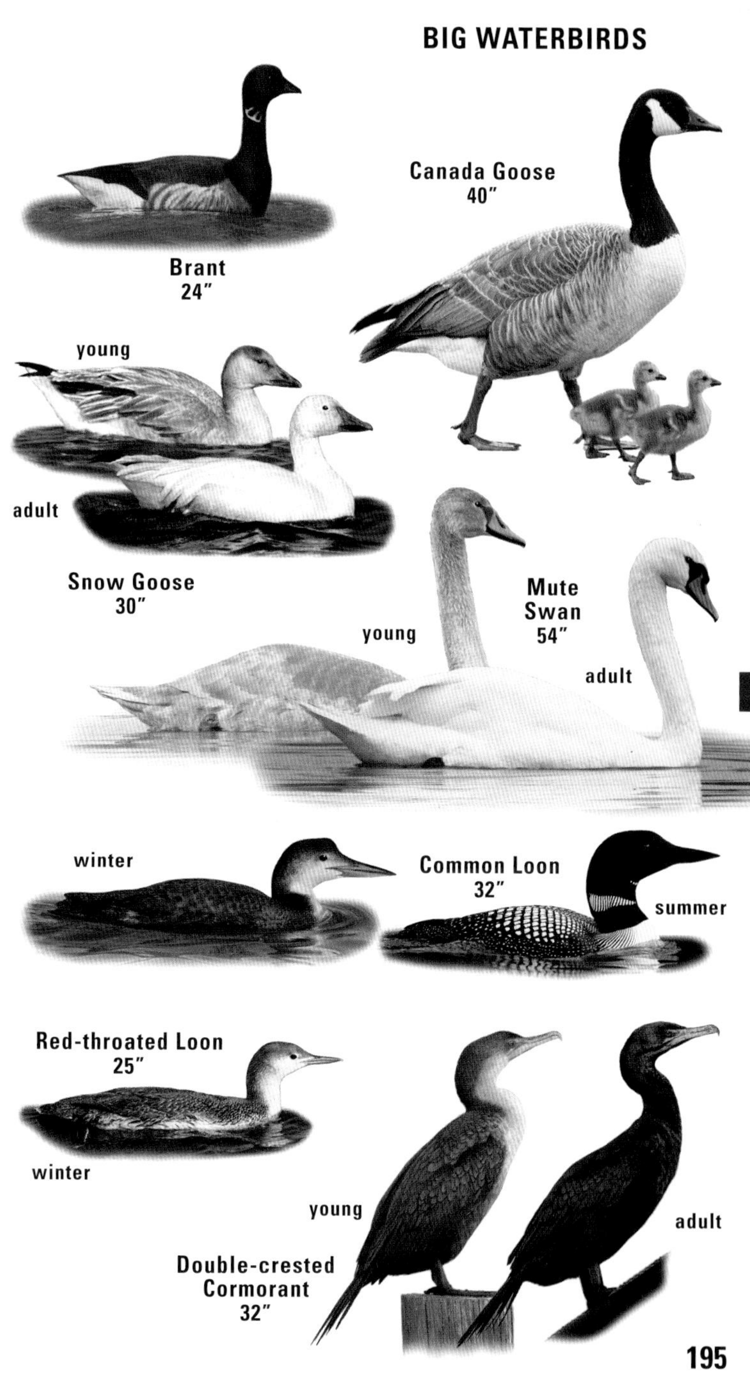

Brant
24″
Canada Goose
40″
young
adult
Snow Goose
30″
young
Mute
Swan
54″
adult
winter
Common Loon
32″
summer
Red-throated Loon
25″
winter
young
Double-crested
Cormorant
32″
adult

Coots and gallinules are in the rail family **(Rallidae).** Grebes (family **Podicipedidae**) are adept divers and underwater swimmers, but helpless on land. The last four species below are in the auk family **(Alcidae).**

AMERICAN COOT ***Fulica americana***

This odd bird flocks with ducks on ponds and marshes, grazes on grassy shores. ▶ Mostly slaty gray with blacker head, very *thick white bill.* Nods its head as it swims. ♪**Voice:** clucks, whines.

COMMON GALLINULE ***Gallinula galeata***

A relative of the coot, usually uncommon on marshes, freshwater ponds. ▶ Slaty with browner back, white side stripe, *thick colorful bill* (red and yellow, or all yellow). ♪**Voice:** varied clucks, whines.

PIED-BILLED GREBE ***Podilymbus podiceps***

Fairly common migrant on ponds, scarce in summer and winter. Can swim with only head and neck above water. Builds floating nest. ▶ Compact, tailless look. In summer, thick bill is black and white ("pied"), throat is black. ♪**Voice:** cooing, gobbling chatter.

HORNED GREBE ***Podiceps auritus***

Common along coast in migration and winter, sometimes seen on inland lakes. ▶ Compact, with thin dark bill. Usually seen here in winter plumage, clean black and white. Breeding plumage more colorful, with buff "horns." **Red-necked Grebe** *(P. grisegena)*, scarce along coast in winter, is larger, grayer on neck.

BLACK GUILLEMOT ***Cepphus grylle***

Seen close to shore more often than other members of auk family. Fairly common along rocky coastlines, diving and swimming underwater. Pronounced GILL-uh-mott. ▶ Black with big white wing patch in summer; compare to White-winged Scoter (p. 192). Winter and young birds much whiter.

ATLANTIC PUFFIN ***Fratercula arctica***

A famous bird of the Maine coast, though it takes special effort to see one at the offshore islands where they nest. Reintroduction of the species to Eastern Egg Rock was a conservation success story. Puffins winter far out at sea, seldom seen from land south of Maine. ▶ Summer adults unmistakable, with *large colorful bill,* white face. In winter, bill is somewhat smaller and duller (after outer plates are shed), face is grayer. Young bird is duller with bill even smaller, but still unlike other local auks.

RAZORBILL ***Alca torda***

Common offshore in winter, a few off Maine coast in summer. ▶ Sharply black and white with big, blunt bill, long tail. Fast wingbeats in flight.

DOVEKIE ***Alle alle***

A tiny Arctic auk, wintering off our coast. Sometimes blown ashore by storms. ▶ Small, with *stubby bill.* White extends up onto side of neck.

American Coot
15″

Common Gallinule
14″

summer

Pied-billed Grebe
13″

winter

summer

Horned Grebe
13½″

winter

Black Guillemot
13″

summer

Atlantic
Puffin
13″

Razorbill
17″

Dovekie
8¼″

GULLS

are among our most familiar birds of the water's edge, especially on the coast. They nest in colonies, mostly on the ground. Along with terns and skimmers (p. 200), they make up the family **Laridae.** Gulls take two to four years to reach adult plumage. Brown gulls are just young birds, not different species; compare sizes and shapes to help identify them.

HERRING GULL ***Larus argentatus***
Abundant all year on coast, less numerous inland. An adaptable scavenger, also predatory on smaller creatures. ▶ Adult gray and white (with mottled head in winter), with white spots in black wingtips. *Legs pink; bill mostly yellow.* Young all-brown at first, gradually changing to adult plumage over the course of 4 years. ♩**Voice:** like most gulls, a variety of harsh cries.

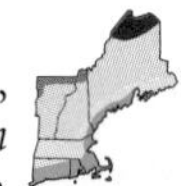

RING-BILLED GULL ***Larus delawarensis***
Widespread on coast and inland, around beaches, docks, ponds, parking lots. ▶ Smaller than Herring Gull, adult has *yellow-green legs, black ring* on bill. Young birds start off grayer and paler than young Herring Gulls and have *pink bill with black tip.*

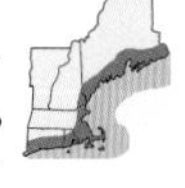

GREAT BLACK-BACKED GULL ***Larus marinus***
Our largest gull, common along coast and offshore, scarcer inland. ▶ Adult unmistakable with huge size, black back, thick bill, pink legs. Young are paler below and on head than young Herring Gull, with strong *checkered pattern* on back at first.

BONAPARTE'S GULL ***Chroicocephalus philadelphia***
Nesting in the far north, this small gull migrates through New England, wintering along coast. ▶ Looks small and delicate in flight, with white wedge in outer part of wing. Adult has black hood in summer, black ear spot in winter. Young shows more pattern on wings. Compare to Black-legged Kittiwake (p. 202).

LAUGHING GULL ***Leucophaeus atricilla***
Common in summer on coast, mostly absent in winter. ▶ Adults have *dark gray* back and wings, *black hood* in spring and summer. Young brown at first, molting to brown and gray; note bill shape, dark legs. ♩**Voice:** loud laughing calls.

LESSER BLACK-BACKED GULL ***Larus fuscus***
Formerly rare, becoming a regular visitor from Europe. ▶ Near size and shape of Herring Gull, but adult with *darker gray back, yellow legs.*

ICELAND GULL ***Larus glaucoides***
Winter visitor from Greenland and Canada (not Iceland), uncommon, mostly on coast. ▶ Near size of Herring Gull but paler, with pale wingtips.

GLAUCOUS GULL ***Larus hyperboreus***
Another scarce winter visitor. ▶ Larger than Herring Gull, with very pale wingtips. Young have bicolored bills. In summer, faded, sun-bleached young of other gulls can be mistaken for Glaucous Gulls.

GULLS

immatures
Herring Gull
25″
spring
adult
immature
adult
spring
adult
Ring-billed Gull
19″
immatures
spring
adult
Great Black-backed Gull
30″
winter
adult
immature
immatures
Bonaparte's Gull
13″
spring
adult
Lauging Gull
17″
spring
adult
SCARCER GULLS (not to scale)
Glaucous Gull
28″
Iceland
Gull
23″
Lesser
Black-backed
Gull
23″

TERNS AND SKIMMERS

are related to gulls, but are mostly smaller, with more pointed bills and often with forked tails. They occur in New England only during the warmer half of the year. Terns feed mostly by plunging into the water to catch small fish in their bills. They nest in colonies, mostly on islands.

COMMON TERN ***Sterna hirundo***

The most numerous tern in New England; thousands nest on some offshore islands. ▶ Typical tern with long forked tail, black cap. In summer, bill is red with black tip. Young bird and fall adult have white forehead. Compare to next two species. **Forster's Tern** *(S. forsteri),* not shown, scarce in New England, is very similar with paler wings, orange bill base. ♩**Voice:** harsh grating cries.

ARCTIC TERN ***Sterna paradisaea***

Uncommon, nesting mostly on islands off Maine, feeding farther offshore than other terns. A long-distance migrant, wintering in the southern hemisphere. ▶ Like Common Tern but has smaller *all-red bill, darker gray below,* longer tail. In flight, wings look more silvery above, with narrower black trailing edge below.

ROSEATE TERN ***Sterna dougallii***

Now considered endangered, nesting in only a few colonies in northeast. ▶ Like Common Tern but looks whiter overall. Bill is *longer, thinner,* mostly black. Flies with quicker shallow wingbeats. ♩**Voice:** distinctive soft *chivvyit,* also harsh notes.

CASPIAN TERN ***Hydroprogne caspia***

The size of a small gull, this hefty tern is an uncommon migrant here, mostly along coast. ▶ Known by *large size, thick red bill.* Shows dark underside of wingtips in flight. May have solid black cap or may have forehead streaked. ♩**Voice:** low harsh *kahhrrr.*

BLACK TERN ***Chlidonias niger***

Uncommon, mostly around inland marshes in spring, along coast in fall. ▶ Spring adult black with silvery wings and tail. Young and fall adults white below, but darker above than other terns.

LEAST TERN ***Sternula antillarum***

Locally common on coast, nesting on many mainland beaches, which puts it at risk except where colonies have been fenced to keep out intruders. ▶ Tiny size, *yellow bill* with black tip, sharply defined *white forehead.* ♩**Voice:** high notes, *zzrreep* and *kvick.*

BLACK SKIMMER ***Rynchops niger***

An odd tern relative with a bizarre feeding style. Flies low over water with long lower mandible submerged, snapping bill shut when it strikes a small fish. ▶ Large size, very long black wings. Unique bill with lower mandible much longer than upper. Young birds browner than adults. ♩**Voice:** low, barking *wurf, wurf.*

Common Tern
14″ w 30″
w = wingspan
Arctic Tern
15½″ w 31″
Roseate Tern
15″ w 29″
Caspian Tern
21″ w 50″
Black Tern
10″ w 24″
Least Tern
8½″ w 20″
Black Skimmer
18″ w 44″

VARIOUS SEABIRDS

These true seabirds, from several families, are seldom found on land in New England. Whale-watching boat trips may offer chances to see them.

NORTHERN GANNET ***Morus bassanus***
Gannets (family Sulidae) are big seabirds, flying high, plunge-diving into the sea headfirst to catch fish. Nesting on Canadian islands, they are common off New England in migration and winter. ► Huge, with pointed wings and tail, spearlike bill. Adults white with black wingtips; young birds all-brown at first, gradually developing white over about 4 years.

PARASITIC JAEGER ***Stercorarius parasiticus***
Jaegers (family Stercorariidae) are related to gulls but more piratic, chasing other seabirds to steal their food. ► Variable in color pattern but usually has *pointed central tail feathers*, white flash in outer part of wing.

BLACK-LEGGED KITTIWAKE ***Rissa tridactyla***
A gull (see p. 198) that actually is a "seagull," nesting on islands of far north, usually staying offshore in New England. ► Adult has small yellow bill, wingtips "dipped in ink." Young has strong wing pattern, dark neck bar.

GREAT SHEARWATER ***Puffinus gravis***
Shearwaters (family Procellariidae) resemble gulls but fly with fast, stiff wingbeats and long glides, far out at sea. This one nests on islands in South Atlantic and is common in summer and fall off New England. ► Contrasting pattern with black cap, pale collar, white rump, dark belly patch.

SOOTY SHEARWATER ***Puffinus griseus***
Another visitor from the southern hemisphere, common offshore in summer. ► Dark sooty gray with silvery flash under wing. Note flight action.

NORTHERN FULMAR ***Fulmarus glacialis***
This shearwater relative is common off New England in winter. ► Patterned like a gull, but with short thick bill, different flight action.

RED-NECKED PHALAROPE ***Phalaropus lobatus***
This odd relative of the sandpipers (see p. 220) nests in the Arctic, spends most of the year out at sea. Migrating flocks occur off our coast in spring and fall. ► Swims buoyantly, picking at surface. Small size, slim black bill, striped back. Red neck patch in spring (brighter on female).

WILSON'S STORM-PETREL ***Oceanites oceanicus***
Storm-petrels (family Hydrobatidae) flit low over the waves far offshore. Wilson's is the one commonly seen off New England, though it nests only on islands far south of the Equator, making a great migration to northern oceans. ► Small, black, with *white rump, short square-tipped tail.* Flies with quick shallow wingbeats. May patter feet on water while hovering.

LEACH'S STORM-PETREL ***Oceanodroma leucorhoa***
Nests on islands off New England coast but seen less often than Wilson's on boat trips offshore, perhaps foraging much farther from land. ► Like Wilson's but has longer, more angled wings, forked tail, more erratic flight.

VARIOUS SEABIRDS

HAWKS

(family **Accipitridae**) are birds that hunt by day, relying mostly on their very keen eyesight to locate prey. Shape and flight style are important for distinguishing among the various kinds of hawks on the next few pages. The first four below, members of the genus *Buteo,* have relatively short tails and broad wings and are often seen soaring high in the open. The Northern Harrier is a very distinctive hawk with long wings and long tail, usually seen gliding low over open meadows and marshes.

RED-TAILED HAWK ***Buteo jamaicensis***

The most familiar of the soaring buteo hawks. Widespread and common in farmland, roadsides, and increasingly also in towns and city parks. ▶ Adult's tail is *reddish brown* above, whitish below, with color showing through in flight overhead. Juvenile's tail is brown with darker bars. At all ages, shows whitish chest, dark "belly-band" of streaks. ♪ **Voice:** squealing *keeyaahh.*

ROUGH-LEGGED HAWK ***Buteo lagopus***

Named for its feathered legs (an adaptation to cold), this hawk nests in the Arctic and reaches New England in winter. Favoring open country at all seasons, it is most often seen here over extensive meadows, farmland, marshes. Unlike most hawks, regularly seen hovering on rapidly beating wings. ▶ Tail is whitish at base, with dark banding at tip. Wings show *dark wrist patch* in flight. Quite variable in body plumage, from very dark to very pale.

BROAD-WINGED HAWK ***Buteo platypterus***

A long-distance migrant, nesting in the forests of the north and east, mostly migrating to the tropics for the winter. ▶ Small and compact. Soars with wings held flat and tapering to a point. From below, wings whitish with narrow dark outline. Adult has *broad black and white tail bands,* reddish chest; juvenile has streaked chest, narrower tail bands. ♪ **Voice:** thin whistle, *eeh-eeeee.*

RED-SHOULDERED HAWK ***Buteo lineatus***

A relatively noisy hawk of forested areas, often heard before it is seen. More widespread in summer than in winter. ▶ Strong *narrow white and black barring* on wings and tail. Reddish wash on shoulders and chest. Flies with quick wingbeats followed by glide. Immature brown, streaked below, similar to young Broad-winged but with longer wings and tail. At all ages, shows pale crescent near wingtips. ♪ **Voice:** repeated clear cries, *keeyar, keeyar.*

NORTHERN HARRIER ***Circus cyaneus***

Hunts by flying slowly and low over fields and marshes, looking and listening for prey. Nests on the ground, now quite scarce as a nesting bird in New England. ▶ In all plumages, recognized in flight by *contrasting white rump,* long-winged shape, low flight with wings angled up. Adult male mostly pearly gray, adult female brown, immature warm brown with orange tinge below.

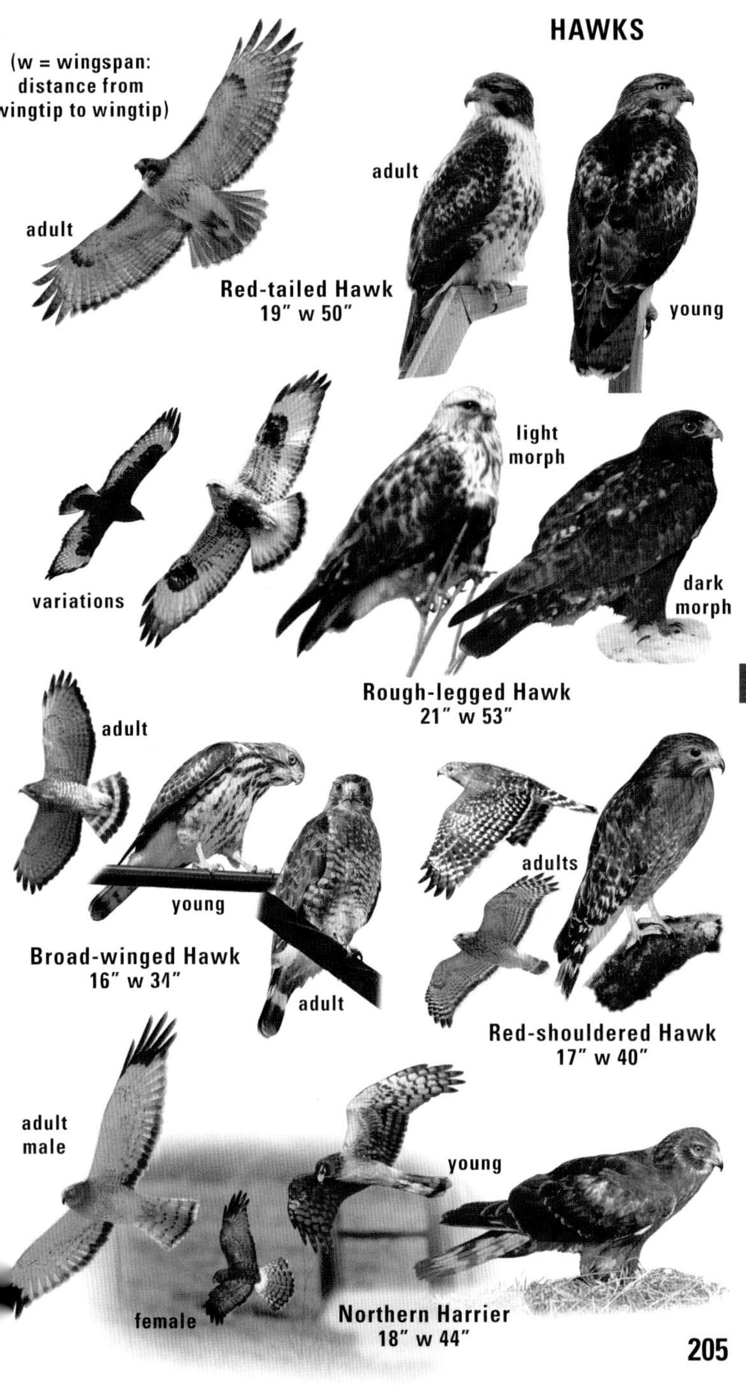
(w = wingspan: distance from wingtip to wingtip)
adult
adult
Red-tailed Hawk
19″ w 50″
young
variations
light morph
dark morph
Rough-legged Hawk
21″ w 53″
adult
young
Broad-winged Hawk
16″ w 34″
adult
adults
Red-shouldered Hawk
17″ w 40″
adult male
young
female
Northern Harrier
18″ w 44″

VULTURES, OSPREYS, AND EAGLES

American vultures (family **Cathartidae**), unrelated to similar birds found in the Old World, are scavengers with naked heads. Soaring for hours at a time seeking dead animals, they could be considered part of nature's cleanup crew. Eagles are in the hawk family, introduced on p. 204, and the Osprey is now placed in its own family **(Pandionidae)**.

TURKEY VULTURE ***Cathartes aura***

Numerous and increasing in southern New England, mainly in summer. Unlike most birds, has a well-developed sense of smell, useful for finding carrion. Nest is well hidden in hollow log, abandoned building, etc. ▸ Huge, with *long wings, long tail, small head.* Wings, held in *shallow V* while soaring, have two-toned look. Head red on adults, gray on young.

BLACK VULTURE ***Coragyps atratus***

A southern bird, established in southern New England, but wanders elsewhere. ▸ Different shape from Turkey Vulture: *short tail,* larger head, broad wings. Soars with wings held flat. Whitish patch near wingtips. Head gray (as on young Turkey Vulture).

OSPREY ***Pandion haliaetus***

This "fish hawk" almost disappeared from New England by the 1970s: effects of DDT and other persistent pesticides kept them from successfully raising young. Conservation efforts brought them back and they are now commonly seen in summer. ▸ *Black face stripe* on white head. In flight, the long wings are held *angled at the wrist.* Strong wing pattern from below, with black wrist patches. ♪ **Voice:** very vocal, loud clear *keyew keyew keyew . . .*

BALD EAGLE ***Haliaeetus leucocephalus***

Another formerly endangered species that has made a comeback. Now fairly common, especially along coast and major rivers. Builds massive nest of sticks in large tree, usually near water. A powerful predator, but also may feed as a scavenger on dead animals or fish. ▸ Adult almost unmistakable. Immatures take 5 years to reach full adult plumage. Youngest juveniles are all dark brown on head and body with some whitish mottling on wings and tail; older immatures may have much white on body. ♪ **Voice:** harsh chatter, rather weak for the size of the bird.

GOLDEN EAGLE ***Aquila chrysaetos***

Mostly a rare migrant through New England, although a few stay through the winter in wilder habitats and a few pairs nest in remote northern areas. Not a close relative of the Bald Eagle, and not so tied to the vicinity of water. ▸ Huge, mostly dark brown, long wings held flat while soaring. Immature has *white patches* in wings and tail. Adult resembles darkest young Bald Eagles (much more numerous in New England); Golden has longer tail, smaller head, lacks white mottling on body and wing-linings.

Black Vulture
25″ w 59″

Turkey Vulture
26″ w 67″

Osprey pair
at nest

Osprey
23″ w 63″

(w = wingspan:
distance from
wingtip to wingtip)

adult

Golden
Eagle
30″ w 80″

young

Bald Eagle
31″ w 80″

adult

young

HAWKS AND FALCONS

The first three species below are in the hawk family (like most of those on pp. 204–207). These three are the Accipiters, the bird-hunting hawks. They spend most of their time inside the forest, where their short, rounded wings and long tails give them the ability to maneuver among the branches in rapid bursts of flight. The latter four birds on this page are in the falcon family **(Falconidae).** These raptors have longer, pointed, more angular wings and long tails, and the larger ones are very fast in flight, usually pursuing their prey in open country.

SHARP-SHINNED HAWK ***Accipiter striatus***

Common during migration, uncommon in summer and winter. Lurks in forest, comes out to nab small birds at feeders. ▶ Adult blue-gray above, reddish below; young bird brown, streaked below. Female larger than male. Tip of tail usually looks *squared.*

COOPER'S HAWK ***Accipiter cooperii***

Another forest hawk, most numerous during migration in spring and fall. ▶ Like Sharp-shinned Hawk but larger (especially female), with larger head. Tip of tail usually looks *rounded.*

NORTHERN GOSHAWK ***Accipiter gentilis***

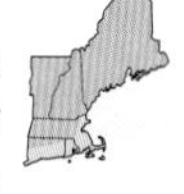

Local and uncommon all year in New England, usually staying in dense forest. A powerful hunter, taking prey as large as rabbits or grouse. ▶ Adult mostly gray, with *white eyebrow* above *black face.* Young bigger than young Cooper's, with zigzag tail bands.

MERLIN ***Falco columbarius***

A compact, fast falcon. Migrates mostly along coast; nests in northern forest. ▶ Bigger than kestrel, with *narrow white bars* across shorter *dark tail.* Adult male blue-gray above, female and young browner. ♪ **Voice:** chattering *ki-ki-ki-ki . . .*

AMERICAN KESTREL ***Falco sparverius***

A small falcon of open country, seen perching on wires, hovering above fields. Catches large insects, rodents, small birds. Nests in holes in trees, or in nest boxes. ▶ *Long reddish tail,* red-brown back. Male has *blue-gray wings.* ♪ **Voice:** shrill *killy killy-killy.*

PEREGRINE FALCON ***Falco peregrinus***

Possibly the world's fastest bird, reaching 200 mph when power-diving at prey. Migrant through New England, especially along coast, and now nests on city building ledges as well as on cliffs in wilderness areas. ▶ Pointed angular wings like other falcons, long tail, broad shoulders, *dark hooded effect.* Adult blue-gray above, narrowly barred below. Young brown, streaked below. ♪ **Voice:** near nest, harsh *kyah kyah . . .*

GYRFALCON ***Falco rusticolus***

This big Arctic falcon is a rare winter visitor to New England, mostly to coastal areas. ▶ Typical falcon shape but *much larger* than Peregrine, with plainer face. Overall color usually gray, can be blackish or mostly white.

adult
young
young
young
Cooper's Hawk
14"–19"
young
adult
young
Sharp-shinned Hawk
9"–13"
adult
Northern
Goshawk
18"–24"
female
ale
Merlin
11"
male
female
American Kestrel
10"
Gyrfalcon
22"
adult
young
Peregrine Falcon
17"

LARGE OWLS

The barn owls (family **Tytonidae**) and typical owls (family **Strigidae**) are mysterious birds, and not often seen, although a few species are fairly common in New England. Although they can see well in daylight, their eyes are especially adapted for seeing in dim light, and their exceptional hearing allows some owls to locate and capture prey in total darkness.

GREAT HORNED OWL ***Bubo virginiensis***

A powerful nighttime predator, common but easily overlooked. Takes prey as large as rabbits, even skunks. Starts nesting as early as February, so often active and vocal in midwinter. ▶ Very large, with ear tufts, white throat, fine *horizontal bars* on belly. ♪ **Voice:** low hoots, often in pattern of 5: *hoo huhoo, hooo, hoooh.*

LONG-EARED OWL ***Asio otus***

Uncommon and elusive, but concentrations are sometimes found roosting in dense evergreens in winter. ▶ Smaller and slimmer than Great Horned Owl, with *stripes* on belly, rusty on face, black around eyes. ♪ **Voice:** low moaning hoots, not often heard.

SHORT-EARED OWL ***Asio flammeus***

An owl of open marshes and fields, sometimes active by day, especially in winter. Flies low with floppy wingbeats. ▶ Pale buffy look, streaked chest, black around eyes. Short "ear" tufts seldom obvious. *Contrasting wing patches* in flight. ♪ **Voice:** wheezy barks.

BARRED OWL ***Strix varia***

Locally common in dense woods and swamps. Sometimes active by day. ▶ Round head with no ear tufts, *brown eyes,* barred chest, stripes on belly. ♪ **Voice:** rich hooting ending in a drawl, *who cooks for you, who cooks for you-allll?* Also odd screams, cackles.

SNOWY OWL ***Bubo scandiacus***

This huge Arctic predator is a regular winter visitor, especially near coast. ▶ Big, round-headed, with *yellow eyes.* Varies from all white (older males) to heavily marked with black (younger females). Compare Barn Owl, white downy young of other owls.

GREAT GRAY OWL ***Strix nebulosa***

This fluffy giant, a very rare winter visitor, is sure to draw attention when it appears. ▶ Huge, with dark face rings, yellow eyes, *white neck spots.*

NORTHERN HAWK OWL ***Surnia ulula***

Another very rare winter visitor, usually perching atop an isolated tree or snag. ▶ *Long tail,* odd posture, finely barred chest, black rim around face.

BARN OWL ***Tyto alba***

Now rare in southern New England, still found on Martha's Vineyard. Nests in abandoned barns, large tree cavities, nest boxes; hunts over open country, eating mice, rats. ▶ Very pale, with heart-shaped face, *dark eyes.* Much smaller than Snowy Owl. ♪ **Voice:** low rasping hiss, harsh shriek.

Long-eared
Owl
15″
Great Horned Owl
23″
Short-eared
Owl
15″
Barred
Owl
21″
Snowy Owl
24″
Great
Gray
Owl
27″
Northern
Hawk Owl
16″
Barn
Owl
16″

SMALL OWLS AND CHICKENLIKE BIRDS

These two tiny owl species are sometimes mistaken for baby owls. Grouse, pheasants, and turkeys all belong to the family **Phasianidae,** while bobwhites are in the New World quail family **(Odontophoridae).**

EASTERN SCREECH-OWL ***Megascops asio***

Fairly common in southern New England in areas with large trees; often overlooked in suburbs. Nests in tree holes. ▸ "Ear" tufts may be raised or flattened, changing appearance of head shape. Usually gray overall (sometimes reddish brown). ♪ **Voice:** quavering wail; long low trill. Despite name, does not really screech.

NORTHERN SAW-WHET OWL ***Aegolius acadicus***

This gnome is not often seen, but when found it is often absurdly tame. Present all year in New England, most common during fall migration. ▸ No "ear" tufts. Warm brown, with reddish streaks on white chest. Juvenile dark, with white eyebrows. ♪ **Voice:** long series of single toots; hoarse note like saw against whetstone.

SPRUCE GROUSE ***Falcipennis canadensis***

This northern forest grouse is so tame that it is easy to miss: it may sit motionless while a hiker walks right past. ▸ Male mostly gray, with black throat, rusty tail tip, red "comb" above each eye. Female shorter-tailed than Ruffed Grouse, lacks black bars on sides. ♪ **Voice:** clucks; deep hoots from displaying male.

RUFFED GROUSE ***Bonasa umbellus***

Fairly common in wooded areas. Usually seen on ground, also perches in trees. In spring courtship, male struts on log with tail spread, neck ruffs puffed up; rapidly drums the air with his wings, producing a deep thumping sound. ▸ Long, fan-shaped tail, *reddish or gray,* with *black band* near tip. *Blackish bars* on sides.

NORTHERN BOBWHITE ***Colinus virginianus***

Formerly common in southern New England, declining in recent years, now mostly found where stocked as a game bird. ▸ Reddish brown, with short tail. *Pale eyebrow and throat* buff on female, white on male. ♪ **Voice:** whistled *er-bob-whoit!* and *quoy-kee.*

RING-NECKED PHEASANT ***Phasianus colchicus***

Native to Asia, introduced here and regularly restocked as a game bird. Locally common in farm country, brushy areas, open woods, marshes. ▸ Flashy male is unmistakable. Female mottled brown, with *long, pointed tail.* ♪ **Voice:** harsh crowing, *khhaa-angk.*

WILD TURKEY ***Meleagris gallopavo***

Domestic turkeys may be dumb, but the Wild Turkey is crafty and a good flier. Once nearly wiped out in New England, has made a comeback, now found even around towns. ▸ Huge, with naked head, long wide tail. Looks trimmer and stronger than domestic turkey, with darker rusty tail tip. ♪ **Voice:** loud gobbling.

SMALL OWLS, CHICKENLIKE BIRDS
(Figures not to scale)
gray morph
red morph
Eastern Screech-Owl 8½″
Northern Saw-whet Owl 8″
female
male
Spruce Grouse 16″
red morph
Ruffed Grouse 17½″
gray morph
female
male
Northern Bobwhite 10″
female
male
Ring-necked Pheasant 21″ (female), 33″ (male)
female
male
Wild Turkey 37″ (female), 46″ (male)

HERONS AND EGRETS

(family **Ardeidae**) are mostly birds of the water's edge, standing motionless or wading slowly in the shallows, waiting to spear fish and other aquatic creatures. Most species nest in colonies in trees near water.

GREAT BLUE HERON ***Ardea herodias***

Our largest and most widespread heron, throughout New England in summer, locally in south in winter. May be seen miles from water, flying with slow flaps, neck hunched back onto shoulders. Often called "crane," but real cranes are unrelated. ▶ Huge, gray, with *black crown stripe* on whitish head. **Sandhill Crane** *(Grus canadensis)*, not shown, has short dark bill, bare red skin on head, flies with neck fully extended. ♪ **Voice**: harsh squawks.

GREAT EGRET ***Ardea alba***

An uncommon nesting bird but a fairly common visitor, wandering widely, especially in late summer. Favors open marshes and lakes, usually standing very still in shallows. ▶ Very large, long-necked, long-legged. All-white with *yellow bill, black legs.*

CATTLE EGRET ***Bubulcus ibis***

Native to the Old World, this chunky heron apparently invaded the Americas on its own, reaching South America by the 1870s and New England by the 1950s. Not aquatic like its relatives; forages in fields, often following cattle to catch insects they flush from the grass. ▶ Stocky, with *short yellow bill.* Legs vary from yellow to blackish. White plumage has *peach patches* in summer.

LITTLE BLUE HERON ***Egretta caerulea***

An uncommon visitor from the south, seen most often in marshes near the coast. ▶ Adult dark slaty all over. Young bird all white at first, with greenish legs, pale bill base, similar to young Snowy Egret. Patchy "calico" phase follows as dark feathers molt in.

SNOWY EGRET ***Egretta thula***

Common in early summer in many coastal areas, wandering widely in late summer. Mostly in open marshes, edges of lakes and ponds. Often moves about actively in shallows. ▶ Known by slender build, *black bill* with yellow in front of eye, and black legs with contrasting *yellow feet* ("golden slippers").

GREEN HERON ***Butorides virescens***

A solitary little heron of wooded streams, tree-lined ponds. Looks crowlike in flight. ▶ Small, dark, with *orange-yellow legs.* Black crown feathers sometimes raised in bushy crest. Dark back glossed blue or green. Neck mostly *chestnut* on adult, striped brown on young bird. ♪ **Voice**: loud *skyowk!* when alarmed.

TRICOLORED HERON ***Egretta tricolor***

An uncommon summer visitor, mostly near coast. ▶ *Long bill; contrasting white belly* and neck stripe. Neck dark blue on adult, rusty on young.

HERONS AND EGRETS

Great Egret 39″

Great Blue Heron 47″

SMALLER HERONS AND EGRETS
(not at same scale as above)

Cattle Egret 19″

Little Blue Heron 24″

Snowy Egret 24″

Tricolored Heron 26″

Green Heron 19″

VARIOUS WADING BIRDS

The first four below are in the heron family (see p. 214). Ibises (family **Threskiornithidae**), unlike herons, fly with their necks outstretched. Rails (family **Rallidae**) are shy marsh birds, heard more often than seen.

BLACK-CROWNED NIGHT-HERON ***Nycticorax nycticorax***

This bulky heron often spends the day roosting in low tree branches near water, flying out at dusk to begin foraging. Waits to spear fish along shores, docks. Common near coast in summer, scarcer inland. A few overwinter in south. ▶ Adult has clean pattern of *black cap* and back, *gray wings.* Juvenile very different, brown with stripes and white spots. ♩**Voice:** low, hollow *wock!*

YELLOW-CROWNED NIGHT-HERON ***Nyctanassa violacea***

An uncommon summer visitor in southern and coastal areas, nesting locally. Active partly at night. ▶ Adult *all-gray* with *black and white face,* tinge of yellow on crown. Juvenile like young Black-crowned but grayer, longer-legged. ♩**Voice:** hollow *wack!*

AMERICAN BITTERN ***Botaurus lentiginosus***

Bitterns are herons that hide in cattail marshes. If disturbed, they "freeze" with bills pointed skyward. ▶ Warm brown, heavily *striped* below. *Black neck mark* (dark brown on young). Compare to young night-herons. ♩**Voice:** deep *ooom-ka-choom,* with sharp middle note (like hammer hitting metal) audible from far away.

LEAST BITTERN ***Ixobrychus exilis***

This scarce, tiny heron is most likely to be seen flying low over marsh. ▶ Buff, with cap and back brown (female) or black (male). Buff wing patch obvious in flight. ♩**Voice:** fast cooing gobble.

GLOSSY IBIS ***Plegadis falcinellus***

Flocks of ibises wade in marshes, probing with their bills. ▶ *Very dark* (with bronze and green sheen) with *curved bill.* Whimbrel (p. 222) is much paler gray-brown with striped head.

CLAPPER RAIL ***Rallus longirostris***

Elusive like other rails, the Clapper hides in salt marshes of our southern coasts. ▶ Chicken-sized, *gray-brown,* long-billed, heavily barred on flanks. ♩**Voice:** clattering *kek-kek-kek-kek . . .*

VIRGINIA RAIL ***Rallus limicola***

Rails look rotund in profile but their bodies are narrow, to slip through dense marsh growth. This one is common in freshwater marshes. ▶ *Reddish brown* with *gray cheeks,* long bill, barred flanks. ♩**Voice:** metallic *kik kidik kidik;* nasal *wenk-wenk-wenk.*

SORA ***Porzana carolina***

This small rail sometimes walks about on open mud beside ponds, twitching its short tail. ▶ *Short yellow bill, black face* contrasting with gray chest. Young are plain-faced. ♩**Voice:** whistle rising at end, *surr-reee!* Also sharp *keek,* descending whinny.

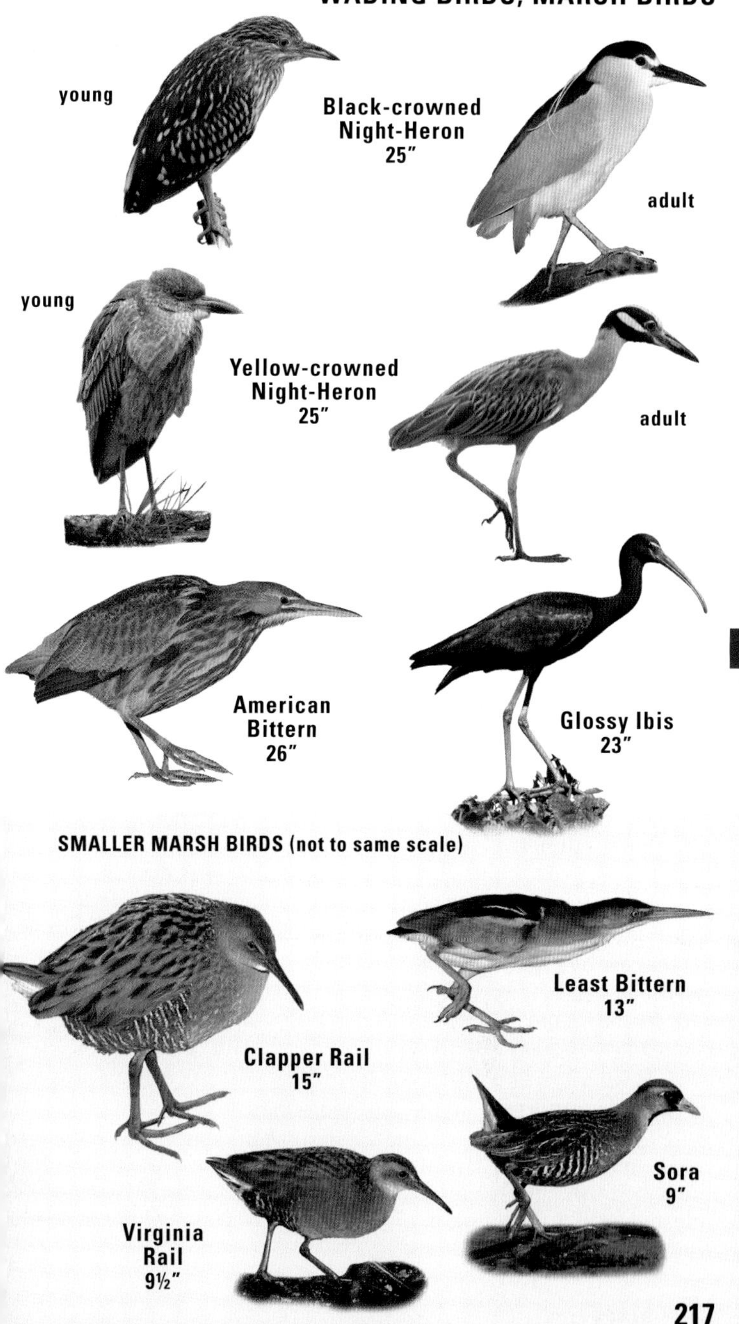
young
Black-crowned
Night-Heron
25″
adult
young
Yellow-crowned
Night-Heron
25″
adult
American
Bittern
26″
Glossy Ibis
23″
SMALLER MARSH BIRDS (not to same scale)
Least Bittern
13″
Clapper Rail
15″
Sora
9″
Virginia
Rail
9½″

In birder language, "shorebirds" are not just birds on the shore: they are plovers, sandpipers, and related birds. Plovers (family **Charadriidae**) may be on shorelines, mudflats, or open fields. They typically run a few paces, then stop to pick at the ground with their short bills. Oystercatchers (family **Haematopodidae**) are large, striking shorebirds that feed mostly on mollusks. Sandpipers are introduced on p. 220.

KILLDEER *Charadrius vociferus*

This noisy plover is common in open fields, grassy places, laying its eggs in a simple scrape on the ground. Sometimes fakes a broken wing to lure intruders away from nest. ▶ Has 2 black chest bands; rather *long* tail is *mostly orange*. Downy young has just 1 chest band. ♪ **Voice:** loud, clear *kil-deeah* and *dee-dee-dee . . .*

SEMIPALMATED PLOVER *Charadrius semipalmatus*

Nests on Arctic tundra, common migrant on New England coastal flats. Scarce migrant inland. ▶ *Single* black chest band, short bill, *dark brown* back, *yellow-orange legs.* ♪ **Voice:** clear *chuweep.*

PIPING PLOVER *Charadrius melodus*

Uncommon and declining, an endangered species. Nests on sandy beaches and vulnerable to disturbance there. ▶ Suggests Semipalmated Plover but *much paler* above (color of *dry* sand), black chest band usually *incomplete.* ♪ **Voice:** piping *peep-loh.*

BLACK-BELLIED PLOVER *Pluvialis squatarola*

Nests only in the Arctic and mostly winters farther south, but very common on our coast as a migrant, and some can be found there all year. Scarce inland. ▶ Bulky, with thick, short bill. Drab most of year, mottled gray-brown. In flight shows black "wingpits," whitish rump. Breeding plumage (seen in late spring) has striking pattern. ♪ **Voice:** mournful whistle, *wheeyou-wee.*

AMERICAN GOLDEN-PLOVER *Pluvialis dominica*

Nests in the Arctic, winters in South America. Migrates through New England, mostly along coast in fall. ▶ Slimmer than Black-bellied, warmer brown above, less contrasting flight pattern.

AMERICAN OYSTERCATCHER *Haematopus palliatus*

Pairs and small groups of oystercatchers haunt beaches, tidal flats, coastal islands, mainly in summer. ▶ *Very large,* with blade-like *red bill.* Striking pattern with black head, dark back, white belly; broad white wing stripe in flight. ♪ **Voice:** clear *wheeep.*

UPLAND SANDPIPER *Bartramia longicauda*

Once called "Upland Plover" (and its short bill does suggest a plover), but really a member of the sandpiper family (p. 220). Not associated with either sand or shore, it haunts fields, dry meadows, blueberry barrens. Now rare and local in New England in summer. ▶ *Habitat and shape* are best clues; note long tail, small head, big-eyed look. ♪ **Voice:** airy whistles.

downy young
Killdeer
Killdeer
10½"
fall
juvenile
Piping Plover
7¼"
Semipalmated Plover
7¼"
spring
adult
fall and
winter
Black-bellied Plover
11½"
fall
juvenile
American
Golden-Plover
10¼"
spring
adult
(not shown
to scale)
American
Oystercatcher
18½"
Upland
Sandpiper
12"

SANDPIPERS

(family **Scolopacidae**) are not typically on sand; most favor tidal flats, estuaries, muddy pond edges. Most sandpipers nest on Arctic tundra, and some migrate as far as southern South America for the winter. Their migration is protracted: some northbound birds linger in New England through early June, some southbound ones appear by early July, and a few stay through summer on our coast. Most juvenile sandpipers on their first fall migration look different from either breeding or winter adults.

SANDERLING ***Calidris alba***
This is one sandpiper that does favor sand beaches, running back and forth chasing the waves. ► Pale in "winter" plumage (most of year), with *stout black bill, black legs,* dark shoulder mark. Piping Plover (p. 218) has much shorter bill, orange legs. Juvenile Sanderling (seen in fall) blacker on back. In breeding plumage, seen briefly in late spring, much *redder.* ♪ **Voice:** hard *kwip.*

DUNLIN ***Calidris alpina***
Common coastal migrant, a few wintering. ► Long bill, *drooped* at tip. Winter plumage (most of year) gray on chest and above. In spring, reddish back, dark belly patch. ♪ **Voice:** rasping *krreez.*

RED KNOT ***Calidris canutus***
Strictly coastal as a migrant, a few wintering. ► Stout, with straight bill. Spring adult *robin red below.* Very plain gray and whitish at other seasons, fall juvenile with *scaly pattern* above.

LEAST SANDPIPER ***Calidris minutilla***
Common in migration on mudflats and marsh edges, both on coast and inland. ► Smaller than Semipalmated, *browner, darker* across chest. Legs yellow (hard to see). ♪ **Voice:** thin *kreeet!*

SEMIPALMATED SANDPIPER ***Calidris pusilla***
The most abundant small shorebird migrant in New England, especially on the coast. ► Very small, plain gray-brown, with short bill, blackish legs. Juvenile more scaly above. ♪ **Voice:** low *chrk.*

PURPLE SANDPIPER ***Calidris maritima***
This "rockpiper" shows up in late fall and winter on rocky shorelines, jetties. ► Chunky with short yellowish legs, fairly long drooping bill. Mostly *dark slaty* in winter, with whitish belly.

PECTORAL SANDPIPER ***Calidris melanotos***
An uncommon migrant, more numerous in fall, favoring grassy mudflats, wet fields. ► Warm brown, streaked. *Sharp contrast* between heavily streaked chest and white belly. ♪ **Voice:** low *krrrek.*

RUDDY TURNSTONE ***Arenaria interpres***
An odd sandpiper that may use its short bill to flip over small rocks as it seeks food on beaches, rocky shores. ► *Short orange legs, wedge-shaped bill.* Unmistakable pattern in spring; brown in fall and winter, with *dark chest pattern.* ♪ **Voice:** sharp rattle.

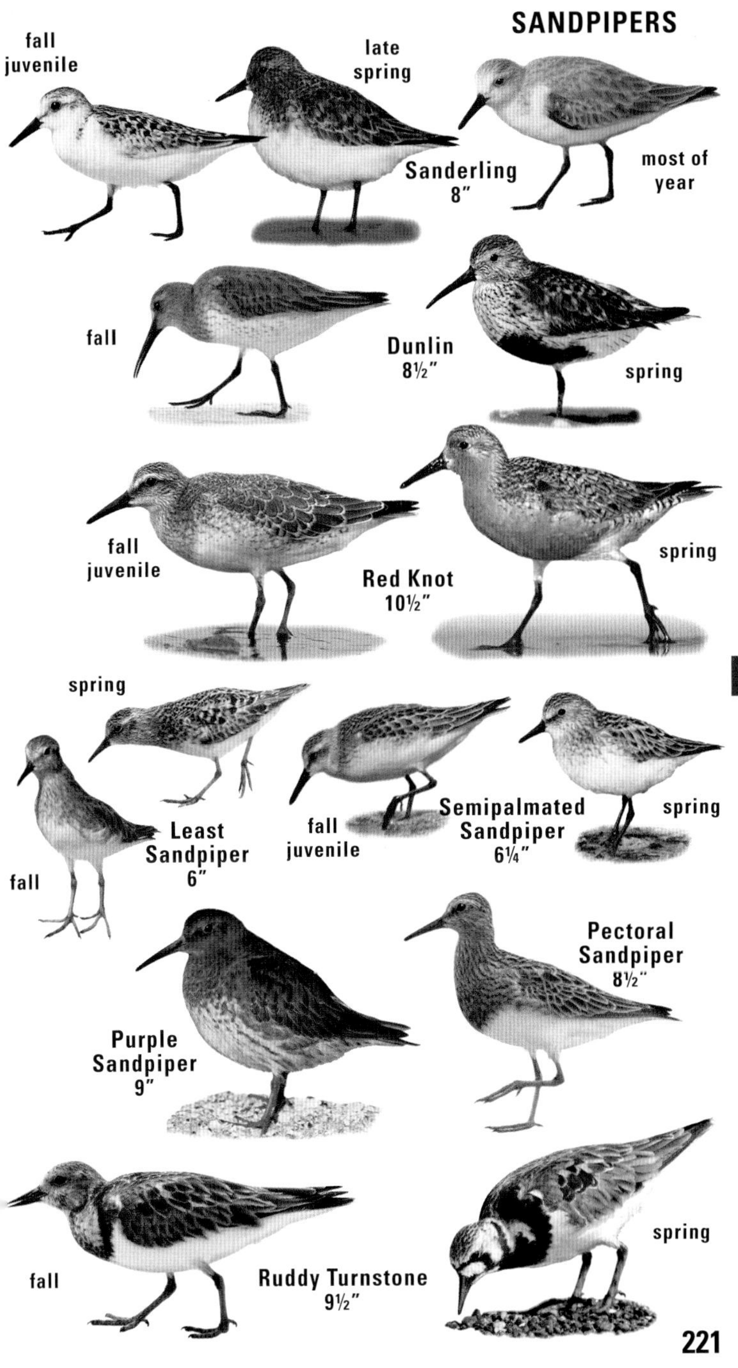
fall
juvenile
late
spring
Sanderling
8″
most of
year
fall
Dunlin
8½″
spring
fall
juvenile
Red Knot
10½″
spring
spring
fall
Least
Sandpiper
6″
fall
juvenile
Semipalmated
Sandpiper
6¼″
spring
Pectoral
Sandpiper
8½″
Purple
Sandpiper
9″
fall
Ruddy Turnstone
9½″
spring

SPOTTED SANDPIPER ***Actitis macularius***

Nests around inland creeks and ponds. Teeters unsteadily while standing; flies with stiff shallow wingbeats. ► *Round black spots* below in breeding plumage. Plainer at other seasons; note *teetering actions,* white shoulder mark. ♪ **Voice:** abrupt *peet-weet.*

SOLITARY SANDPIPER ***Tringa solitaria***

A migrant, mostly inland at ponds and creeks. ► Resembles fall Spotted (and bobs head when excited) but *darker,* slimmer, with white eye-ring. ♪ **Voice:** shrill *pit-weet!,* higher than Spotted's.

LESSER YELLOWLEGS ***Tringa flavipes***

The two species of yellowlegs are slim sandpipers that wade in shallows of marsh edges, tidal flats. ► *Bright yellow* legs, slim straight bill. In flight, shows whitish tail. ♪ **Voice:** mellow *tu tu tu.*

GREATER YELLOWLEGS ***Tringa melanoleuca***

A common migrant, especially near the coast, and sometimes stays in winter. ► Like Lesser but larger with thicker, longer, more upturned bill, louder voice. ♪ **Voice:** ringing *whee whee wheew!*

WILLET ***Tringa semipalmata***

This big sandpiper is a common migrant on mudflats, beaches, also nests locally in salt marshes. ► Bulky, with *straight heavy bill.* Barred in spring plumage, drab in fall, but *spectacular in flight* when wing pattern shows. ♪ **Voice:** ringing *pill will willet.*

WHIMBREL ***Numenius phaeopus***

Uncommon migrant on the coast, more frequent in fall. ► A big gray-brown sandpiper with a downcurved bill, dark head stripes. Wings and tail look plain in flight. ♪ **Voice:** rippling whistle.

SHORT-BILLED DOWITCHER ***Limnodromus griseus***

Common in migration. Flocks of dowitchers wade slowly or stand in shallows, head down, probing with their bills. ► Stout, short-necked, long-billed. (Called "Short-billed" by contrast to **Long-billed Dowitcher,** *L. scolopaceus,* rare here.) Orange and white below in spring, grayer in fall. ♪ **Voice:** mellow *tututu.*

WILSON'S SNIPE ***Gallinago delicata***

Lurks in marshes; if disturbed, flushes almost underfoot into zigzag flight. Common migrant, scarce in summer and winter. ► *Long bill. Striped head* and back, barred sides. ♪ **Voice:** when flushed, *zzkah.* Hooting trill in flight display in nesting season.

AMERICAN WOODCOCK ***Scolopax minor***

This weird sandpiper hides in forest by day, probing for worms in wet fields at night. In spring, males make musical courtship flights at night. ► Long bill, orange-buff below, *crosswise bars* on head. ♪ **Voice:** nasal *pzeent;* twittering sounds in display flight.

spring
Solitary
Sandpiper
8½″
fall
Spotted Sandpiper
7½″
spring
Greater
Yellowlegs
14″
spring
fall
juvenile
Lesser
Yellowlegs
10½″
fall
Willet
15″
Whimbrel
17″
spring
Willet
in flight
fall
Short-
billed
Dowitcher
11″
spring
American Woodcock
11″
Wilson's
Snipe
10½″

MEDIUM-SIZED LAND BIRDS

These eight birds represent five different and unrelated families.

ROCK PIGEON ***Columba livia***

Pigeons and doves (family Columbidae) have rather small round heads and short bills. This species is the familiar city pigeon, native to the Old World, introduced here and now common in U.S. cities and farms. ▶ Typically gray with white rump, 2 black bars on wings, but color varies from white to reddish to black.

MOURNING DOVE ***Zenaida macroura***

Common in open country toward the south, but scarce in northern forest. Perches on roadside wires, comes to bird feeders for seeds. ▶ Mostly plain, with black spots on wings. *Long, pointed tail* shows *white spots* along edge in flight. Young bird has scaly pattern at first. ♪ **Voice:** mournful *coowah, cooo, coo, coooo.*

YELLOW-BILLED CUCKOO ***Coccyzus americanus***

Two cuckoos (family Cuculidae) occur regularly in New England, both fairly common but often hard to see as they lurk in dense woodland. ▶ Slender, long-tailed. Bill *partly yellow,* underside of tail with *big white spots,* wings show *reddish* in flight. ♪ **Voice:** clatter slowing toward end, *kakakaka-kah-kah-kah-kowp kowp.*

BLACK-BILLED CUCKOO ***Coccyzus erythropthalmus***

Both of our cuckoos feed heavily on caterpillars, including hairy ones that most birds avoid. ▶ Like Yellow-billed Cuckoo but bill *all-black,* narrow *red eye-ring,* underside of tail has *narrow* white spots, wings *lack* reddish. ♪ **Voice:** hollow *cucucu, cucucucu . . .*

EASTERN WHIP-POOR-WILL ***Caprimulgus vociferus***

A member of the nightjar family (Caprimulgidae), calling loudly on summer nights, hiding on the forest floor by day. Has declined in numbers in recent years. ▶ Big-headed, mottled brown and gray. ♪ **Voice:** rolling *whip, prrr-WEEL,* last note highest.

COMMON NIGHTHAWK ***Chordeiles minor***

Not a hawk but a relative of the Whip-poor-will, and not active just at night. Pursues insects in high erratic flight, often near dusk. ▶ Long angular wings crossed by *white bar.* Heavily *barred* below. ♪ **Voice:** buzzy *pzeent.* In diving display flight, rushing *voom.*

BELTED KINGFISHER ***Megaceryle alcyon***

Our only kingfisher (family Alcedinidae). Perches or hovers over water, plunges headfirst to catch small fish in bill. Nests in burrows in dirt banks. ▶ Shaggy head, big bill, short neck, small feet. (Blue Jay, p. 234, also blue-gray and crested, but *very* different in shape.) Female has rusty band across chest. ♪ **Voice:** loud rattle.

MONK PARAKEET ***Myiopsitta monachus*** **(family Psittacidae)**

Native to southern South America. Escaped cage birds live in noisy colonies, build big stick nests. ▶ Long-tailed, green with gray front.

SOME MEDIUM-SIZED BIRDS

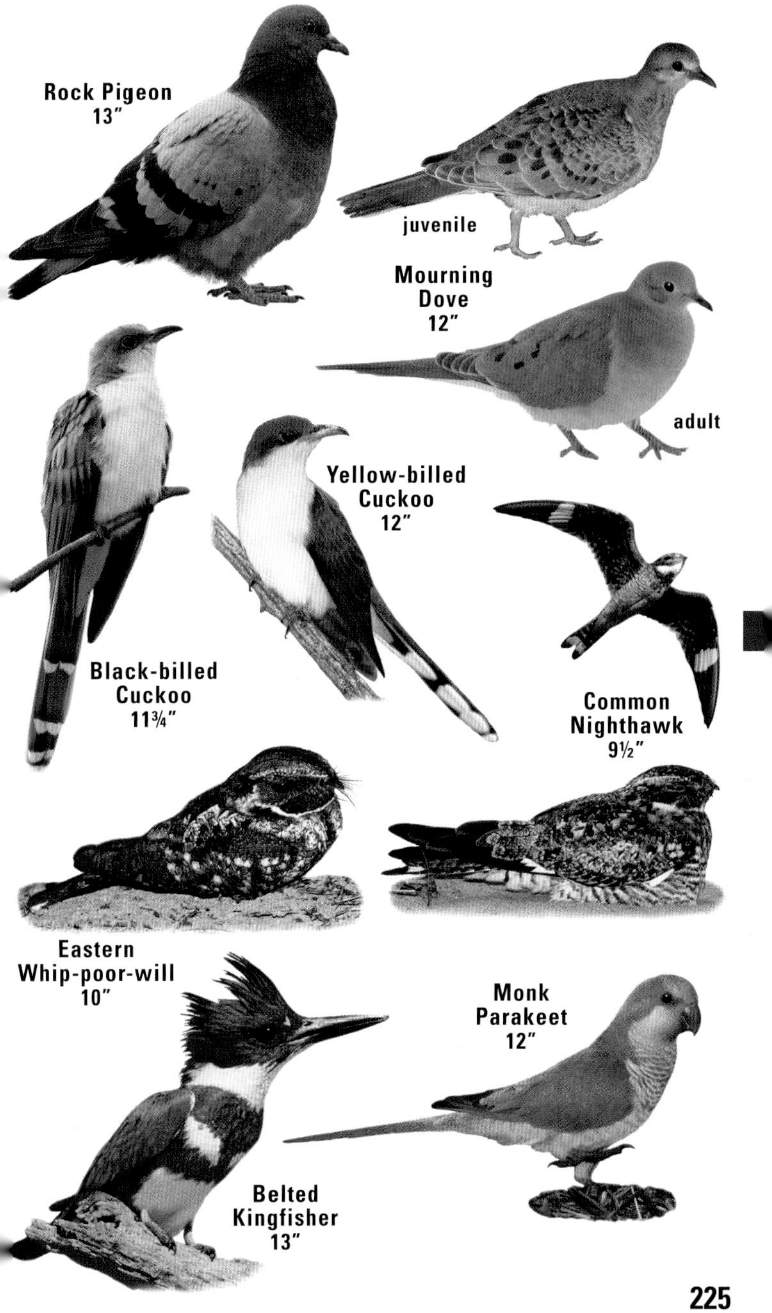
Rock Pigeon
13″
juvenile
Mourning
Dove
12″
adult
Black-billed
Cuckoo
11¾″
Yellow-billed
Cuckoo
12″
Common
Nighthawk
9½″
Eastern
Whip-poor-will
10″
Monk
Parakeet
12″
Belted
Kingfisher
13″

WOODPECKERS

(family **Picidae**) climb trees, clutching with strong feet, bracing themselves with stiff tail feathers. They use their chisel-like bills to drill for insects below the bark, to excavate nest holes in dead trees, and to advertise their presence by drumming loudly on resonant dead wood.

DOWNY WOODPECKER ***Picoides pubescens***

Common in woods, towns, city parks, often visiting bird feeders for suet. In winter, often in mixed flocks with chickadees (p. 236) and other birds. ▶ Small, with *stubby bill.* Patterned black and white, with big spots on wings, barred outer tail feathers. Male has red nape. ♪ **Voice:** flat *pik;* chattering, descending whinny.

HAIRY WOODPECKER ***Picoides villosus***

Less common than Downy Woodpecker, usually in forests. ▶ Like Downy but slightly larger with distinctly *longer bill.* White outer tail feathers lack dark bars. ♪ **Voice:** sharp *peek!* and shrill rattle.

RED-BELLIED WOODPECKER ***Melanerpes carolinus***

A southern bird that has increased here in recent decades. Found in forests, towns. ▶ *Zebra-backed pattern,* red stripe running up nape (female) or all the way to forehead (male). Red on belly is hard to see. ♪ **Voice:** loud *chiff, chiff,* and rolling *churrrr.*

YELLOW-BELLIED SAPSUCKER ***Sphyrapicus varius***

Its name sounds like a joke, but this is a real bird that drills neat rows of holes in bark, returning to drink the sap. Mainly evergreen woods in summer. ▶ Striped face, mottled back, *long white stripe* on wing. Young bird much browner. ♪ **Voice:** catlike *meeyah.*

NORTHERN FLICKER ***Colaptes auratus***

This big woodpecker sometimes abandons tree trunks to forage on the ground, eating ants. Common in summer and migration in open woods. ▶ Brown with bars and spots, *black chest patch,* red nape. Male has black moustache. In flight shows white rump, *yellow in wings and tail.* ♪ **Voice:** ringing *kleeyah!* and *wikwikwik.*

PILEATED WOODPECKER ***Dryocopus pileatus***

Our biggest woodpecker. Uncommon, in forests with large trees. Digs in dead wood for carpenter ants, other insects. ▶ Unmistakable. White wing linings flash in flight. Forehead and moustache red on male, black on female. ♪ **Voice:** loud, ringing notes.

BLACK-BACKED WOODPECKER ***Picoides arcticus***

Scarce in northern forest, rarely wandering south. May inhabit areas of trees killed by fire or flood. ▶ Solid *black back,* barring on sides. Male has yellow crown spot. ♪ **Voice:** sharp *pik.*

RED-HEADED WOODPECKER ***Melanerpes erythrocephalus***

Rare and local in New England, in open oak groves. ▶ Solid red head (both sexes), white wing patch. Young are brown-headed. ♪ **Voice:** raspy *kreeyer!*

Hairy Woodpecker 9″

male

male

female

Downy Woodpecker 6½″

Red-bellied Woodpecker 9½″

LARGER WOODPECKERS (not shown to same scale)

Northern Flicker 13″

male

female

Yellow-bellied Sapsucker 8½″

male

male

male

Black-backed Woodpecker 9″

Pileated Woodpecker 17″

Red-headed Woodpecker 9¼″

HUMMINGBIRDS, SWIFTS, SWALLOWS

Hummingbirds (family **Trochilidae**) are only distantly related to swifts **(Apodidae)** and not at all to swallows **(Hirundinidae)**, but all make their living on the wing: hummingbirds hovering at flowers for nectar, swifts and swallows catching insects in midair during graceful flight.

CHIMNEY SWIFT ***Chaetura pelagica***

Our most aerial bird. Incapable of perching, can only cling to vertical surfaces; nests inside chimneys. Winters in Amazon Basin. ► Very short tail, blunt head, long curved wings. Flies with rapid wingbeats and long glides. ♪**Voice**: metallic chippering.

RUBY-THROATED HUMMINGBIRD ***Archilochus colubris***

Common but easily overlooked. Hovers at flowers or sugar-water feeders; males perch high. ►More likely to be mistaken for an insect than another bird; see hawkmoths (p. 318). Iridescent green above, whitish below. Male's *red throat* often just looks black. Female has white tail spots. **Rufous Hummingbird** *(Selasphorus rufus)*, very rare fall visitor, is strongly marked with orange.

BARN SWALLOW ***Hirundo rustica***

Very common in summer, building its mud nest inside barns and all manner of other structures. ► *Long, forked tail* with white spots; chestnut throat and forehead. ♪**Voice**: musical twittering.

TREE SWALLOW ***Tachycineta bicolor***

Common in summer. Nests in holes in trees and in houses put up for bluebirds. Eats insects like other swallows, but also berries; flocks gather near coast in fall to eat bayberries. ► *Clean white* below, blue-black above; young browner. ♪**Voice**: clear *tdeet.*

CLIFF SWALLOW ***Petrochelidon pyrrhonota***

Uncommon. Nesting colonies today are mostly under bridges or on buildings, not on cliffs. Gathers mud to make jug-shaped nest with entrance on side. ► Short, square-tipped tail, *buffy rump patch,* dark throat, white forehead. ♪**Voice**: *churr* and creaks.

BANK SWALLOW ***Riparia riparia***

Locally common. Nests in holes in dirt banks (riverbanks, quarries); many pairs often nest close together in colony. ► Brown back, sharp *brown band* below *white throat.* ♪**Voice**: dry buzzes.

N. ROUGH-WINGED SWALLOW ***Stelgidopteryx serripennis***

Like Bank Swallows, Northern Rough-wings nest in holes in dirt banks, but as isolated pairs, not in colonies. ► Bigger than Bank Swallow, throat and chest *entirely dusky.* ♪**Voice**: buzzy *fzzzt.*

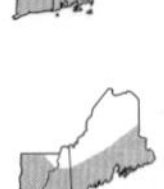

PURPLE MARTIN ***Progne subis***

Our biggest swallow. Uncommon and local, nesting in multi-roomed houses put up for it. ► Male all-black (with purple sheen); compare to starlings (p. 246). Female and young grayer below, with white belly. ♪**Voice**: burry *dzeeb-dzurr,* other notes.

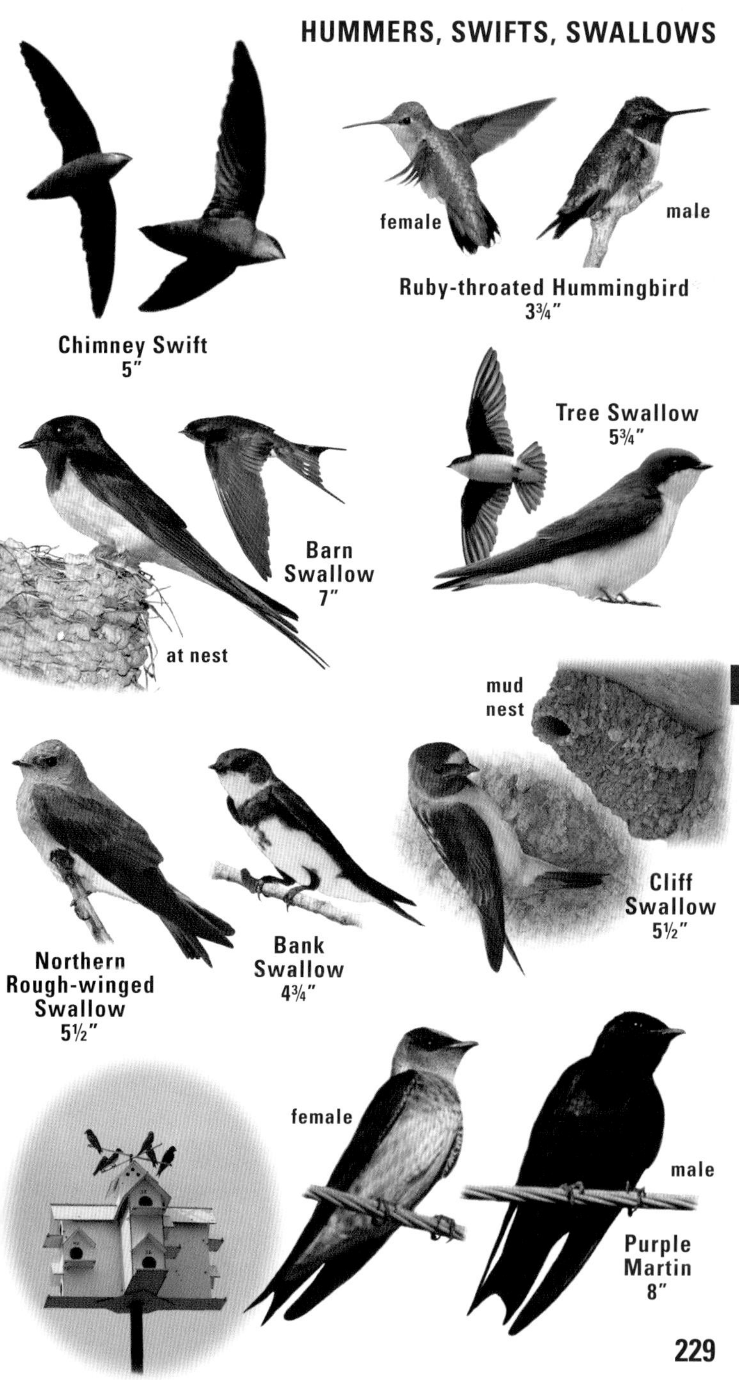
female
male
Ruby-throated Hummingbird
3¾″
Chimney Swift
5″
Tree Swallow
5¾″
Barn
Swallow
7″
at nest
mud
nest
Cliff
Swallow
5½″
Bank
Swallow
4¾″
Northern
Rough-winged
Swallow
5½″
female
male
Purple
Martin
8″

FLYCATCHERS AND WAXWINGS

Tyrant flycatchers (family **Tyrannidae**) are named for aggressive behavior of kingbirds and others, and for their habit of perching and watching for flying insects, then darting out to catch them in midair. Waxwings (family **Bombycillidae**) also do some flycatching, but mostly eat berries.

GREAT CRESTED FLYCATCHER ***Myiarchus crinitus***
A forest flycatcher, heard more often than seen. Nests in holes in trees. ► Yellow belly contrasts with gray chest, bright reddish brown in tail and wings. ♩**Voice:** whistled *wheeap!*, rough *berrg.*

EASTERN KINGBIRD ***Tyrannus tyrannus***
Common in open country in summer, perching on fences and wires, often driving away hawks and other large birds that come too near its nest. ► Broad *white band* at tip of black tail. Blackish above, white below. ♩**Voice:** high *bzzeent,* often run into chatter.

EASTERN PHOEBE ***Sayornis phoebe***
Arrives early in spring along streams, forest edge, often placing nest on porches or under bridges. Rare in winter. ► Rather plain, gray above, whitish below. Known by *gentle tail-wagging action,* contrasting dark face. ♩**Voice:** says its name, *fee-bee.* Also *pip.*

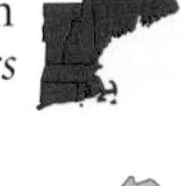

EASTERN WOOD-PEWEE ***Contopus virens***
Common in mature forests in summer, heard more often than seen. ► Compact, with long wingtips. Gray, with pale *wing bars* but *no eye-ring.* ♩**Voice:** plaintive *peeyeeer* and *peey-ya-weee.*

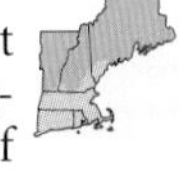

OLIVE-SIDED FLYCATCHER ***Contopus cooperi***
Uncommon in summer in northern bogs, uncommon migrant throughout. Usually seen perched at top of dead stub. ► Big-headed, short-tailed. *Dark sides* contrast with white center of belly (like *unbuttoned vest*). ♩**Voice:** whistled *quick-three-beers!*

LEAST FLYCATCHER ***Empidonax minimus***
Five species of *Empidonax* flycatchers occur regularly in New England, all so similar that they are safely identified only by voice. Even serious birders often call them all "Empids." This one favors second growth, edges. ► All our Empids are tiny, with white *eye-rings,* contrasting *wing bars.* ♩**Voice:** snappy *che-bek!*, dry *pit.*

ALDER FLYCATCHER ***Empidonax alnorum***
Another confusing Empid, this one favoring dense thickets (especially of alder) near ponds and streams. ► Like Least, slightly larger, paler. ♩**Voice:** buzzy *freeBEEyeer,* musical *kep.*

CEDAR WAXWING ***Bombycilla cedrorum***
Flocks of waxwings wander unpredictably in search of food, may swarm where berries are abundant. ► Crested, with *yellow band on tail tip,* yellow belly, red waxy tips on wing feathers. **Bohemian Waxwing** *(B. garrulus),* a rare winter visitor, is larger, grayer, with chestnut under tail. ♩**Voice:** high thin *ssseeee.*

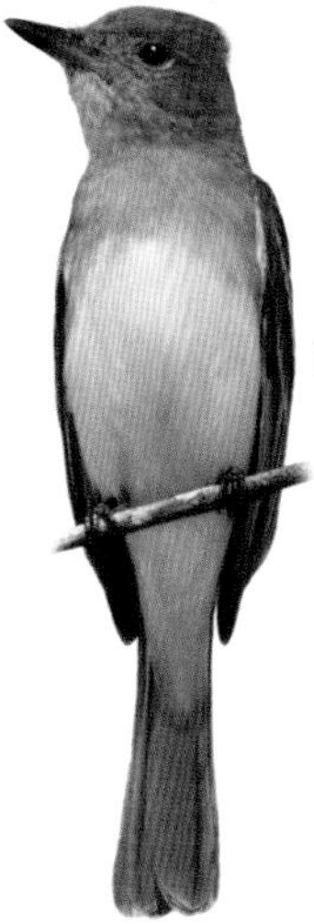

Great Crested Flycatcher
8½″

Eastern Kingbird
8½″

Eastern Phoebe
7″

Olive-sided Flycatcher
7½″

Least Flycatcher
5¼″

Eastern Wood-Pewee
6½″

Alder Flycatcher
5¾″

Cedar Waxwing
7″

Thrushes (family **Turdidae**) and thrashers **(Mimidae)** include many superb singers. Larks **(Alaudidae)** are usually on the ground in open country.

AMERICAN ROBIN ***Turdus migratorius***
Familiar almost everywhere, hunting earthworms on lawns, building its mud-based nest on windowsills. During winter, flocks roam in search of berries, wild fruits. ▶ Brick red chest, gray back, streaks on white chin. Juvenile is heavily spotted at first. ♪ **Voice:** rich caroling, often starting well before dawn.

WOOD THRUSH ***Hylocichla mustelina***
Declining, but still fairly common in summer in forests, shady suburbs. ▶ Rich *reddish brown* above, bold *eye-ring, round black spots* on white chest. ♪ **Voice:** fluting *eeyoh-lay;* sharp *pep-pep-pep.*

HERMIT THRUSH ***Catharus guttatus***
Common migrant, early spring and late fall. A few stay in winter. Uncommon in summer in evergreen and mixed forest. ▶ *Red-brown tail,* duller back, strong eye-ring. ♪ **Voice:** long clear note followed by soft quick warble; repeated on different pitch.

VEERY ***Catharus fuscescens***
Common in summer in damp leafy woods. ▶ *Warm tawny brown* above, with only faint spots on chest. Face looks pale and plain. ♪ **Voice:** breezy, spiraling whistles, *veeyurr, veeyur, veeer, veer.*

SWAINSON'S THRUSH ***Catharus ustulatus***
Common migrant, nesting in spruce woods. ▶ Dull olive-brown above, buff eye-ring, buff at sides of chest. ♪ **Voice:** song starts with short clear note, then short phrases ending higher.

BICKNELL'S THRUSH ***Catharus bicknelli***
Very local in summer on highest peaks. ▶ Dull brown back, pale *grayish face,* lightly spotted chest. **Gray-cheeked Thrush** *(C. minimus),* an uncommon migrant, is almost identical.

BROWN THRASHER ***Toxostoma rufum***
Lurks in thickets, thrashing fallen leaves on the ground. ▶ Bigger, longer-tailed than Wood Thrush, *striped* (not spotted) below, with *yellow eyes.* ♪ **Voice:** short rich phrases, usually doubled.

GRAY CATBIRD ***Dumetella carolinensis***
Common, mainly in summer, in forest undergrowth, swamps, suburban gardens. Lurks in bushes but also can be boldly inquisitive. ▶ Slim, gray, with long tail, black cap, *rusty* under tail. ♪ **Voice:** catlike *meyeww;* disjointed song of whistles, squeaks, whines.

HORNED LARK ***Eremophila alpestris***
Flocks of larks live on barren open ground: plowed fields, airports, shores. ▶ Black *chest crescent* and *ear mark;* tiny "horns" hard to see. Face may be white or yellow. ♪ **Voice:** song is a musical tinkling twitter, often given in high flight.

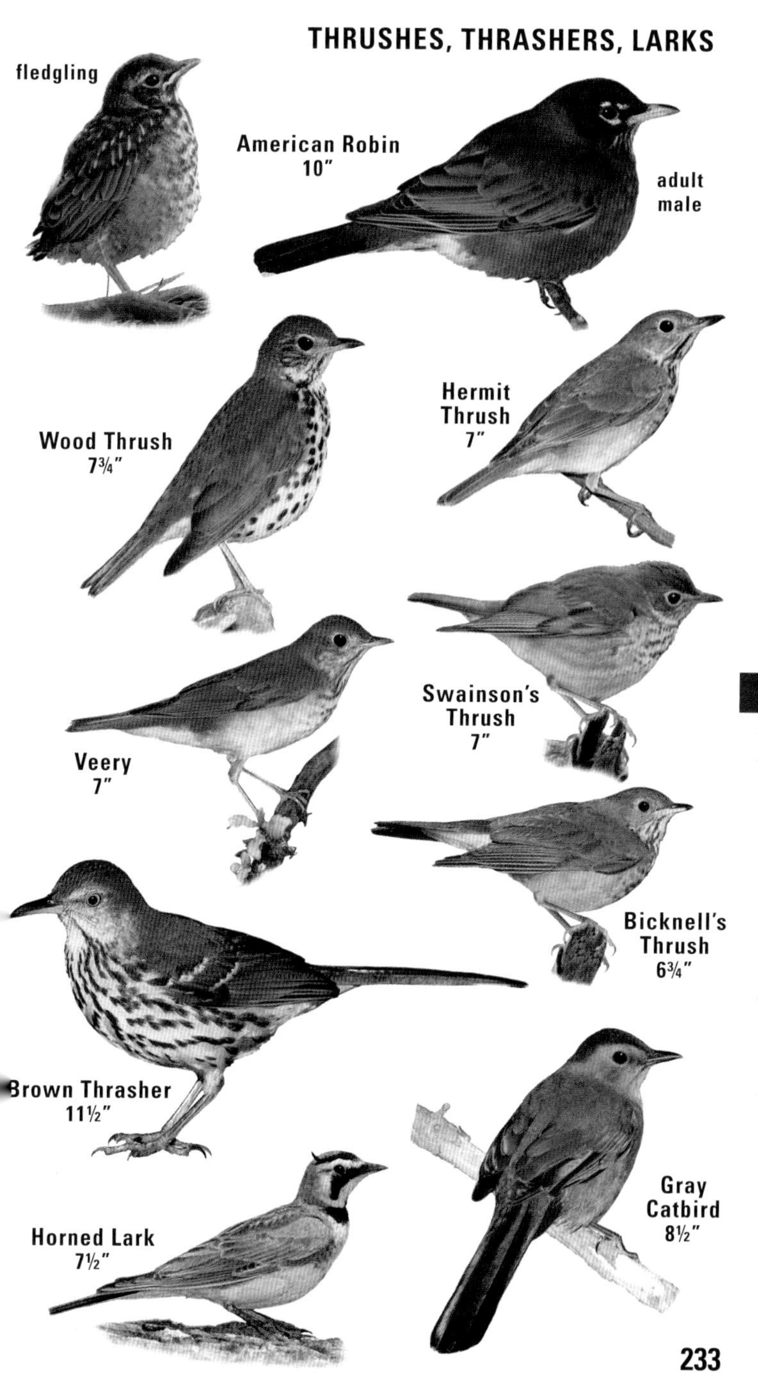
fledgling
American Robin
10″
adult
male
Hermit
Thrush
7″
Wood Thrush
7¾″
Swainson's
Thrush
7″
Veery
7″
Bicknell's
Thrush
6¾″
Brown Thrasher
11½″
Gray
Catbird
8½″
Horned Lark
7½″

VARIOUS SONGBIRDS

The mockingbird is related to the thrashers on p. 232, the bluebird is one of the thrushes, while the shrike is in a separate family **(Laniidae)**. Jays, crows, and ravens (family **Corvidae**) are omnivores that are thought to be among the most intelligent of birds.

EASTERN BLUEBIRD ***Sialia sialis***

One of America's favorite birds. Uncommon in open country and farmland, seen mainly in summer. Often uses manmade nest boxes. ► Small, short-tailed, with blue back, rusty chest, white belly. Female paler, duller. ♩**Voice:** soft warbling song; *true-lee* call.

NORTHERN MOCKINGBIRD ***Mimus polyglottos***

A southern bird ("Northern" by contrast to tropical relatives) gradually invading our area. May sing all night on moonlit nights. Eats many berries in winter. ► Slim, long-tailed. *White in wings and tail* obvious in flight. ♩**Voice:** repeats phrase over and over, then switches to another, on and on. Often mimics other birds.

NORTHERN SHRIKE ***Lanius excubitor***

Catches rodents, small birds, impales the carcasses on thorns or barbed wire. Scarce winter visitor in open areas. ► Gray or tan with *dark mask, hooked bill,* black and white wings and tail.

GRAY JAY ***Perisoreus canadensis***

In the north woods, this jay may be oddly tame, entering campsites for scraps. ► Gray, paler below, with black nape patch. Juvenile sooty with pale whisker mark. ♩**Voice:** whistles, low notes.

BLUE JAY ***Cyanocitta cristata***

A brash, noisy, colorful bird, present all year in New England, although migrating flocks pass over in spring and fall. ► Our only *crested blue bird.* Long tail, *black necklace,* patterned wings. ♩**Voice:** screaming *jaayy!,* musical *beadle-beadle,* other notes.

COMMON RAVEN ***Corvus corax***

Classified as a songbird, but as big as a hawk. A bird of northern wilderness, now expanding south in New England. ► Much larger than crows with heavy bill, shaggy throat feathers, wedge-shaped tail. ♩**Voice:** deep echoing croak, plus screams, whistles, gurgles.

FISH CROW ***Corvus ossifragus***

Tied to waterside habitats of the coast and river valleys. ► Smaller than American Crow, best recognized by sound. ♩**Voice:** high, nasal *kah-hah.* Note that young American Crows also sound nasal.

AMERICAN CROW ***Corvus brachyrhynchos***

Very common in open country, increasingly in cities also, as this adaptable bird adjusts to urban life. In winter, large numbers may gather in night roosts. ► Large, all-black. Size, shape, voice are best distinctions from starlings and blackbirds (p. 246). See 2 preceding species. ♩**Voice:** familiar harsh *caw! caw!,* other notes.

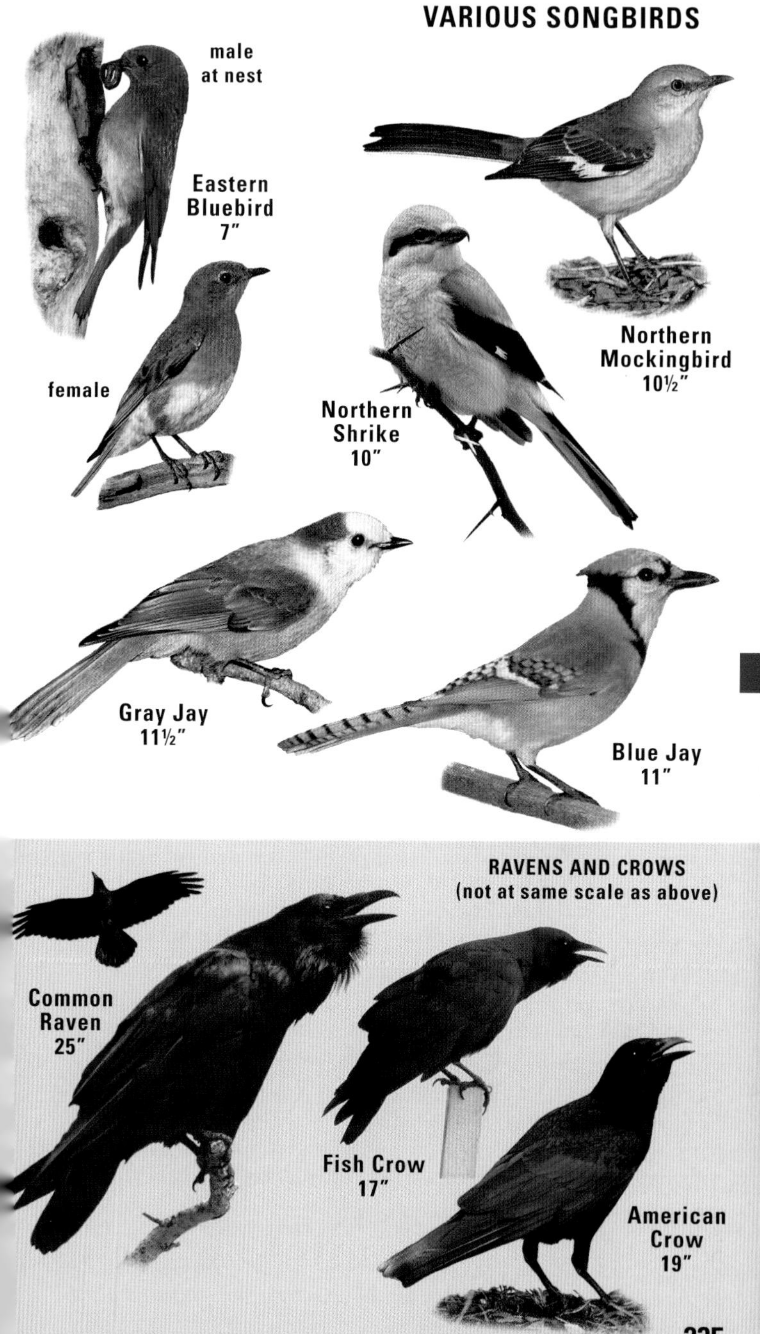
male
at nest
Eastern
Bluebird
7″
female
Northern
Mockingbird
10½″
Northern
Shrike
10″
Gray Jay
11½″
Blue Jay
11″
RAVENS AND CROWS
(not at same scale as above)
Common
Raven
25″
Fish Crow
17″
American
Crow
19″

VARIOUS SMALL BIRDS

These belong to different families: chickadees and titmice **(Paridae)**, nuthatches **(Sittidae)**, creepers **(Certhiidae)**, and wrens **(Troglodytidae)**, but all are very small, mostly insect-eaters, and usually quite active.

BLACK-CAPPED CHICKADEE ***Poecile atricapillus***

Common year-round in woods and towns, in busy flocks in winter. Nuthatches, titmice, and others flock with chickadees, visit bird feeders with them. ► Gray and white, with black cap and bib. **Boreal Chickadee** (*P. hudsonica*, not shown), uncommon in spruce forest of north, has *dusty* look, *brown cap.* ♪ **Voice:** whistled *fee bee-ee,* first note higher; chattering *chik-a-deedeedee.*

TUFTED TITMOUSE ***Baeolophus bicolor***

Found in pairs or small flocks in woods, parks. More common southward. ► Gray above with *crest,* pale face, wash of *orange* on sides. ♪ **Voice:** whistled *peeto-peeto-peeto;* scolding callnotes.

WHITE-BREASTED NUTHATCH ***Sitta carolinensis***

An acrobatic tree-climber that walks down trees as well as up. Common all year in leafy woods, parks. ► Note behavior, short-tailed shape, clean *white face.* ♪ **Voice:** nasal *yaank, yaank.*

RED-BREASTED NUTHATCH ***Sitta canadensis***

A tame little tree-climber of evergreen forest. Many may migrate south in some fall seasons. ► Nuthatch shape and actions, *orange wash* below, *black eye-stripe.* ♪ **Voice:** soft, whining *henk, henk.*

BROWN CREEPER ***Certhia americana***

Like an animated bit of bark, creeping up one tree, then flying down to base of another. ► Streaked brown above, white below. Best known by shape and behavior. ♪ **Voice:** high, reedy *tsseeee.*

HOUSE WREN ***Troglodytes aedon***

Common summer bird of gardens, woods. Fusses about in brush piles, often holding tail up. Nests in birdhouses, sheds. ► Rather plain, with thin bill, *faint eyebrow, eye-ring.* Bars on wings and tail. ♪ **Voice:** fast, jumbled, bubbling song. Harsh nasal callnotes.

WINTER WREN ***Troglodytes hiemalis***

A stub-tailed gnome, hard to see as it scoots about fallen logs, forest thickets. ► Shorter-tailed, darker than House Wren. Voice differs. ♪ **Voice:** long, varied, tinkling trill. Squeaky *kimp-kimp* call.

CAROLINA WREN ***Thryothorus ludovicianus***

In thickets and woods, more common toward south, usually in pairs. ► Rich colors, chestnut and buff, with white eyebrow. ♪ **Voice:** rollicking *liberty-liberty-liberty-whew.* Varied metallic calls.

MARSH WREN ***Cistothorus palustris***

Common in marshes but hard to see. Nest is a spherical mass in stems above water. ► Bold white eyebrow, *white stripes* on dark back. ♪ **Voice:** varied, sputtering, bubbling song; *chuk-chuk* call.

Tufted
Titmouse
6½″
Black-capped
Chickadee
5¼″
White-breasted
Nuthatch
5½″
Red-breasted
Nuthatch
4½″
Brown
Creeper
5″
House Wren
4¾″
Winter Wren
4″
Carolina
Wren
5¾″
Marsh
Wren
5″

VIREOS, KINGLETS, GNATCATCHERS

Vireos (family **Vireonidae**) may be heard more than seen as they search among foliage for insects. Mostly larger than warblers (p. 240), they also have thicker bills. Kinglets (family **Regulidae**) are among our tiniest birds, but surprisingly cold-hardy, migrating early in spring and late in fall. Gnatcatchers are placed in their own family **(Polioptilidae)**.

RED-EYED VIREO ***Vireo olivaceus***

A very common summer resident in New England, singing almost constantly, but unnoticed by many because it stays in dense leafy treetops. ▶ Strong head pattern, with *black stripes* setting off gray crown, white eyebrow. Red eyes (brown on young birds) hard to see. ♪ **Voice:** short whistled phrases separated by pauses.

WARBLING VIREO ***Vireo gilvus***

Fairly common in summer in wood edges, streamsides, isolated groves. ▶ Confusingly plain, gray above, white below, with pale eyebrow. ♪ **Voice:** fast musical warble, rising at middle and end.

BLUE-HEADED VIREO ***Vireo solitarius***

Fairly common in summer in mixed forest, pine or hemlock with oak. ▶ Blue-gray hood contrasting with *white "spectacles,"* yellow sides. ♪ **Voice:** short whistled phrases, like Red-eyed but higher.

WHITE-EYED VIREO ***Vireo griseus***

A vireo of low growth, hiding in thickets, scrub. ▶ *Yellow "spectacles"* around *white eyes.* Gray above, whitish below, with 2 wing bars. ♪ **Voice:** snappy jumble, *pick-up-a-real-chick!*

YELLOW-THROATED VIREO ***Vireo flavifrons***

A southern bird, uncommon in New England in summer, mostly in oaks. ▶ *Yellow throat, yellow "spectacles," white wing bars.* See Pine Warbler (p. 244). ♪ **Voice:** short phrases with hoarse sound.

RUBY-CROWNED KINGLET ***Regulus calendula***

Kinglets constantly flick their wings partly open and shut, especially when alarmed. The Ruby-crowned is a common migrant, more local in summer and winter. ▶ Tiny, hyperactive, with bold *white eye-ring,* white and black wing bars. Ruby "crown" of male is usually hidden. ♪ **Voice:** *chi-dit* call; loud bubbling song.

GOLDEN-CROWNED KINGLET ***Regulus satrapa***

This kinglet favors evergreens at all seasons and regularly stays in New England through winter. ▶ Tiny, active. Wing pattern and wing-flicking action like Ruby-crowned, but has *striped face* (no eye-ring), yellow or orange crown. ♪ **Voice:** high thin *see-see-see.*

BLUE-GRAY GNATCATCHER ***Polioptila caerulea***

This long-tailed little sprite is uncommon in summer in leafy woods. ▶ Blue-gray above, white below, with *white eye-ring,* no wing bars. Long black tail has white outer feathers. ♪ **Voice:** thin, whining *shpeew* call. Song is a thin squeaky warble.

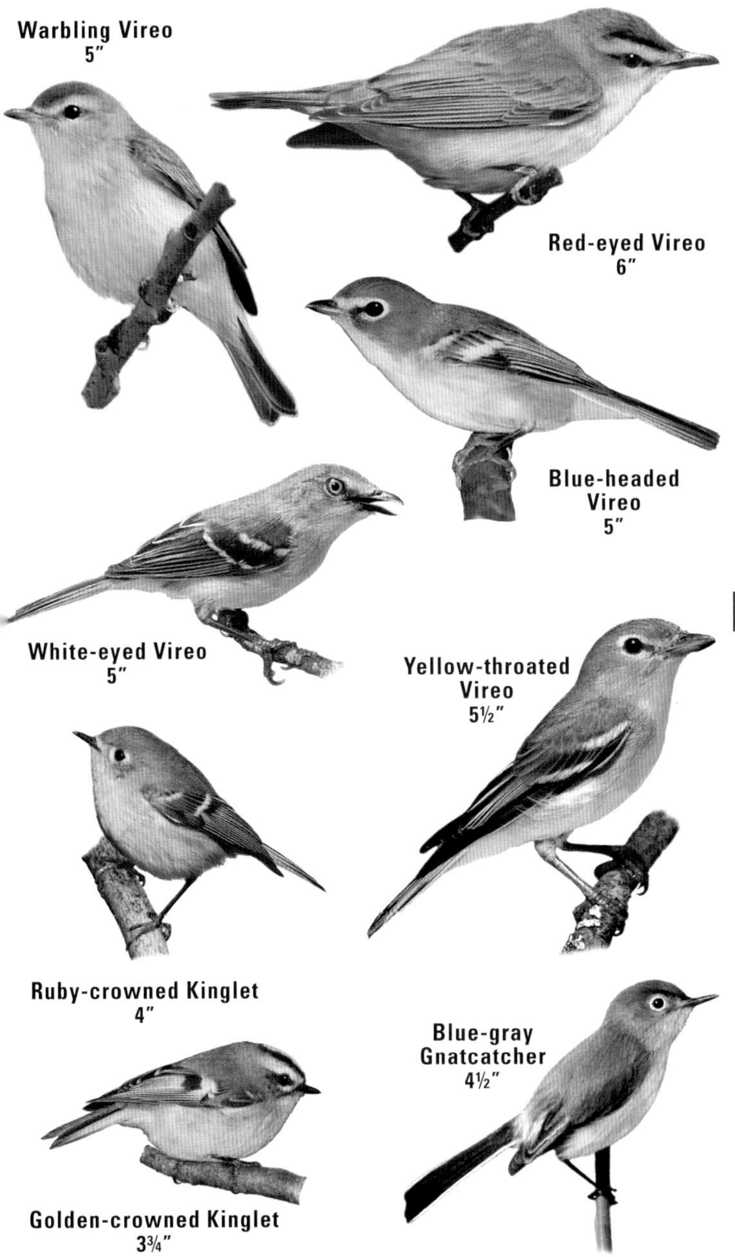
Warbling Vireo
5″
Red-eyed Vireo
6″
Blue-headed
Vireo
5″
White-eyed Vireo
5″
Yellow-throated
Vireo
5½″
Ruby-crowned Kinglet
4″
Blue-gray
Gnatcatcher
4½″
Golden-crowned Kinglet
3¾″

WARBLERS

(family **Parulidae**), favorites of many birders, are small, active, colorful insect-eaters. Three dozen species occur regularly in New England, and it is possible to find 20 or more species in a day at the peak of spring migration. Their songs and calls are mostly thin and high-pitched. Warblers are harder to identify in fall migration, when some wear duller plumages.

YELLOW-RUMPED WARBLER ***Setophaga coronata***
Also called Myrtle Warbler. Migrates earlier in spring and later in fall than other warblers, even stays through winter in some areas, feeding on berries. ► *Yellow rump* (obvious as bird flies away), white tail spots (shared by many warblers). Overall color varies from crisp gray, black, and white of spring males to pale brown of some fall birds. Look for *yellow patches at sides of chest* and on crown. ♪ **Voice**: rambling, warbling song. Call, loud *check.*

MAGNOLIA WARBLER ***Setophaga magnolia***
Common in summer in spruce forest; spring and fall migrant throughout. Often flits about low branches. ► Yellow below, with *stripes along sides. Square-edged white tail band.* Adult males black above, females grayer. ♪ **Voice**: sweet *wayta wayta wayteeh.*

CAPE MAY WARBLER ***Setophaga tigrina***
Migrant throughout, nesting in northern spruce forest. ► Adult male has *chestnut ear patch,* black stripes on yellow chest. Female and young duller, well striped below. ♪ **Voice**: very high thin song.

BLACK-THROATED GREEN WARBLER ***Setophaga virens***
Common in summer in evergreen and mixed forest; migrates throughout. ► *Bright yellow face,* green back, white wing bars. Adult male has black throat. ♪ **Voice**: buzzy *zoo-zee-zoozoo-zee.*

BLACK-THROATED BLUE WARBLER ***Setophaga caerulescens***
Summers in undergrowth of mixed forest. ► Male dark blue and black, white below, with *white wing spot.* Female plain and dull, but usually has wing spot. ♪ **Voice**: lazy *zhur zhur zhur zhree?*

YELLOW WARBLER ***Setophaga petechia***
Very common in summer in willows near ponds, streams. ► Yellow all over, adult male with *red stripes* on the chest. Goldfinches (p. 252) have *thicker* bills. ♪ **Voice**: fast *sweet sweet weetaweet.*

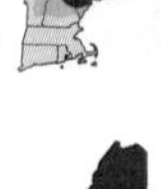

NORTHERN PARULA ***Setophaga americana***
This tiny warbler tucks its nest in *Usnea* lichen (p. 160) in northern spruces. ► Blue-gray above, white wing bars, yellow on chest. Male has rusty chest band. ♪ **Voice**: snappy *zz-zz-zzzeee-wup.*

AMERICAN REDSTART ***Setophaga ruticilla***
Common in summer in leafy woods. Active, flitting about with wings and tail partly spread, showing off colors. ► Adult male black with *orange patches,* female gray with *yellow patches* in wings and tail. ♪ **Voice**: varied phrases, *weesa weesa weesa,* etc.

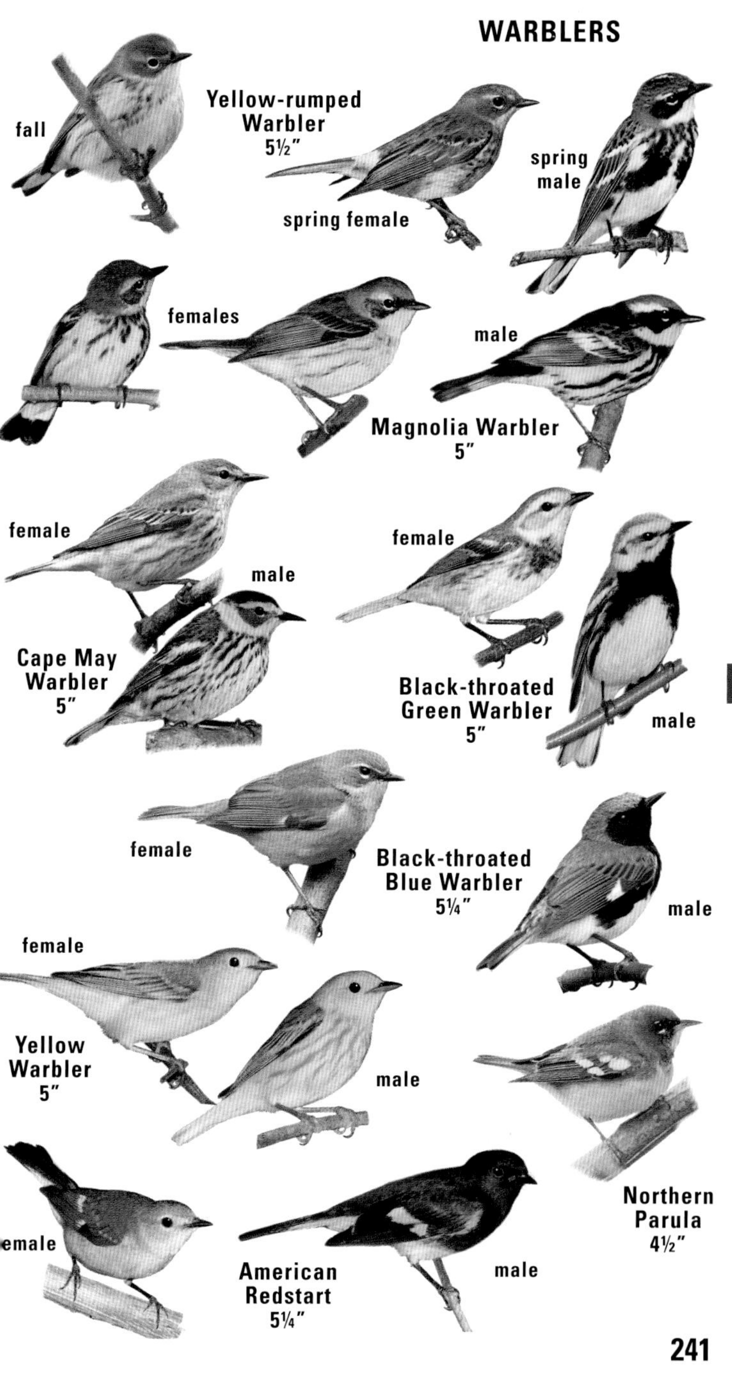
fall
Yellow-rumped Warbler 5½″
spring female
spring male
females
male
Magnolia Warbler 5″
female
male
Cape May Warbler 5″
female
Black-throated Green Warbler 5″
male
female
Black-throated Blue Warbler 5¼″
male
female
Yellow Warbler 5″
male
Northern Parula 4½″
emale
American Redstart 5¼″
male

COMMON YELLOWTHROAT ***Geothlypis trichas***

Our only warbler that nests in marshes. Also seen in thickets, wet woods, especially in migration. ▸ Male's *bandit mask* is set off by *yellow throat,* white upper outline. Female duller; yellow throat contrasts with plain face. ♪**Voice:** fast *wichity-wichity-wichity.*

MOURNING WARBLER ***Geothlypis philadelphia***

Nests in thickets, raspberry tangles of the north. Uncommon migrant, hiding in dense low growth. ▸ Yellow below, with *gray hood.* Male has black on chest. ♪**Voice:** rolling, 2-parted chant.

WILSON'S WARBLER ***Cardellina pusilla***

Nests in streamside thickets, willows of northern New England, migrates throughout. ▸ Yellow, plain-faced, no white in wings or tail. *Round black cap* of male diagnostic. ♪**Voice:** rising chatter.

BLUE-WINGED WARBLER ***Vermivora cyanoptera***

A summer bird of old fields, thickets. Increasing here in recent decades. Often interbreeds with Golden-winged Warbler where their ranges meet and has mostly replaced that species in New England. ▸ Yellow with *black line* through eye; blue-gray wings with white wing bars. ♪**Voice:** *bzzeee-buzzzz,* second note lower.

NASHVILLE WARBLER ***Oreothlypis ruficapilla***

Fairly common in summer in second-growth woods, edges. Migrant throughout. ▸ *Gray head* contrasts with *white eye-ring, yellow throat,* olive back. ♪**Voice:** double notes followed by trill.

TENNESSEE WARBLER ***Oreothlypis peregrina***

Nests in northern spruce forest, bogs. A common migrant elsewhere. ▸ Spring male with gray cap, green back, white eyebrow. Female duller. See vireos (p. 238). ♪**Voice:** rapid staccato series.

CANADA WARBLER ***Cardellina canadensis***

Common in summer in leafy thickets of wet woods, maple swamps. Migrates late in spring, usually staying low. ▸ *Necklace of black streaks* on yellow breast, most obvious on adult male. Bold eye-ring, blue-gray back. ♪**Voice:** fast, jumbled song.

CERULEAN WARBLER ***Setophaga cerulea***

Rare and local in summer in treetops of tall deciduous forest. ▸ Male *blue above,* white below with thin black necklace. Female duller, with pale eyebrow, white wing bars, tinge of blue above. ♪**Voice:** buzzy rising song.

GOLDEN-WINGED WARBLER ***Vermivora chrysoptera***

Now rare in New England, apparently pushed out by its close relative, Blue-winged Warbler. ▸ Black mask and bib, yellow cap and wing bars.

HOODED WARBLER ***Setophaga citrina***

Nests in forests of southern New England, strays farther north. ▸ *Black hood* (faint on female) around *yellow face,* white tail edges.

WARBLERS

(adult males unless otherwise noted)

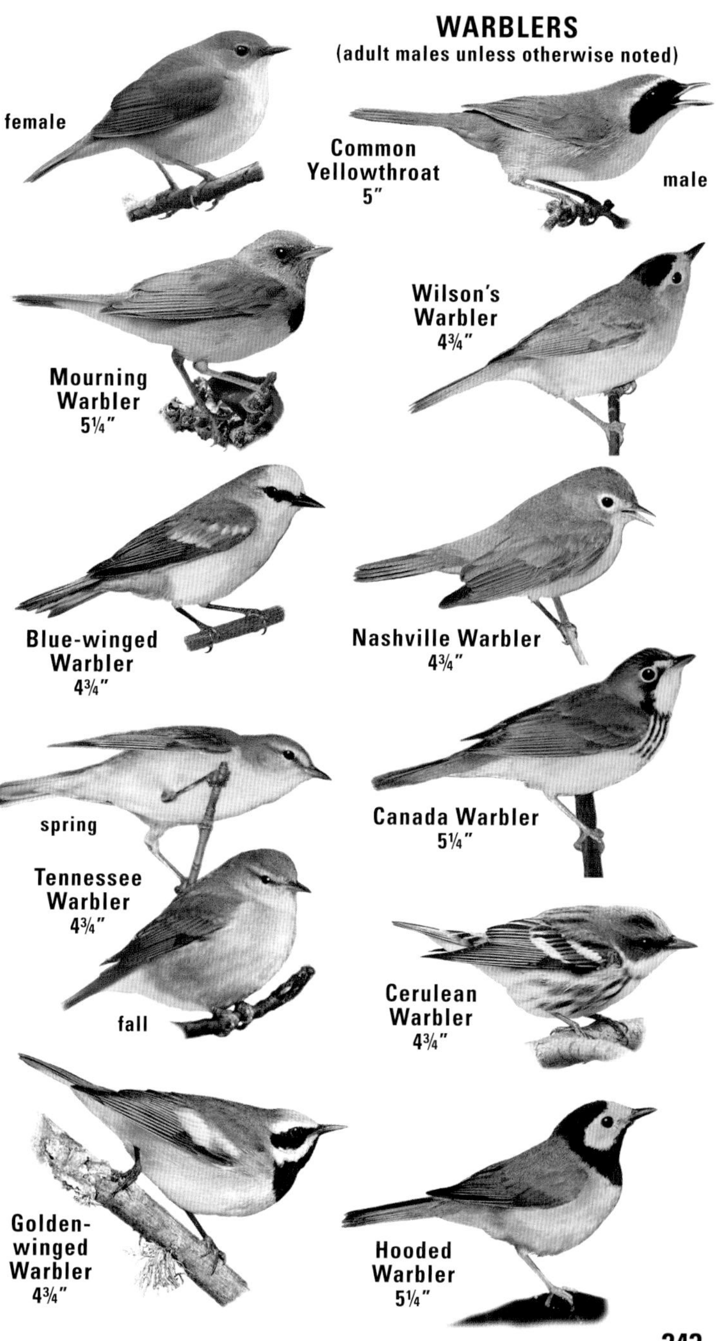

CHESTNUT-SIDED WARBLER ***Setophaga pensylvanica***
Fairly common in second growth, open leafy woods. ▶ *Yellow crown,* small black face mask, chestnut stripe on sides (less on female). Fall birds *lime green above,* whitish below, with white eye-ring. ♪ **Voice:** lively song, *sweet sweet sweet seesaWEETchew.*

BLACKBURNIAN WARBLER ***Setophaga fusca***
Like a glowing flame among dark spruces in summer. ▶ Spring male orange and black, with white back stripes. Female and fall birds duller. ♪ **Voice:** thin wiry song like a "mouse with a toothache."

BLACK-AND-WHITE WARBLER ***Mniotilta varia***
A warbler that acts like a nuthatch (p. 236), often creeping along trunks and limbs. Nests on ground. ▶ Striped pattern, including *white central crown stripe.* ♪ **Voice:** thin *weesee weesee weesee.*

BLACKPOLL WARBLER ***Dendroica striata***
A champion migrant, wintering south to Brazil. ▶ Spring male has *black cap,* white cheeks. Female and fall birds greenish with wing bars, often yellow legs. ♪ **Voice:** thin *zi-zi-zi-zi-zi-zi.*

BAY-BREASTED WARBLER ***Setophaga castanea***
Nests in northern forest, migrant elsewhere. ▶ Spring male chestnut and buff, female duller. Fall birds greenish with white wing bars, hint of chestnut on flanks. ♪ **Voice:** thin high-pitched song.

PINE WARBLER ***Setophaga pinus***
A rather slow-moving warbler, almost always in pines. ▶ Adult male olive above, yellow below; female duller. Young female very drab, with hint of face pattern. ♪ **Voice:** slow musical trill.

PALM WARBLER ***Setophaga palmarum***
Migrates early in spring and late in fall, often seen low in open areas. ▶ *Bobs tail up and down* constantly. May be bright or dull yellow, with pale eyebrow, *yellow under tail.* ♪ **Voice:** rough trill.

PRAIRIE WARBLER ***Setophaga discolor***
Lives in thickets, not prairies, especially scrub oak woods in sandy places. ▶ *Bobs tail* up and down. Olive above, yellow below, with strong face pattern. ♪ **Voice:** wiry rising *zee zee zee zee zee . . .*

NORTHERN WATERTHRUSH ***Parkesia noveboracensis***
Another brown ground warbler, bobbing tail as it walks along streams, swamps. ▶ Dark above, yellow or white with dark stripes below, strong pale eyebrow. Note habitat, tail-bobbing. ♪ **Voice:** ringing fast chant ending in low emphatic notes. Callnote, *chink.*

OVENBIRD ***Seiurus aurocapilla***
This brown warbler walks slowly on the ground, tail often held up. Builds domed nest like old-fashioned oven. ▶ *White eye-ring,* orange crown stripe. ♪ **Voice:** ringing *chertea chertea chertea . . .*

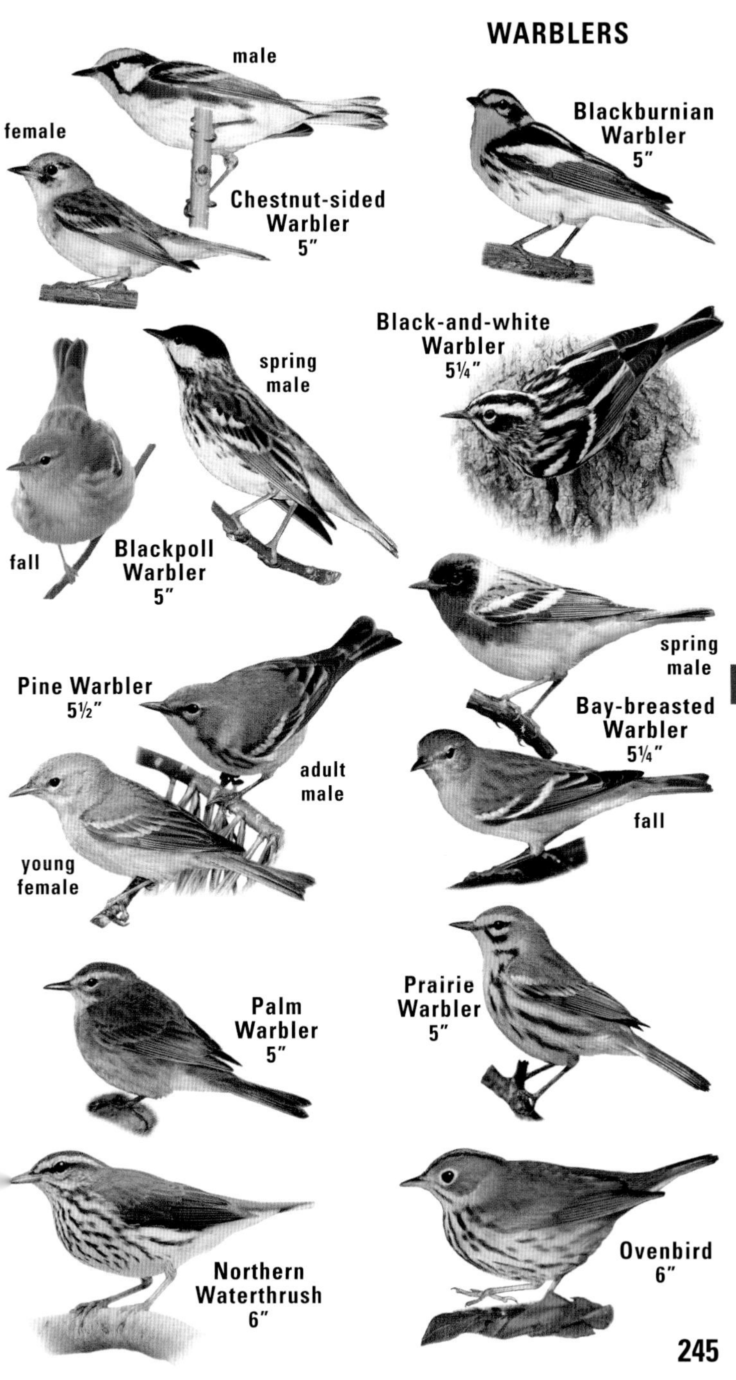
male
female
Chestnut-sided
Warbler
5″
Blackburnian
Warbler
5″
Black-and-white
Warbler
5¼″
spring
male
fall
Blackpoll
Warbler
5″
spring
male
Bay-breasted
Warbler
5¼″
fall
Pine Warbler
5½″
adult
male
young
female
Palm
Warbler
5″
Prairie
Warbler
5″
Northern
Waterthrush
6″
Ovenbird
6″

EUROPEAN STARLING ***Sturnus vulgaris***

Our only member of an Old World family (Sturnidae), introduced here, now abundant. Lives in farm country, towns, cities; huge flocks of migrants gather near coast in fall. Nests in holes, sometimes displacing native birds. ▶ Stocky, *short-tailed.* Spiky bill dark in winter, *yellow* in spring. Winter plumage heavily spangled white and buff. ♩**Voice:** chatters, whistles, imitations.

RED-WINGED BLACKBIRD ***Agelaius phoeniceus***

Like all the birds below, a true blackbird (family Icteridae). Redwings arrive in March, are common all summer in every wet field and marsh. A few stay in winter. ▶ Red on males can be mostly hidden. Females brown, streaked. ♩**Voice:** nasal *awnk-ah-rrhee.*

EASTERN MEADOWLARK ***Sturnella magna***

Uncommon and declining in meadows, farmland. ▶ Stocky, with *white outer feathers* of short tail, visible in flight. Striped head, *black V on yellow chest.* ♩**Voice:** whistled *te-seeyeer seeyayy.*

BOBOLINK ***Dolichonyx oryzivorus***

The male's bubbling flight song is a delight of summer meadows. In hayfields, nests often destroyed by mowing. ▶ Summer male unmistakable. Female and fall male sparrowlike, buff, streaked.

BALTIMORE ORIOLE ***Icterus galbula***

Common in summer in towns, open woods, making hanging nest in shade trees. ▶ Male unmistakable. Female dull orange below, white wing bars; note bill shape. ♩**Voice:** rich whistles, chatters.

ORCHARD ORIOLE ***Icterus spurius***

Uncommon summer resident of woodland edges, towns. ▶ Adult male *chestnut and black.* Female greenish yellow, young male similar but with *black throat.* ♩**Voice:** fast jumbled song.

BROWN-HEADED COWBIRD ***Molothrus ater***

A brood parasite, laying its eggs in nests of other birds. Flocks forage in open fields. ▶ Male glossy black with brown head. Female confusingly plain; note bill shape. ♩**Voice:** gurgles, whistles.

COMMON GRACKLE ***Quiscalus quiscula***

Abundant in summer, scarce in winter, in open country, woods, towns. ▶ Pale eyes, *long* creased tail. Blue-black head contrasts with *bronzy body.* ♩**Voice:** gurgling *kssh-kaleeah,* hard *chack.*

BOAT-TAILED GRACKLE ***Quiscalus major***

A southern marsh bird, found locally on Connecticut coast. ▶ Larger, rounder-headed than Common Grackle; female brown.

RUSTY BLACKBIRD ***Euphagus carolinus***

Mostly a migrant. A few nest in northern bogs. ▶ Dull black with yellow eyes. Distinctive in fall, with *rusty cap, buff eyebrow.* ♩**Voice:** high creaking.

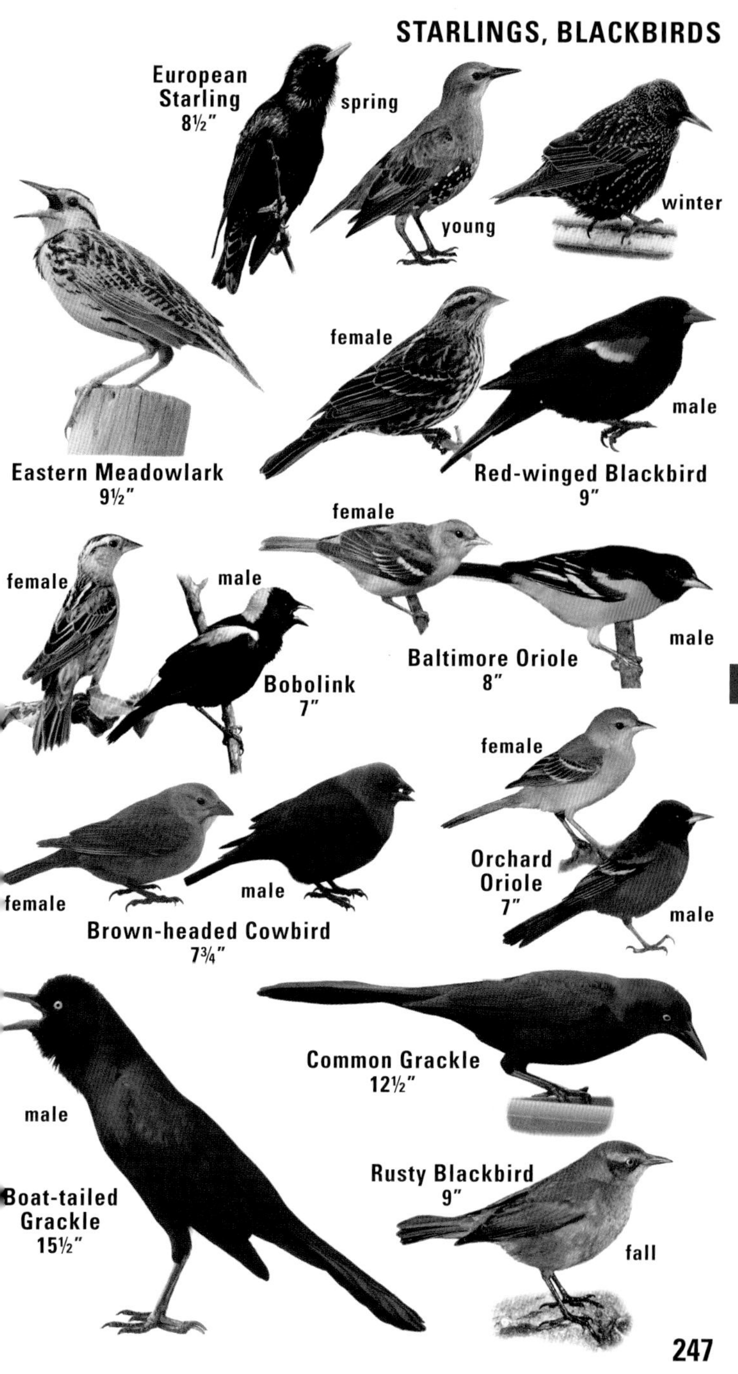
European Starling
8½″
spring
young
winter
Eastern Meadowlark
9½″
female
male
Red-winged Blackbird
9″
female
female
male
Bobolink
7″
Baltimore Oriole
8″
male
female
Orchard Oriole
7″
male
female
male
Brown-headed Cowbird
7¾″
Common Grackle
12½″
male
Boat-tailed Grackle
15½″
Rusty Blackbird
9″
fall

SPARROWS

The House Sparrow belongs to an Old World family **(Passeridae)** and is not related to our many native sparrows (family **Emberizidae**).

HOUSE SPARROW ***Passer domesticus***
Introduced from Europe, common where humans live, but rare in natural habitats. ► Male has *black bib,* white cheeks, chestnut nape. Female has buff eyebrow, striped back. ♪**Voice:** chirps.

FIELD SPARROW ***Spizella pusilla***
This baby-faced sparrow lives in brushy old fields, thickets. More common and widespread in summer. ► *Pink bill,* rusty cap, plain face. ♪**Voice:** short plaintive whistles speeding up to a trill.

AMERICAN TREE SPARROW ***Spizella arborea***
Favors weedy fields, not trees. Visits in winter, sometimes flocking with juncos (p. 250). ► Like Chipping Sparrow but with *chest spot,* rusty eyeline, *bicolored bill.* ♪**Voice:** musical *twiddle-eat.*

CHIPPING SPARROW ***Spizella passerina***
Common in summer in towns, farms, forest edges. Rare in winter. ► Small with plain chest, *chestnut cap,* white eyebrow, *black line* through eye. Fall birds duller. ♪**Voice:** rapid, dry trill.

SWAMP SPARROW ***Melospiza georgiana***
A dark sparrow that hides in marshes, dense thickets. ► Cap is *chestnut* in summer, brown in winter. Dark with contrasting *reddish wings and back,* white throat. ♪**Voice:** slow musical trill.

SONG SPARROW ***Melospiza melodia***
Common in dense low cover; may become rather tame around gardens, parks. ► Strong face pattern, streaked below, chest often with central blotch. ♪**Voice:** short notes followed by musical trill.

SAVANNAH SPARROW ***Passerculus sandwichensis***
Open areas: dunes, coastal meadows, farm fields. ► Strong face pattern, heavily streaked below. Like Song Sparrow but with shorter tail, *yellow* in front of eye. A pale form ("Ipswich Sparrow") winters along coast. ♪**Voice:** song, *sip sip sip sreeeee, sip.*

FOX SPARROW ***Passerella iliaca***
Mostly an uncommon migrant, a few wintering. Scratches with its feet in leaf-litter under thickets. ► Big, beautiful, mostly *foxy red,* brightest on tail. ♪**Voice:** musical song with rich whistles.

WHITE-THROATED SPARROW ***Zonotrichia albicollis***
Often very common in forest undergrowth, especially in migration. ► *White* throat, *contrasting* head stripes (can be either white or tan). ♪**Voice:** whistled *oh, sweet, Kimberly-Kimberly-Kimberly.*

WHITE-CROWNED SPARROW ***Zonotrichia leucophrys***
Migrant through New England, rarely wintering, in brushy areas. ► *Striped head* (black and white on adults, tan on young birds), *pink bill,* gray chest.

SPARROWS

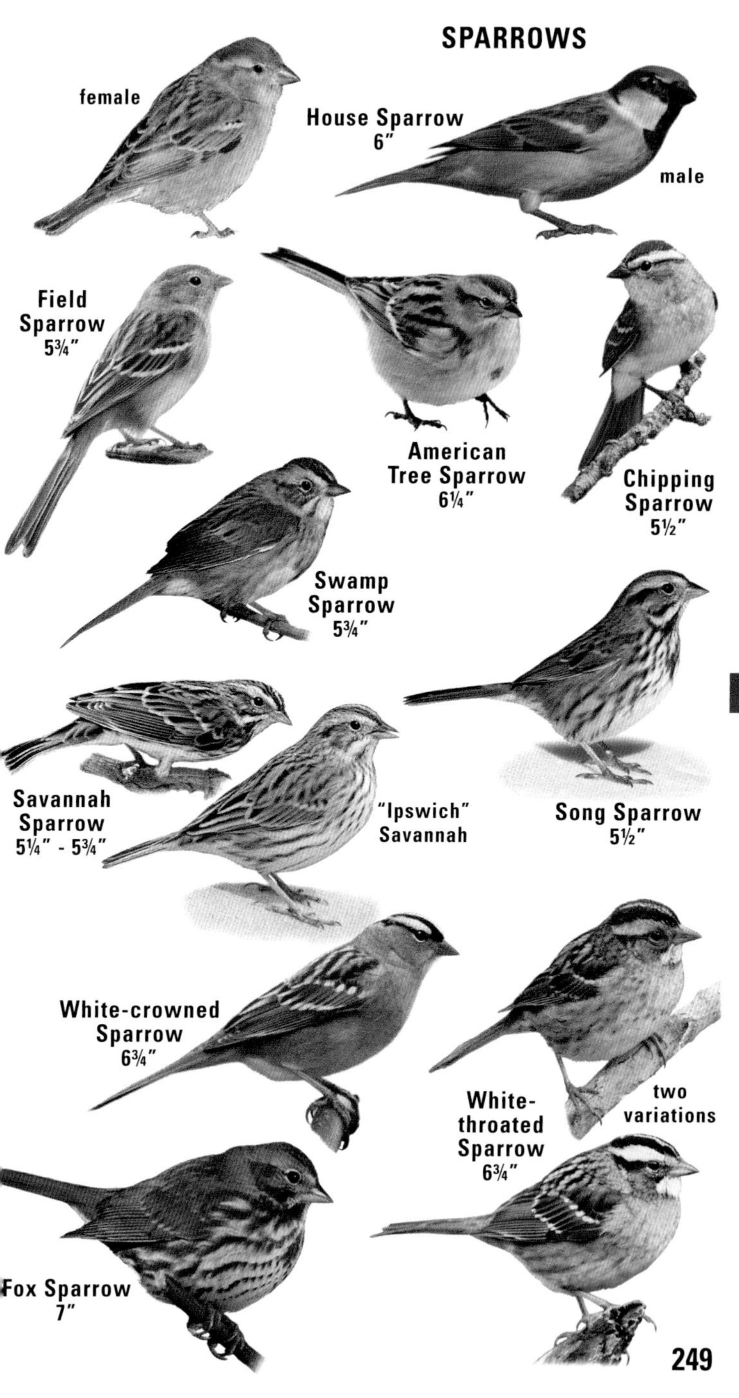
female
House Sparrow
6″
male
Field
Sparrow
5¾″
American
Tree Sparrow
6¼″
Chipping
Sparrow
5½″
Swamp
Sparrow
5¾″
Savannah
Sparrow
5¼″ - 5¾″
"Ipswich"
Savannah
Song Sparrow
5½″
White-crowned
Sparrow
6¾″
White-
throated
Sparrow
6¾″
two
variations
Fox Sparrow
7″

TANAGERS, GROSBEAKS, BUNTINGS, ETC.

The first four colorful species below are in the small family **Cardinalidae.** Towhees and juncos are related to the native sparrows on p. 248, while Snow Bunting and longspurs, despite their similarity to sparrows, are now placed in a separate family, **Calcariidae.**

SCARLET TANAGER ***Piranga olivacea***

Fairly common in summer in oak woods but can be surprisingly hard to see among the treetop foliage. ► Summer male unmistakable. Female and fall male greenish with darker wings and tail. ♪**Voice:** whistling song, like hoarse robin; *chip-brr* call.

NORTHERN CARDINAL ***Cardinalis cardinalis***

A favorite backyard bird, visiting feeders for sunflower seeds, brightening winter days with whistled song. Colonized New England from the south during 20th century. ► Male is our only *crested red bird.* Female duller but shares *crest,* massive *orange bill.* ♪**Voice:** varied song, *what-cheer, what-cheer,* etc. Callnote, *tchip.*

INDIGO BUNTING ***Passerina cyanea***

Common in summer in brushy clearings, where males sing from high perches. The shy brown females are seen less often. ► Male is our only *dark blue songbird.* Female warm brown, with *faint streaks* on chest. ♪**Voice:** bright, quick song, notes often in pairs.

ROSE-BREASTED GROSBEAK ***Pheucticus ludovicianus***

A striking summer bird of leafy woods, often hard to see among foliage. ► Adult male black and white with rose patch on chest. Female more sparrowlike, but note heavy bill, strong face pattern, treetop habits. ♪**Voice:** fast caroling song, like a nervous robin.

EASTERN TOWHEE ***Pipilo erythrophthalmus***

In second-growth woods or oak scrub, this big sparrow scratches among leaf-litter on the ground with both feet. ► Dark hood and *rusty sides* contrast with *white stripe* down center of belly. Eyes *red.* ♪**Voice:** ringing *drink-your-teeeeeee.* Callnote, *chwink.*

DARK-EYED JUNCO ***Junco hyemalis***

Nests in evergreen and mixed forest, winters throughout New England. Small flocks forage on the ground under feeders with other native sparrows. ► Slaty gray with white belly, *white outer tail feathers.* Females browner. ♪**Voice:** musical trill, *tic* callnote.

SNOW BUNTING ***Plectrophenax nivalis***

Nests on Arctic tundra, winters in small flocks on open beaches, barren fields. ► Pale brown and white with yellow bill, *big white wing patches* obvious in flight. ♪**Voice:** rattles, soft whistles.

LAPLAND LONGSPUR ***Calcarius lapponicus***

Another winter visitor to open ground. Often flocks with Horned Larks (p. 232) or Snow Buntings. ► Dark above, white below, with *red-brown on nape and wings.* ♪**Voice:** rattles, whistles.

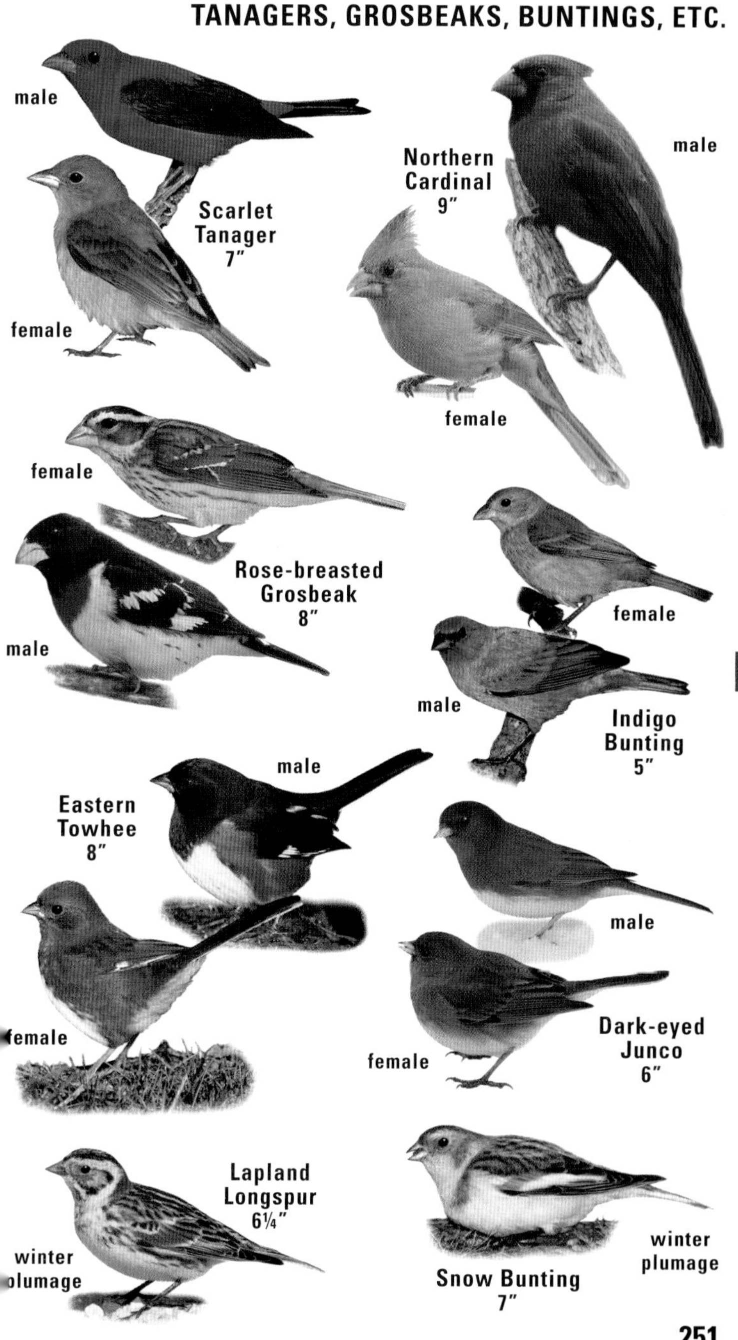
male
Scarlet
Tanager
7″
female
Northern
Cardinal
9″
male
female
female
Rose-breasted
Grosbeak
8″
male
female
male
Indigo
Bunting
5″
male
Eastern
Towhee
8″
female
male
female
Dark-eyed
Junco
6″
Lapland
Longspur
6¼″
winter
plumage
winter
plumage
Snow Bunting
7″

FINCHES

Technically known as Cardueline finches, part of the family **Fringillidae,** these birds feed mostly on plant material (seeds, buds, berries, etc.) at all seasons. Most are erratic in their migrations, and flocks may wander far (in undulating flight) in response to changing food supplies.

HOUSE FINCH ***Carpodacus mexicanus***

Native to the southwest, this finch was accidentally introduced to New York in 1940 and is now common throughout the east, in towns, cities, farmland. ▸ Male brown with variably *red* chest and eyebrow, stripes on flanks. Female striped below, plain on face. ♪ **Voice:** rich warbling song, usually ending on rough note.

PURPLE FINCH ***Carpodacus purpureus***

Fairly common, but less so in towns than House Finch. ▸ Like House Finch but heavier, shorter-tailed. Male *lacks* streaks on flanks, female has *stronger face pattern.* ♪ **Voice:** warbling song.

COMMON REDPOLL ***Acanthis flammea***

Nesting in the Arctic, this finch visits weedy fields and feeders in New England in winter, sometimes in large numbers. ▸ *Red forehead, black chin,* streaks. Male pink on chest. ♪ **Voice:** rattles, soft notes.

AMERICAN GOLDFINCH ***Spinus tristis***

Common all year, flocks of goldfinches wander in weedy fields, come to feeders for thistle seed. Nests later in summer than most birds. ▸ Summer male gold with *black forehead,* wings, tail. Summer female duller greenish. In winter, buff with contrasty black wings. ♪ **Voice:** Musical twitter. In bouncing flight, *po-ta-to-chip.*

PINE SISKIN ***Spinus pinus***

Like a goldfinch in camouflage. Often flocks with American Goldfinches, acts like them. ▸ Suggests a sparrow but has *thinner bill, yellow in wings,* plainer face. ♪ **Voice:** musical and harsh notes.

EVENING GROSBEAK ***Coccothraustes vespertinus***

Uncommon. Flocks wander erratically in winter, appearing at feeders to eat sunflower seeds. ▸ Gray and gold, with big white patch on black wing, big pale bill. ♪ **Voice:** ringing *peeyr.*

PINE GROSBEAK ***Pinicola enucleator***

Scarce in northern forest, rarely wanders in winter throughout New England. ▸ Stubby black bill, long tail. Adult male pink and gray, female and young mostly gray. ♪ **Voice:** clear whistled calls.

WHITE-WINGED CROSSBILL ***Loxia leucoptera***

An odd bill shape enables crossbills to pry open cones to eat conifer seeds. This species shows up to exploit big crops of spruce cones. ▸ Adult male *rose red,* female dull yellow, with big *white wing bars.* ♪ **Voice:** slow rattle.

RED CROSSBILL ***Loxia curvirostra***

Another nomad, wandering in flocks to feed on cones. ▸ Adult male *brick red,* female dull yellow, with darker wings and tail. ♪ **Voice:** hard *kep-kep.*

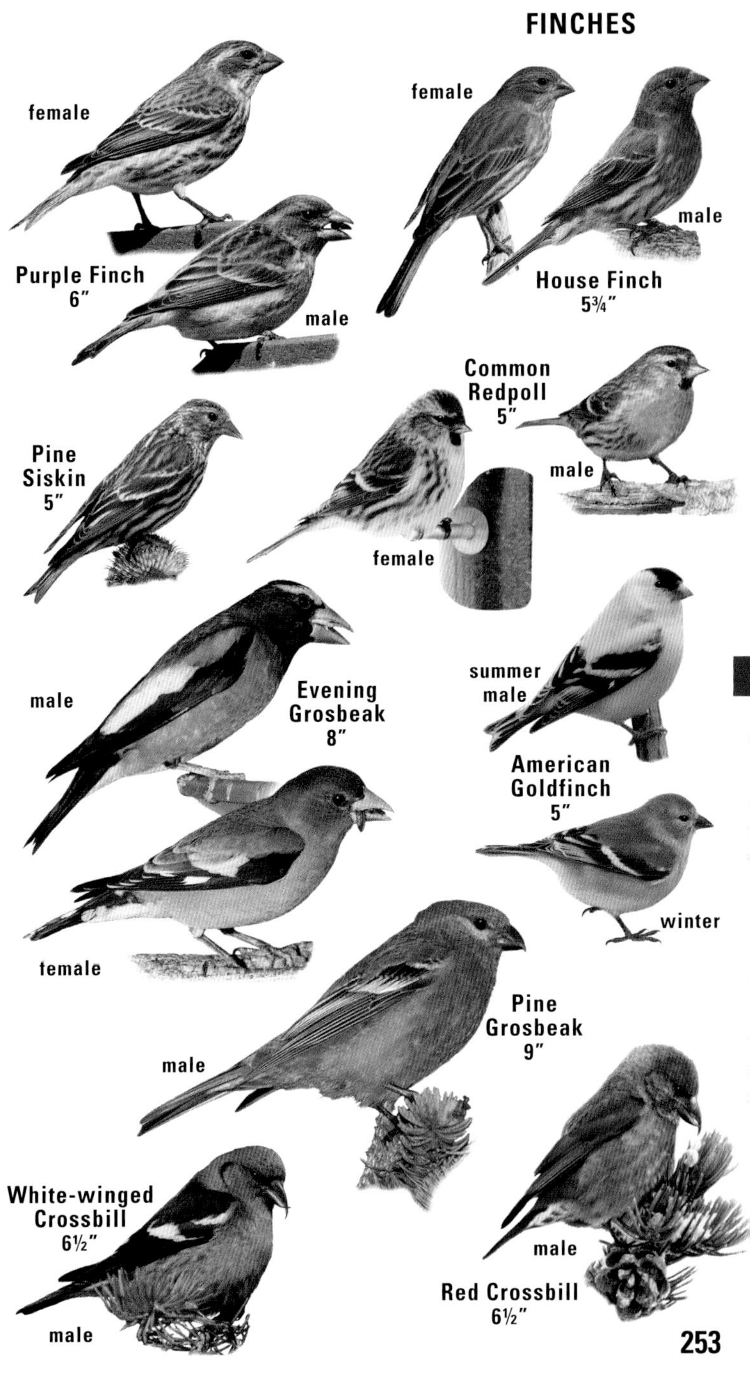
female
Purple Finch
6″
male
female
male
House Finch
5¾″
Common
Redpoll
5″
Pine
Siskin
5″
male
female
male
Evening
Grosbeak
8″
female
summer
male
American
Goldfinch
5″
winter
Pine
Grosbeak
9″
male
White-winged
Crossbill
6½″
male
male
Red Crossbill
6½″

represent two distinct classes of animals, with reptiles thought to have branched off from amphibians more than 300 million years ago. Still, the science of Herpetology treats amphibians and reptiles as a group, and these creatures may be collectively known as herptiles (or "herps"). **Reptiles (class Reptilia)** are represented in New England by turtles, snakes, and lizards. Their skin is relatively dry and usually at least partly covered with scales. Those with feet usually have claws on their toes. Young reptiles are shaped like smaller versions of adults. **Amphibians (class Amphibia)** are represented here by salamanders, toads, and frogs. These have relatively moist skin without scales, and have no claws on their toes. Young amphibians are often aquatic and may be shaped very differently from adults (compare tadpoles to adult frogs, for example).

REPTILES

Turtles (order Testudines) are famously slow-moving but may be very long-lived. In other parts of the world, giant tortoises may live over 150 years, and even the humble box turtle may live more than half a century. Most of our turtles are highly aquatic, spending most of their time in the water and hibernating underwater during the winter; one exception is the box turtle, which spends the summer wandering through woods and fields and hibernates underground in winter. However, all female turtles come out on land to dig holes in which to lay their eggs.

The shells of turtles are made of numerous bony plates, usually fused together; the upper shell (carapace) and lower shell (plastron) are joined by a bridge of bone or cartilage. The bony plates of the carapace and plastron are usually covered by large scales, called scutes. To identify turtle species in some regions, it's necessary to examine fine details of the scutes, but turtles in New England usually can be identified by their color patterns.

Snakes (order Squamata, in part) are feared by some, but they are fascinating creatures with important roles to play in natural habitats. All snakes lack legs, eyelids, and external ear openings. But their lack of limbs does not prevent some species from moving very fast — some are even excellent climbers — and many have sharp eyesight. They use their long, forked tongues to pick up chemical clues from their surroundings and deliver them to a specialized organ in the roof of the mouth, called Jacobson's organ, which operates like a sophisticated sense of smell. Some snakes lay eggs (like most other reptiles), while others bear live young.

Snakes are most diverse in the tropics. They cannot tolerate subfreezing temperatures, so those in New England hibernate in winter in sheltered sites, usually underground or in caves. These sites (called hibernacula) may be shared by many individuals and more than one species.

Only two venomous snakes, the Copperhead and Timber Rattlesnake, occur in New England, and neither is common. However, some other snakes can deliver nasty bites if cornered or handled. The vast majority of snakebite cases occur when people are trying to catch snakes. It is usually more rewarding to observe snakes from a distance in the wild.

Lizards (order Squamata, in part) are most common and diverse in hot climates, including some very dry regions such as the American southwest; New England has only one species. Most lizards are alert, fast-moving animals, with keen senses of eyesight, hearing, and smell. Many have tails that detach easily if the animal is attacked: if grabbed by a predator, the tail breaks off and continues to wiggle and thrash while the lizard itself escapes; the lizard usually can grow a new tail to replace it.

AMPHIBIANS

Salamanders (order Caudata) look superficially like lizards but are totally unrelated. They have moist skin without scales, their toes lack claws, and most have a larval stage that lives in water. While lizards can survive in very arid climates, salamanders must remain in moist or wet environments to avoid drying out, and some are aquatic throughout their lives.

Female salamanders lay their eggs in the water or in damp places, and they often guard or brood the eggs until they hatch. Most species have an aquatic larval stage, living underwater and breathing with gills, before transforming to the terrestrial adult stage. Two of our species hatch out on land, and one, the Mudpuppy, spends its whole life in the water.

All salamanders are predatory, feeding mostly on insects, worms, and other small invertebrates, although the largest aquatic species may take small fish or other creatures in the water.

Frogs and toads (order Anura) are familiar creatures, often seen and even more often heard; the voices of frogs are typical spring and summer sounds in New England.

Female frogs and toads lay their eggs in the water, and the eggs hatch out into small, legless, swimming creatures called tadpoles. Tadpoles are mostly vegetarians, feeding on algae and other submerged plant matter for a period of a few weeks to many months, until they go through metamorphosis and emerge as small froglets or toadlets. These tiny versions of the adults (often with partial tails at first) may be abundant near water for brief periods, and it may take up to three years for these young ones to grow to full size. The adults are carnivorous, mostly preying on insects and other invertebrates, although Bullfrogs regularly take other frogs, snakes, rodents, and even birds.

As we might expect of such vocal creatures, many of the frogs and toads have excellent hearing. Many have a conspicuous eardrum, or tympanum, on the side of the head, and its size or pattern may be a field mark. Also worth noticing is the presence or absence of ridges or raised bumps on the back.

American Bullfrog, showing the tympanum, or eardrum, behind the eye

All the turtles on this page are classifed in the family **Emydidae** except for the Eastern Musk Turtle, which belongs to the family **Kinosternidae.**

PAINTED TURTLE ***Chrysemys picta***

A common turtle of many kinds of shallow, marshy ponds and slow-moving streams, often seen basking on logs or islands. Seldom wanders far from water. ▶ Shell mostly dark with paler edges of large scutes and with *red markings along edges.* Yellow stripes and spots on head, yellow and red stripes on legs.

SPOTTED TURTLE ***Clemmys guttata***

This beautiful little turtle lives in shallow marshes, wet meadows, vernal pools, and other damp places. Fairly common and widespread, seen basking in the open mainly in spring. ▶ Dark shell has scattered small round spots. Yellow or orange spots on head.

EASTERN MUSK TURTLE ***Sternotherus odoratus***

Also known by the more colorful name of "Stinkpot." Exudes a smelly liquid when handled, and can bite hard, so take care if you catch one of these on your fishing line. This small turtle spends most of its time crawling on the bottom of ponds, sometimes basking in the open on logs. ▶ Small, with rounded shell, two *thin pale stripes on head.*

BLANDING'S TURTLE ***Emydoidea blandingii***

Uncommon and local (and considered threatened) in eastern New England, in shallow ponds and marshes, swamps, vernal pools. ▶ Shell dark with yellow dots and streaks (may be obvious or obscure). *Bright yellow chin and throat* obvious at a distance.

EASTERN BOX TURTLE ***Terrapene carolina***

Often found away from water, plodding through woods, especially on warm spring days or after summer rains. Burrows under logs or rests in ponds in hot weather. ▶ Known by its high domed shell, variably patterned with yellow or orange. The lower shell is hinged and can close up tight when the turtle is threatened.

WOOD TURTLE ***Glyptemys insculpta***

Another "land turtle" often seen far from water, wandering in woods and fields. ▶ Adults have *orange* on neck and legs. *Very rough shell,* each large scute with raised center surrounded by ridges. Compare to Diamond-backed Terrapin (p. 258).

POND SLIDER (RED-EARED SLIDER) ***Trachemys scripta***

A turtle of the south-central U.S., not native to New England, but found in the wild here after people "liberate" pet turtles. A troublesome invasive in some areas, possibly competing with native species. Favors marshy ponds or slow-moving streams, often seen basking on logs. ▶ Patterned shell, yellow head stripes, broad red "ear" stripe (less obvious on adult males).

TURTLES

(size given is average shell length of adults)

Spotted Turtle (2 examples)
4″

Painted Turtle
5¼″

Eastern Musk Turtle
4″

Blanding's Turtle
6″

Eastern Box Turtle
5¼″

Pond Slider
6″

Wood Turtle
6½″

The four highly distinctive creatures shown here are from four different families. Snapping Turtle is in the family **Chelydridae;** Diamond-backed Terrapin is in the family **Emydidae** like most on p. 256. Loggerheads (like most sea turtles) are in the family **Cheloniidae,** while the Leatherback is the only member of the family **Dermochelyidae.**

SNAPPING TURTLE ***Chelydra serpentina***

A big, tough turtle with a bad temper and strong jaws. Common in most freshwater habitats (and even brackish marshes). Usually in the water, not basking in the sun like other turtles, but will wander far on land. Can be dangerous if cornered on land, lunging with lightning reflexes and strong jaws, but usually docile and harmless if encountered in the water. In early summer, females come out on land to dig holes for laying eggs. ▶ Can be huge, with shell more than a foot long. Big ugly head, small eyes, *long tail with saw-toothed upper ridge.* Baby Snappers are small (shell about an inch long at hatching) and long-tailed; the shell is rougher than the adult's, dark with *pale spots along the edge.*

DIAMOND-BACKED TERRAPIN ***Malaclemys terrapin***

A coastal turtle, limited to salt and brackish marshes, tidal creeks, bays. In the early 1900s it was endangered because it was too popular as a gourmet food item; it has made a comeback since but is now threatened by destruction of its habitat. ▶ Strong pattern, each large scute of shell with *raised concentric rings.* Head and legs pale gray with *dark dots.* Habitat is a good clue.

LOGGERHEAD SEA TURTLE ***Caretta caretta***

Sea turtles are magnificent reptiles of the open ocean, swift and graceful in their swimming. Most populations around the world have been severely reduced by hunting, overharvesting of their eggs, disturbance of nesting beaches, and accidental drowning in commercial fishing and shrimping nets. Five species of sea turtles occur in the western North Atlantic; all have been found in New England waters, but the Loggerhead is the one that is seen most regularly. ▶ Very different in shape from land turtles, with legs modified into flippers. Plain shell, mottled head, with an overall yellow-brown or red-brown tinge. Three other species of sea turtles that occur as rare visitors have a more gray-green or marbled appearance.

LEATHERBACK SEA TURTLE ***Dermochelys coriacea***

The largest species of turtle on earth today, regularly over 5' long and weighing more than half a ton. Occurs in New England waters in small numbers during summer; usually stays far out at sea, but may come closer to shore following schools of jellyfish, its main food item. ▶ Very large size, overall *dark slaty color,* with narrow lighter ridges and sometimes with pale patches. Hard shell is replaced by leathery skin.

TURTLES

(size given is average shell length of adults)

not all shown at same scale

Snapping Turtle
15″

Diamond-backed Terrapin
6″

Loggerhead Sea Turtle
38″

Leatherback Sea Turtle
62″

SNAKES

Most of the snakes in the world are classified in the family **Colubridae,** including the first five below and all of those on p. 262. The Copperhead and Timber Rattlesnake, the only venomous reptiles in New England, are in the family **Viperidae.**

NORTH AMERICAN RACER ***Coluber constrictor***

A well-named snake, speedy and alert. When hunting, it often raises its head and fore part of its body to look around. Surprise one and it will make an amazingly quick getaway. If cornered it may fight back, striking repeatedly and perhaps vibrating its tail, or it may climb up into low branches. ▶ Adult is black above, dark gray below, usually with white on chin and throat. Scales are smooth. Young is gray at first, with dark blotches on back.

EASTERN RATSNAKE ***Pantherophis alleghaniensis***

Mostly uncommon, in rocky woods or field edges. May be seen climbing about in trees; eats many rats and other rodents but also raids birds' nests. ▶ Adult is mostly black above, white on chin and throat; *whitish belly has checkered dark pattern.* Young pale gray at first, with dark blotches.

MILKSNAKE ***Lampropeltis triangulum***

The odd name comes from the old myth that it milks cows. Milksnakes do enter barns — to hunt rats and mice. Fairly common in open woods, fields. ▶ Pale tan with large brown blotches on back and sides. Top of head brown with *Y-shaped pale mark.*

EASTERN HOG-NOSED SNAKE ***Heterodon platirhinos***

Startle this harmless snake and it may puff itself up with loud hissing — and if that doesn't scare you away, it may roll over and play dead. Mainly in sandy habitats, feeding on toads. ▶ *Upturned snout,* blotchy pattern, distinctive behavior.

NORTHERN WATERSNAKE ***Nerodia sipedon***

A superb swimmer, common in ponds, marshes, slow-moving rivers. Avoids people in the water but may bite if cornered on land. ▶ Stout-bodied, dingy, with broad darker brown bands.

COPPERHEAD ***Agkistrodon contortrix***

Uncommon, usually slow-moving, on rocky wooded hillsides. **Venomous and should be avoided.** ▶ Coppery with dark brown crossbands in an *hourglass shape,* usually narrowest at center of back. Wedge-shaped head, vertical pupils.

TIMBER RATTLESNAKE ***Crotalus horridus***

Uncommon, mostly around hillsides in dense forest. Numbers gather in rocky dens in winter. **Venomous. Most snakebites occur when people are unwisely trying to catch snakes.** ▶ Big wedge-shaped head, rattles on tail, dark crossbands. Ground color may be yellowish or very dark.

SNAKES
(size given is average length of adults)

North American Racer 45″

Eastern Ratsnake 50″

Milksnake 30″

Eastern Hog-nosed Snake 24″

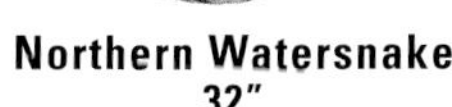

Northern Watersnake 32″

Copperhead 30″

Timber Rattlesnake 45″

SNAKES AND LIZARD

Most of these snakes are smaller or more slender than those on p. 260. Our sole lizard belongs to the skink family **(Scincidae)**.

COMMON GARTERSNAKE ***Thamnophis sirtalis***

A common and widespread snake in many habitats, even found in suburbs and city parks. ▸ Quite variable in color and pattern. Usually has 3 conspicuous pale stripes, with rows of darker spots in the areas between, but some or all of the stripes may be missing. Square spots can be so prominent that pattern looks checkered, especially in northeastern part of our area.

EASTERN RIBBONSNAKE ***Thamnophis sauritus***

Fairly common, but mostly in habitats near water. Seemingly nervous, active, and fast-moving, usually much harder to catch than a gartersnake. ▸ Patterned like some Common Gartersnakes, with 3 contrasting pale stripes, but more slender and elongated, with extremely long tail. Lacks dark spots on belly.

RING-NECKED SNAKE ***Diadophis punctatus***

Common in wet woods but often overlooked, spending much time hiding under logs, rocks, debris. ▸ Smooth gray or brown above with *yellow neck ring,* bright yellow belly. Young of next species also have pale collar but lack bright color on belly.

DEKAY'S BROWNSNAKE ***Storeria dekayi***

Another common but overlooked snake, usually hiding under objects in woods, swamps, city parks. ▸ Brown with vertical stripe on face, parallel rows of black spots down back.

RED-BELLIED SNAKE ***Storeria occipitomaculata***

Locally common in woods, but often hides under logs or rocks. May come out on rainy nights. ▸ Brown above (vaguely striped), usually with *reddish belly, 3 pale spots* on nape.

EASTERN WORMSNAKE ***Carphophis amoenus***

Local in southern New England, almost always under objects or underground in moist soil. ▸ Suggests a large earthworm, brown above and pinkish below, with small head and pointed tail tip.

SMOOTH GREENSNAKE ***Opheodrys vernalis***

Widespread in New England, including some offshore islands. Often in open grassy areas. ▸ Small and slender, *bright green above,* creamy or pale yellow below. Young may be darker.

COMMON FIVE-LINED SKINK ***Plestiodon fasciatus***

One lizard barely reaches New England, living in damp woods around brushpiles, fallen logs. ▸ Easily recognized as our only lizard; compare to salamanders (p. 264). Young are very dark with 5 sharp pale lines, blue tail. Adult female has duller stripes. Adult male may be almost unstriped, with red-orange on head.

variation
(young)

Common Gartersnake
22″

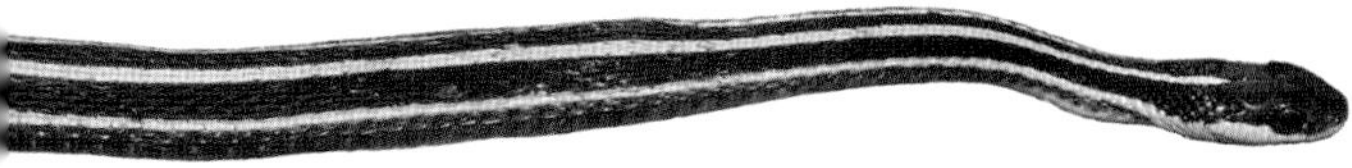

Eastern Ribbonsnake
22″

Ring-necked
Snake
13″

DeKay's
Brownsnake
11″

Red-bellied
Snake
9″

Eastern
Wormsnake
9″

Smooth Greensnake
17″

Common
Five-lined Skink
7″

often go unnoticed by most people, but they are common in some areas of New England, espcially in wet forest and along streams and swamps. All on this page are in the family **Plethodontidae,** salamanders that lack lungs altogether, breathing through their skin and mouth lining.

NORTHERN DUSKY SALAMANDER ***Desmognathus fuscus***

Very common near streams and springs in forested areas, usually found hiding under logs, rocks, or debris close to the water or at the water's edge. ► Tail laterally compressed (higher than wide). Variable in pattern, gray or brown, with darker spots and pale belly. Usually a *pale line* from eye to corner of mouth.

EASTERN RED-BACKED SALAMANDER ***Plethodon cinereus***

Another abundant salamander in New England, regularly found under rocks or logs near streams. Unlike the other salamanders in our area, this species and the next one *lack* an aquatic larval stage; the young hatch out of the eggs with their legs already developed. ► Small and slender, with tiny legs. Color pattern varies: typically dark with a straight-edged reddish stripe down the back ("redback"), but sometimes all dark ("leadback"), occasionally all reddish. Belly *heavily mottled* black and white.

FOUR-TOED SALAMANDER ***Hemidactylium scutatum***

Uncommon, usually found in areas with sphagnum and other mosses, such as bogs, peatlands, wet woods. ► Small, yellowish brown to orange-brown with obscure marks above, but belly is *white with bold black specks.* Base of tail *sharply constricted.* Has 4 toes on each foot (most salamanders have 5 toes on hind feet).

NORTHERN TWO-LINED SALAMANDER ***Eurycea bislineata***

Common almost throughout New England, usually found hiding under stones, logs, or debris close to running streams or swamps. Will wander far from water in rainy weather. ► Mostly some shade of *yellow,* with 2 *irregular dark lines,* running from each eye to the tail. Usually has dark dotting and mottling on the back between the 2 lines.

NORTHERN SLIMY SALAMANDER ***Plethodon glutinosus***

Uncommon and localized in New England, found mainly on rocky hillsides in forested areas. If you pick up this salamander, you may get slimed with a whitish goo from its skin glands; wash this off before it dries, or you may be wearing it for days. ► Mostly *glossy black* with many *sharply defined white spots.*

SPRING SALAMANDER ***Gyrinophilus porphyriticus***

Localized and usually uncommon around flowing springs and clear, cold mountain streams, sometimes found under rocks at the water's edge. ► Relatively large, *pinkish brown* to dull reddish overall, with vague pattern of darker mottling.

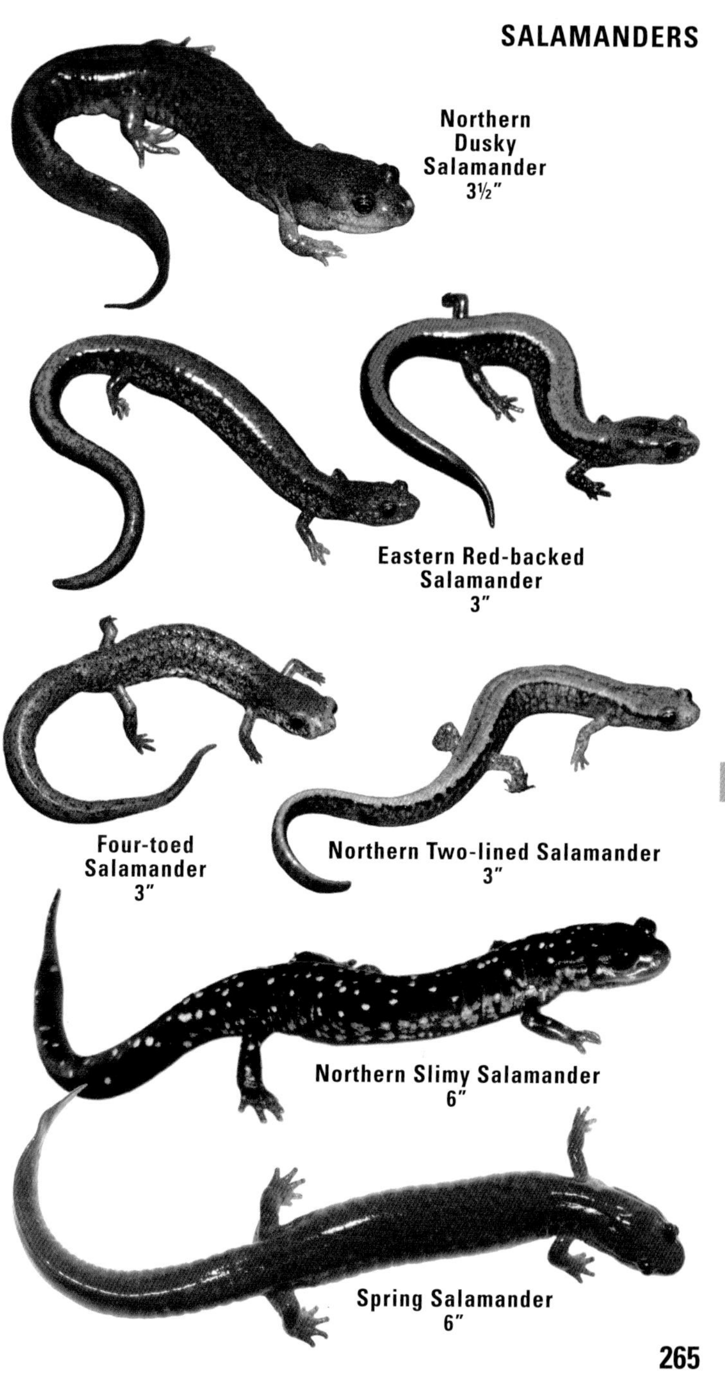

Northern Dusky Salamander
3½″

Eastern Red-backed Salamander
3″

Four-toed Salamander
3″

Northern Two-lined Salamander
3″

Northern Slimy Salamander
6″

Spring Salamander
6″

SALAMANDERS

The first four species below are in the family **Ambystomatidae** (Mole salamanders). Newts (family **Salamandridae**) and Mudpuppies (family **Necturidae**) are distinctly odd, even more so than other salamanders.

MARBLED SALAMANDER ***Ambystoma opacum***

Uncommon. Most often seen in forest in early fall. Female lays eggs in dried-up pond, stays with them until autumn rains flood the pond and the eggs hatch. ▶ Beautifully and variably patterned with white (male) or gray (female) bands on glossy black.

BLUE-SPOTTED SALAMANDER ***Ambystoma laterale***

This species and the next interbreed where their ranges come in contact, and some experts say that all of New England is occupied by a hybrid zone. Many seen here will look intermediate, but we show typical examples of the two parental forms. Both breed in early spring in woodland pools. ▶ Glossy black, very heavily marked with *blue* or bluish white *spots*. Toes are relatively long.

JEFFERSON SALAMANDER ***Ambystoma jeffersonianum***

(not shown) The southern replacement for Blue-spotted Salamander, hybridizing with it throughout New England and nearby areas. ▶ Averages larger than Blue-spotted, with longer toes and longer snout. Very plain overall, grayish to brownish, usually with fine blue speckles on sides. Many seen here will look intermediate between the two species and will not be identifiable.

SPOTTED SALAMANDER ***Ambystoma maculatum***

Most likely to be noticed the night of the first warm rain of early spring, when large numbers may migrate to the vernal pools where they will breed. Sometimes found under logs or rocks at other seasons. ▶ Glossy black with numerous *round, yellow spots,* often tending more toward orange on head.

EASTERN NEWT ***Notophthalmus viridescens***

Aquatic as a larva and as an adult, but in between there is usually — not always — a terrestrial stage, the Red Eft, that wanders on land for as long as 3 years. Foul secretions from skin glands apparently protect it from predators. ▶ Adults yellowish green with red spots, the male in spring with a high tail fin. Red Eft is rough-skinned, orange to dull red, with red spots.

MUDPUPPY ***Necturus maculosus***

It looks like a grotesque little space alien, but it's actually a big salamander. The Mudpuppy is not often seen because it is active mostly at night and entirely aquatic, living in rivers, lakes, and large ponds. Populations in New England are mostly introduced. Sometimes caught on fishing lines; completely harmless despite its gross appearance. ▶ Large, stout, with laterally flattened tail. Variably gray-brown with dark spots, reddish brown gills.

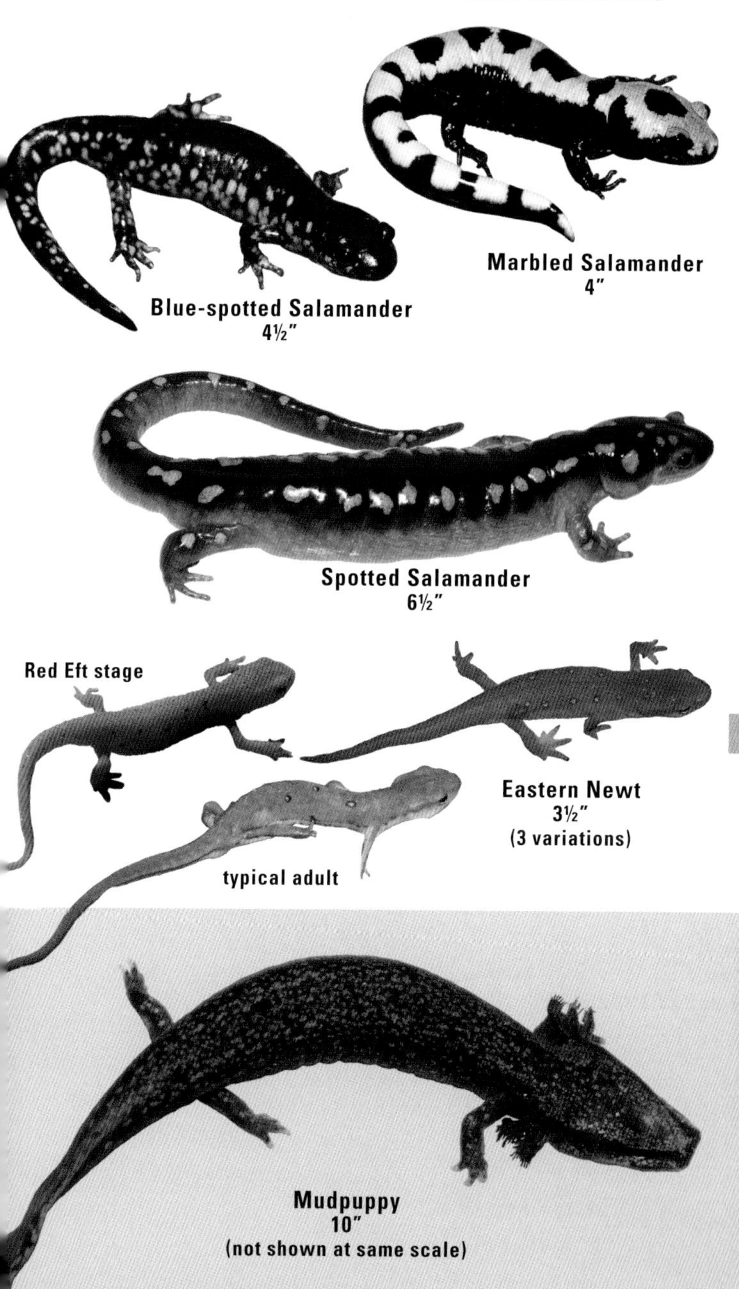

Blue-spotted Salamander
4½″

Marbled Salamander
4″

Spotted Salamander
6½″

Red Eft stage

Eastern Newt
3½″
(3 variations)

typical adult

Mudpuppy
10″
(not shown at same scale)

TOADS AND FROGS

are familiar sights and sounds throughout New England. Those on this page represent three families: Toads **(Bufonidae)**, spadefoots **(Pelobatidae)**, and treefrogs and related species **(Hylidae)**.

AMERICAN TOAD ***Anaxyrus americanus***

Common and widespread in practically any habitat, including back yards; this is the toad commonly found in gardens. Contrary to legend, toads don't cause warts, but their skin secretions can irritate the eyes or mouth; if you handle a toad, be sure to wash hands thoroughly. ▶ Toads differ from frogs in shorter hind legs, bumpy skin. On this species, large dark spots on back have only 1 or 2 "warts" each, and chest has dark spots. ♪ **Voice:** a long, musical trill, lasting up to half a minute.

FOWLER'S TOAD ***Anaxyrus fowleri***

Locally common in parts of southern New England, mostly in sandy areas. ▶ Similar to American Toad, but largest dark spots on back usually have *3 or more* raised warts, not just 1 or 2, and the chest usually lacks dark spots. ♪ **Voice:** a short, nasal *wrraaah,* lasting up to 4 seconds.

EASTERN SPADEFOOT ***Scaphiopus holbrookii***

Rare and mysterious, spending most of its life underground, in regions of sandy soil. Emerges mainly after heavy rains have fallen at any time during the warmer months. ▶ Stout-bodied, big-eyed. Fairly dark, with pair of pale lines on back. A sharp-edged black "spade" on the underside of each hind foot, good for digging. ♪ **Voice:** sharp, bleating grunt.

SPRING PEEPER ***Pseudacris crucifer***

Common throughout most of New England, Spring Peepers begin calling at night from marshes, ponds, and vernal pools very early in spring. At other times of year they are mostly in woods, thickets. Sometimes heard calling at any season, even on warm days in midwinter. ▶ Very small and relatively plain, but with a rough × pattern on its back. ♪ **Voice:** a sharp, high-pitched *peep* repeated at intervals of 1 or 2 seconds. Large concentrations of peepers can be incredibly loud at close range.

GRAY TREEFROG ***Hyla versicolor***

Often goes unseen, spending most of its time up in trees and shrubs. Comes down to water's edge in swamps, ponds, or wet meadows for breeding season in spring. ▶ Highly variable in color. Usually green or dark gray, but may be brown, tan, or pale gray, and an individual may change color. Usually has a *pale spot* below each eye. ♪ **Voice:** a loud, rough trill.

American Toad
2¾″

Fowler's Toad
2½″

Eastern Spadefoot
2″

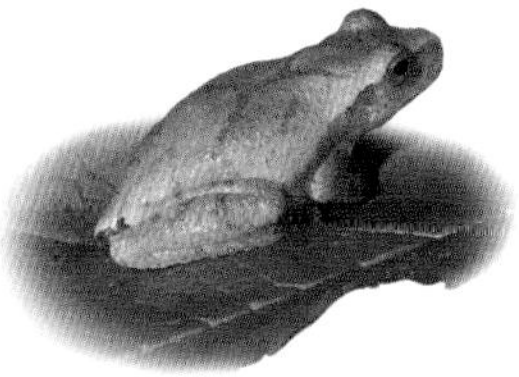

Spring Peeper
1″

Gray Treefrog
1¾″

(examples of 2 colors)

TYPICAL FROGS

(family **Ranidae**) have relatively smooth skin and long legs, compared to the species on p. 268. All of the frogs below were formerly classified in the genus *Rana,* and this name is still used in some books.

AMERICAN BULLFROG ***Lithobates catesbeianus***

Our largest frog, found around larger marshes, ponds, lakes, rivers, more common toward the south. ▶ Large size and relatively unpatterned look are good marks. Lacks ridges on back shown by Green Frog. Male has yellowish throat, and tympanum ("eardrum") larger than eye. ♪ **Voice**: deep, rolling bass, *jug-a-rumm.*

GREEN FROG ***Lithobates clamitans***

Very common around ponds, marshes, streams, other fresh waters throughout our area. ▶ Variable in color, may be mostly green or mostly brown (or rarely blue!). Male has bright yellow throat, larger eardrum. Dark blotches on back may be heavy. Differs from Bullfrog in prominent *raised ridge* down either side of back. ♪ **Voice**: a sudden, twangy *glunk,* sometimes repeated.

MINK FROG ***Lithobates septentrionalis***

Cold northern lakes and streams are home to this darkly patterned frog. Named for the smell given off by its skin (useful if you happen to know what a mink smells like!). ▶ Greenish with heavy dark spots above. Green Frog can be very similar, but always has raised ridges on back (Mink Frog sometimes lacks them), and has cross-bands on hind legs (Mink Frog has dark blotches there). ♪ **Voice**: throaty *tuk-tuk-tuk-tuk-tuk.*

WOOD FROG ***Lithobates sylvaticus***

Common in moist forests, often found far from open water. Our most cold-hardy frog, gathering at shallow ponds very early in spring, then dispersing into surrounding area. ▶ Variable in color, from tan to pinkish to brown, with a *dark brown mask* behind the eye. ♪ **Voice**: a hoarse and rather weak quacking sound.

PICKEREL FROG ***Lithobates palustris***

Common around ponds, bogs, and slow-flowing streams in spring, wandering out into open habitats in summer. ▶ Known by the *parallel rows* of *squarish spots* down the back. Bright yellow on inner surface of hind legs may show when the frog is hopping. ♪ **Voice**: a rough, snoring sound, lasting up to 2 seconds.

NORTHERN LEOPARD FROG ***Lithobates pipiens***

Widespread, but usually less common than Pickerel Frog. Found around marshes, ponds, and vernal pools in spring, wandering widely through open habitats in summer. ▶ Patterned above with pale-edged dark spots, much more irregular than those of Pickerel Frog. ♪ **Voice**: irregular deep snore, up to 3 seconds long, broken up with rattling clucks.

American Bullfrog
4½″

Green Frog
3″

Mink Frog
2½″

Wood Frog
2¼″

Pickerel Frog
2½″

Northern Leopard Frog
2¾″

FISHES

As a group, fishes have been vitally important to the economy of New England, with some coastal communities having been supported for many generations by commercial fishing operations. Recreational fishing is now also a mainstay of many areas, both along the coast and on inland lakes and rivers. Fish-watching as a hobby is still in its infancy, but it may be expected to grow as more people become fascinated with the sheer diversity of underwater life.

New England has several hundred species of fish; we treat only a few of the more common or interesting ones here.

Identifying fish is something that we often do in the hand, after catching a fish with hook and line or with a net. In some situations, we can watch wild fish in the water. In either situation, to identify them, we should start by looking at shape and structure, following up with color and markings as secondary clues.

Although we avoid technical jargon in this guide, it's useful to know a few terms for the parts of the fish, as labelled on the diagram below.

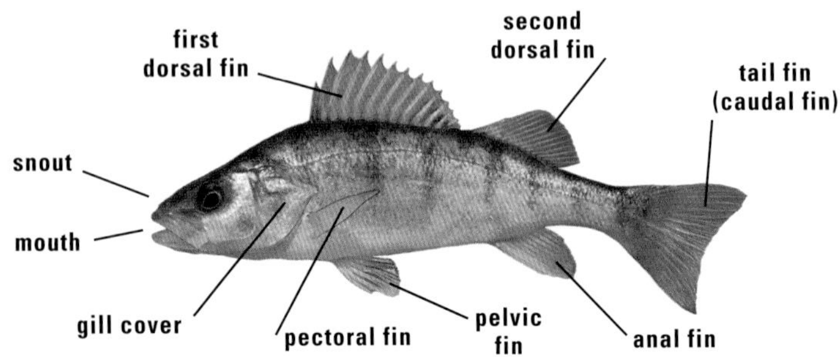

Size is a useful clue in fish ID, but it varies quite a lot within species. In this guide, we give sample lengths of typical adults, but these are intended only to give a very general idea.

Color and pattern are also helpful in identification, as long as we keep in mind that they can vary. In some cases, young fish are strikingly different in pattern from adults of their species. Individuals may vary in color depending on whether they live in fresh or salt water, or depending on other factors in their environment. Males and females may differ in color. And in some species, males in breeding condition may become very brightly colored, enough so that they look utterly different from their normal state.

Location is another good clue in identifying fish. The distinction between inland and oceanic species is important, and in this guide we make a point of indicating whether a fish is found in fresh or salt water, or both. Even within these broad categories, locations and habitats differ. Some freshwater fish, for example, live in deep, cold lakes, others in marshy ponds, while others favor fast-flowing streams and rivers. Among saltwater fish, some live in the shallows close to the coast, while others tend to stay far offshore and seldom come close to land.

There are a number of fish that migrate regularly between fresh and salt water. For example, American Shad live at sea for most of the year, but in spring they swim up rivers in order to spawn (that is, to lay their eggs), with the adults returning to the sea if they survive the trip. A species that reproduces in this way is said to be anadromous.

Behavior would be an excellent way to identify fish, if it were not so hard for us to observe most of the time! Avid anglers learn many things about fish behavior in an indirect way. For example, some fish will go only for bait that is dragged along the bottom, while others will go for a lure at the surface. Some fish are solitary, scattered through the habitat, while others travel in loose groups or in dense concentrations called schools. In fact, skilled anglers generally have very detailed knowledge about the lives of various fishes, and you can learn a lot by talking with them, or by going fishing yourself.

Conservation is a concern with fish, as with other groups of living things. Some species that were formerly abundant, such as Atlantic Cod and Atlantic Bluefin Tuna, have been seriously depleted by overfishing. Laws to protect populations of fish have been improving, and most U.S. fishing fleets now harvest fish at sustainable levels. Sport fishing, too, can be practiced in a sustainable way, and there is no reason not to enjoy fishing in New England as long as we adhere to established limits and seasons.

In New England's inland and coastal waters, threats to fish populations are more likely to come from things like water pollution and introduction of invasive species. In some cases, fish species that were stocked intentionally have turned out to have negative impacts on native species. Common Carp, for example, often degrade the habitat in shallow ponds, rooting out vegetation and muddying the water. Brown Trout, introduced from Eurasia, may outcompete our native Brook Trout.

Some of the most serious problems are caused by commercial fishing in international waters, which is often poorly regulated. Currently the most critical issue involves killing of sharks for the supposed "delicacy" of shark fin soup. There are many documented cases of people cutting the fins off of live sharks and then throwing the helpless fish back in the water to die. We need more public pressure to stop this barbaric practice. Not only is it obviously inhumane, but many shark species around the world are rapidly disappearing. As in any other ecosystem, these top predators are necessary for maintaining the balance of nature in the oceans.

LAMPREY, SKATES, AND SMALLER SHARKS

Lampreys probably should not be considered fish at all; recent studies place them in a completely different group. To put this in perspective, a typical fish such as a trout may be more closely related to dogs, cats, or robins than it is to a lamprey! Skates, rays, and sharks also make up a class separate from the typical fishes. They are referred to collectively as cartilaginous fishes because their skeletons are made of cartilage, not bone. They lack the swim bladders of the bony fishes, so they must be actively swimming at all times to keep from sinking to the bottom.

SEA LAMPREY ***Petromyzon marinus***
A lamprey has no jaws. Its mouth is a round disk like a suction cup, which it uses to attach to other fish, rasping a hole in the skin and sucking its blood and body juices. This species occurs at sea off the New England coast, entering rivers to spawn. Lamprey family (Petromyzontidae). ► Snakelike but with 2 dorsal fins, small tail fin. Mostly brown, often with heavy darker mottling.

LITTLE SKATE ***Leucoraja erinacea***
Skates are broad, flat fishes, roughly diamond-shaped but with long tails. They spend most of their time on the ocean floor, and they swim by flapping their fins, appearing to "fly" underwater. They feed on small fishes and other small bottom-dwelling creatures. Skates lay their eggs in rectangular cases that are often found washed up on beaches (see p. 380). Skate family (Rajidae). ► Distinctive shape; brown to gray above, with irregular pattern of scattered darker spots.

BARNDOOR SKATE ***Dipturus laevis***
One of the largest species of skates (up to 5' long), the Barndoor was formerly common off the New England coast, but its numbers have declined seriously and it is now considered endangered. Some are still caught as incidental bycatch by trawling operations. Skate family. ► Similar to Little Skate but gets *much larger;* tips of "wings" and snout more pointed.

SMOOTH DOGFISH ***Mustelus canis***
This small shark was formerly common along the New England coast, mainly over muddy bottoms near shore. Numbers have been depleted by overfishing. Hound shark family (Triakidae). ► Slender body with 2 large dorsal fins. Tail fin with *distinct notch;* some lower fins white-edged. Uniformly dark gray above, whitish on belly.

SPINY DOGFISH ***Squalus acanthias***
Formerly very common off New England, from near shore out to edge of continental shelf, often hunting in large schools. Now much depleted by overfishing. Dogfish shark family (Squalidae). ► Long and slender, with narrow, pointed snout. Some fins pale-edged, but tail fin *lacks* obvious notch. Gray to blue-gray above, usually with pattern of small white spots; whitish below.

LAMPREY, SKATES, SHARKS

(sizes given are *average* lengths of adults; some individuals can be much larger or smaller)

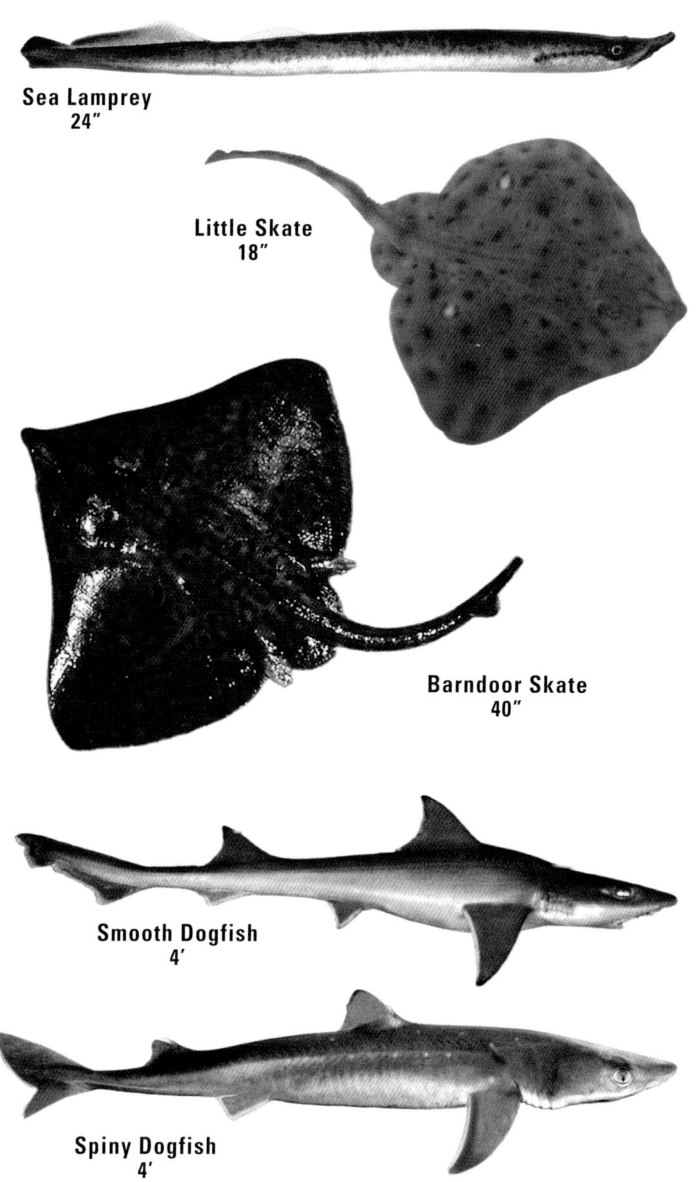

Sea Lamprey
24″

Little Skate
18″

Barndoor Skate
40″

Smooth Dogfish
4′

Spiny Dogfish
4′

LARGE SHARKS

As mentioned on p. 274, sharks belong to a group known as cartilaginous fishes, having skeletons made of cartilage rather than bone.

WHITE SHARK ***Carcharodon carcharias***

A powerful swimmer, usually staying well offshore but sometimes coming into coastal waters. Curious and aggressive, has been known to attack humans in New England waters, although it is hardly the bloodthirsty monster that has been portrayed in popular fiction. Mackerel shark family (Lamnidae). ▶ Dark blue-gray to pale gray above, whitish below. Bluntly pointed snout. Lower lobe of tail fin nearly as large as upper lobe.

SHORTFIN MAKO ***Isurus oxyrinchus*** **(not shown)**

A shark of the open ocean, usually near the surface. Popular as a sport fish because of its active and acrobatic behavior, leaping and fighting when hooked, but populations are now at risk because of overfishing. Mackerel shark family. ▶ Blue gray to slaty above, whitish below. Pointed snout. As in White Shark, lower lobe of tail fin nearly as large as upper lobe.

BLUE SHARK ***Prionace glauca***

Uncommon but widespread out at sea, seldom coming close to shore. Requiem shark family (Carcharinidae). ▶ Dark slaty blue above, paler blue-gray on sides, whitish below. Elongated and slender, with a long, pointed snout. Upper lobe of tail fin longer than lower (as in most sharks). *Long,* slender pectoral fins.

SAND TIGER ***Odontaspis taurus***

A shark of shallow waters, generally foraging close to the bottom, from areas near shore out to the edge of the continental shelf. Slow-moving and not aggressive, although some of its relatives elsewhere in the world can be dangerous. Sand tiger family (Odontaspididae). ▶ Brownish gray above, with *darker spots,* mainly concentrated toward tail. Second dorsal fin near *same size* as first.

THRESHER SHARK ***Alopias vulpinus***

Widespread at sea, but mostly far offshore. Threshers are fast swimmers that reportedly use their very long tails to herd and stun their prey. Thresher shark family (Alopiidae). ▶ *Very long* upper lobe of tail fin, nearly as long as body. Dark brownish gray to bluish gray above, with white (often broken up into patches) below.

BASKING SHARK ***Cetorhinus maximus***

A very large, sluggish shark, often found resting (or "basking") near the water's surface. Not aggressive, but its large size and habit of swimming just below the surface may pose a hazard for small boats. Basking shark family (Cetorhinidae). ▶ Dusky gray, sometimes with hint of stripes. Large head and large mouth, with tip of snout rounded. Gill slits on side of head are *very long.*

LARGE SHARKS
(not all shown at same scale)

White Shark
12′

Blue Shark
8–10′

Sand Tiger
10′

Thresher Shark
19′

Basking Shark
30′

SALTWATER FISH

Most on this page are popular with anglers.

ATLANTIC COD ***Gadus morhua***

Widespread in the North Atlantic, this was once the most important commercial fish in our region. Overfishing led to a general population collapse in the 1990s. Numbers have not recovered, even though an adult female can lay millions of eggs in a single spawning season. A generalized feeder, found from near shore to deep water. Cod family (Gadidae). ▸ Body tapered at both ends, heaviest toward front. Has 3 dorsal fins. Tail fin *straight-edged*. Single barbel on chin. Color variable, brownish to olive, but usually with *numerous dark spots* on back and sides.

POLLOCK ***Pollachius virens***

A popular sport fish, traveling in large schools. Younger fish are often near shore, adults in deeper water. Cod family. ▸ Has 3 dorsal fins. Tail fin with *shallow fork*. Lower jaw projects *beyond* upper; tiny barbel on chin, or none. Dark on back, fading to dull olive on sides and paler below, with whitish lateral line.

HADDOCK ***Melanogrammus aeglefinus***

Another fish of importance to sport anglers and commercial fishing, although numbers have been reduced. Adults are usually in deep water, younger fish are more often in the shallows. Cod family. ▸ Has 3 dorsal fins, the first one taller. Small barbel on chin. Pale silvery gray overall with *dark* lateral line, usually with dark spot on side just above pectoral fin.

BLACK SEA BASS ***Centropristis striata***

Mostly in fairly shallow water, often around jetties, piers, and other structures. Common north to Cape Cod, scarcer north to southern coast of Maine. Sea bass family (Serranidae). ▸ Spiny dorsal fin with *pale bars* and small *white tips*. Tail fin rounded but with short trailing streamers at top and bottom. Dark gray overall with irregular darker bars.

TAUTOG ***Tautoga onitis***

Common in waters along the coast, especially in rocky areas and around piers and docks. May move to deeper water in winter. This and the next species may swim by flapping their broad pectoral fins. Wrasse family (Labridae). ▸ Rounded head, blunt snout. Full-grown males mostly dark, with *white chin*, pale belly, *white spot* on side. Females (and small males) paler and heavily mottled.

CUNNER ***Tautogolabrus adspersus***

Common close to shore, also found over offshore shallows such as Georges Bank. Around rocky areas or eelgrass beds. Aggressive and active, adept at stealing bait. Wrasse family. ▸ Snout more pointed than on Tautog. Thick lips. Quite variable in color, dull reddish or orange to dull olive, usually glossy overall and with some darker mottling.

SALTWATER FISH

(sizes given are average lengths of adults)

Atlantic Cod
35″

Pollock
30″

Haddock
20″

Black Sea Bass
14″

Tautog
18″

Cunner
10″

MOSTLY SALTWATER FISH

All of these are found in coastal waters of New England. The first three are also found in fresh water, at least in spawning season.

STRIPED BASS ***Morone saxatilis***
Common from late spring through early fall all along the New England coast, also moving upstream along many major rivers. Most of the population migrates farther south for the winter. Also called "Striper" and "Rockfish." Temperate bass family (Moronidae). ▶ Slightly elongated shape, 2 dorsal fins. Adults blue-gray to grayish green on back, pale on sides, with about 7 *distinct dark stripes* along sides.

WHITE PERCH ***Morone americana***
Widespread in New England, both on inland waters and along the immediate coast, favoring fresh and brackish waters. Despite the name, not a true perch, but a member of the temperate bass family. ▶ Body compact in profile, deep and laterally compressed, with 2 dorsal fins. Mostly silvery white, darker along center of back, especially on large individuals. Juveniles may have pale stripes along sides.

ATLANTIC TOMCOD ***Microgadus tomcod***
Fairly common along the coast, including brackish water of estuaries, entering rivers to spawn in winter. Cod family (Gadidae). ▶ Has 3 dorsal fins, rounded tail fin. Overall yellowish brown with darker mottling, including on dorsal and tail fins. One ray of pelvic fin is greatly elongated.

SILVER HAKE ***Merluccius bilinearis***
Common and widespread offshore, generally closer to the coast in late spring and summer, in deeper water in winter. A fast-swimming predator, hunting mostly at night. Merlucciid hake family (Merlucciidae). ▶ Has 2 dorsal fins, first short, second running almost to tail, but with *dip* in edge. Large mouth, large teeth. Mostly pale silvery, slightly darker on back.

RED HAKE ***Urophycis chuss***
Another common offshore fish that comes closer to the coast in summer. Usually stays close to areas with a sandy or muddy bottom. Phycid hake family (Phycidae). ▶ Has 2 dorsal fins, first one short but with long streamer, second running almost to tail. Pelvic fins reduced to long, narrow streamers. Mostly brown to reddish, with pale mottling.

WHITE HAKE ***Urophycis tenuis*** **(not shown)**
Very common offshore, especially near muddy bottom areas in the Gulf of Maine. Phycid Hake family. ▶ Similar to Red Hake but grows significantly larger, regularly to 28", up to 50" or larger. Variable in color, brown to olive to gray. Young individuals difficult to separate from Red Hake.

SCUP (PORGY) ***Stenotomus chrysops***
Fairly common along coast and offshore, traveling in schools, mostly near bottom. Porgy family (Sparidae). ▶ Very *rounded* shape in profile. Pale silvery, sometimes with darker bars. Vague blue spot above eye, bluish line along center of back.

Striped Bass
26″

White Perch
11″

Atlantic Tomcod
11″

Silver Hake
14″

Red Hake
12″

Scup
12″

HERRINGS AND OTHERS

The first two species below support major fishing industries; the next two are most famous for their upriver runs in late spring.

ATLANTIC HERRING ***Clupea harengus***
Abundant in waters over the continental shelf, more numerous off Maine in summer, off southern New England in winter. Herring travel in schools, often with vast numbers of individuals. They feed on plankton, tiny creatures drifting in the water, especially copepods and other extremely small crustaceans. Although full-grown herring themselves are not large, their sheer abundance has made them the center of an important commercial fishery, and they are also a significant food source for many larger species of fish. Herring family (Clupeidae). ▶ Elongated and small-headed, with upturned mouth, jutting lower jaw. Has 1 dorsal fin, forked tail fin. Silvery overall, slightly darker on back.

ATLANTIC MENHADEN ***Brevoortia tyrannus***
Another small, abundant fish that forms immense schools in coastal waters and offshore, usually traveling near the surface. Like the preceding species, menhaden support a major commercial fishing industry, and they are also important prey for larger fish. Herring family. ▶ Deeper body and larger head than Atlantic Herring. Mostly pale silvery, with *dark spot* behind gills and smaller dark spots scattered on sides. Fins tinged yellowish.

ALEWIFE ***Alosa pseudoharengus***
Common offshore most of the year, traveling in schools, coming closer to the surface at night. It draws more attention in spring, however, from early May to early June, when large numbers of Alewives travel up coastal rivers to spawn. Herring family. ▶ Like related species, has 1 dorsal fin, forked tail fin. Noticeably large eyes. Dull blue-gray on back, pale silvery on sides, with *dark spot* behind gills; some have narrow darker stripes along sides.

AMERICAN SHAD ***Alosa sapidissima***
Another common offshore fish that is noticed mainly in late spring, when it swims up rivers to spawn, mainly in May and June. After spawning, the adults return to the ocean. At sea, they may travel in schools of thousands. This is the official state fish of Connecticut. Herring family. ▶ Like preceding species, has 1 dorsal fin, forked tail fin. Body looks deep in profile. Unlike Alewife, eyes are relatively small. Mostly pale silvery, with dark spot behind gills, often followed by row of smaller, fainter spots.

SAND LANCE ***Ammodytes* sp.**
These odd little fish are very adept at burying themselves in soft sand. In shallow coastal waters they may simply bury themselves at low tide, emerging again after the tide comes in. Large schools of sand lances offshore may travel close to surface and may attract feeding concentrations of birds and larger fish. We have 2 very similar species in the sand lance family (Ammodytidae). ▶ Long, narrow shape, with pointed snout. Single dorsal fin runs most of length of body.

HERRINGS AND OTHERS

(sizes given are average lengths of adults)

Atlantic Herring
10″

Atlantic Menhaden
10″

Alewife
11″

American Shad
20″

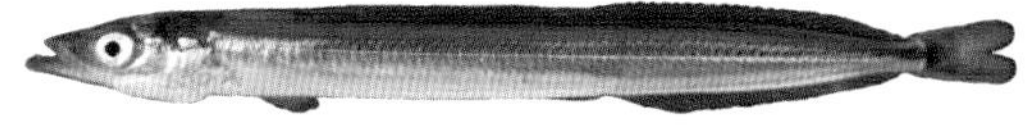

Sand Lance
6″

LARGE SALTWATER FISH

The first four species below are important to commercial fisheries, sport anglers, or both.

BLUEFISH ***Pomatomus saltatrix***
Widespread and common over the continental shelf off New England during the warmer months, moving farther south for the winter. Adults hunt actively in groups, pursuing smaller fish and squid, voraciously snapping at them. At times, when Bluefish have chased schools of small fish into the shallows near public beaches, swimmers caught in the melee have been bitten. Bluefish family (Pomatomidae). ▶ Torpedo-shaped with large head, jutting lower jaw, numerous teeth. Mostly pale silvery, with dark spot at base of pectoral fin, dark blue-gray back.

ATLANTIC MACKEREL ***Scomber scombrus***
Large schools of Mackerel are common over the outer continental shelf, often swimming fast near the surface. Some move in closer to shore, especially in summer. Mackerel family (Scombridae). ▶ Long-bodied and streamlined, but with fairly large head and large mouth. Has 2 dorsal fins, well separated. Blue to blue-green above, silvery below; back patterned with *wavy black lines* extending about halfway down body.

ATLANTIC BLUEFIN TUNA ***Thunnus thynnus***
These magnificent ocean fish are long-distance migrants, spawning mostly in the Gulf of Mexico and then moving north to colder waters. Schools may travel thousands of miles, even crossing the Atlantic. Slow to mature, they may not spawn until they are several years old, but they may live for 40 years. Their populations have been seriously depleted by overfishing. Mackerel family. ▶ Large head and deep body tapering to narrow base before crescent-shaped tail fin. Blue-black on back, sides silvery with angled paler bars. Tiny yellow finlets near base of tail.

SWORDFISH ***Xiphias gladius***
A fast-swimming, predatory fish, usually traveling alone or in very loose groups. Typically well offshore. Swordfish family (Xiphiidae). ▶ Long "bill" is flattened, swordlike, in cross-section. Crescent-shaped tail fin. Mostly dark gray above, pale below. Note: 2 species that occur north to our region, **Blue Marlin** *(Makaira nigricans)* and **White Marlin** *(Kajikia albida)*, are similar, but their "bills" are rounded in cross-section and they usually show a barred pattern on the sides.

OCEAN SUNFISH ***Mola mola***
This bizarre creature, essentially looking like a gigantic fish head with a couple of fins attached, is widespread in warm oceans of the world. In New England waters it is uncommon, seen mainly in summer and fall. Feeding mainly on jellyfish, it may be a strong swimmer underwater, but in our region it is most often seen basking and drifting near the water's surface. Mola family (Molidae). ▶ Distinctive shape makes it almost unmistakable. **Sharptail Mola** *(Masturus lanceolatus)*, which may occur north to Massachusetts, is similar but smaller, with a pointed projection on the tail fin.

LARGE SALTWATER FISH
(not all shown at same scale)

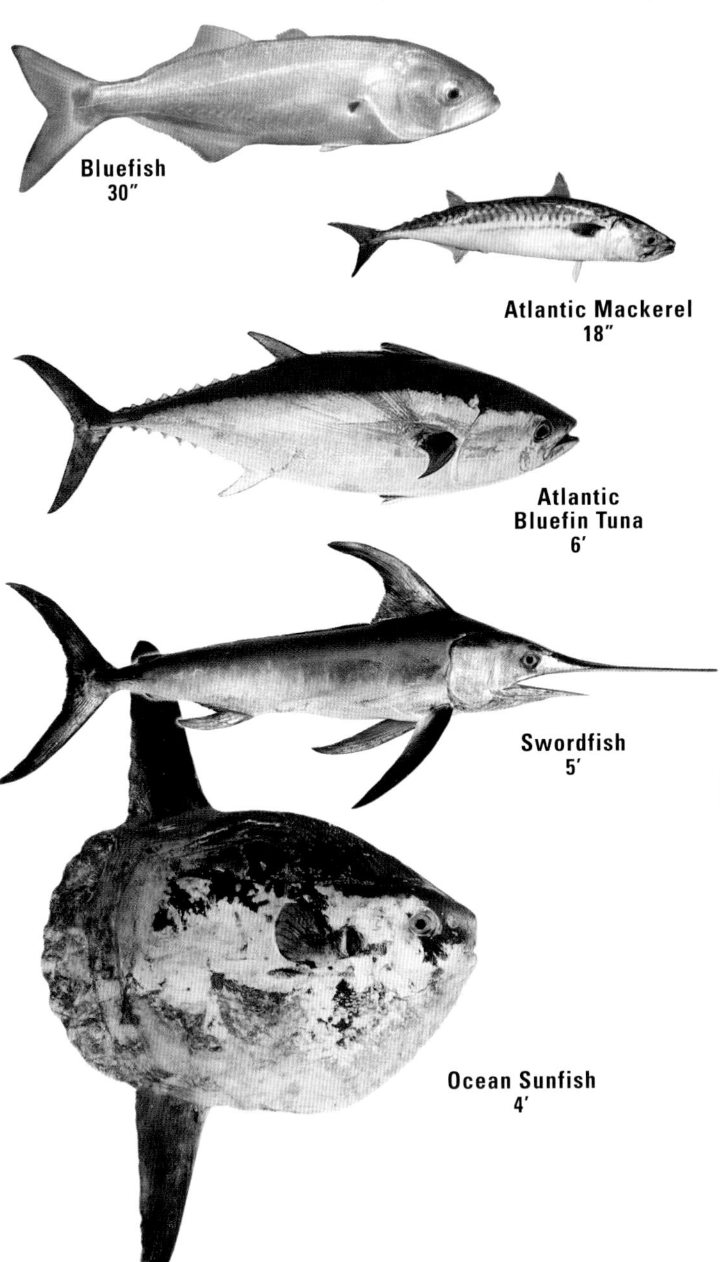

Bluefish
30″

Atlantic Mackerel
18″

Atlantic
Bluefin Tuna
6′

Swordfish
5′

Ocean Sunfish
4′

LINED SEAHORSE ***Hippocampus erectus***
We might imagine them dwelling only in aquaria or cartoons, but real seahorses live off our coast, in shallow waters with much vegetation. Female lays eggs, male broods them in special pouch. Pipefish family (Syngnathidae). ▶ Distinctive shape with horselike head, prehensile tail (which it coils around plant stems). Body may sport fleshy filaments.

LUMPFISH ***Cyclopterus lumpus***
This rotund, sluggish fish hugs the bottom, mainly in rocky areas. Modified fins on the underside may act as a suction cup to hold it in place. Lumpfish family (Cyclopteridae). ▶ Round shape, body covered with *knobby bumps,* including rows on sides. Gray to brown; breeding male red below.

LONGHORN SCULPIN ***Myoxocephalus octodecemspinosus***
Common near the bottom in bays, estuaries, and offshore banks. Sculpin family (Cottidae). ▶ Large, blunt head, with long spines. Color varies with surroundings; always marked with darker bars on body, banding on fins. **Shorthorn Sculpin** *(M. scorpius)* and **Grubby** *(M. aeneus)* are similar.

OYSTER TOADFISH ***Opsanus tau***
Mostly close to shore, over rocky bottoms, around jetties, debris. Whistles and grunts during courtship. Toadfish family (Batrachoididae). ▶ Color variable (can change with surroundings). Fleshy protuberances around head, heavily mottled body, banded pattern on fins.

ATLANTIC WOLFFISH ***Anarhichas lupus***
An aggressive and voracious predator, living over hard, rocky bottoms, often near shore. Wolffish family (Anarhichadidae). ▶ *Large head* with protruding teeth, body tapering to small tail. Mostly gray to blue-gray, with darker bars most obvious toward front; smaller ones more mottled.

SUMMER FLOUNDER ***Paralichthys dentatus***
This and the next 2 species represent 3 families of flatfishes — which are, in a word, flat, with both eyes on one side and the other side featureless. This one lies on sandy or muddy bottoms of bays and estuaries, mostly in southern New England. Sand flounder family (Paralichthyidae). ▶ Variable in color, usually mottled brown, often with neat pattern of *ringed spots.*

WINDOWPANE ***Scophthalmus aquosus***
Also called "Sand Dab." Common on sandy bottoms close to the coast. Turbot family (Scophthalmidae). ▶ Body has round outline, but fins give it an overall diamond shape. Usually reddish brown to buff, heavily marked with darker spots. Body is so flat as to be translucent, hence the name.

ATLANTIC HALIBUT ***Hippoglossus hippoglossus***
Formerly common in New England's offshore waters, this big flatfish was heavily overfished years ago and its population has never recovered; it remains scarce here. Righteye flounder family (Pleuronectidae). ▶ Broadly diamond-shaped. Large adults dark above, with faint mottling; smaller ones more obviously mottled. Tail fin broad, with *concave edge.*

DISTINCTIVE SALTWATER FISH
(not all shown at same scale)

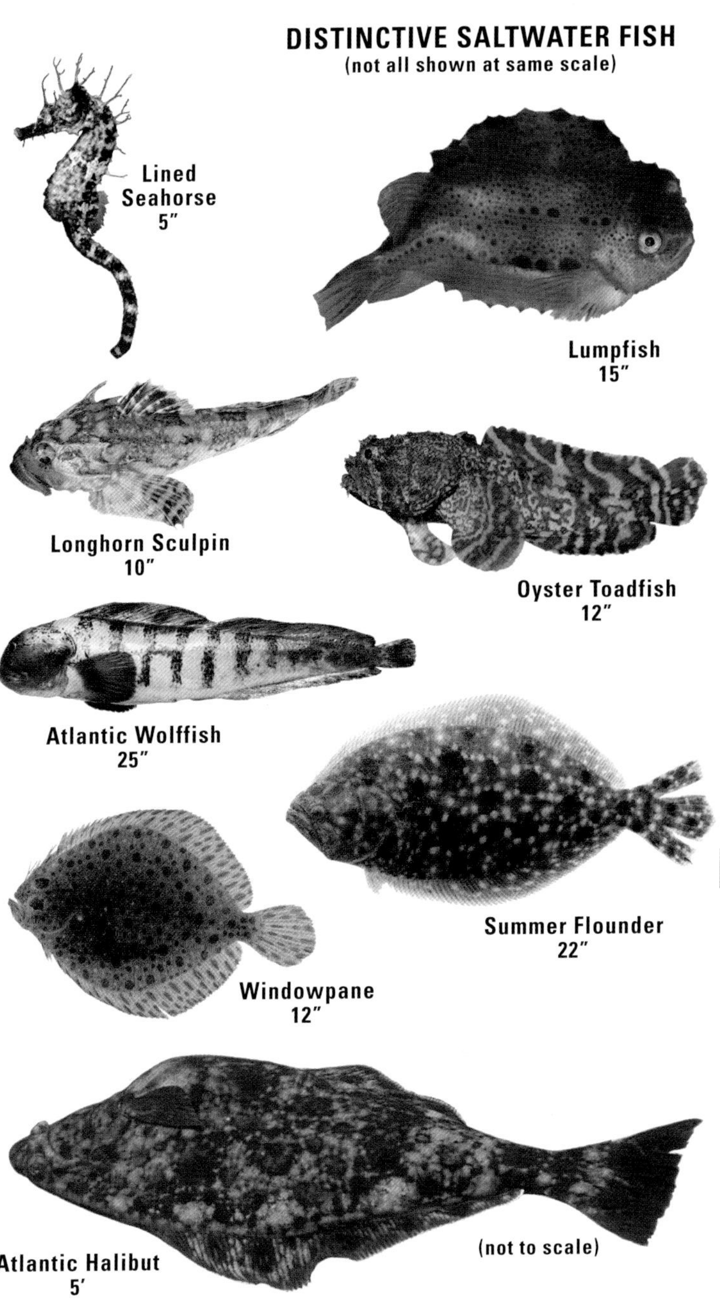

Lined Seahorse
5″

Lumpfish
15″

Longhorn Sculpin
10″

Oyster Toadfish
12″

Atlantic Wolffish
25″

Summer Flounder
22″

Windowpane
12″

Atlantic Halibut
5′

(not to scale)

MUMMICHOG ***Fundulus heteroclitus***
Common along the coast, in shallow bays and salt marshes, entering estuaries and sometimes coming into fresh water. Topminnow family (Fundulidae). ▶ Small, with blunt head, wide-based tail, rounded edge to tail fin. Mostly olive-gray, male with paler bars and spots, female usually with less distinct dark bars.

BANDED KILLIFISH ***Fundulus diaphanus***
Related to the Mummichog but mostly a *freshwater* species, common in lakes, ponds, and slow-moving rivers; may move into brackish water in estuaries. Topminnow family. ▶ Similar to Mummichog but with more pointed head, base of tail not as wide, heavier bars on side.

THREESPINE STICKLEBACK ***Gasterosteus aculeatus***
A small but adaptable fish, widespread in both salt and fresh water. Common in shallow areas of lakes and rivers, also in coastal bays and estuaries and offshore. Males build nests, engage in courtship displays, and care for the young. Stickleback family (Gasterosteidae). ▶ Has 3 *dorsal spines* (last one short), narrow tail base. Blue-gray to olive above, silvery on sides, with variable dark bars. Male becomes more colorful when breeding.

RAINBOW SMELT ***Osmerus mordax***
Schools of these small fish are common in both salt and fresh water. In New England they are widespread in coastal waters, moving up rivers to spawn, also found on inland lakes. Smelt family (Osmeridae). ▶ Slender, with large mouth and large teeth. May look relatively plain, with *iridescent silvery stripe* on side, or may show reflections of green and violet.

ATLANTIC SILVERSIDE ***Menidia menidia***
Along sandy beaches, shallow bays, and estuaries, schools of these small fish are common. They often become the focal point for feeding groups of larger fish, such as Striped Bass, and of birds such as terns. New World silverside family (Atherinopsidae). ▶ Small, long, and slender. Pale green to grayish green on back; *silver stripe* on side, with faint darker margins.

ROCK GUNNEL ***Pholis gunnellus***
These slender fish are common along shorelines, mainly rocky shores in northern New England, and are sometimes found in tidepools. Gunnel family (Pholidae). ▶ Long and slender, with *long dorsal fin* running back to the base of the tail. Series of 10 or more *pale-ringed dark spots* along base of dorsal fin. Overall color varies, greenish to reddish to brown, with mottling on sides.

ATLANTIC NEEDLEFISH ***Strongylura marina***
Common in shallow water along the coast, coming into estuaries and into the lower stretches of rivers. Actively pursues smaller fish and crustaceans. Needlefish family (Belonidae). ▶ Greatly elongated, with long, slender jaws. Blue-green on back, silvery on sides, with bluish lateral line.

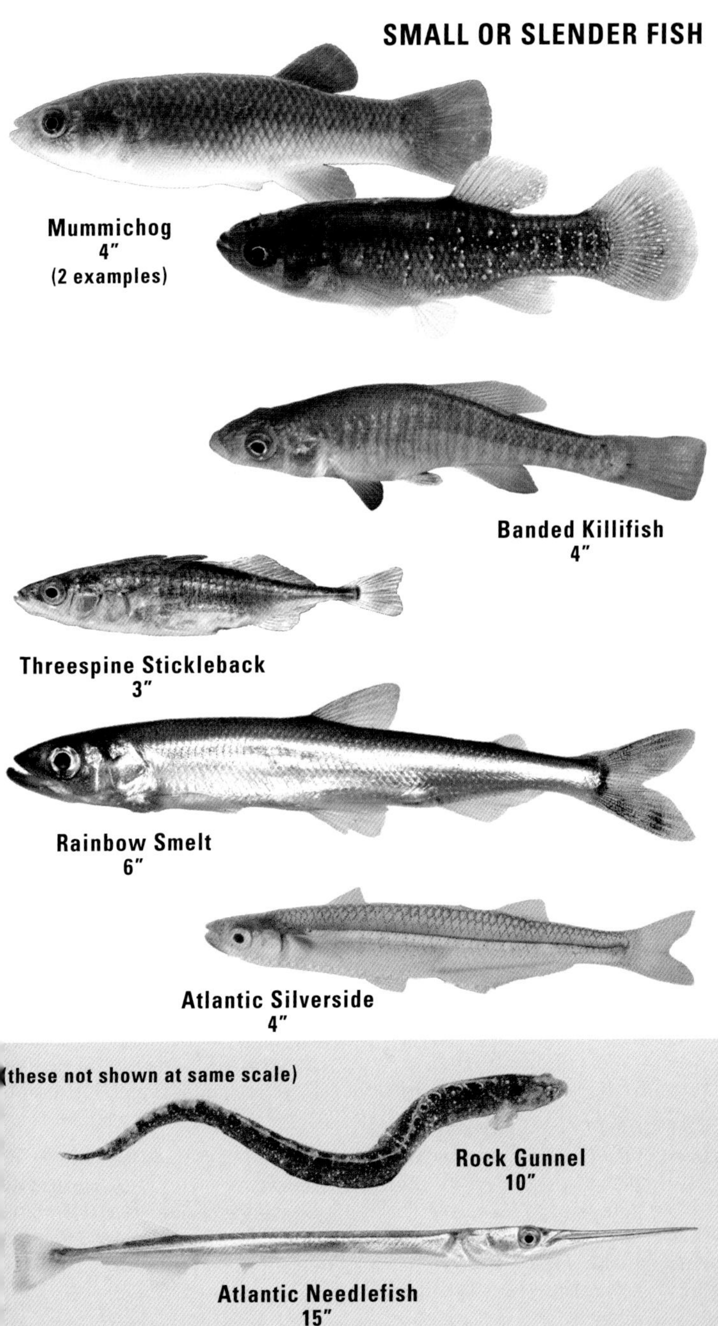

Mummichog
4″
(2 examples)

Banded Killifish
4″

Threespine Stickleback
3″

Rainbow Smelt
6″

Atlantic Silverside
4″

(these not shown at same scale)

Rock Gunnel
10″

Atlantic Needlefish
15″

Only one of these is not confined to fresh water. American Eels live in rivers but go to sea to spawn, the opposite of the life cycle of some fish.

COMMON CARP ***Cyprinus carpio***

Native to Eurasia, this fish was introduced to the U.S. intentionally in the 1800s. Now widespread and abundant in shallow lakes, ponds, and slow-moving rivers, it is considered a nuisance in most places, as it stirs up the muddy bottom, destroys plant life, and degrades the habitat for native fish. Carp and Minnow family (Cyprinidae). ▸ Stout body with long dorsal fin; 2 barbels at each corner of mouth. Varies from gray to bronze-green above, paler below. Large adults may have lower fins tinged red-orange.

WHITE SUCKER ***Catostomus commersoni***

Generally in clear streams and small rivers, sometimes in lakes, and may enter brackish waters near coast. The mouth, wide and thick-lipped on the underside of the head, is modified for sucking up small food items from the bottom. Sucker family (Catostomidae). ▸ Long, narrow body. Dusky on back, silvery to cream on sides; breeding male becomes more colorful.

BROWN BULLHEAD ***Ameiurus nebulosus***

Catfishes, as a group, are common in the southeastern and central U.S., but only this one is widespread in New England. Lives near the bottom in quiet areas of rivers and streams, also lakes and ponds. North American catfish family (Ictaluridae). ▸ Has 4 pairs of barbels ("whiskers") around mouth. Rounded first dorsal fin. Mostly brown, with or without dark spotting.

NORTHERN PIKE ***Esox lucius***

In western New England, this low-slung fish is common in slow-moving rivers, cold lakes with much plant growth. Pike family (Esocidae). ▸ Large head with jutting lower jaw; long body, dorsal fin set far back. Olive-green patterned with yellow spots, bars, or both.

MUSKELLUNGE ***Esox masquinongy***

Native farther west, Muskies have been introduced into lakes and rivers in northern New England. Pike family. ▸ Like Northern Pike but has pattern of dark bars and blotches on pale yellow-green body. A hybrid between the 2 species, "Tiger Muskie," also barred, has been stocked in some areas.

CHAIN PICKEREL ***Esox niger***

Widespread in swamps, marshes, quiet rivers, in areas with much plant growth. Pike family. ▸ Shaped like 2 preceding species, but averages smaller. Pale olive sides have *chainlike* pattern. *Dark stripe* under eye.

AMERICAN EEL ***Anguilla rostrata***

Lives in freshwater rivers for most of year, hunting at night and hiding by day. Males stay near river mouths, but female may spend years far upriver before going out to sea to spawn. Young develop at sea for several months then enter rivers. Freshwater eel family (Anguillidae). ▸ Long and flexible with narrow, snakelike head; has *long* dorsal fin, continuous with fins of tail and underside. Mostly unmarked olive to yellowish brown.

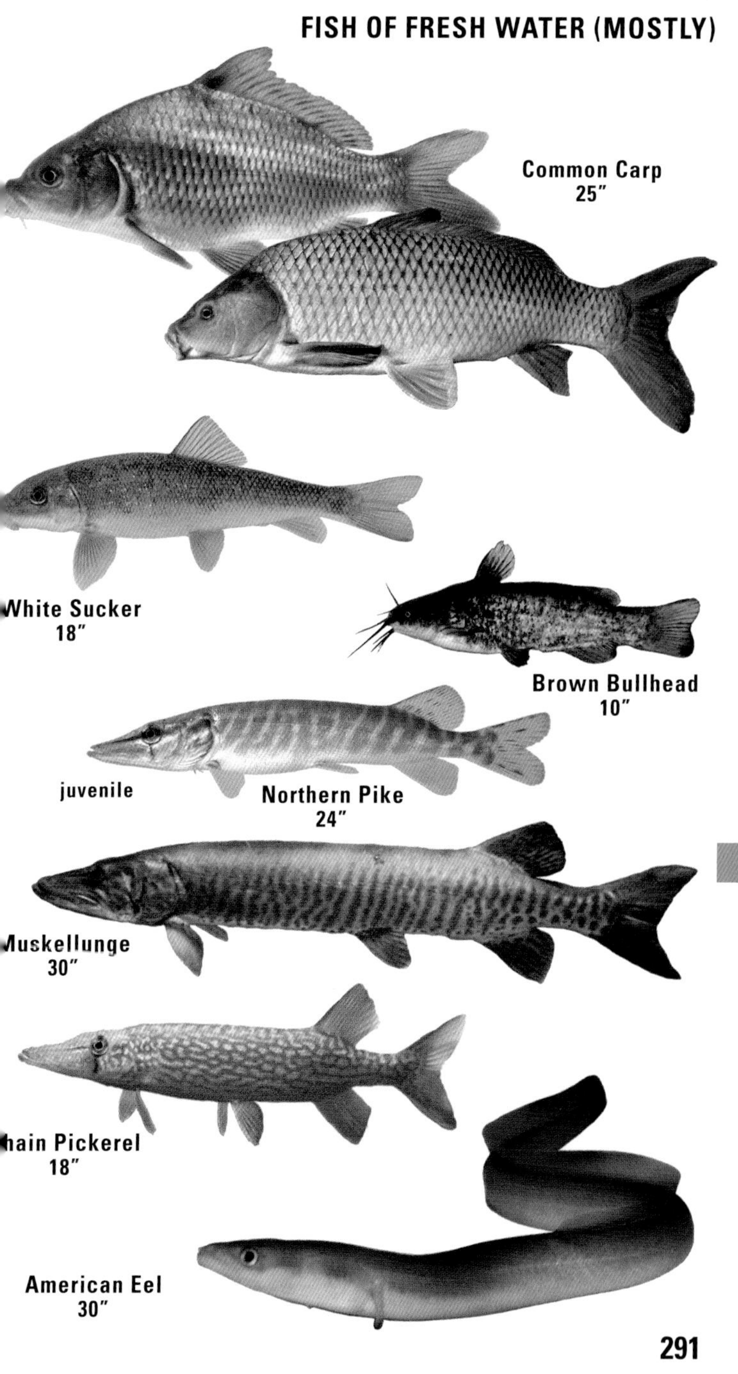

Common Carp
25″
White Sucker
18″
Brown Bullhead
10″
juvenile
Northern Pike
24″
Muskellunge
30″
Chain Pickerel
18″
American Eel
30″

TROUT, CHAR, AND SALMON

These are all members of the family **Salmonidae,** fish that thrive in cool streams and lakes of the Northern Hemisphere. Some populations are migratory, moving to the ocean for part of their life cycle, then returning upstream to spawn. Extremely popular with anglers, they often have been introduced into areas far outside their original distributions.

RAINBOW TROUT ***Onchorhynchus mykiss***
Native to western North America, but introduced and now common ir New England rivers and lakes. ▶ Quite variable in color. Usually blue-gray to olive above, silvery on sides, creamy white below, patterned with smal black spots. Typically a *broad wash of pink to reddish* on side.

ARCTIC CHAR ***Salvelinus alpinus***
The principal range of this trout is the high Arctic, where it occurs farthe north than any other freshwater fish. In New England it occurs mostly i lakes in Maine and does not grow as large there as in the far north. ▶ Bod shape similar to other trout; tail fin slightly forked. Color variable, olive t silvery, but usually with small *pink or red spots* on back and sides.

BROOK TROUT ***Salvelinus fontinalis***
Widespread in cold lakes, streams, rivers, with some going out to ocean fo part of year. ▶ Tail fin straight-edged or slightly forked. Variable in colo Dark dorsal fin and back are usually marked with wavy pale lines an spots; red or pink spots on sides, surrounded by blue rings. Breeding mal may be very brightly colored, orange or orange-red below.

LAKE TROUT ***Salvelinus namaycush***
Mainly found in relatively deep lakes in northern and western New Eng land. The largest native trout in North America. ▶ Long body, forked ta fin. Fairly dark gray to olive head, body, and fins, heavily marked wit small, yellowish, round or oval spots. Variable, and some may be plain silvery overall. Breeding male develops a dark stripe along the side.

BROWN TROUT ***Salmo trutta***
Native to the Old World, introduced to North America in the 1880s. No widespread, stocked in many lakes and streams; some river populatior may go out to sea. ▶ Tail fin straight-edged or rounded. Mainly pale brow or olive, variably marked with pale-ringed, black or reddish spots. Breec ing male may be bright reddish below.

ATLANTIC SALMON ***Salmo salar***
At one time this was an abundant fish in New England, spawning an growing up in rivers, then going to the ocean for a time before returnir upriver to spawn. Pollution, damming of rivers, and overfishing all toc their toll on salmon populations, and they remain scarce today. ▶ Tail fi has slightly concave edge. Variable in color. Brown to olive to bluish abov silvery on sides, with numerous black spots. Breeding adult may be mo brightly colored, bronze to brown with red spots.

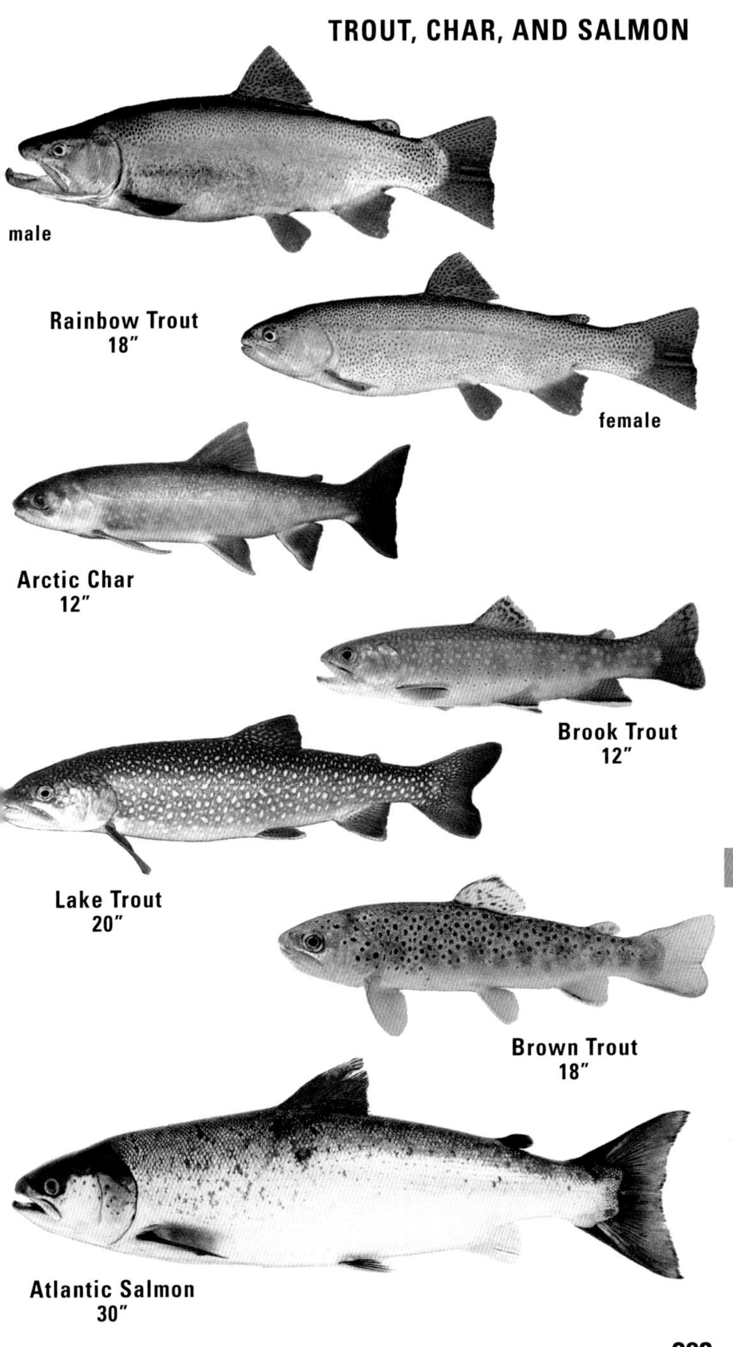
male
Rainbow Trout
18″
female
Arctic Char
12″
Brook Trout
12″
Lake Trout
20″
Brown Trout
18″
Atlantic Salmon
30″

VARIOUS SMALL FRESHWATER FISH

These are a few of the most numerous small fish to be found in lakes, ponds, streams, and rivers in New England.

FATHEAD MINNOW ***Pimephales promelas***
Widespread and common in ponds, streams, and rivers of western and southern New England. Because it is able to adapt to a wide range of water conditions and is often used as live bait, it has been accidentally introduced into many areas beyond its original range. Carp and minnow family (Cyprinidae). ► Small and stout, with blunt head. Dark stripe and angled lines on sides. Breeding male becomes dark-headed, with white or yellow patches on side of body.

SLIMY SCULPIN ***Cottus cognatus***
Common around rocky areas at the bottoms of cold lakes or streams. Sculpin family (Cottidae). ► Long-bodied, flat-headed, with bulging eyes on top of head. The 2 dorsal fins run most of the length of the back. Blackish mottling on brown body; dark bands on fins and tail.

BANDED SUNFISH ***Enneacanthus obesus***
Sunfish, as a group, have oval bodies, laterally compressed. This species is common in southern New England, in quiet sections of creeks and rivers or in ponds or lakes, mainly where there is heavy plant growth over sandy or muddy bottoms. Sunfish family (Centrarchidae). ► Wide dark bands on sides, overlaid with small pale spots. Dark "teardrop" spot below eye.

BLUEGILL ***Lepomis macrochirus***
This sunfish has been widely introduced and is now common in the shallows of many ponds, lakes, and streams in New England. Despite their small size, Bluegills are popular with anglers and are often called "panfish." Sunfish family. ► Dark spot near back of dorsal fin. Dark, vertical bands on body; small *blue-black ear flap* at rear of gill cover. Breeding male becomes brightly colored with blue on head, orange on underparts.

PUMPKINSEED ***Lepomis gibbosus***
Widespread over most of New England except northern Maine, in ponds, lakes, and quiet stretches of rivers, in areas with plenty of plant growth. Sunfish family. ► Blackish ear flap has *red-orange spot,* pale margin. Rows of spots on dorsal fin and tail fin. Colorful body, pale green to yellowish with spots of blue, gold, or orange, and with wavy blue lines on the darker face.

REDBREAST SUNFISH ***Lepomis auritus***
Widespread in New England, in creeks and small rivers and in shallow lake edges, mainly in sandy or rocky areas or spots with lots of plant growth. Sunfish family. ► Fins may be tinged yellow or orange, but generally unspotted. Solid black ear flap is *longer* than that of Bluegill. Mostly olive on back and sides, with orange-brown spots; underside may be whitish to orange, becoming bright orange on breeding male.

Fathead Minnow
2½"
Slimy Sculpin
2"
Banded Sunfish
2½"
illustrations below
at different scale
Bluegill
7"
Pumpkinseed
7"
(2 examples)
Redbreast Sunfish
6"

POPULAR GAME FISH OF FRESH WATER (MOSTLY)

Of the fishes on this page, only the sturgeon also occurs in salt water.

SMALLMOUTH BASS ***Micropterus dolomieu***

Mostly native to areas farther west, this popular and feisty fish has been introduced to rivers and lakes throughout New England. It is most common in areas of clear water over a rocky or gravel bottom. Sunfish family (Centrarchidae). ▶ The dorsal fins (first one spiny, second more rounded) run together. Mouth is not small except by comparison to next species; upper jaw extends back to a point even with front of eye. Mostly pale olive, with irregular dark brown bars on sides.

LARGEMOUTH BASS ***Micropterus salmoides***

Introduced widely in New England waters, now common in lakes, ponds, swamps, quiet stretches of rivers. Sunfish family. ▶ Similar to the preceding species, but averages larger; 2 dorsal fins nearly separate. Upper jaw extends back to a point well *past the eye*. Olive to brown overall, with ragged *blackish stripe* along side rather than vertical bars.

BLACK CRAPPIE ***Pomoxis nigromaculatus***

A popular fish, despite what the name might suggest to the uninitiated (it's pronounced like *croppy,* not *crappy!*). Widely introduced, now common in western and southern New England, in ponds, lakes, quiet areas of streams, usually where there is much plant growth. Sunfish family. ▶ Large dorsal fin set rather far back on body. Forehead indented above eye. Olive to brown, paler below, heavily blotched with blackish; fins spotted or barred.

YELLOW PERCH ***Perca flavescens***

Widespread and common in clear water of lakes, ponds, quiet sections of streams. Perch family (Percidae). ▶ Fairly long body and small head. Has 2 separated dorsal fins, forked tail fin. Pale greenish brown to yellowish, with darker bars extending down sides as irregular wedges or triangles.

WALLEYE ***Sander vitreus***

Mostly native to areas farther west, but introduced into many lakes and rivers in New England. Large and feisty, popular with inland anglers who enjoy a challenge. Perch family. ▶ Long body, long head, large mouth. Has 2 separated dorsal fins, with dark spot at back of first one. Tail fin forked with white at tip of lower lobe. Olive to yellowish brown, marked with dusky bars, scattered dark spots.

ATLANTIC STURGEON ***Acipenser oxyrhynchus***

Sturgeons are primitive fishes with a long history, with fossils known from as long as 200 million years ago. This species, formerly common in coastal New England, was seriously depleted by overfishing. Now uncommon in shallow waters along the coast, it moves up rivers to spawn. Sturgeon family (Acipenseridae). ▶ Distinctive shape, with long body, pointed snout, rows of knobby plates on back, dorsal fin set far back, upper lobe of tail fin longer than lower lobe. Mostly dark brown to blackish, paler below.

FISH OF FRESH WATER (MOSTLY)

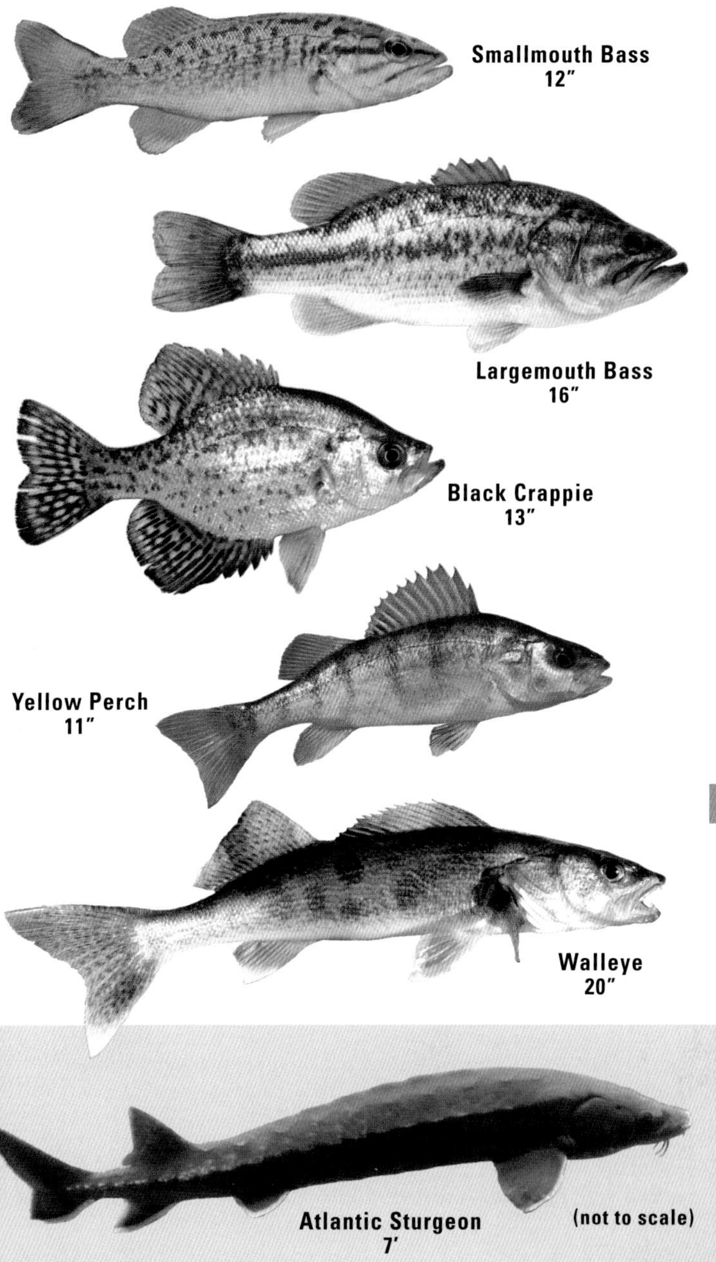

Smallmouth Bass
12″

Largemouth Bass
16″

Black Crappie
13″

Yellow Perch
11″

Walleye
20″

Atlantic Sturgeon
7′

(not to scale)

BUTTERFLIES AND MOTHS

(order **Lepidoptera**) are undoubtedly the most popular of insects (well, at least the butterflies are), and they are so conspicuous that we have placed them in their own section. For more information about insects in general — most of which will apply equally well to butterflies and moths — please see the introduction to the next section.

Lepidoptera life cycles are similar for both butterflies and moths. They go through a complete metamorphosis, changing utterly in appearance and form during their lives. All begin life as an egg, which hatches into a caterpillar, also called a larva (plural, larvae). The larva has six legs like other insects but usually appears to have more, with several pairs of prolegs down the length of the body. The larva is a little eating machine, munching away on a specific kind of food (usually a certain plant, or members of a certain group of plants) and growing. As the larva grows, it sheds its exoskeleton (or "skin") several times; the stages between these molts are called instars. After it is full grown, it pupates. The pupa of a butterfly is often called a chrysalis, while the pupa of a moth is often enclosed in a cocoon. Finally, the winged adult will emerge from the pupa, to begin the cycle again.

LIFE CYCLE OF A BUTTERFLY (Black Swallowtail)

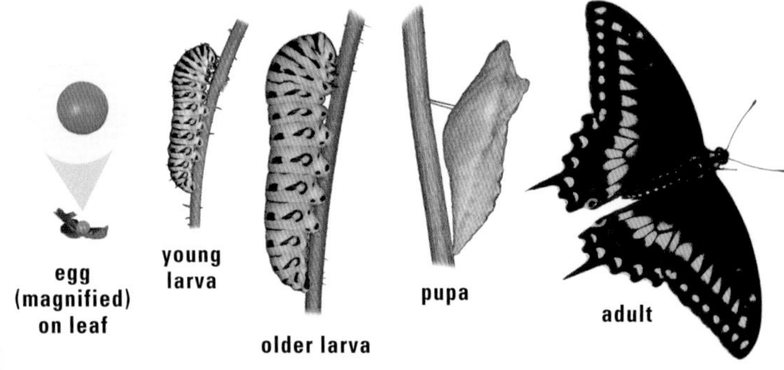

In the rest of this section, when we mention butterflies or moths, we'll be talking about the adults unless specified otherwise.

Butterflies vs. Moths: We may react differently to the idea of these two groups, but actual differences between them are minor. Butterflies are often considered to be more colorful, but there are many drab butterflies and many colorful moths. Butterflies in New England are active only by day while most moths are active mainly at night; however, a number of day-flying moths are common here. Butterflies usually rest with their wings spread out to the sides or raised straight above their backs, while moths often rest with their wings folded rooflike over their backs, but many moths are exceptions to this usual posture.

The most consistent, visible difference is in the antennae. Butterflies have thickened "knobs" at the tip of each antenna, while the antennae of moths in North America are threadlike or fernlike, with no thickened tip.

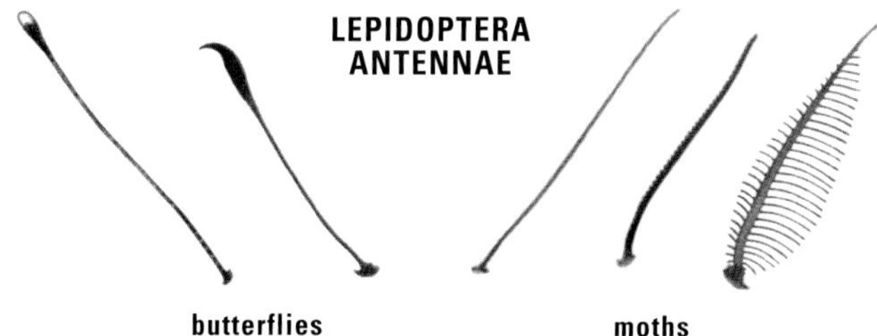

A less-obvious distinction is in the diversity of each group. About 125 species of butterflies occur regularly in New England. The number of moth species here is probably well over 3,000! Many are tiny "micro-moths," but that still leaves a rich variety for moth-watchers to enjoy.

Finding butterflies is a warm-season activity; many butterflies are active only when the sun is shining, although a few will fly on cloudy days or in deep shade. Most butterflies will come to flowers for nectar, so gardens or fields of wildflowers are good places to look. There are a few kinds that rarely visit flowers but may come to rotten fruit or animal droppings. And some, especially blues and sulphurs, will gather in "puddle parties" at the muddy margins of ponds, finding nutrients in the wet mud.

Finding moths is possible for much of the year in New England; a few cold-tolerant species will fly late into the fall or very early in the spring. Most nocturnal moths (but not all) are attracted to lights at night. Hanging a light up next to a white sheet or wall, close to a woodlot or other natural habitat, is a good way to attract a variety of moths. Some species come to "moth bait": our favorite recipe is a combination of rotten bananas, brown sugar, and stale beer, stirred up and painted on tree trunks. This is one of the best ways to attract underwing moths (p. 322).

Rearing butterflies or moths is a great way to learn about them. If you find the eggs or larvae in the wild, you can bring them indoors to raise and observe — just make sure you keep them supplied with fresh foliage from the same species of plant on which you found them. Cleaning out the container frequently will help to prevent mold and fungal infections. When the larvae stop eating and start crawling around inside the container, they are probably looking for a place to pupate. Most will either hang from an upright stem or burrow under dirt to pupate, so if you don't know what species you have, give them several options. Later, when the adult emerges from the pupa, you'll have a better chance of identifying it.

SWALLOWTAILS

(family **Papilionidae**) include the largest butterflies in New England. Those in our area have "tails" on the hindwings. Young caterpillars of many swallowtails resemble bird droppings, but larger caterpillars often have distinctive patterns.

EASTERN TIGER SWALLOWTAIL ***Papilio glaucus***

Widespread and common in southern New England in towns, woodland edges. Flies in summer, visiting flowers and puddles. Some females are very dark, with only a shadow of striping, but this melanistic form is scarce as far north as New England, more common in the south. ► Black-striped yellow adults are unlikely to be mistaken for any species except the very similar Canadian Tiger Swallowtail. **Larval foodplant:** tuliptree, cherry, other trees.

CANADIAN TIGER SWALLOWTAIL ***Papilio canadensis***

Common in northern New England, where it replaces the preceding species. ► Very similar to Eastern Tiger, but tends to be smaller and slightly paler yellow. The pale stripe near the edge of the forewing on the underside tends to be more *continuous,* not broken into spots. The 2 species may interbreed where their ranges overlap. **Larval foodplant:** birch, apen, other trees.

BLACK SWALLOWTAIL ***Papilio polyxenes***

Widespread and common in open country and farmland, less common in clearings in forested regions. ► Blackish above with 2 rows of yellow spots, generally larger and brighter on males. Blue sheen on hindwing, and orange spots on underside of hindwing. Compare to next 2 species. **Larval foodplant:** members of parsley family, including Queen Anne's Lace, dill, parsley.

SPICEBUSH SWALLOWTAIL ***Papilio troilus***

Locally common in southern New England, in meadows, gardens, woodland clearings. ► Similar to Black Swallowtail (including double row of orange spots on underside of hindwing), but with *pale green* clouding on upperside. **Larval foodplant:** mainly Spicebush, also Sassafras, other members of laurel family.

PIPEVINE SWALLOWTAIL ***Battus philenor***

Only a scarce visitor to New England but its influence is felt here: several other dark butterflies may gain protection by "mimicking" this swallowtail, which carries distasteful compounds from its larval feeding. ► Like Spicebush Swallowtail but with *blue* sheen (not pale green), *single* row of orange spots on hindwing below (not a double row). **Larval foodplant:** pipevine *(Aristolochia).*

GIANT SWALLOWTAIL ***Papilio cresphontes***

Another southern butterfly that wanders north to our area, especially in late summer. ► Very large, wings dark above, crossed by 2 pale yellow spot bands that *cross* near wingtip. Wings pale yellow below. **Larval foodplant:** citrus and rue relatives.

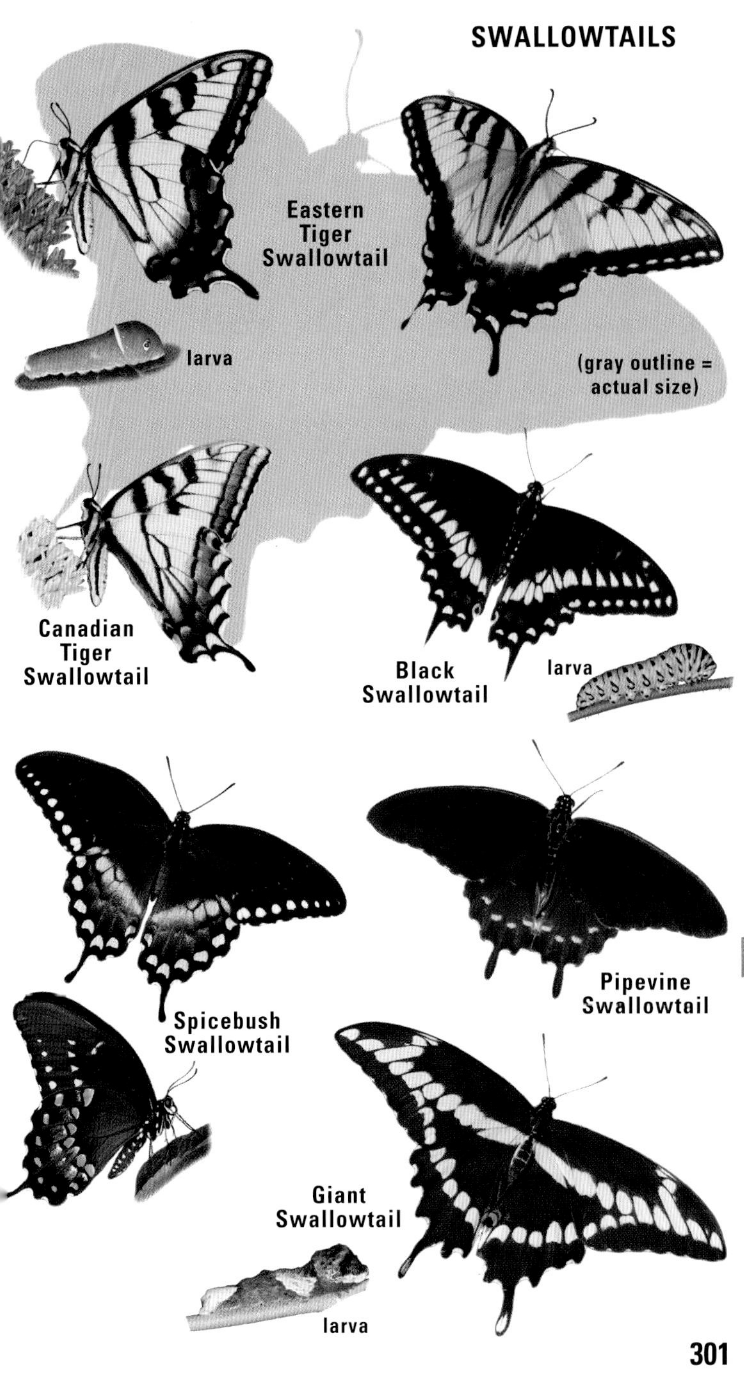
Eastern Tiger Swallowtail
larva
(gray outline = actual size)
Canadian Tiger Swallowtail
Black Swallowtail
larva
Spicebush Swallowtail
Pipevine Swallowtail
Giant Swallowtail
larva

WHITES AND SULPHURS

(family **Pieridae**) are familiar fliers of open country, most colored some shade of white, yellow, or orange. Some are among our most numerous butterflies. Most species keep their wings tightly closed above their backs when at rest, showing their bright uppersides mainly in flight.

CABBAGE WHITE ***Pieris rapae***

Native to the Old World, arrived here in the 1860s and soon became abundant throughout New England, flying from early spring to late fall. ▶ Forewing with 1 (male) or 2 (female) black dots in center, dark tip. Hindwing below plain yellowish white. **Larval foodplant:** cabbage, watercress, many others in mustard family.

MUSTARD WHITE ***Pieris oleracea***

Mostly uncommon in northern forest, flying in late spring and summer. ▶ Plain white above; below with gray scaling along veins, darker in spring. **Larval foodplant:** toothwort, other mustards.

FALCATE ORANGETIP ***Anthocharis midea***

A rare treat of spring in southern New England forests. ▶ Pointed forewing, with *orange tip* on male. Hindwing below with delicate marbling. **Larval foodplant:** Rock Cress, other mustards.

ORANGE SULPHUR ***Colias eurytheme***

Also called Alfalfa Butterfly and arrived in New England following that crop. Now abundant in open country. ▶ Orange-yellow to orange above with black borders (spotted paler in female). Some females are mostly white. Plainer below with red-rimmed spot on hindwing. **Larval foodplant:** alfalfa, others in pea family.

CLOUDED SULPHUR ***Colias philodice***

Widespread and abundant in open country. ▶ Very much like the Orange Sulphur, but *lacks orange above* (but this is hard to judge when they are at rest). The two sometimes interbreed, producing intermediate hybrids. **Larval foodplant:** alfalfa, others in pea family.

PINK-EDGED SULPHUR ***Colias interior***

Locally common in northern New England, in bogs, blueberry barrens. ▶ Like Clouded Sulphur but with more obvious pink wing edges, plainer hindwing below. **Larval foodplant:** blueberry.

LITTLE YELLOW ***Pyrisitia lisa***

Southern, invading northward in summer; may reach northern New England. ▶ *Small.* Yellow with black edges above. Brown spot on hindwing below. **Larval foodplant:** senna, others in pea family.

CLOUDLESS SULPHUR ***Phoebis sennae***

This big, pale sulphur, resident in the southern U.S., strays northward every summer, often reaching New England. ▶ *Twice the size* of our other sulphurs. Pale yellow to whitish above (slight dark edge on females), variable brown markings below. **Larval foodplant:** senna, others in pea family.

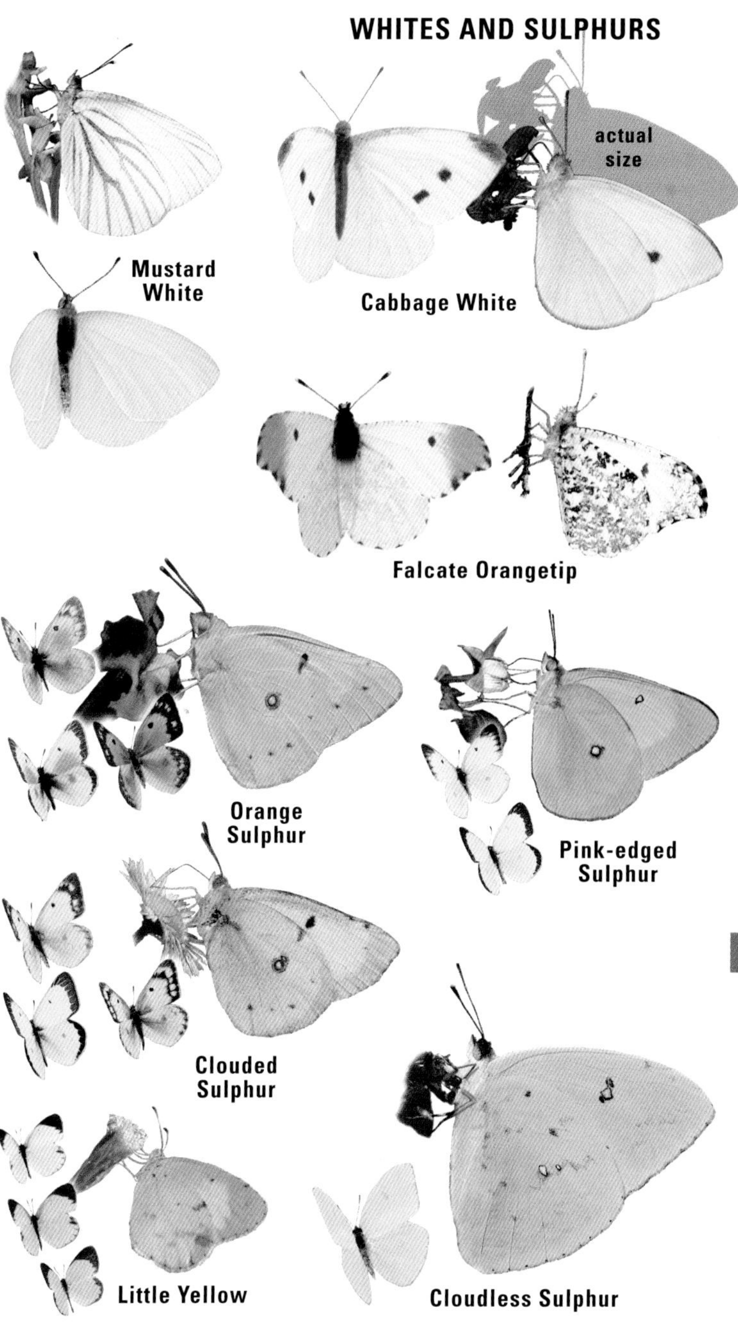
actual size
Mustard White
Cabbage White
Falcate Orangetip
Orange Sulphur
Pink-edged Sulphur
Clouded Sulphur
Little Yellow
Cloudless Sulphur

BLUES, COPPERS, AND HARVESTER make up three different subfamilies under the family of gossamer-wings **(Lycaenidae)**. These tiny butterflies are easy to overlook, although blues draw attention when dozens gather in "puddle parties" at damp mud.

EASTERN TAILED-BLUE ***Cupido comyntas***

Common in gardens, parks, open country, with multiple broods of adults from spring to fall. ► Threadlike "tails" on hindwing are distinctive but hard to see. Pale underside with fine dark marks, *orange spot* on hindwing. Upperside deep blue on male, mostly gray on female. **Larval foodplant:** flowers of clover, other legumes.

SPRING AZURE ***Celastrina ladon***

A welcome sight in early spring is this small, pale butterfly, fluttering along the edges of dark woods. ► Variable, may represent more than one species. Usually very pale below, but some are more heavily marked. Pale blue above, female with wider blackish margins. **Larval foodplant:** buds and flowers of many plants.

SUMMER AZURE ***Celastrina neglecta***

Common and widespread, mostly in open habitats. ► Like Spring Azure but averages paler. Best identified by later flight season, in summer, not spring. **Larval foodplant:** dogwood and other plants.

SILVERY BLUE ***Glaucopsyche lygdamus***

Now common in northern New England, but present there only since the 1960s. Flies in early summer. ► Gray below, with row of white-edged round black spots. Upperside silvery blue on male, dusky on female. **Larval foodplant:** Cow Vetch, other legumes.

"KARNER BLUE" ***Plebejus melissa samuelis***

Seriously endangered, confined to oak-pine barrens, savannahs. Conservationists are working to preserve a colony near Concord, New Hampshire. ► Row of *orange spots* near rim of hindwing. **Larval foodplant:** wild lupine.

AMERICAN COPPER ***Lycaena phlaeas***

Locally common in meadows, roadsides, vacant lots, often seen visiting flowers. Males perch in the open and chase other insects. ► Flame orange on forewing, mostly gray hindwing. Compare to Bronze Copper. **Larval foodplant:** Sheep Sorrel, other buckwheats.

BRONZE COPPER ***Lycaena hyllus***

Uncommon and local, in marshes, wet meadows. ► Duller above than American Copper, but with much more distinct orange band on underside of hindwing. **Larval foodplant:** docks.

HARVESTER ***Feniseca tarquinius***

Famous as our only "carnivorous" butterfly, but not often seen. Adults live around alder thickets, swamps, streamsides, seldom or never visiting flowers. ► Orange above with black blotches. Underside reddish with many circular white marks. **Larval foodplant:** not a plant! Feeds on woolly aphids, mostly on alders.

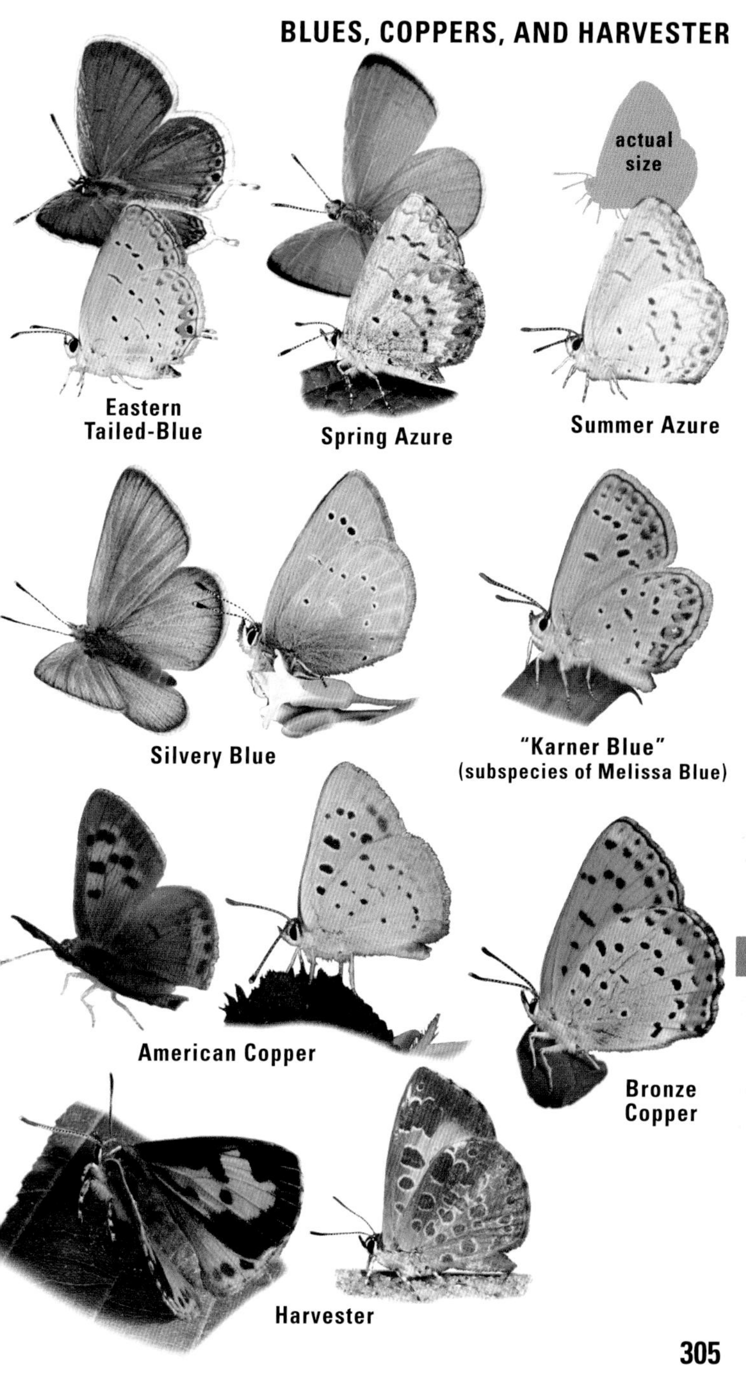

Eastern Tailed-Blue

Spring Azure

Summer Azure

Silvery Blue

"Karner Blue" (subspecies of Melissa Blue)

American Copper

Bronze Copper

Harvester

HAIRSTREAKS

are small, subtle butterflies, making up a distinct subfamily **(Theclinae)** of the gossamer-wing group. Most have thin "tails" on the hindwing, waving when they rub the hindwings back and forth. Most (except the first one below) perch with their wings tightly closed above their backs.

GRAY HAIRSTREAK ***Strymon melinus***

Widespread in southern New England in gardens, parks, woods, seen regularly but not in large numbers. Unlike other hairstreaks, often basks with wings open. ▶ Distinctly *gray* below, with orange spot near base of tails. Thin black and white hindwing line often *edged orange.* **Larval foodplant:** flowering parts of many plants.

WHITE-M HAIRSTREAK ***Parrhasius m-album***

Uncommon in summer in southern New England. ▶ Narrow white M (or W) and red spot on hindwing. Best mark is brilliant *blue upperside* (visible only in flight). **Larval foodplant:** oaks.

BANDED HAIRSTREAK ***Satyrium calanus***

Common in June and July along forest edges, clearings. ▶ Brown with variable darker bands, edged outwardly with white. Orange and dull blue spot on hindwing. **Larval foodplant:** oaks, hickories.

STRIPED HAIRSTREAK ***Satyrium liparops***

Usually uncommon in midsummer around edges of clearings, swamps. ▶ Like Banded, but with *more stripes,* dark bands edged on *both sides* with white. **Larval foodplant:** cherry, rose, others.

CORAL HAIRSTREAK ***Satyrium titus***

Often fairly common in midsummer in brushy places, old fields. Favors flowers of Butterfly Weed. ▶ *Row of orange-red spots* along edge of hindwing; no "tails." **Larval foodplant:** cherry, plum.

BROWN ELFIN ***Callophrys augustinus***

Flies in spring and early summer around pine barrens, bogs, open woods. ▶ Rich brown below, with hindwing dark toward base, reddish toward outer edge. **Larval foodplant:** blueberry.

EASTERN PINE ELFIN ***Callophrys niphon***

Common in pine woods, flying in spring and early summer, visiting flowers at forest edge. ▶ Striking pattern of *irregular black and brown bands* with white edges. **Larval foodplant:** pines.

JUNIPER HAIRSTREAK ***Callophrys gryneus***

Uncommon around stands of Eastern Redcedar, perching on trees, visiting nearby flowers. ▶ Variably *green* on underside with white lines, cinnamon tinges. **Larval foodplant:** Eastern Redcedar.

HESSEL'S HAIRSTREAK ***Callophrys hesseli***

Rare and local, flying in early summer in swamps dominated by Atlantic White-Cedar. ▶ Like Juniper Hairstreak but more blue-green, forewing line bent. **Larval foodplant:** Atlantic White-Cedar.

actual size

Gray Hairstreak

White-M Hairstreak

Banded Hairstreak

Striped Hairstreak

Coral Hairstreak

Brown Elfin

Eastern Pine Elfin

Juniper Hairstreak

Hessel's Hairstreak

FRITILLARIES, CRESCENTS, CHECKERSPOTS

are all in the family **Nymphalidae,** or brushfooted butterflies, like all the species on the next two spreads. This is a highly diverse family, known for the fact that the front legs are reduced to short brushy appendages, so that these butterflies appear to have only four legs.

GREAT SPANGLED FRITILLARY ***Speyeria cybele***

Common and widespread, a beautiful splash of color in summer fields. ► Bright orange with intricate pattern. Hindwing below has silver spots, *broad pale band.* **Larval foodplant:** violets.

APHRODITE FRITILLARY ***Speyeria aphrodite***

Usually less common than the preceding species. ► Like Great Spangled but a little smaller. On hindwing below, pale band paralleling outer edge looks *narrower.* **Larval foodplant:** violets.

ATLANTIS FRITILLARY ***Speyeria atlantis***

Mainly in northern New England, sometimes common in open meadows. ► Smaller than the 2 preceding species, and uppersides of wings show a distinct *dark outer border.* **Larval foodplant:** violets.

MEADOW FRITILLARY ***Boloria bellona***

Fairly common from spring to early fall in most of New England, in open fields of all kinds. ► A "lesser fritillary," smaller than the 3 preceding species, with forewings more square-tipped. Underside of hindwing has *muted pattern.* **Larval foodplant:** violets.

SILVER-BORDERED FRITILLARY ***Boloria selene***

Widespread but uncommon, mostly in wet meadows, marshes, bogs. ► Like Meadow Fritillary but hindwing has darker border above, pattern of *silver marks* below. **Larval foodplant:** violets.

PEARL CRESCENT ***Phyciodes tharos***

Very small, very common, flitting actively and visiting flowers in fields, roadsides, gardens. ► Orange with intricate pattern above. Hindwing below usually pale yellow, lightly marked; darker in spring and fall individuals. **Larval foodplant:** many kinds of asters.

NORTHERN CRESCENT ***Phyciodes cocyta (not shown)***

A close relative of the preceding, also very common. ► Averages slightly larger than Pearl Crescent, may fly more slowly. Best identified by range (see map). **Larval foodplant:** asters.

HARRIS'S CHECKERSPOT ***Chlosyne harrisii***

Locally common around meadows, marsh edges. ► Like Pearl Crescent above but slightly larger, less finely marked above; *very different pattern below.* **Larval foodplant:** Parasol Whitetop.

BALTIMORE CHECKERSPOT ***Euphydryas phaeton***

This stunning creature lives in local colonies around damp meadows or dry wood edges. ► Unmistakable pattern of black, white, and orange-red. **Larval foodplant:** turtlehead, plantain, others.

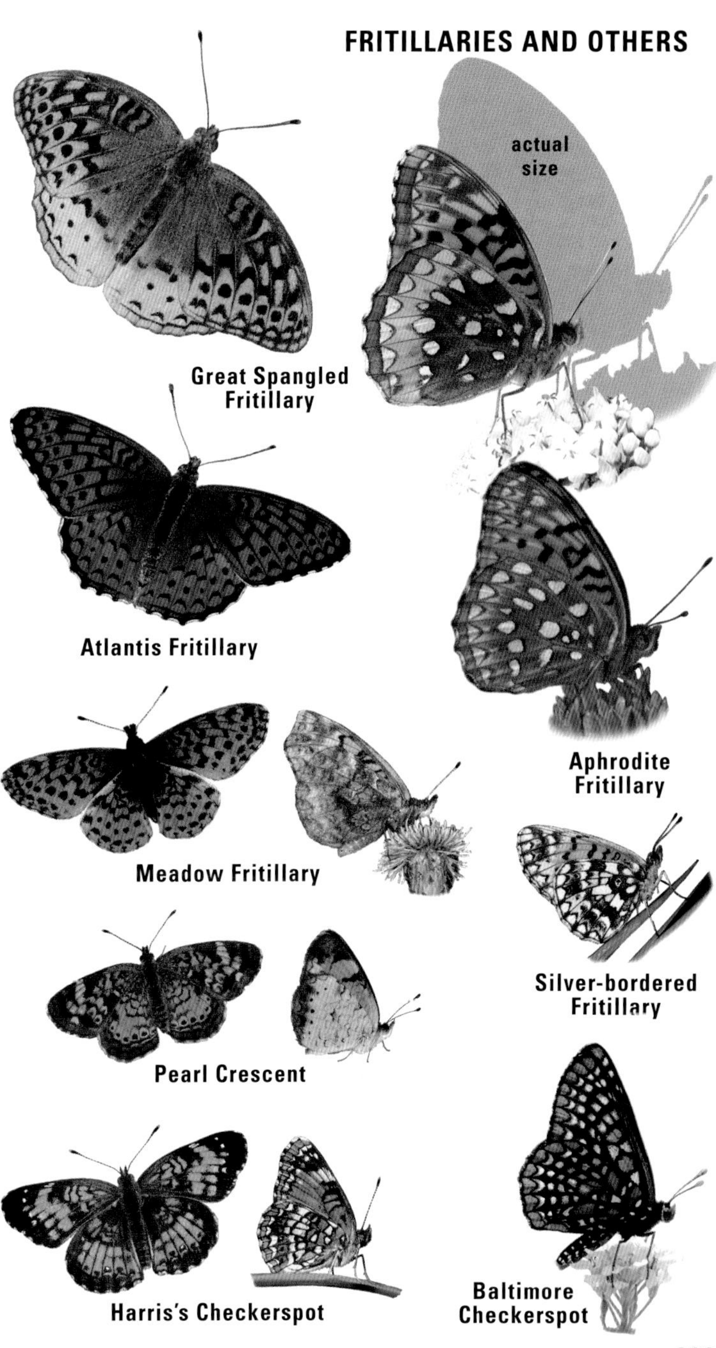

Great Spangled Fritillary

Atlantis Fritillary

Aphrodite Fritillary

Meadow Fritillary

Silver-bordered Fritillary

Pearl Crescent

Harris's Checkerspot

Baltimore Checkerspot

This diverse family was introduced on p. 308.

EASTERN COMMA ***Polygonia comma***

In woods, usually at puddles or sap flows, not flowers. ▶ Angular wings; hindwing above may be black or orange. Silvery "comma" in center of hindwing below. **Larval foodplant:** nettles, elms, hops.

QUESTION MARK ***Polygonia interrogationis***

Hibernates as adult, sometimes flies in winter thaws. ▶ Forewing with 1 more black spot than Eastern Comma; silvery "question mark" in center of hindwing below. **Larval foodplant:** nettles, hops.

MILBERT'S TORTOISESHELL ***Aglais milberti***

A common summer visitor to flowers in northern meadows. Numbers vary from year to year. ▶ Dark below; above wings dark at base with orange-yellow outer band. **Larval foodplant:** nettles.

COMPTON TORTOISESHELL ***Nymphalis l-album***

Hibernates as adult, may fly early in spring in forest. ▶ Angular wings, gray below, orange and black above. *White spot* near leading edge of hindwing. **Larval foodplant:** aspens, birches, willows.

MOURNING CLOAK ***Nymphalis antiopa***

Widespread, common. Hibernates as an adult, may fly in early spring or even in winter thaws. ▶ Rich brown above, gray below, with *cream-yellow borders.* **Larval foodplant:** willows, birches, others.

RED ADMIRAL ***Vanessa atalanta***

Variable in numbers, sometimes invading in large numbers, in all kinds of open country. ▶ Dark with *red-orange slashes* across wings, cryptic below. **Larval foodplant:** nettles and related plants.

AMERICAN LADY ***Vanessa virginiensis***

Fairly common in summer in open areas. ▶ On hindwing above, spots near trailing edge seem *smeared together.* Underside of hindwing has *2 large spots.* Forewing above shows more open pattern than next species. **Larval foodplant:** everlastings, others.

PAINTED LADY ***Vanessa cardui***

An irregular migrant to New England, common at times. ▶ Like American Lady but spots near hindwing edge *more separated,* both above and below. **Larval foodplant:** thistles, mallows, others.

COMMON BUCKEYE ***Junonia coenia***

A migrant from the south, often common in late summer in open areas. ▶ Brown, with distinct pattern of *bars and round spots* above, plainer below. **Larval foodplant:** plantains, vervains, others.

AMERICAN SNOUT ***Libytheana carinenta***

Another stray into New England from the south. ▶ Long *snoutlike palpi,* forewings square-tipped. Orange and white marks above, underside variable. **Larval foodplant:** hackberries.

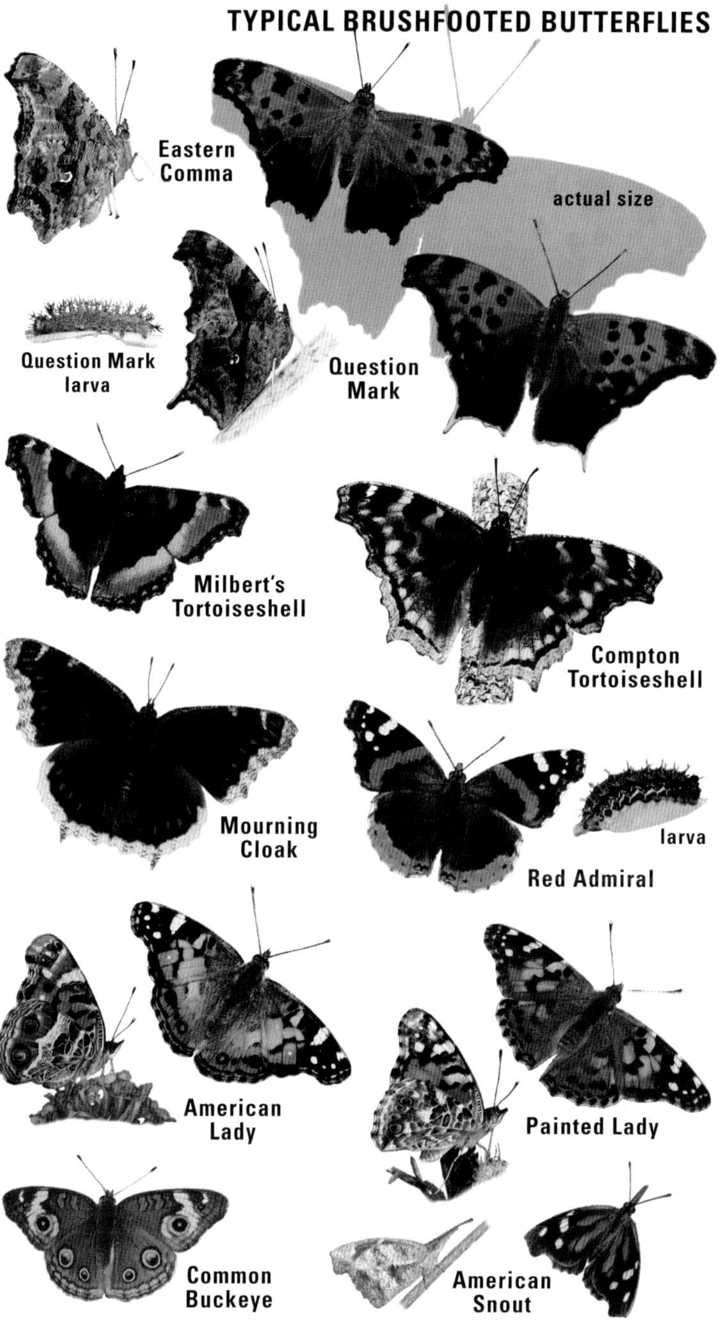
Eastern Comma
actual size
Question Mark larva
Question Mark
Milbert's Tortoiseshell
Compton Tortoiseshell
Mourning Cloak
Red Admiral
larva
American Lady
Painted Lady
Common Buckeye
American Snout

VARIOUS BRUSHFOOTS

The last four species below were once considered a separate family.

WHITE ADMIRAL ***Limenitis arthemis arthemis***
Common in northern forest edges, clearings. Classified in same species as Red-spotted Purple, and they interbreed across central New England, producing many intermediates. ▶ Wide *white band* across wings is distinctive. **Larval foodplant:** leaves of many trees.

RED-SPOTTED PURPLE ***Limenitis arthemis astyanax***
Southern woodlands. A mimic of Pipevine Swallowtail (p. 300). ▶ Blue iridescence, orange-red spots. Intermediates with White Admiral are frequent. **Larval foodplant:** leaves of many trees.

VICEROY ***Limenitis archippus***
Related to the preceding species, but gains protection from predators by mimicking the Monarch. Fairly common around streams, willow groves. ▶ Pattern like Monarch but with an extra black bar on hindwing. Flies differently, with quick flaps and flat-winged glides. **Larval foodplant:** mostly willows, also poplars, aspens.

MONARCH ***Danaus plexippus***
Our most famous butterfly, common here in late summer. Multiple generations move north in spring and summer from Mexican wintering sites; final late-summer generation migrates from New England south to Mexico. ▶ Large size, orange wings, black veins, white spots on body and wing edges. Easily recognized, but many people apply the name "monarch" to any orange butterfly. **Larval foodplant:** milkweeds. Chemicals in the plant make caterpillars and adults distasteful to birds and other predators.

COMMON RINGLET ***Coenonympha tullia***
This and the next 3 butterflies are in the subfamily Satyrinae. The Ringlet is a recent arrival in New England, first found here in the 1960s, now common in meadows. ▶ Gray and orange-brown, with small spot near tip of forewing. **Larval foodplant:** grasses.

LITTLE WOOD-SATYR ***Megisto cymela***
A woodland butterfly with low, bouncy flight, seen in spring and early summer. ▶ Small black wing spots with yellow rings. Reddish brown bands on underside of wings. **Larval foodplant:** grasses.

COMMON WOOD-NYMPH ***Cercyonis pegala***
Common in meadows, woodland edges. ▶ Two large eyespots on forewing; fine wavy lines on underside. Some have large yellow patch surrounding forewing spots. **Larval foodplant:** grasses.

EYED BROWN ***Satyrodes eurydice***
Fairly common in sedge meadows, marsh edges. ▶ Many round spots near wing edges. The very similar **Appalachian Brown** (*S. appalachia*), locally common in southern New England, tends to live in more wooded areas. **Larval foodplant:** sedges.

White Admiral

actual size

Red-spotted Purple

Viceroy

Monarch larva on milkweed

Monarch

Common Ringlet

Little Wood-Satyr

Common Wood-Nymph

Eyed Brown

SKIPPERS

(family **Hesperiidae**) are thick-bodied butterflies with hooked antenna tips. New England has about 45 species, most challenging to identify.

SILVER-SPOTTED SKIPPER ***Epargyreus clarus***
The easiest skipper to recognize, common in summer in open habitats. ▶ A big skipper with gold bands on forewings above, *white spot* on hindwing below. **Larval foodplant:** various legumes.

NORTHERN CLOUDYWING ***Thorybes pylades***
Fairly common in open spots in early summer. ▶ Dusky brown with tiny white spots on forewing. Usually sits on flowers with wings *half-opened.* **Larval foodplant:** various legumes.

JUVENAL'S DUSKYWING ***Erynnis juvenalis***
Duskywings are dark, fast-flying skippers that sit with wings spread out flat. At least 6 similar species occur in New England; this one is often most common in late spring. **Larval foodplant:** oaks.

ARCTIC SKIPPER ***Carterocephalus palaemon***
A sharp little skipper of clearings in the north woods. May rest with wings spread flat or folded above back. ▶ Orange *checkered* pattern above, *outlined* pale spots below. **Larval foodplant:** grasses.

EUROPEAN SKIPPER ***Thymelicus lineola***
Accidentally introduced from Europe around 1910, now abundant in open country, wet meadows. ▶ Very small. Orange above with veins blackened inward from edges; plain pale orange below. Antennae very short. **Larval foodplant:** timothy and other grasses.

LEAST SKIPPER ***Ancyloxypha numitor***
In damp meadows and marsh edges, this tiny skipper flutters weakly through the grass. ▶ Rounded wings mostly dark on upperside, pale orange below. **Larval foodplant:** grasses.

PECK'S SKIPPER ***Polites peckius***
Common in early to midsummer in open fields, roadsides, gardens, often seen in quick, darting flight from one flower to the next. ▶ Underside rich brown with two big yellow patches on hindwing; a central blotch juts out from outer one. Above orange and black like many other skippers. **Larval foodplant:** grasses.

LONG DASH ***Polites mystic***
Fairly common in fields, especially damp sites. ▶ Underside of hindwing orange-brown with curved yellow spot band separated from single basal spot. **Larval foodplant:** grasses.

HOBOMOK SKIPPER ***Poanes hobomok***
Fairly common in woodland clearings and edges in early summer. ▶ Underside of hindwing mostly brown, with broad yellow blotch on outer half. Above orange with broad dark edges. Some females are dark brown overall. **Larval foodplant:** grasses.

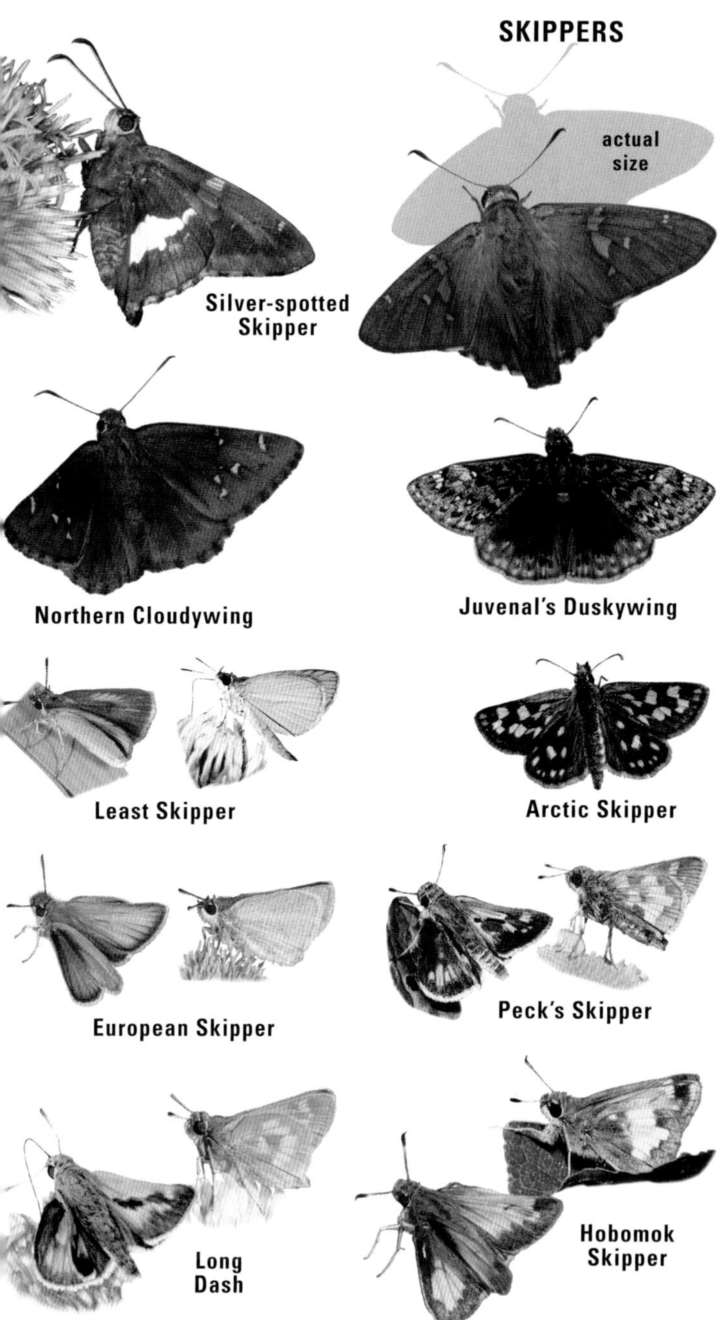

Silver-spotted Skipper

Northern Cloudywing

Juvenal's Duskywing

Least Skipper

Arctic Skipper

European Skipper

Peck's Skipper

Long Dash

Hobomok Skipper

GIANT SILKMOTHS

(family **Saturniidae**) include some impressively large lepidoptera, but some are only medium-sized. They do all their feeding as larvae: adults have only rudimentary mouthparts and do not feed. Adult females "call" to males by releasing a pheromone; males may follow this faint scent on the breeze for almost a mile. Silkmoth populations have declined in many areas, partly because of control measures aimed at Gypsy Moths.

LUNA MOTH ***Actias luna***
Still common in forested regions, this lovely moth often comes to lights, mainly in June and July. ▶ Unmistakable: large, pale green, long-tailed. **Larval foodplant:** Paper Birch, also hickories and others.

IMPERIAL MOTH ***Eacles imperialis***
Uncommon in deciduous forest, flying between mid-June and early August. ▶ Very large, with patches of yellow and violet-brown. **Larval foodplant:** many, including oak, maple, pine.

POLYPHEMUS MOTH ***Antheraea polyphemus***
Adults fly between late May and late July. If disturbed, they flash the startling eyelike spots on the hindwings. ▶ Huge, pale brown, with *large spots* on wings. **Larval foodplant:** many trees and shrubs.

ROSY MAPLE MOTH ***Dryocampa rubicunda***
A common visitor to porch lights in early July, but might be seen from late May to early August. ▶ Variable. Usually *pink wings* crossed by *yellow stripe,* sometimes mostly creamy wings. Fuzzy body is yellow to white. **Larval foodplant:** maple, sometimes oak.

PROMETHEA MOTH ***Callosamia promethea***
Adults are seen between late May and mid-July. Females may be active day or night, but males fly mostly by day. ▶ Females are reddish brown. Males (not shown) are *almost black,* with few light markings. **Larval foodplant:** many trees and shrubs.

IO MOTH ***Automeris io***
Common in southern New England forests and towns, flying in summer. ▶ Looks like a dead leaf until it spreads its wings, showing the *brilliant eyespots* and *red stripes* on the hindwings. Females are browner than males. **Larval foodplant:** many trees and shrubs.

PINK-STRIPED OAKWORM MOTH ***Anisota virginiensis***
Named for its colorful caterpillar, this moth flies mostly in June. ▶ Sluggish yellow-brown females have *white wing spots.* The fast-flying males, active by day, look like bees. **Larval foodplant:** oaks.

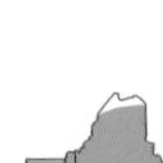

CECROPIA MOTH ***Hyalophora cecropia***
Widespread and fairly common in forest and in well-wooded suburbs, mostly flying between late May and late July. ▶ Huge and colorful, gray-brown with big *white spots* and *red bands* on wings. **Larval foodplant:** many trees and shrubs, especially maple, wild cherry, birch, alder, dogwood, and willow.

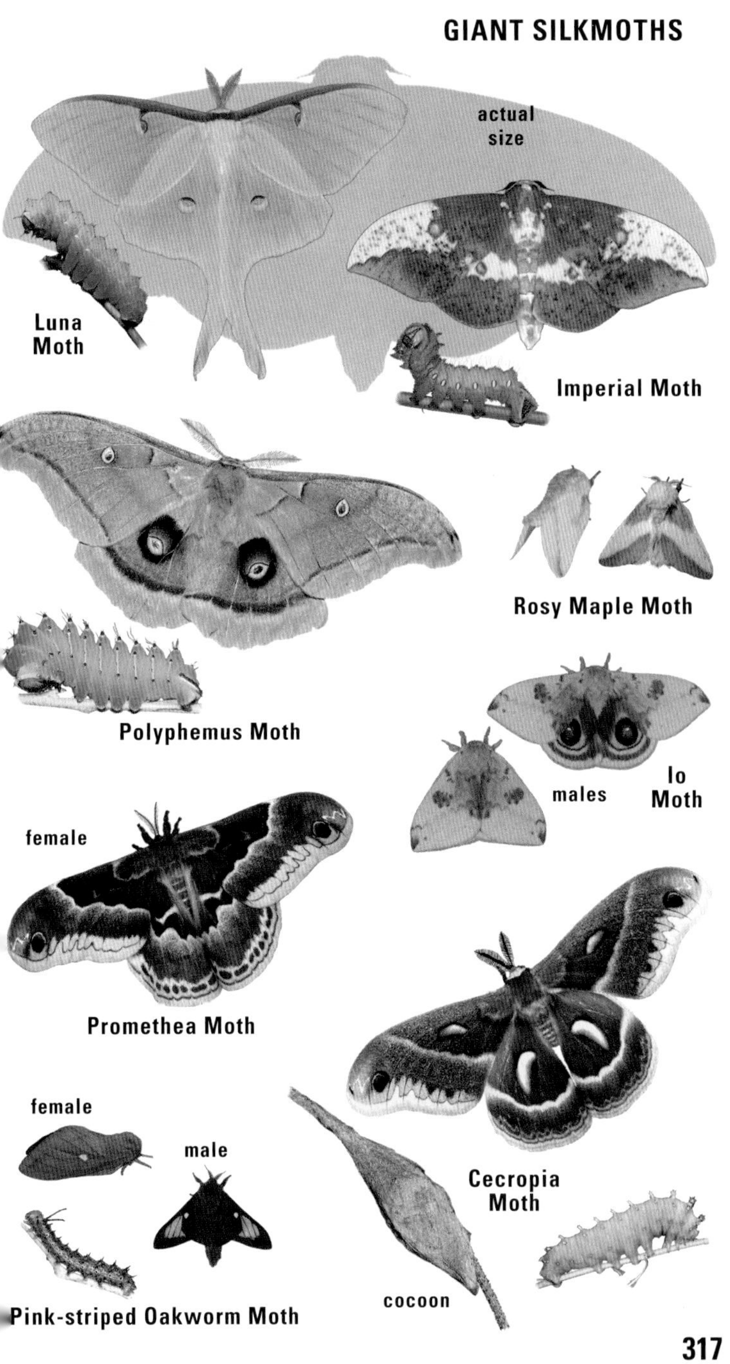
actual
size
Luna
Moth
Imperial Moth
Rosy Maple Moth
Polyphemus Moth
males
Io
Moth
female
Promethea Moth
female
male
Cecropia
Moth
cocoon
Pink-striped Oakworm Moth

SPHINX MOTHS

or hawkmoths (family **Sphingidae**) are strong, fast fliers that may hover at flowers. Their larvae are commonly called hornworms.

FIVE-SPOTTED SPHINX ***Manduca quinquemaculata***

Sometimes common in southern New England. ▶ Adult has 5 pairs of yellow spots on abdomen. Larva has *green "horn"* (red in next species). **Larval foodplant:** tomato and others in nightshade family.

CAROLINA SPHINX ***Manduca sexta***

Most familiar for its larva, the common hornworm on tomatoes in southern New England. ▶ Adult has 6 pairs of yellow spots on abdomen. **Larval foodplant:** tomato and others in nightshade family.

WHITE-LINED SPHINX ***Hyles lineata***

Often active by day, sometimes mistaken for a hummingbird as it hovers at garden flowers. ▶ Striped forewing, pink-barred hindwing. Larva variable. **Larval foodplant:** wide variety of plants.

SMALL-EYED SPHINX ***Paonias myops***

Common in summer. "Eyes" in the names of this and the next 2 are eyespots on the hindwings. ▶ Dark brown. Blue eyespots on *yellow hindwings.* **Larval foodplant:** hawthorn, cherry, and others.

BLINDED SPHINX ***Paonias excaecatus***

Common in hardwood forests, scarcer northward, often coming to lights at night. ▶ Warm brown. Blue eyespot (with no "pupil") in *pinkish hindwing.* **Larval foodplant:** various trees.

ONE-EYED SPHINX ***Smerinthus cerisyi***

Mostly northern New England, uncommon around woods and streamsides. ▶ Grayish brown. Blue eyespot (with one "pupil") in pink hindwing. **Larval foodplant:** poplar, willow, others.

FAWN SPHINX ***Sphinx kalmiae***

Also called Laurel Sphinx. Common around woods in early to midsummer. ▶ Forewings warm brown, streaked darker, blackish on inner margin. **Larval foodplant:** ash, lilac, privet, and others.

WAVED SPHINX ***Ceratomia undulosa***

Common around woodland edges and towns, often coming to lights at night. ▶ Brown forewing with blackish *wavy lines,* dark-ringed white central spot. **Larval foodplant:** ash and lilac.

HOG SPHINX ***Darapsa myron***

Also called Virginia Creeper Sphinx. Common, especially southward. ▶ Marked with *green* (duller when worn), with *orange* on hindwing. **Larval foodplant:** Virginia creeper, grape, and others.

SNOWBERRY CLEARWING ***Hemaris diffinis***

This day-flying sphinx mimics a bumble bee. ▶ *Hovers* in front of flowers (bees alight to feed). Has longer antennae than bumble bees. **Larval foodplant:** honeysuckle, snowberry, others.

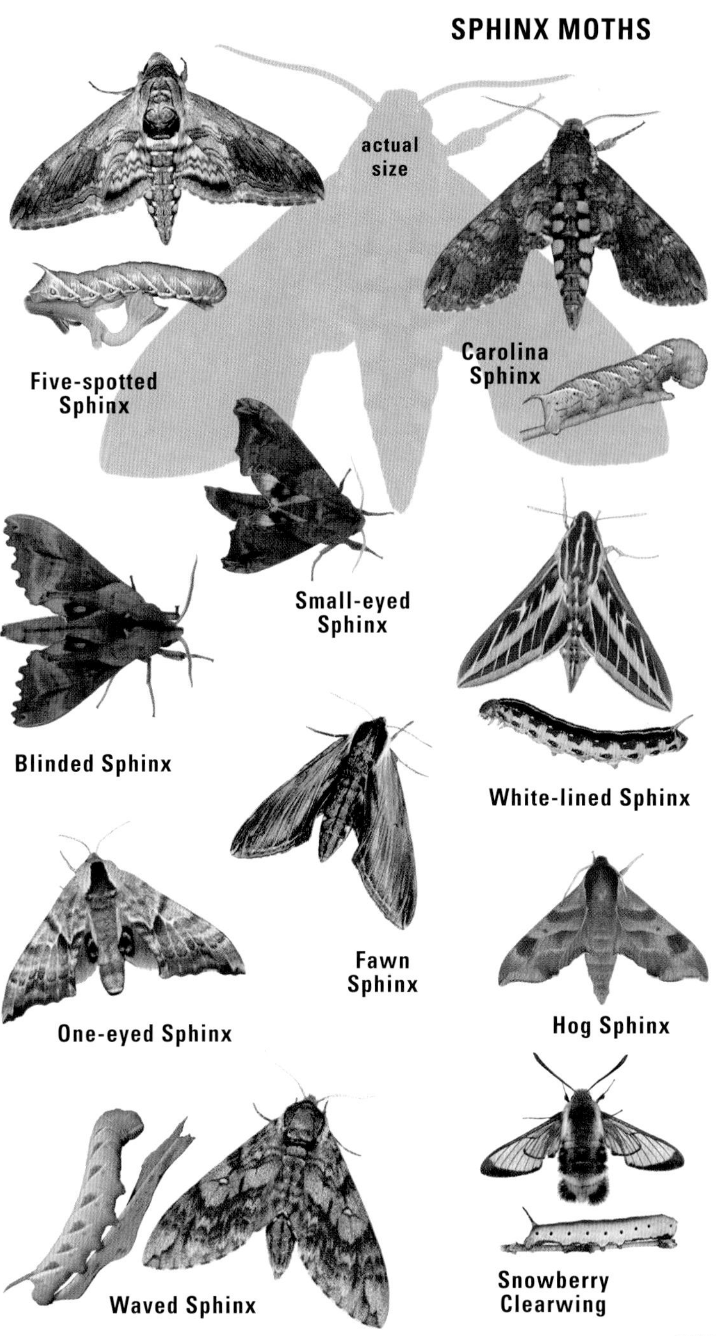

Five-spotted Sphinx

Carolina Sphinx

Small-eyed Sphinx

Blinded Sphinx

White-lined Sphinx

Fawn Sphinx

One-eyed Sphinx

Hog Sphinx

Waved Sphinx

Snowberry Clearwing

OWLET MOTHS

(also called Noctuids) make up the **Noctuidae,** our largest family of moths, containing roughly a quarter of all North American species (including hundreds in New England). The family is extremely diverse, but most (as on this page) are shades of brown or gray.

GREATER OAK DAGGER MOTH ***Acronicta lobeliae***
Common; one of many species of dagger moths in New England. ▶ Gray with black dashes. Other daggers are similar. **Larval foodplant:** oaks.

DINGY CUTWORM MOTH ***Feltia jaculifera***
Very common in fall, coming to lights. ▶ Rich brown, with detailed pattern of black. **Larval foodplant:** grasses, beans, corn, many others.

CORN EARWORM MOTH ***Helicoperva zea***
Common, especially in early fall, when large numbers may invade from the south. ▶ Tan with subtle pattern across forewing, gray patch on hindwing. **Larval foodplant:** corn (feeds on end of ear under husk), tomatoes, others.

COMMON LOOPER MOTH ***Autographa precationis***
Common in fields, open country. ▶ Brown with *doubled white spot* on forewing. Some other loopers are similar. **Larval foodplant:** many low plants.

CELERY LOOPER MOTH ***Anagrapha falcifera***
Another moth of open fields, often visiting flowers by day. ▶ Brown patch on forewing set off by *white line and spot.* **Larval foodplant:** many low plants.

IPSILON DART ***Agrotis ipsilon***
Found worldwide, common in New England, invading from the south in summer. ▶ Slim shape, dark with *paler band* near wingtips. **Larval foodplant:** larva digs underground, comes out at night to feed on many low plants.

ARMYWORM MOTH ***Mythimna unipuncta***
Another migratory moth, abundant in New England. ▶ Tan with *white dot;* wingtip has dark line. **Larval foodplant:** larva ("Armyworm") feeds at night on many plants, sometimes "marching" *en masse* to new fields.

BALTIMORE BOMOLOCHA ***Hypena baltimoralis***
Common around edges of woods, swamps. ▶ Sharply defined *dark brown patch* on each forewing, dark line near wingtip. Other bomolochas are similar. **Larval foodplant:** Red Maple and Silver Maple.

DIMORPHIC BOMOLOCHA ***Hypena bijugalis***
Common, spring to fall. ▶ Female (shown) has strong pattern, male dark with single white spot on each forewing. **Larval foodplant:** dogwood.

EYED PAECTES ***Paectes oculatrix***
Locally common in summer around forest edges. ▶ Small, with a big eyelike spot on each forewing. **Larval foodplant:** Poison Ivy.

EASTERN PANTHEA ***Panthea furcilla***
Now in a separate small family, the Pantheidae. Common in forested areas. ▶ Grayish with *crossed* black lines. **Larval foodplant:** pine, larch, spruce.

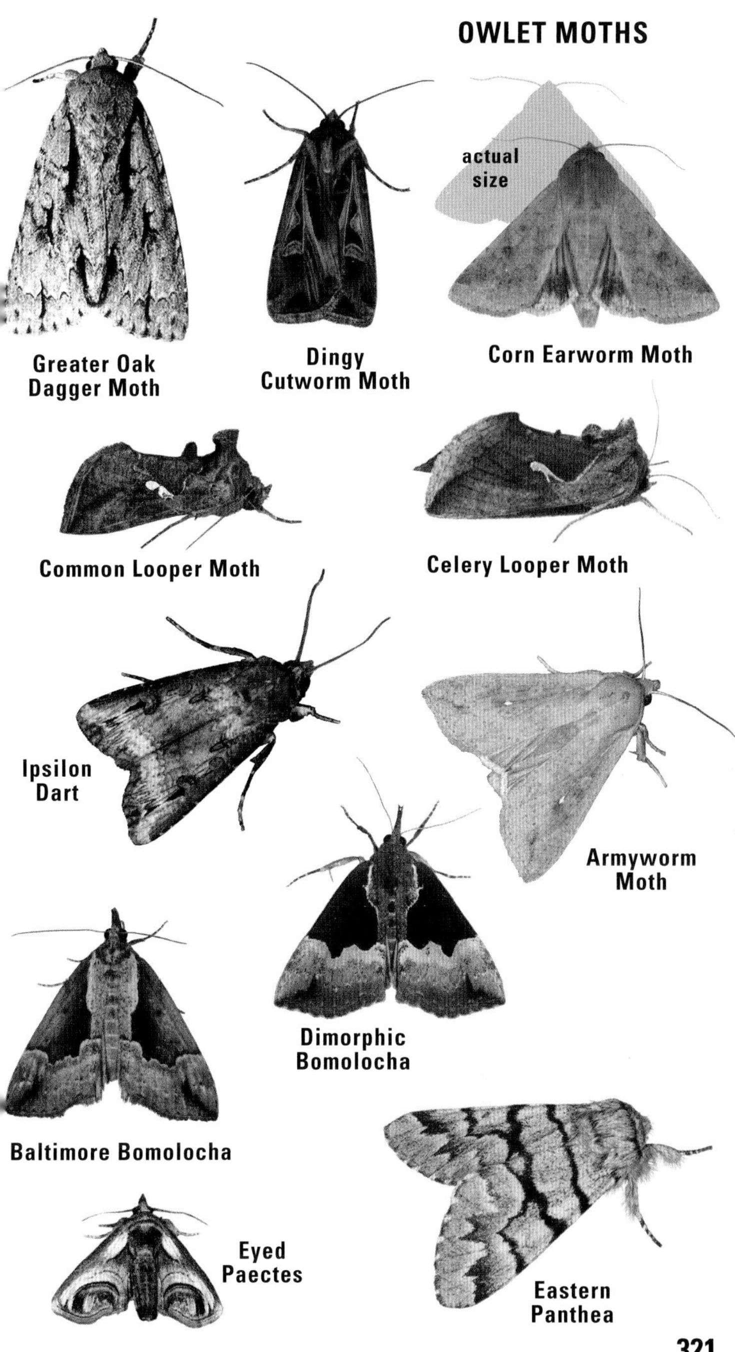

Greater Oak Dagger Moth

Dingy Cutworm Moth

Corn Earworm Moth

Common Looper Moth

Celery Looper Moth

Ipsilon Dart

Armyworm Moth

Dimorphic Bomolocha

Baltimore Bomolocha

Eyed Paectes

Eastern Panthea

EIGHT-SPOTTED FORESTER ***Alypia octomaculata***
A day-flier, visiting flowers. ▶ Two *pale yellow* spots on each forewing, two white spots on each hindwing. **Larval foodplant:** grape, Virginia Creeper.

BEAUTIFUL WOOD-NYMPH ***Eudryas grata***
By day, rests on leaves in the open, looking like a bird dropping. Also visits lights at night. ▶ Forewings white with *smooth-edged* brown border and markings, hindwings yellow. **Larval foodplant:** grape, Virginia Creeper.

PEARLY WOOD-NYMPH ***Eudryas unio***
▶ Like preceding but with *wavy* border. **Larval foodplant:** many low plants.

FORAGE LOOPER ***Caenurgina erechtea***
Common in fields, active by day, also comes to lights at night. ▶ Pale brown with curved darker bars. **Larval foodplant:** grass, clover, other low plants.

DECORATED OWLET ***Pangrapta decoralis***
Common around woodland edges, clearings. ▶ Small, with *whitish triangles* on outer edge, golden brown pattern. **Larval foodplant:** blueberries.

LUNATE ZALE ***Zale lunata***
Very common from spring to fall. ▶ Brown wings crossed by jagged pattern. Suggests a geometer (p. 324). **Larval foodplant:** many.

HORRID ZALE ***Zale horrida***
Not as bad as it sounds: "horrid" also means "bristly." ▶ Broad *pale border* on dark wings, bristles on thorax. **Larval foodplant:** viburnum.

DARLING UNDERWING ***Catocala cara***
More than 40 species of underwings *(Catocala)* are in New England. Most have colorful hindwings, hidden by camouflaged forewings at rest (we show them with wings partly spread). Most fly in late summer. ▶ *Pink* hindwing stripes, dark forewings. **Larval foodplant:** willow, poplar.

BRIDE UNDERWING ***Catocala neogama***
Common in forest, especially southward. ▶ Wavy *orange* bands on hindwings; strong pattern on gray forewings. **Larval foodplant:** hickory, walnut.

YELLOW-GRAY UNDERWING ***Catocala retecta***
Common in forests in late summer. ▶ Hindwings *black;* forewings gray, sometimes with yellow marks. **Larval foodplant:** hickory, walnut.

YELLOW-BANDED UNDERWING ***Catocala cerogama***
▶ *Even-edged, ochre-yellow* hindwing bands. **Larval foodplant:** basswood.

WHITE UNDERWING ***Catocala relicta***
Often rests on birch or aspen trunks, where well camouflaged. ▶ *Whitish* forewings, *white-striped* hindwings. **Larval foodplant:** aspen, poplar, willow.

LARGE YELLOW UNDERWING ***Noctua pronuba***
Not a true underwing and not very large. Introduced from Europe, now common. ▶ Yellow hindwings with black near border, variable forewings.

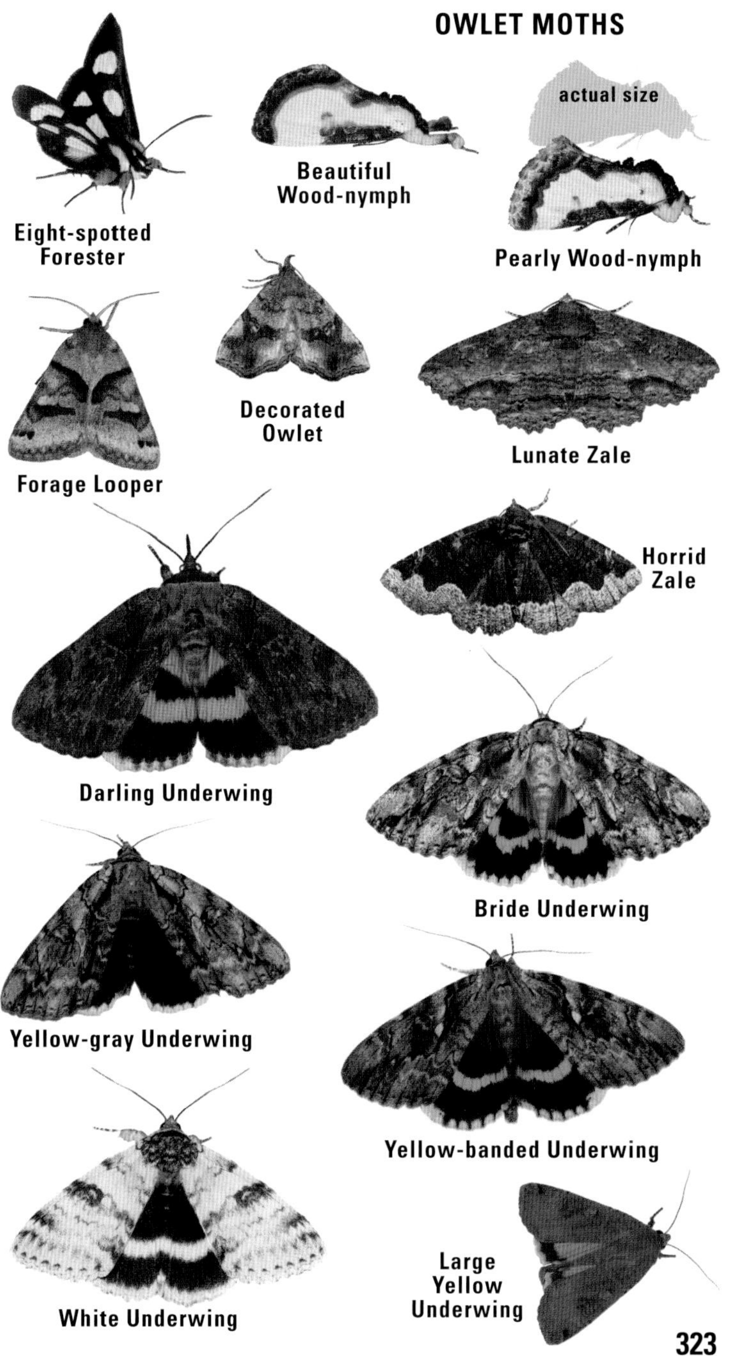

Eight-spotted Forester

Beautiful Wood-nymph

Pearly Wood-nymph

Forage Looper

Decorated Owlet

Lunate Zale

Horrid Zale

Darling Underwing

Bride Underwing

Yellow-gray Underwing

Yellow-banded Underwing

White Underwing

Large Yellow Underwing

GEOMETER MOTHS

(Geometridae) make up our second-largest moth family, with hundreds of species in New England. Adults of many species rest with wings spread to the sides. Larvae are "inchworms" that loop along stems and leaves.

TULIP-TREE BEAUTY ***Epimecis hortaria***
Common all summer in forests of southern New England. ► *Large* size, *scalloped hindwing edge,* intricate pattern. **Larval foodplant:** Tulip-tree, others.

LARGE MAPLE SPANWORM ***Prochoerodes transversata***
Common throughout New England from spring to fall. ► Suggests a dead leaf when at rest. Brown with darker lines. **Larval foodplant:** maples, others.

FALSE CROCUS GEOMETER ***Xanthotype urticaria***
Flies in summer and fall, common. ► Yellow with brown mottling. **Crocus Geometer** *(X. sospeta)* is very similar. **Larval foodplant:** many.

FERGUSON'S SCALLOP SHELL ***Rheumaptera prunivorata***
Locally common in forested areas. ► Sharp pattern of *scalloped wavy lines.* **Larval foodplant:** groups of larvae build nests in leaves of black cherry.

LARGE LACE-BORDER ***Scopula limboundata***
A common visitor to lights in summer. ► Creamy wings with variable lacy pattern near border. **Larval foodplant:** twiglike larvae feed on many plants.

NORTHERN PINE LOOPER ***Caripeta piniata***
Common. ► Orange-brown, with whitish pattern. **Larval foodplant:** pines.

CHICKWEED GEOMETER ***Haematopis grataria***
Common in open grassy places, active by day but also coming to lights at night. ► Yellow with *pink* lines. **Larval foodplant:** clover, other low weeds.

PALE BEAUTY ***Campaea perlata***
Common at lights, especially in late summer. ► Silky whitish, wings crossed by faint, *nearly straight* lines. **Larval foodplant:** many shrubs and trees.

LESSER MAPLE SPANWORM ***Itame pustularia***
A common visitor to lights in summer. ► Silky white with *coppery lines* across wings, sharpest at *leading edge* of forewing. **Larval foodplant:** maples.

LESSER GRAPEVINE LOOPER ***Eulithis diversilineata***
Common from Massachusetts south. ► Orange-brown with sharp pattern. Often rests with *abdomen raised.* **Larval foodplant:** grape, Virginia Creeper.

BLUISH SPRING MOTH ***Lomographa semiclarata***
Active by day in spring, visiting flowers. ► Whitish with black markings, bluish tinge. Suggests a small butterfly. **Larval foodplant:** various shrubs.

COMMON SPRING MOTH ***Heliomata cycladata***
Flies by day in spring. ► Black and cream pattern. **Larval foodplant:** locusts.

WAVY-LINED EMERALD ***Synchlora aerata***
Common in summer. ► *Small, pale green,* with wavy white lines. **Larval foodplant:** asters and others. Larva covers itself with plant fragments.

Tulip-tree Beauty

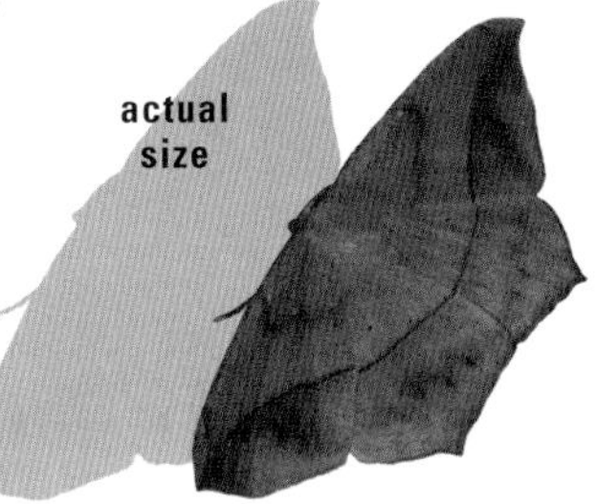

Large Maple Spanworm

False Crocus Geometer

Ferguson's Scallop Shell

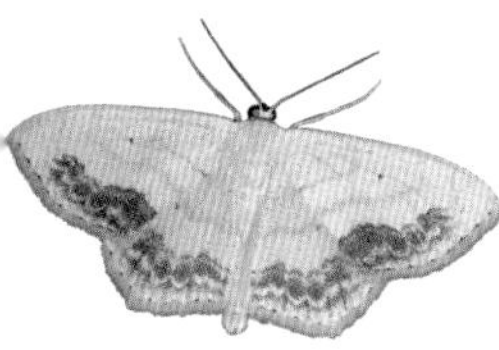

Large Lace-border

Northern
Pine Looper

Chickweed
Geometer

Pale Beauty

Lesser
Maple Spanworm

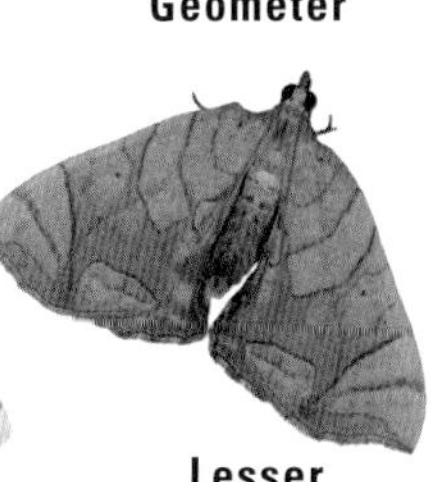

Lesser
Grapevine Looper

Bluish
Spring Moth

Common
Spring Moth

Wavy-lined
Emerald

TIGER MOTHS

(family **Arctiidae**) mostly have fuzzy caterpillars, well-patterned adults.

ISABELLA TIGER MOTH ***Pyrrharctia isabella***
Famous for its larva, the "Woolly Bear" that wanders across autumn roads. ▶ Mustard colored with brown dots, pinkish wash. **Larval foodplant:** many.

SALT MARSH MOTH ***Estigmene acraea***
Despite the name, common and widespread in many habitats. ▶ Male smaller than female, with *yellow hindwings.* **Larval foodplant:** many.

VIRGINIAN TIGER MOTH ***Spilosoma virginica***
Common, often comes to lights. ▶ Adult white with black dots, some *yellow on body and legs.* Larva variable, long-haired. **Larval foodplant:** many.

BANDED TUSSOCK MOTH ***Halysidota tessellaris***
Common in woods, often comes to lights. ▶ Distinct but *pale* pattern of bands on wings. **Larval foodplant:** many trees and shrubs.

VIRGIN TIGER MOTH ***Grammia virgo***
This tiger-striped moth is a prize find at porch lights in summer. ▶ Several tiger moths are similar; this is the largest. **Larval foodplant:** many low plants.

HARNESSED TIGER MOTH ***Apantesis phalerata***
Another beautiful tiger, fairly common in summer. ▶ Simpler pattern than the preceding, fewer white stripes. **Larval foodplant:** many low plants.

MILKWEED TUSSOCK MOTH ***Euchaetes egle***
Often found by people seeking Monarch larvae (p. 312). ▶ Tufts of rust, cream, and black. Adult gray, inconspicuous. **Larval foodplant:** milkweed.

NEIGHBOR HAPLOA ***Haploa contigua***
Haploas fly day or night, come to flowers, lights. ▶ Brown lines on white. Three other similar haploas in New England. **Larval foodplant:** asters, others.

CLYMENE HAPLOA ***Haploa clymene***
Often seen by day on flowers, also visits lights. ▶ Stronger pattern than other haploas. Hindwings *yellow.* **Larval foodplant:** asters and others.

VIRGINIA CTENUCHA ***Ctenucha virginica***
Visits flowers by day, also comes to lights. ▶ Suggests a wasp at first glance; note long antennae, *blue sheen* on body. **Larval foodplant:** grasses.

YELLOW-COLLARED SCAPE MOTH ***Cisseps fulvicollis***
Common by day on early fall flowers such as goldenrod. ▶ Smaller than Virginia Ctenucha, duller, less blue. **Larval foodplant:** grasses and sedges.

BELLA MOTH ***Eutetheisa bella***
A day-flier of meadows, more common toward the south. ▶ Dotted forewings; *bright pink hindwings* show in flight. **Larval foodplant:** legumes.

PAINTED LICHEN MOTH ***Hypoprepia fucosa***
Locally common in woodlands, coming to lights at night. ▶ Slaty stripes on wings washed yellow and red. **Larval foodplant:** lichens on trees and rocks.

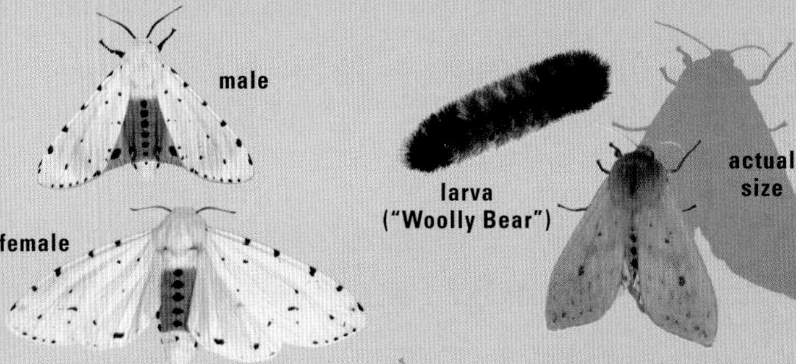

Salt Marsh Moth

Isabella Tiger Moth

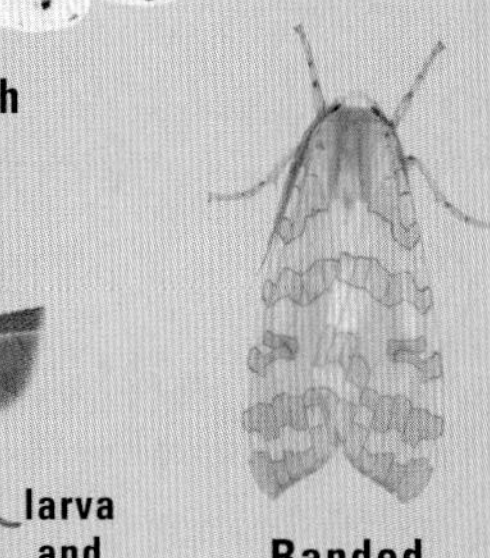

Banded Tussock Moth

Virgin Tiger Moth

larva and adult

Virginian Tiger Moth

Harnessed Tiger Moth

Milkweed Tussock Moth larva

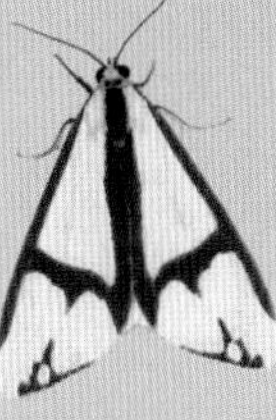

Neighbor Haploa

Clymene Haploa

Virginia Ctenucha

Yellow-collared Scape Moth

Bella Moth

Painted Lichen Moth

The first four below are in the Prominent family **(Notodontidae),** while the remaining six are all from different families. The last three families are among the many that are classified as Microlepidoptera, a diverse group of mostly tiny moths that are not covered in detail in this book.

WHITE FURCULA ***Furcula borealis***
Fairly common in wooded areas, flying in late spring and summer, attracted to lights at night. ▸ Beautiful pattern, white with gray median band and black dots. **Larval foodplant:** wild cherry.

DOUBLE-TOOTHED PROMINENT ***Nerice bidentata***
Fairly common around woodland edges, clearings. ▸ Rich brown outer part of each forewing has 2 "teeth" pointing inward. **Larval foodplant:** elms.

WHITE-DOTTED PROMINENT ***Nadata gibbosa***
Common in oak woodlands and edges throughout New England. ▸ Rich orange-brown, each forewing crossed by two lines and with two *central white dots.* **Larval foodplant:** oak and other trees and shrubs.

DATANA PROMINENT ***Datana* sp.**
Several species in this genus occur in New England. ▸ Tan wings with darker lines, *dark brown* furry thorax. **Larval foodplant:** various trees and shrubs.

ARCHED HOOKTIP ***Drepana arcuata***
Common in forested areas. (Family Drepanidae) ▸ Strongly *hooked wingtips,* curved dark lines. **Larval foodplant:** alder and birch.

EASTERN TENT CATERPILLAR MOTH ***Malacosoma americanum***
Common and widespread. (Family Lasiocampidae) ▸ Warm brown wings crossed by *2 pale bands.* **Larval foodplant:** hawthorn, apple, other trees, shrubs. Larvae spin communal web in fork of branch during late spring.

GYPSY MOTH ***Lymantria dispar***
Introduced from Europe to Boston in 1869, now abundant throughout New England, sometimes a major forest pest. Larvae can defoliate large areas, although efforts to control them may cause damage of other kinds. (Family Lymantriidae) ▸ Female much larger, paler than male; both with similar pattern of lines and dots. **Larval foodplant:** oak, beech, 500+ others.

GRAPE LEAF-FOLDER ***Desmia funeralis***
Common, widespread, active day and night. (Family Crambidae) ▸ White spots on narrow black wings. Compare Eight-spotted Forester, p. 322. **Larval foodplant:** larvae fold over edges of grape leaves, feed inside the fold.

PLUME MOTHS **family Pterophoridae**
Common, often attracted to lights. ▸ Recognized by their resting posture, wings out to the side, like tiny airplanes. **Larval foodplant:** various.

AILANTHUS WEBWORM MOTH ***Atteva punctella***
Common in southern New England. (Family Yponomeutidae) ▸ Orange with *network of black-ringed white spots.* **Larval foodplant:** Ailanthus.

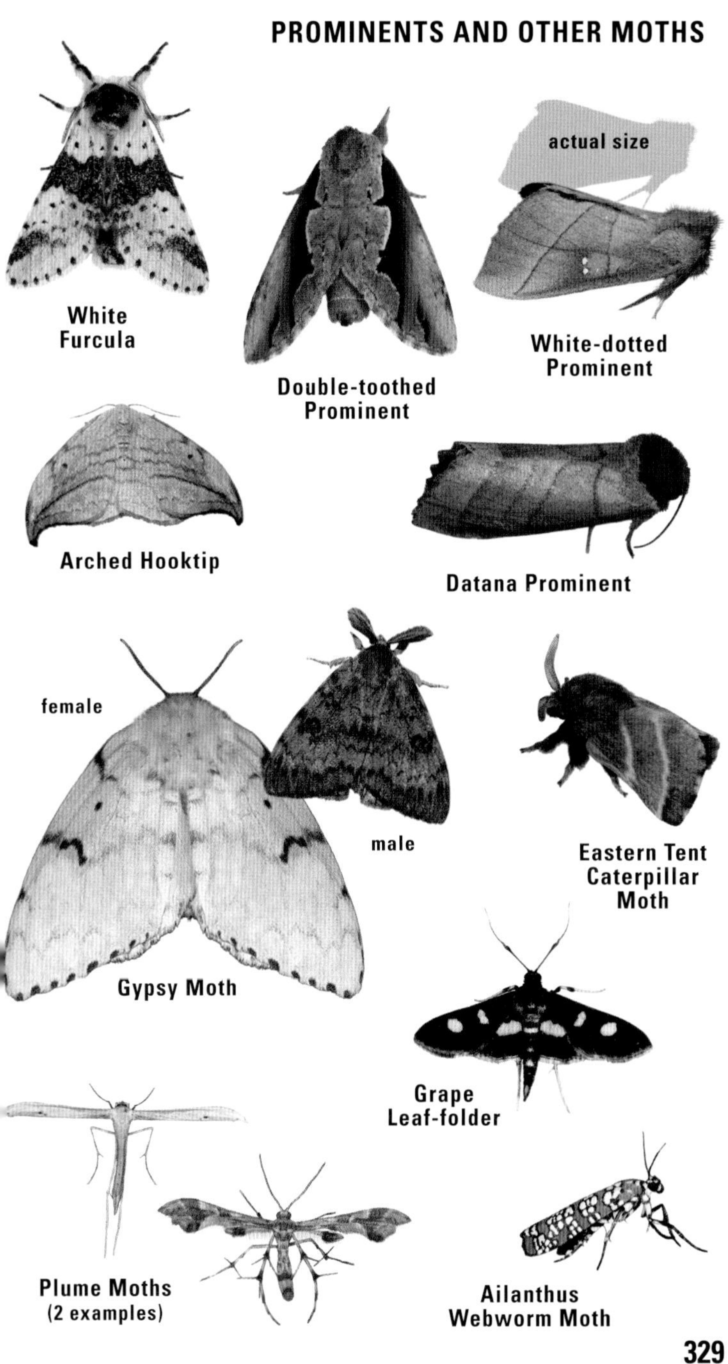

White Furcula

Double-toothed Prominent

White-dotted Prominent

Arched Hooktip

Datana Prominent

Gypsy Moth

Eastern Tent Caterpillar Moth

Grape Leaf-folder

Plume Moths (2 examples)

Ailanthus Webworm Moth

Butterflies and moths, because they are so popular, are treated in their own separate section (starting on p. 298). The present section covers everything else: all the other insect orders besides the Lepidoptera.

Insects section contributed by Eric R. Eaton

Insects are wildlife, too! We tend to lump them all as pests, or dismiss them as a nuisance at best, but only a tiny fraction are garden-chomping, forest-destroying, garbage-infesting, blood-sucking terrors. The bulk of those are also nonnative, brought here from Europe or Asia by our own accident or intent. Insects are, overwhelmingly, necessary to the functioning of natural ecosystems and increasingly indispensable allies in agriculture, medicine, national defense, and other human enterprises.

What exactly is an insect? Insects are invertebrate animals in the phylum Arthropoda, which translates to "joint-footed." Other examples of arthropods include arachnids like spiders and scorpions, myriapods (centipedes and millipedes), and crustaceans (crabs, lobsters, shrimp). All arthropods have an exoskeleton, in contrast to the internal skeleton of vertebrates.

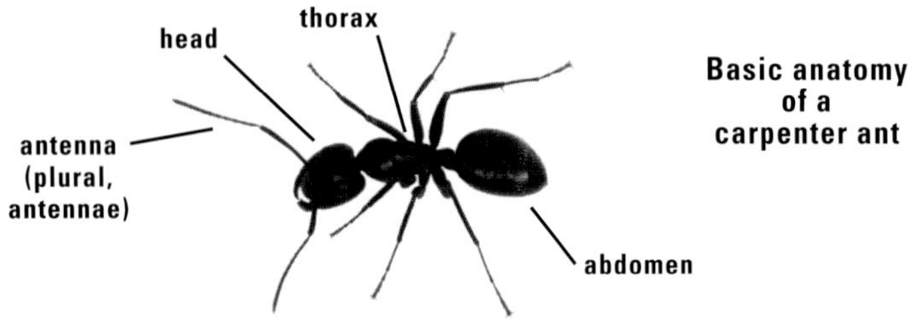

Basic anatomy of a carpenter ant

The body of an insect is divided into three segments: the head is the sensory center, with the compound eyes, antennae, and mouthparts located there. The thorax is locomotion central, as all six legs and two pairs of wings (one pair in flies and some other insects) arise from the midsection of the insect. Lastly, the abdomen functions in digestion, excretion, and reproduction. Antennae act like the insect's nose, picking up scents and other chemical cues in the environment. The eyes are superb at detecting motion and can see in the ultraviolet end of the light spectrum. The mouthparts can taste morsels before the insect ever takes a bite. Most insects do not hear, but they can readily detect vibrations. Legs of various insects are modified for running, jumping, swimming, digging, or climbing, facilitating the exploitation of a variety of habitats. Wings allow adult insects to disperse across vast distances.

Metamorphosis is among the most remarkable traits of insects. After hatching from an egg, the nymphs of grasshoppers, cockroaches, and true bugs simply grow incrementally larger, gradually accruing reproductive organs and often wings. This is termed "simple," "gradual," or "incomplete" metamorphosis. More advanced insects experience "complete metamorphosis," going through an egg, larva, and pupa stage before graduating to adulthood. (See the illustration of complete metamorphisis in a butterfly on p. 298.) Growth in all instances is achieved by molting: shedding the exoskeleton. The animal gets larger in the brief time before the new cuticle hardens. Intervals between molts are called "instars." A typical larval insect will pass through 4–6 instars before pupating. The pupal stage is considered the resting stage because it is typically an inert organism on the exterior. Inside, however, genes are being turned on and turned off, and the cellular structure of the animal is being reorganized. Adult insects do not molt and the insect cannot increase in size. Therefore, something like a "baby lady beetle" is actually a small species or individual; it won't ever "grow up." The real "baby" would be the larval stage.

The diversity of insects can hardly be overstated. They comprise well over 80 percent of the animal kingdom. There is scarcely any climate or niche that insects have not conquered, save for Antarctica and the open ocean (oh, wait; there are marine water striders). There are, in fact, so many species that very few have been assigned official common (English) names. The scientific name, in Latin, Greek, or a combination of the two, is the best way to avoid confusion when discussing a given species anyway.

Successful as insects are, there are some species that are endangered. This is especially true of certain aquatic insects, cave insects, and those species that inhabit unique, vulnerable habitats such as dune systems and wetlands. The Karner Blue Butterfly and American Burying Beetle are federally endangered species found in New England, but there are numerous insect species on state threatened and endangered lists.

Identifying insects is complicated by their small size (the average insect is 5 millimeters or less), metamorphosis (many larvae and adults have yet to be associated with one another), and mimicry (flies, beetles, moths, and other insects may closely resemble bees or wasps, for example). Take a picture. No, take several pictures from different angles and see if you can use this guide to at least place the insect to order level. Use more specific guides, like the *Kaufman Field Guide to Insects of North America,* to narrow the insect to a family or genus, or even species in rare instances. Supplementing field guides with online resources like Bugguide.net can be even more helpful.

So many species, so little time, the experts cry, and they are right. There is always the chance that you, yes, *you,* could find a species new to your county or state, or even new to science. Your digital video could record behaviors and associations completely unknown even to experts. Above all, enjoy the thrill of satisfying your own curiosity.

SOME PRIMITIVE INSECTS

The insects on these pages are among the most primitive. Springtails are not even considered insects any longer. All go through "simple" metamorphosis, with the young resembling miniature versions of adults.

Earwigs (order Dermaptera) are perhaps named for a corruption of "ear wing," describing the appearance of the folded wings of species like the **European Earwig** *(Forficula auricularia)*. Yes, some species can fly. At rest the wings are so intricately folded as to make origami look simple. While the European Earwig is nonnative and considered a pest of roses and other flowers, it is mostly a scavenger. Females guard their eggs and the young earwigs that hatch from them.

Termites and Cockroaches (order Blattodea) include some of our worst pests and most valuable decomposers. Formerly placed in their own order (Isoptera), termites are now considered "social cockroaches." Beneficial in the forest where they turn decaying wood back into soil, termites are structural pests when they eat our homes. The chief pest species in New England is the **Eastern Subterranean Termite** *(Reticulitermes flavipes)*. Watch for soil tubes creeping across your home's foundation from the soil that indicate termites are invading. "Alates," winged males and females that will found new nests, rise in massive swarms from existing termite colonies.

Cockroaches include native "wood roaches" that stick to the outdoors. Indoors we encounter immigrant species that probably originated in tropical Africa and arrived here on slave ships. The **American Cockroach** *(Periplaneta americana)* is one of these. The much smaller **German Cockroach** *(Blattella germanica)* and **Brown-banded Cockroach** *(Supella longipalpa)* are likewise common indoor pests. The **Oriental Cockroach** *(Blatta orientalis)*, aka "waterbug," prefers sewers and other moist niches. Roaches are implicated in the mechanical transmission of bacteria, and their molts (shed exoskeletons), body parts, and feces are proven allergens that can also aggravate asthma.

Silverfish and their allies **(order Zygentoma)** are mostly an indoor nuisance but can be genuine pests in libraries. They have an appetite for starchy materials, such as the paste used in bookbinding. The **Firebrat** *(Thermobia domestica)* likes warm, dry areas such as near furnaces and the insulation around water heaters. The **Four-lined Silverfish** *(Ctenolepisma lineata)* is common under wood shingles, in garden mulch, and in garages, attics, and voids in walls.

Springtails (class Collembola) are named for a hinged organ ("furcula" or "furca") at the rear of the abdomen that the organism uses to propel itself into a jump. Not all springtails "spring," however. They are tiny but incredibly numerous, especially in soil, leaf litter, compost heaps, and on the surface of water and snow. They can be a nuisance indoors in potting soil of houseplants and around the drains of bathtubs, showers, and basins. They feed on decaying organic matter and/or spores of molds and mildews. "Snow fleas," genus *Hypogastrura*, can cover the snow in unimaginable numbers, but smaller gatherings are a common winter sight.

female

European Earwig

male

actual size

mud tubes along wall

swarm of winged adults

workers and soldiers

subterranean termites *(Reticulitermes)*

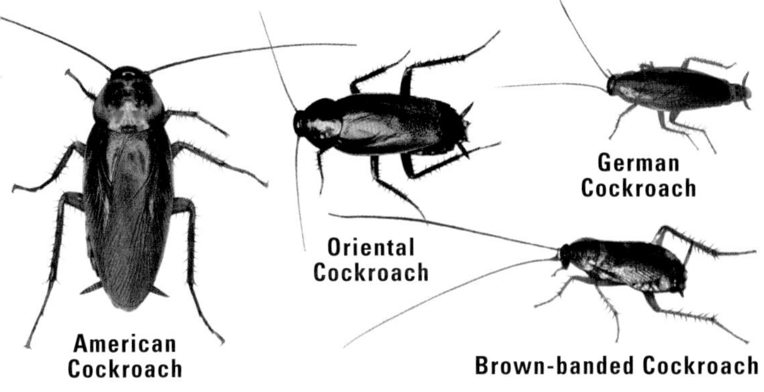

American Cockroach

Oriental Cockroach

German Cockroach

Brown-banded Cockroach

snow fleas *(Hypogastrura)*

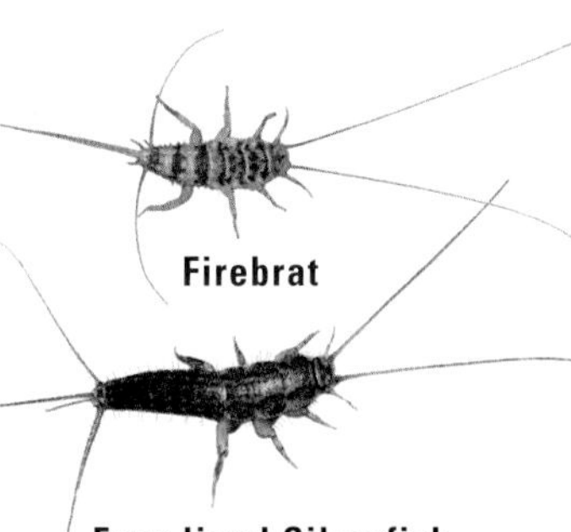

Firebrat

Four-lined Silverfish

DRAGONFLIES are second only to butterflies as our most popular insects. Along with the damselflies (p. 336), they make up the order **Odonata.** Harmless to humans, they do not sting, and they will attempt to bite (not very hard) only if captured. Adults are exceptional fliers, larvae live underwater, and all stages are predatory. They undergo a partial metamorphosis, with mature larvae crawling out of the water and winged adults emerging from the split exoskeleton. Seven families of dragonflies occur in New England, but most of the noticeable types belong to two or three of those.

Darners (family Aeshnidae) include our largest dragonflies. They have huge eyes that meet on the tops of their heads, and their abdomens are long and narrow. When at rest, they hang vertically. At least 20 darner species occur in New England, but the most frequently seen is the **Common Green Darner** *(Anax junius).* Adult males show contrast between the bright green thorax and bright blue abdomen; females and younger males are duller but show the same "bull's-eye" pattern on the forehead. These darners are strongly migratory, and major southward flights may be seen along the coast in fall.

Most **emeralds (family Corduliidae)** have bright green eyes and most are uncommon, but the **Common Baskettail** *(Epitheca cynosura)* is an exception to both rules. It may be seen feeding in swarms in early summer.

Most noticeable dragonflies around ponds and marshes are **skimmers (family Libellulidae).** The **Halloween Pennant** *(Celithemis eponina),* with its strikingly patterned wings, is common in marshes in summer. The **Common Pondhawk** *(Erythemis simplicicollis)* is an aggressive hunter, even catching other dragonflies larger than itself. Mature males are dull powder blue; female and younger males are bright green, with black rings on the abdomen. Smaller but often abundant around still waters is the **Blue Dasher** *(Pachydiplax longipennis).* Mature males have the abdomen pale blue with a black tip, green eyes, and black and yellow stripes on the thorax. Young females are mostly black and yellow, with reddish brown eyes. Blue Dashers often perch with the wings angled downward.

The **Common Whitetail** *(Plathemis lydia)* is numerous around ponds and rivers but is also found in open fields, far from water. Only mature males show the bright white on the abdomen. Also quite wide-ranging in open country is the **Widow Skimmer** *(Libellula luctuosa).* Both sexes have black at the base of the wings and white bands outward from that, but the mature male is much more strongly marked and has a white abdomen. One of our most stunning dragonflies is the **Twelve-spotted Skimmer** *(Libellula pulchella),* in which the mature male has 12 black spots and 10 white spots on the wings.

Among the smallest of our skimmers is the **Eastern Amberwing** *(Perithemis tenera).* Only males have amber wings; females have clear wings with brown spots. Both sexes can look like wasps as they perch on twigs near water. Small reddish skimmers active late in the season are **meadowhawks** (genus *Sympetrum*). They fly mostly in late summer and fall, and some may be active on warm days even in November.

Common
Green
Darner

Common
Baskettail

Halloween
Pennant

Blue
Dasher

Common
Pondhawk

Common
Whitetail

Widow Skimmer

Twelve-spotted
Skimmer

Eastern
Amberwing

meadowhawk
sp.

MORE INSECTS WITH AQUATIC LARVAE

Like the dragonflies on p. 334, the young stages of these four groups all develop underwater.

Damselflies are related to dragonflies but are typically smaller and more slender, and most kinds rest with the wings folded over the back. **Broad-winged Damselflies (family Calopterygidae)** perch on vegetation at the edge of streams and rivers. The **Ebony Jewelwing** *(Calopteryx maculata)* is the most common species. **Spread-winged Damselflies (Lestidae)** are named for their splayed-wings resting posture. The **Northern Spreadwing** *(Lestes disjunctus)* is typical, found around ponds, bogs, and slow-moving streams. **Narrow-winged Damselflies (Coenagrionidae)** are the most abundant of damselflies. The **Familiar Bluet** *(Enallagma civile)* is a fixture around the edges of ponds, but other bluets resemble this species. The diminutive **Eastern Forktail** *(Ischnura verticalis)* has a weaving flight through cattails, reeds, and grasses.

Mayflies (order Ephemeroptera) are the only insects that molt once they become adults. The "subimago" ("dun" in the language of anglers) emerges from the aquatic naiad stage, followed shortly by the imago, or "spinner," the final adult stage. Naiads eat mostly algae and organic debris. Adults live perhaps a day, just long enough to reproduce. Males often swarm over water, mating with females in midair. **Small Minnow Mayflies (family Baetidae)** are small but diverse and abundant. Males have divided eyes, the upper half resembling a mushroom. **Spiny Crawler Mayflies (Ephemerellidae)** are named for the aquatic naiad stage. They are diverse and common, especially in trout streams. Naiads of **Common Burrowing Mayflies (Ephemeridae)** burrow in the sediments of rivers and lakes. Adults are medium to large with three streaming "tails" (caudal filaments).

Stoneflies (order Plecoptera) occupy moving water as aquatic naiads. Most have a short pair of caudal filaments at the rear of the abdomen. **Common Stoneflies (family Perlidae)** are typical. Naiads are predatory on other aquatic organisms. Adults emerge in summer and are sometimes attracted to lights at night. ***Perlesta*** is a common genus. Adults of **Small Winter Stoneflies (Capniidae)** can be found on snow or bridges and streamside vegetation, even at subfreezing temperatures in late winter and early spring. Males of some species have the wings reduced. Naiads of **Giant Stoneflies (Pteronarcyidae)** live in rivers and eat decaying leaves. Adults ("salmonflies") emerge in late spring or early summer.

Caddisflies (order Trichoptera) resemble moths. Their aquatic larvae are master architects. Most build "mobile homes" of sand, pebbles, or plant material. **Netspinning Caddisflies (family Hydropsychidae)** live in fast-flowing streams and spin silk nets to intercept the algae, debris, and small animals they eat. The adult **Zebra Caddisfly** *(Macrostemum zebratum)* comes to lights at night. **Giant Casemakers (Phryganeidae)** make tubular cases of various materials. Young larvae are vegetarians, but they become voracious predators later on. Adults fly May through August and sometimes come to lights. **Longhorned Caddisflies (Leptoceridae)** are named for the long antennae of the small adults.

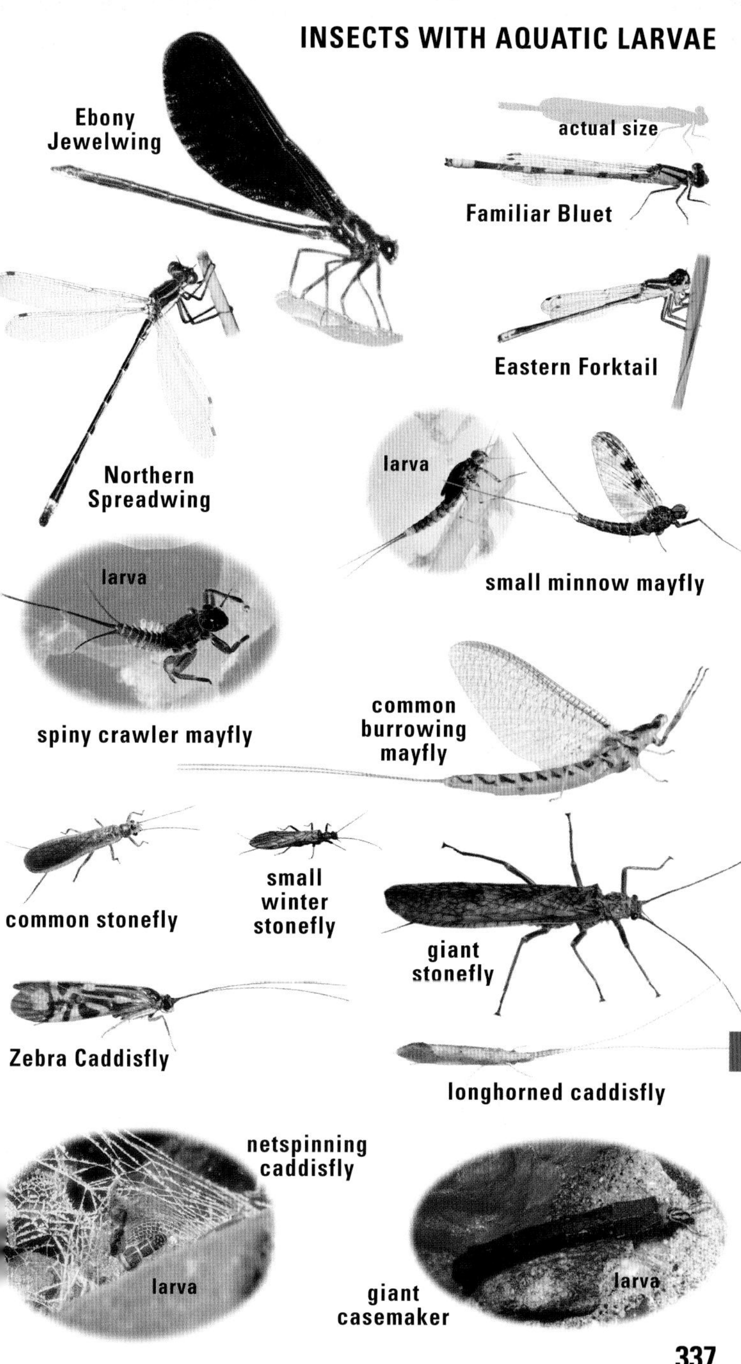
Ebony Jewelwing
actual size
Familiar Bluet
Eastern Forktail
Northern Spreadwing
larva
small minnow mayfly
larva
spiny crawler mayfly
common burrowing mayfly
common stonefly
small winter stonefly
giant stonefly
Zebra Caddisfly
longhorned caddisfly
netspinning caddisfly
larva
giant casemaker
larva

GRASSHOPPERS, KATYDIDS, AND CRICKETS

Grasshoppers and their allies (order **Orthoptera**) are common insects with strong hind legs for jumping. All go through gradual metamorphosis. Adults of some are wingless. Most are omnivores and seldom become true pests of crops.

Short-horned grasshoppers (family Acrididae) are day-active insects with short antennae. Most abundant in summer and fall, they can be incredibly cryptic and are often nearly invisible on soil or vegetation. Many species fly well. The **Carolina Locust** or Carolina Grasshopper *(Dissosteira carolina)* is large and conspicuous in flight, with black hind wings margined in pale yellow. Gray or brown otherwise, it is hard to spy on the ground. The **Northern Green-striped Grasshopper** *(Chortophaga viridifasciata)* is a springtime species, with nymphs overwintering. It can generate loud crackling sounds in flight. The **Sulphur-winged Grasshopper** *(Arphia sulphurea)* is likewise noisy, and its hind wings are bright yellow. The **Seaside Grasshopper** *(Trimerotropis maritima)* occurs inland, too, but likes dunes and sand pits — and with good reason: its camouflage there is perfect. The **Differential Grasshopper** *(Melanoplus differentialis)* is large and lumbering. The herringbone pattern on the hind femur (thigh) is distinctive. It may be gray-green or bright yellow. The **Two-striped Grasshopper** *(M. bivittatus)* is somewhat less common. The **Red-legged Grasshopper** *(M. femurrubrum)* is abundant in fields and vacant lots.

Katydids (family Tettigoniidae) are also called long-horned grasshoppers for their ultra-long antennae. Most are nocturnal, and males sing by rubbing a "scraper" on one front wing against a "file" on the other. The **Common True Katydid** *(Pterophylla camellifolia)* provides night music in southern New England, the males singing a rasping *ka-ty-did, ka-ty-didn't* from high in trees on hot, humid nights. The **Slender Meadow Katydid** *(Conocephalus fasciatus)* can be found in dry fields and vacant lots. It may dodge to the other side of a stem at your approach. The **Drumming Katydid** *(Meconema thalassinum)* is native to Europe but is now common in our region. Males can't "sing" but rapidly tap a hind foot to produce sound. Six species of **bush katydids** (genus *Scudderia*) occur in New England and are common in yards and gardens. **Roesel's Katydid** *(Metrioptera roeselii)* is introduced here from Europe. Look for it in old fields.

Camel Crickets (family Rhaphidophoridae) are wingless and are found in cool, damp places like cellars, basements, old wells, mineshafts, and caves. Members of the genus ***Ceuthophilus*** are abundant, but the **Greenhouse Stone Cricket** *(Diestramenna asynamora)* is becoming increasingly common since its introduction here from its native China.

Crickets (family Gryllidae) include the big **field crickets** (genus *Gryllus*) and much smaller "ground crickets" *(Allonemobius, Eunemobius,* and *Neonemobius)* that are found on the ground, under stones and logs, and similar situations. Look on foliage for the slender and more delicate **tree crickets** (*Oecanthus* spp.). "If moonlight could be heard, it would sound like that," wrote Nathaniel Hawthorne of the trilling choruses of tree crickets.

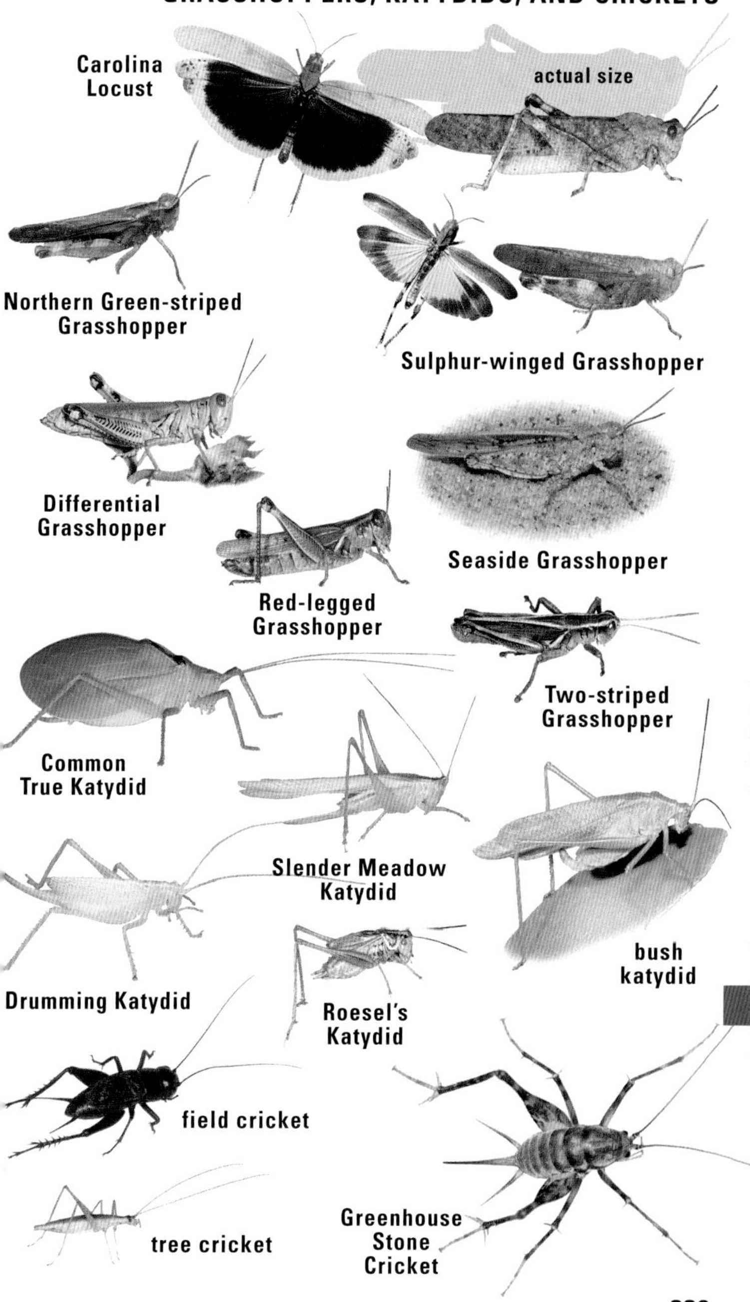
Carolina
Locust
actual size
Northern Green-striped
Grasshopper
Sulphur-winged Grasshopper
Differential
Grasshopper
Seaside Grasshopper
Red-legged
Grasshopper
Two-striped
Grasshopper
Common
True Katydid
Slender Meadow
Katydid
bush
katydid
Drumming Katydid
Roesel's
Katydid
field cricket
tree cricket
Greenhouse
Stone
Cricket

MANTIDS, STICK INSECTS, CICADAS

These are large and conspicuous insects from three different orders. Mantids (order **Mantodea**) and stick insects (order **Phasmatodea**) have a simple metamorphosis, with freshly hatched young looking like smaller versions of the adults. Cicadas belong to the order **Hemiptera** (the true bugs), introduced on p. 342. They also have a simple metamorphosis, but young cicadas have a lifestyle very different from that of adults, tunneling underground and sucking sap from roots.

As a group, mantids are among our easiest insects to recognize. Their front legs are specially modified for grasping prey; when not in use capturing or holding a victim, these legs are folded up in what looks like an attitude of prayer, suggesting the common name of "praying mantis." Normally they hunt by stalking very slowly through vegetation or by lying in wait near flowers, capturing other insects with a sudden grab of their front legs.

The two species seen commonly in New England are both introduced. The **European Mantis** *(Mantis religiosa)*, native to temperate regions of the Old World, may be either brown or green; it is recognized with certainty by the black-and-white "bull's-eye" on the inside of the front thigh. It grows to nearly 3" long. The **Chinese Mantis** *(Tenodera aridifolia sinensis)* gets even larger, up to 4"; it may be green or brown but usually has green edging on the wing. Like other mantids, females of these two species lay eggs in masses on vertical stems, covered with a foam that hardens into a protective capsule. Egg cases of these two species are widely sold to provide pest control in gardens, but mantids eat whatever insects they can catch, most of which are not pests.

Stick insects are masters of camouflage, shaped and patterned like sticks, and moving so slowly that they are incredibly hard to spot in bushes and trees. They feed on leaves. In New England the **Northern Walkingstick** *(Diapheromera femorata)* is most commonly seen in late summer.

Cicadas (family Cicadidae) are heard far more often than they are seen. Especially in southern New England, their grinding, buzzing whines in the treetops are typical sounds of hot summer days. Males make the sound with membranes called tymbals on both sides of their bodies.

Like all true bugs, cicadas have mouthparts adapted to piercing and sucking. Their immature stages, called nymphs, live underground (for 2–5 years in most species), drinking sap from roots. When mature, they crawl to the surface, climb a vertical object, and shed their last nymphal exoskeleton as a winged adult emerges. The empty husks are often found on tree trunks. Although the life cycle takes at least 2 years, some adults emerge every year, so most species are referred to as "annual cicadas."

Remarkable are the **periodic cicadas** (genus *Magicicada*), which live underground as nymphs for 13 or 17 years! New England has two broods of 17-year cicadas found locally in Connecticut and Massachusetts. When they emerge en masse, their abundance makes headlines, the noise of the singing males is deafening, and the stench of the dead adults a month later can be extreme. But these insects are harmless, and most naturalists would regard this mass emergence as a memorable sighting.

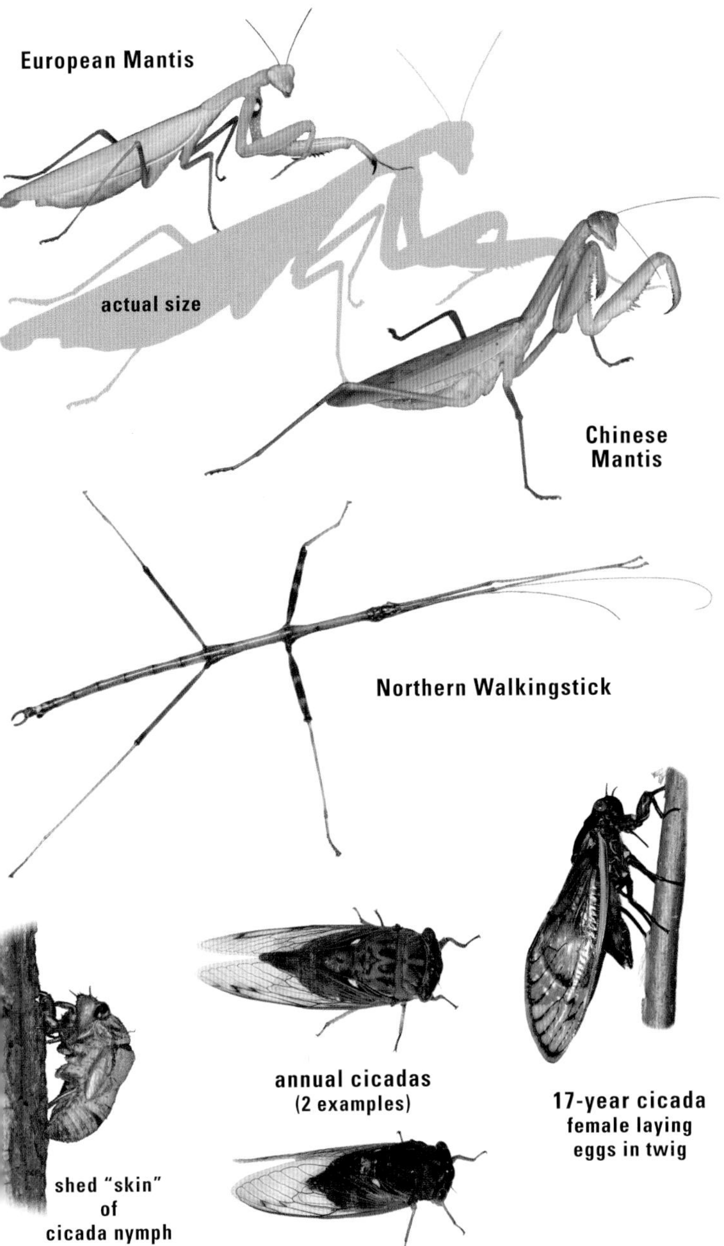
European Mantis
actual size
Chinese Mantis
Northern Walkingstick
annual cicadas (2 examples)
17-year cicada female laying eggs in twig
shed "skin" of cicada nymph

LEAFHOPPERS, APHIDS, AND OTHERS

True Bugs (order **Hemiptera**) have piercing-sucking mouthparts and feed on plant sap. Many are regarded as pests of gardens, farms, or forest. All go through gradual metamorphosis.

Leafhoppers and sharpshooters (Cicadellidae) are very diverse and highly variable in color and pattern, even within a single species. The genus *Graphocephala* includes the **Red-banded Leafhopper** *(G. coccinea)*, also called the Candystriped Leafhopper. ***Coelidia olitoria*** is common in fields. Native to Europe, the **Silver Leafhopper** *(Athysanus argentinus)* feeds on grasses. Look for it in lawns and hay fields, and sometimes at lights at night. ***Gyponana*** is a diverse genus of relatively large leafhoppers that are usually green, sometimes pink. Members of the genus ***Draeculacephala*** have sharp, pointed "noses." They feed mostly on grasses and sedges.

Spittlebug (family Cercopidae) nymphs create blobs of "spittle" by blowing air and liquid waste out their anal opening. The froth protects the soft insects from desiccation and predators. The **Meadow Spittlebug** *(Philaenus spumarius)*, introduced from Europe, is known to feed on over 400 plant species. Look for members of the genus *Aphrophora* on conifers. *Clastoptera* occur mostly on hardwoods like dogwood and alder.

Planthoppers of several families occur in New England. Among the most likely you will encounter are the Cixiidae, Acanaloniidae, and Derbidae. Many occur on shrubs and vines, and a few come to lights at night.

Treehoppers (family Membracidae) look more like thorns or buds than insects. The top of the thorax, called the pronotum, extends over the abdomen and is modified into bizarre shapes. Look for treehoppers in groups on trees, shrubs, and briars. Some may fly to lights at night. ***Entylia carinata*** is often tended by ants. This species is common on perennials in the daisy family. ***Campylenchia latipes*** is a common thorn mimic. ***Telemona*** species are large and occur mostly on oak trees.

Aphids (family Aphididae) are tiny but overwhelmingly populous. They secrete a sweet, liquid waste product called "honeydew" that coats your car in sticky goo, breeds sooty molds, and attracts all kinds of other insects, especially ants. Aphids reproduce sexually and asexually, and a female may be capable of either laying eggs or giving "live birth" to nymphs. A given species may switch host plants over a year, creating a winged generation to fly to the alternate host.

Scale insects (not shown) are typically immobile, attached to a plant, and hardly resemble insects. There are several families, and their collective life cycles and behaviors are beyond the scope of this book.

Galls are abnormal plant growths that are stimulated by bacteria, viruses, fungi, mites, nematode worms, or insects as varied as gall wasps, flies, aphids, adelgids, and psyllids (the latter two both related to aphids). Insects that form galls use them mostly as a nursery for their offspring. Galls are both a protective capsule and a vast reservoir of nutritious food. Oaks and plants in the rose family are especially targeted by gall-makers. Galls rarely do more than cosmetic "damage" to a host.

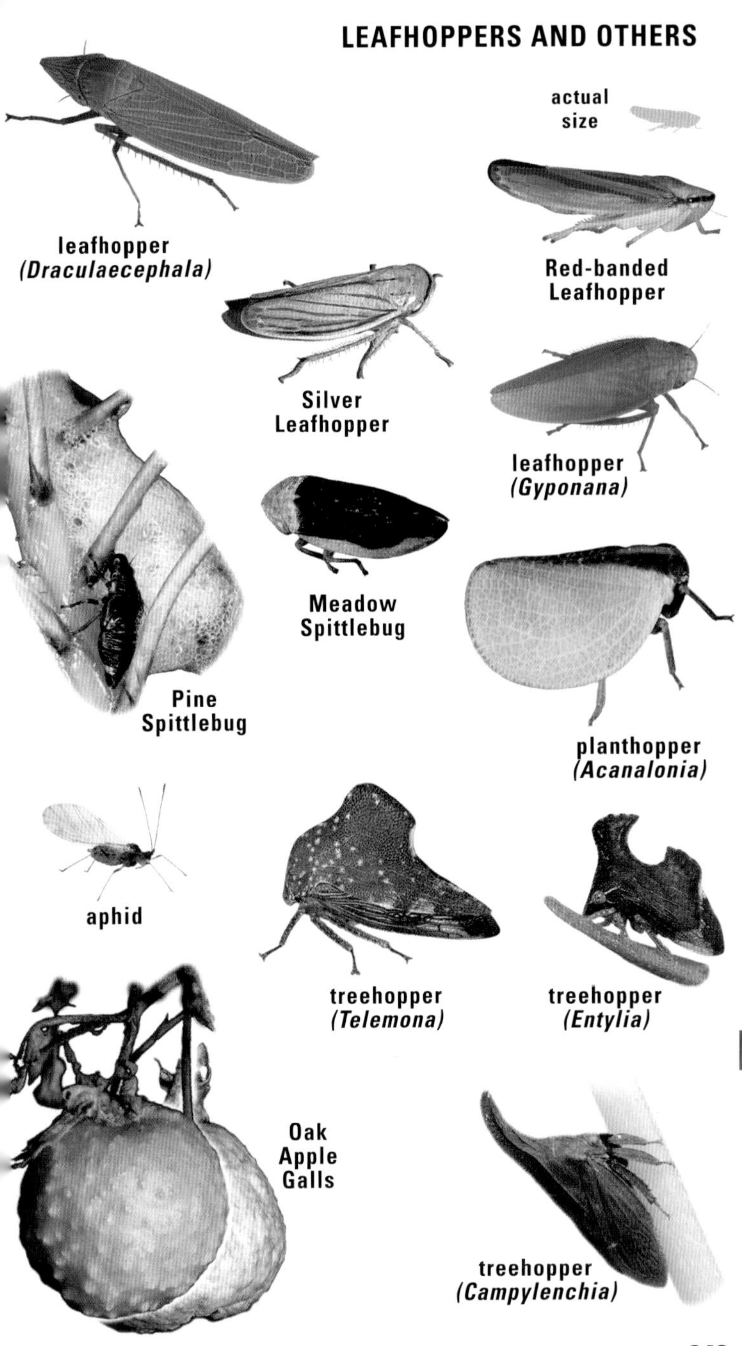

leafhopper
(Draculaecephala)

Red-banded
Leafhopper

Silver
Leafhopper

leafhopper
(Gyponana)

Meadow
Spittlebug

Pine
Spittlebug

planthopper
(Acanalonia)

aphid

treehopper
(Telemona)

treehopper
(Entylia)

Oak
Apple
Galls

treehopper
(Campylenchia)

TRUE BUGS

Like those on p. 342, these are insects that we can call "bugs" without being incorrect. Species on this page are in the suborder Heteroptera. Many resemble beetles, but they have piercing-sucking mouthparts, and they go through gradual metamorphosis, with even the youngest stages suggesting small, wingless versions of the adults.

Water striders (family Gerridae) skate across ponds, lakes, and slow sections of rivers, using their middle and hind legs to spread their weight across the surface film. They use their clamplike front legs to grab prey.

Underwater, **backswimmers (Notonectidae)** swim upside down in pursuit of mosquito larvae and other prey. They are often confused with **water boatmen (Corixidae),** but the latter bugs are smaller, swim right side up, and mostly scavenge bottom debris.

It is a pity **lace bugs (Tingidae)** are so small, for their intricate structure makes them resemble tiny Tiffany lamps. Look (closely) for them on the undersides of leaves on trees and shrubs, where they can be numerous.

Plant bugs (Miridae) are a diverse set of small, often brightly colored insects. Look for a wide variety on flowers of sumac. Many species have several color forms. The **Two-spotted Grass Bug** *(Stenotus binotatus),* introduced from Europe, is abundant in fields. Members of the genus ***Lopidea*** are usually black and red or orange and can be common on trees and shrubs. The **Tarnished Plant Bug** *(Lygus lineolaris)* is exceedingly abundant almost everywhere.

Don't worry, the only things that **assassin bugs (Reduviidae)** kill are other insects. The **Masked Hunter** *(Reduvius personatus)* is named for the habit of the nymphs to mask their appearance by coating themselves in dust and lint. This species may stray indoors. **Ambush bugs** (genus *Phymata*) lie in wait on goldenrod and other flowers. They can kill bees and other insects many times their size.

The family **Lygaeidae** includes the **Small Milkweed Bug** *(Lygaeus kalmii)* and the bigger, brighter **Large Milkweed Bug** *(Oncopeltus fasciatus).* They are common on their host plants, and their bright colors may signal to predators that they are distasteful. Formerly considered a lygaeid, the **Long-necked Seed Bug** *(Myodocha serripes)* is now placed in the family **Rhyparochromidae.** Look for it at lights at night.

The **Western Conifer Seed Bug** *(Leptoglossus occidentalis)* is in the family **Coreidae.** Despite the name, it ranges east to Maine. In autumn it may invade homes, where it will hibernate. When molested, this and other species of leaf-footed bugs emit a strong smell from glands in the thorax.

Scentless Plant Bugs (Rhopalidae) include the **Eastern Boxelder Bug** *(Boisea trivittata),* another bug that infiltrates homes. At least it doesn't smell. Boxelder Bugs disperse quickly come early spring.

Stink bugs (Pentatomidae) live up to their name. Glands in the thorax produce a pungent odor if the insect is handled. Most feed on plants and are occasional pests, but some, like the **Anchor Stink Bug** *(Stiretrus anchorago),* are predators of other pest insects. The **Green Stink Bug** *(Chinavia hilaris,* formerly *Acrosternum hilare)* is more typical.

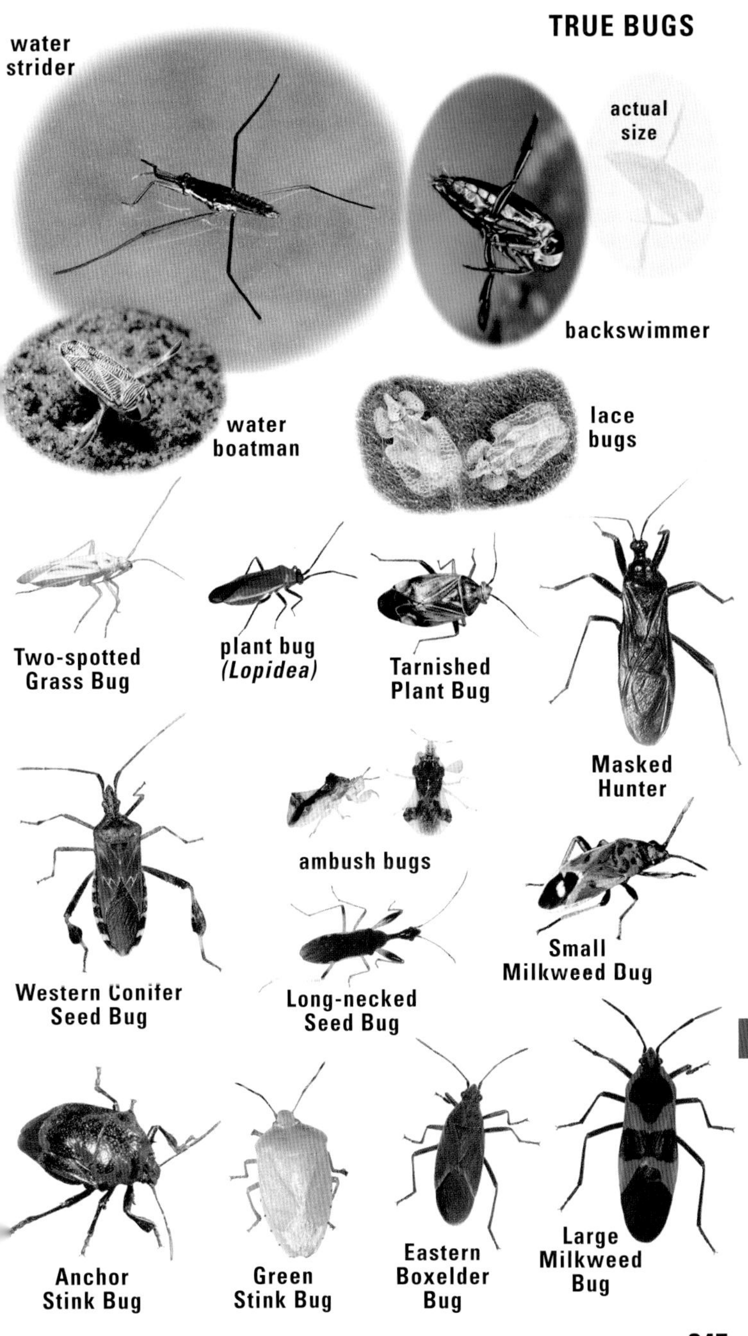
water strider
actual size
backswimmer
water boatman
lace bugs
Two-spotted Grass Bug
plant bug (Lopidea)
Tarnished Plant Bug
Masked Hunter
ambush bugs
Small Milkweed Bug
Western Conifer Seed Bug
Long-necked Seed Bug
Anchor Stink Bug
Green Stink Bug
Eastern Boxelder Bug
Large Milkweed Bug

BEETLES

(order **Coleoptera**) are the most diverse of all organisms. Of all the known species of living things on Earth, one of every five is a beetle! They have exploited nearly every niche in every habitat on land and fresh water. New England has many thousands of species, and we can treat only a small selection of them here. Beetles have chewing mouthparts and go through complete metamorphosis. Most have their forewings hardened into stiff plates, which protect the abdomen at rest, and which they hold out to the side as they use their hindwings for flight.

Ground and Tiger Beetles (family Carabidae) are predatory as larvae and adults. Most tiger beetles are diurnal. Look for **Six-spotted Tiger Beetles** *(Cicindela sexguttata)* on woodland paths. The **Common Shore Tiger Beetle** *(Cicindela repanda),* and most other species, prefer sandy shores, dunes, and blowouts. The **Pennsylvania Dingy Ground Beetle** *(Harpalus pensylvanicus)* is typical of ground beetles: shiny black or brown, nocturnal, and common. Look for many ground beetles at lights at night.

Whirligig beetles (Gyrinidae) spin and swirl across the surface of ponds, lakes, and rivers. Just don't get dizzy watching them.

Stag beetles (Lucanidae) feed in decaying wood as larvae. Males of the **Pinching Beetle** *(Lucanus capreolus)* have enormous jaws used to do battle over females. Both sexes fly to lights at night.

Scarab Beetles (Scarabaeidae) include the familiar **May beetles** (genus *Phyllophaga*) and "June bugs" like the **Variegated June Beetle** *(Polyphylla variolosa).* Male June beetles have fanlike antennae that resemble ears when the segments are folded. Larvae of many scarabs feed underground on plant roots. Adults may eat foliage and are often referred to as chafers. The **Japanese Beetle** *(Popillia japonica)* is a notorious invasive pest of grapevines, roses, and other plants. The native **Grapevine Beetle** *(Pelidnota punctata)* may come to lights at night.

Metallic Woodborers (Buprestidae) tunnel beneath bark as larvae ("flathead borers"). They are rarely pests, but look for them around recently felled timber. Those in the genus ***Chrysobothris*** are common. The top of the abdomen is brilliant metallic green or blue, concealed by the wing covers at rest.

Click Beetles (Elateridae) are common at lights at night. Larvae are "wireworms," and different species have different habits. Adults snap a ventral spine into a groove in their "chest," a maneuver that can buck them out of a predator's grasp. If turned on its back, a click beetle may use this "click trick" to pop itself into the air.

Fireflies (Lampyridae) are bioluminescent as larvae and often as adults. Those in the genus ***Photinus*** are among the most common, blinking in meadows and fields just after sunset. The glow is produced in a chemical reaction catalyzed by an enzyme and produces almost no heat.

Soldier Beetles (Cantharidae) are also called leatherwings for their soft texture. Larvae are predatory on other insects, and adults are, too, though many also feed on nectar and pollen. Watch for the **Goldenrod Soldier Beetle** *(Chauliognathus pensylvanicus)* on flowers in late summer.

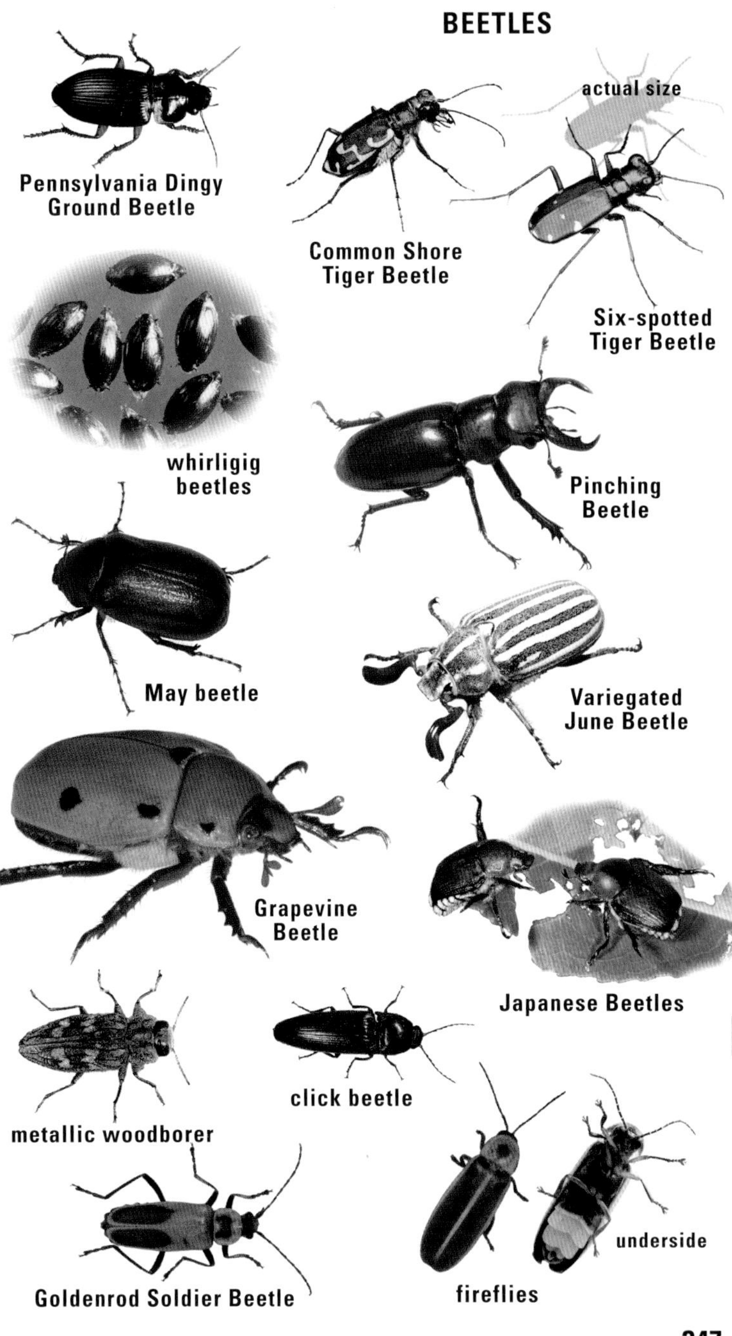

Pennsylvania Dingy Ground Beetle

Common Shore Tiger Beetle

Six-spotted Tiger Beetle

whirligig beetles

Pinching Beetle

May beetle

Variegated June Beetle

Grapevine Beetle

Japanese Beetles

metallic woodborer

click beetle

Goldenrod Soldier Beetle

fireflies

Lady Beetles (Coccinellidae) are among our best-loved insects. Their bright colors and their appetite for aphids endear them to us. Not all are red with black spots: the **Orange-spotted Lady Beetle** *(Brachiacantha ursina),* for example, has the opposite pattern. The **Multicolored Asian Lady Beetle** *(Harmonia axyridis)* is a highly variable introduced species that enters homes to hibernate. "C-7" is the **Seven-spotted Lady Beetle** *(Coccinella septempunctata),* native to Europe and implicated in the decline of native lady beetles.

Blister Beetles (Meloidae) "bleed" a toxic substance from their joints. The chemical, cantharidin, can raise blisters on human skin. Larvae of the genus ***Meloe*** are parasitic on the larvae of certain solitary bees. The adults are flightless and antlike. The **Black Blister Beetle** *(Epicauta pennsylvanica)* is common on goldenrod flowers.

Long-horned Beetles (Cerambycidae) are known in their larval stage as roundhead borers. Nearly all species bore in wood as larvae, but few are pests. The **Northeastern Sawyer** *(Monochamus notatus)* is frequently mistaken for the notorious **Asian Long-horned Beetle** *(Anoplophora glabripennis).* The latter species came to the U.S. inside the wood of crates and pallets from China. An outbreak of this beetle occurred in Worcester, Massachusetts, in 2008. Be vigilant, and do not move firewood outside of quarantine areas. The **Red Milkweed Beetle** *(Tetraopes tetrophthalmus)* is closely associated with its food plant, Common Milkweed (p. 78). The **Locust Borer** *(Megacyllene robiniae)* is common on goldenrod flowers.

Leaf Beetles (Chrysomelidae) are often mistaken for lady beetles. Most are very host-specific, feeding only on plants in one particular family or genus. The **Golden Tortoise Beetle** *(Charidotella sexpunctata)* is often described as a "gold ladybug," but the insect feeds on morning glory foliage. The **Lily Leaf Beetle** *(Lilioceris lilii)* is native to Europe but is now abundant in New England, where it is a major pest of native and cultivated lilies. The **Dogbane Beetle** *(Chrysochus auratus)* is a brilliant metallic beetle found exclusively on Dogbane. The **Spotted Cucumber Beetle** *(Diabrotica undecimpunctata)* has an appetite for many different crops and garden plants. It is often seen on flowers, such as those of Wild Carrot.

Weevils (Curculionidae) make up a diverse group. The jaws of nut and acorn weevils in the genus ***Curculio*** are at the end of a very long snout. The female has a longer "nose" than the male and uses it to cut a hole in a nut so she can deposit an egg inside. The **Black Vine Weevil** *(Otiorhynchus sulcatus)* is native to Europe but is now abundant here. Larvae feed on roots of various plants. Adults are flightless and nocturnal, sometimes straying indoors. This family also includes bark and ambrosia beetles, most of which are small and seldom observed. The **Red Turpentine Beetle** *(Dendroctonus valens)* attacks pines, especially in the wake of fires or logging operations. Larvae feed in groups under bark. Look for long "pitch tubes," the leaking resin that the tree uses to run the beetles out.

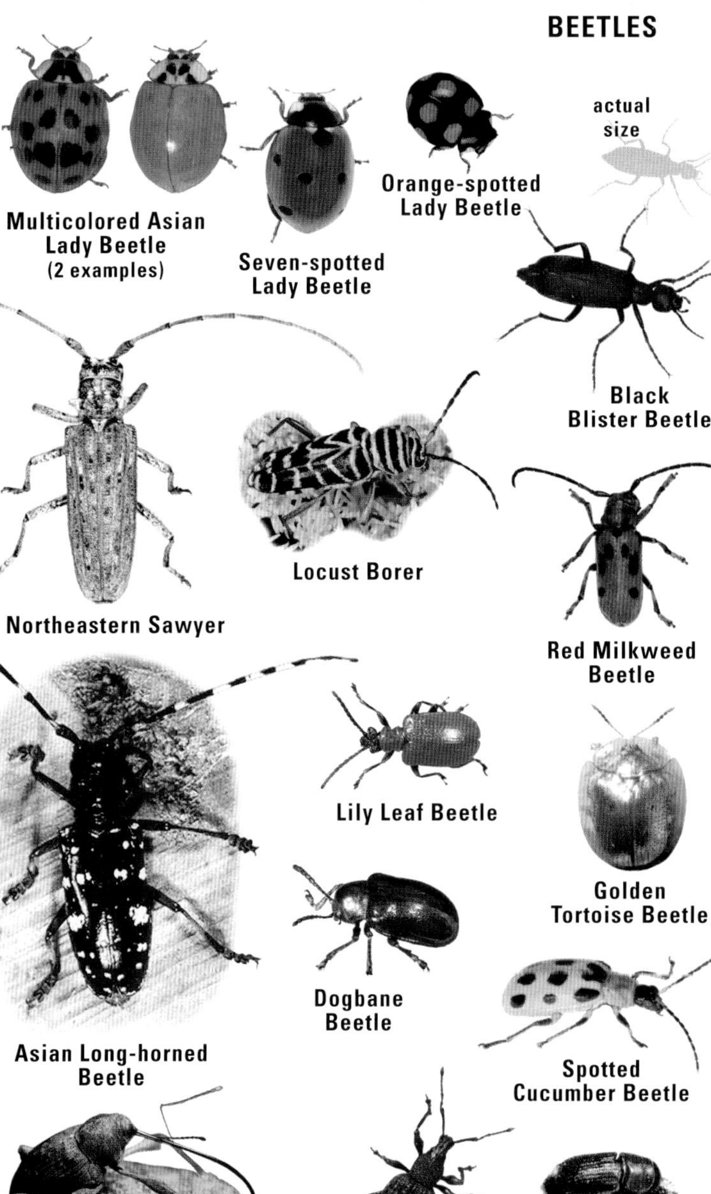

Multicolored Asian Lady Beetle (2 examples)

Seven-spotted Lady Beetle

Orange-spotted Lady Beetle

Black Blister Beetle

Northeastern Sawyer

Locust Borer

Red Milkweed Beetle

Asian Long-horned Beetle

Lily Leaf Beetle

Golden Tortoise Beetle

Dogbane Beetle

Spotted Cucumber Beetle

weevil *(Curculio)*

Black Vine Weevil

Red Turpentine Beetle

The "nerve-winged insects" in the order **Neuroptera** include mostly predatory insects that go through complete metamorphosis. Some are aquatic in the larval stage. The term *nerve-winged* refers to the dendritic pattern of their wing veins, not that the wings of these insects are more sensitive to touch than those of other insects. At the bottom of this page, scorpionflies and hangingflies are in a distinct order, **Mecoptera.**

Dobsonflies, fishflies, and their allies (family Corydalidae) are sometimes placed in their own order, Megaloptera. They are indeed large insects, aquatic as larvae. The male **Eastern Dobsonfly** *(Corydalus cornutus)* has tonglike jaws. Females have "normal" hardware but can bite much harder than the males. Both sexes fly to lights at night. Larvae are the predatory "hellgrammites" of fast-flowing rivers, prized as bait by fishermen. The **Spring Fishfly** *(Chauliodes rasticornis)* and **Summer Fishfly** *(C. pecticornis)* are virtually identical. Larvae of both are omnivores that prefer calmer water than hellgrammites. Look for **dark fishflies** (genus *Nigronia*) from April to July on vegetation near streams.

Green lacewings (family Chrysopidae), also called golden-eyed lacewings, are slow-flying insects that often come to lights at night. New England has several species, but the differences among them are subtle. The larvae are known as "aphidlions" for their voracious appetite for those pests. Some larvae camouflage themselves under a pile of debris, lichens, and/or dead victims. They occasionally bite when they fall out of trees and onto people. The distinctive eggs are laid in small groups, each at the tip of a hairlike filament. **Brown lacewings (family Hemerobiidae)** are typically smaller, darker, and less common than green lacewings. Larvae eat aphids and other small insects.

Antlions (Mymeleontidae) resemble damselflies in their adult stage but have thick, clubbed antennae. Larvae of the genus ***Myrmeleon*** are the "doodlebugs" that live at the bottom of funnel-like pits that they dig in dry, powdery soil. They eat ants and other insects that tumble into their traps. Larvae of other genera of antlions simply bury themselves in the soil and wait for potential victims to pass by.

Mantidflies (Mantispidae) resemble a botched experiment to fuse a praying mantis with a lacewing. The adult insects are a little bigger than lacewings and are predatory on smaller creatures. Larvae of many species eat spider eggs, infiltrating the egg sac when the female spider creates it.

The remaining insects on this page are in the order **Mecoptera.** They undergo complete metamorphosis. **Common Scorpionflies (Panorpidae)** are scavengers as adults, frequently stealing prey from spider webs. Adults have an elongated, beaklike face, and males have enlarged, upturned claspers that give the abdomen a scorpion-like appearance. Look for them along forest edges and cleearings. **Hangingflies (Bittacidae)** can be mistaken for crane flies, hanging from vegetation in the forest understory and manipulating prey with the hind legs. **Snow Scorpionflies (Boreidae),** not shown, are very small, wingless, and active in the dead of winter.

LACEWINGS AND OTHERS

actual size

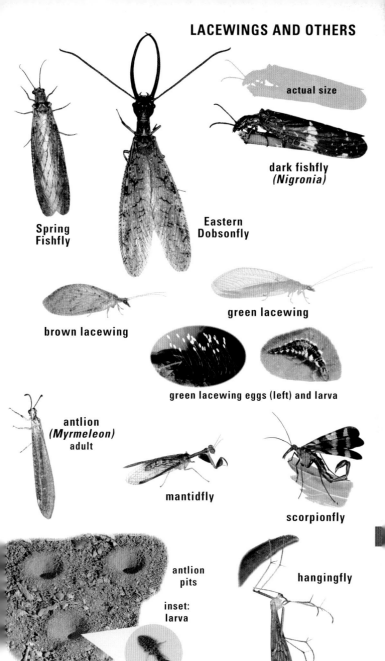

dark fishfly *(Nigronia)*

Spring Fishfly

Eastern Dobsonfly

green lacewing

brown lacewing

green lacewing eggs (left) and larva

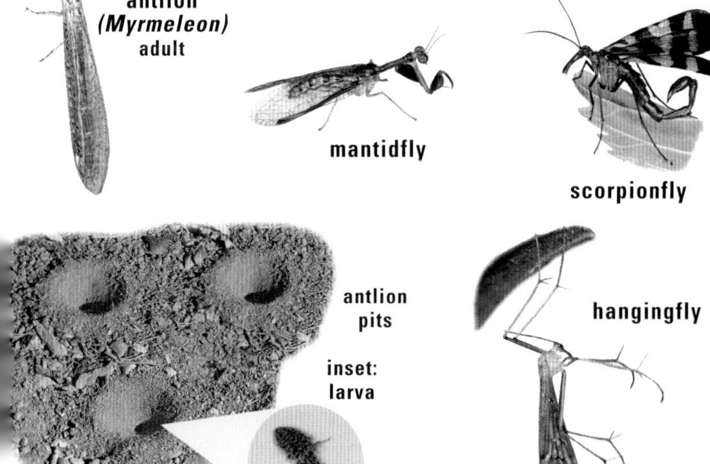

antlion *(Myrmeleon)* adult

mantidfly

scorpionfly

antlion pits

inset: larva

hangingfly

FLIES

The true flies (order **Diptera**) are as diverse as mosquitoes, midges, gnats, no-see-ums, greenheads, and bots. Thousands of species occur in New England, representing many more families than can be addressed here. Most are beneficial. Flies have sponging or piercing-sucking mouthparts as adults. They go through complete metamorphosis.

The syllable "fly" appears in the names of many unrelated insects, such as dragonfly or butterfly. Members of this group are distinguished by having "fly" as a separate word in their names, such as horse fly, crane fly, and so on, rather than as part of a compound word.

Crane Flies (families Tipulidae, Limoniidae) may suggest gigantic, long-legged mosquitoes, but they do not bite. They are exceedingly diverse in larval habits. The adults often fly to lights at night.

Mosquitoes (Culicidae) are abundant, diverse, and unpopular. Larvae ("wrigglers") and pupae ("tumblers") are aquatic. Eliminate puddles in containers and other objects to reduce breeding sites. Apply repellents with DEET to discourage bites. Only the females bite, and most mosquito species would rather feed on birds, or on mammals other than us.

Midges (Chironomidae) are frequently mistaken for mosquitoes but do not bite. Males often gather in enormous airborne swarms over lakes or tall objects to attract females around dusk. Larvae are aquatic, living mostly in bottom sediments. Midges are more common at lights than mosquitoes.

Black Flies or "buffalo gnats" **(Simuliidae)** live near streams where the aquatic larvae filter organic matter from swift current. Blood-feeding adults can be relentless biters in the north woods in early summer.

Horse flies and deer flies (Tabanidae) often have eyes banded or spotted in rainbow colors. Adult females cut victims and then lap up the blood. Larvae are predatory on tiny creatures and usually live in water or mud.

Robber flies (Asilidae) assume many forms, including bumblebee mimics, but most are slim and medium-sized. They perch on foliage, twigs, or the ground and scan the sky above. They intercept other insects in midair and return to their perch to feed.

Bee flies (Bombyliidae) look and act like bees, often hovering. The beak of some species, like ***Bombylius major,*** is used to sip flower nectar. Larvae of different species lead parasitic or predatory lives on other insects.

Flower flies (Syrphidae) are astonishing mimics of wasps and bees. They are abundant in yards, gardens, fields, and forests. The sluglike larvae of many species feed voraciously on aphids.

Blow flies (Calliphoridae) include "greenbottles" (*Lucilia* spp.) and "bluebottles" (*Calliphora* spp.). Larvae are major decomposers of carrion. These are exceedingly abundant flies.

Muscids (Muscidae) include the **House Fly** *(Musca domestica)* and biting **Stable Fly** *(Stomoxys calcitrans)* (not shown). Both are associated with farms, ranches, and zoos where animal waste (the larval food) accumulates. **Flesh Flies (Sarcophagidae)** are often mistaken for house flies but are larger, with scarlet eyes and "tails." They are also more urban than house flies. Larvae of common species feed on carrion.

FLIES

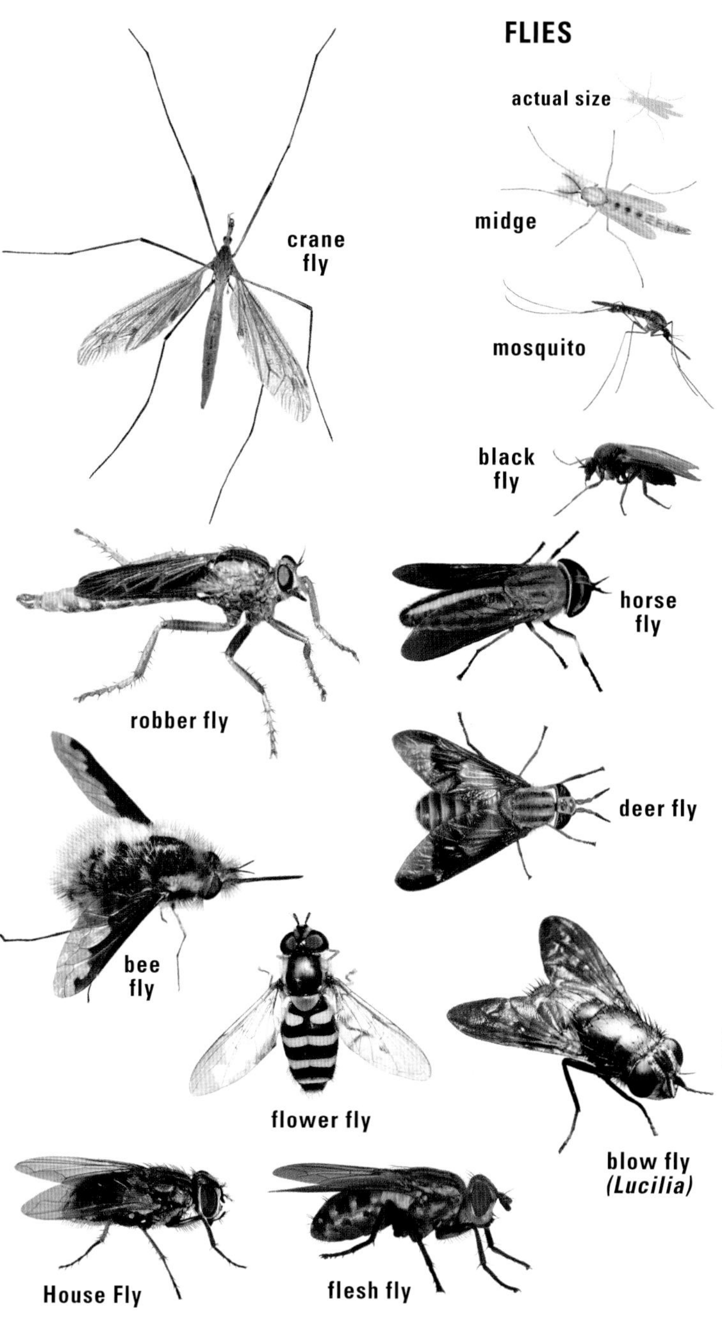
actual size
midge
crane
fly
mosquito
black
fly
horse
fly
robber fly
deer fly
bee
fly
flower fly
blow fly
(Lucilia)
House Fly
flesh fly

WASPS AND SAWFLIES

These insects, along with the bees and ants on p. 356, belong to the order **Hymenoptera.** Collectively these are often called social or stinging insects, but the majority are solitary and many lack stingers (only females sting anyway). All undergo complete metamorphosis and have chewing mouthparts. Many families of tiny, inconspicuous wasps are omitted here.

Sawflies include several families of stingless wasps. Females use a sawlike organ to deposit eggs in twigs or foliage, hence the name. Members of the family **Argidae** have the last antennal segment very long, and many of the species are red and black. Larvae resemble caterpillars and feed on plants. **Elm Sawfly** *(Cimbex americana)* is in the family **Cimbicidae.** Cimbicids are medium to large in size, with short, clubbed antennae. The caterpillar-like larvae feed on foliage and coil up when disturbed. **Common sawflies (Tenthredinidae)** are abundant and diverse. The adults do not sting and the larvae are plant feeders. The genus ***Tenthredo*** is typical, with many species mimicking stinging wasps. Adult *Tenthredo* prey on small insects but also visit flowers.

Horntails (family Siricidae) are large, stingless wasps. Our most common and conspicuous horntail is the **Pigeon Tremex** *(Tremex columba).* Females drill into dead or dying trees and lay their eggs there. The larvae that hatch bore through the wood. Giant ichneumon wasps *(Megarhyssa),* introduced below, are parasites of horntails.

Braconids (Braconidae) are small, stingless parasites of other insects, especially larvae of moths and butterflies. If you find a caterpillar covered in egglike cocoons, it has been parasitized by braconids.

Ichneumons (Ichneumonidae) include giant ***Megarhyssa*** wasps that are parasites of horntails. The long "stinger" is actually the female's egg-laying organ, inserted into trees and logs to reach horntail grubs boring within. Most ichneumons are parasites of caterpillars, the adult wasp emerging from the chrysalis (pupa) stage. Some ichneumons sting, but the stinger is retracted whereas an ovipositor is a visible spearlike appendage.

The **Mymaridae** are "fairy flies," the smallest insects in the world. You are unlikely to ever see these parasites of insect eggs, but they are not uncommon. It is said some species can fly through the eye of a needle.

Gall wasps (Cynipidae) create odd growths on plants, especially oaks. The tiny female wasp lays an egg that stimulates an abnormal growth, furnishing a protective refuge and food for her larva. Many other wasps are parasites of cynipids, so the galls you collect may or may not yield actual gall wasps.

The female **American Pelecinid** *(Pelecinus polyturator)* is an odd, stingless, long-bodied wasp. The shorter-bodied males are rare, so this species can probably reproduce without them. Larvae are parasites of scarab grubs and maybe of other insect larvae as well.

Cuckoo Wasps (Chrysididae) are small and brightly metallic. Look for them around aphid colonies and the exterior of barns. They are stingless parasites of wasps such as mud daubers and sand wasps.

larva

Elm Sawfly

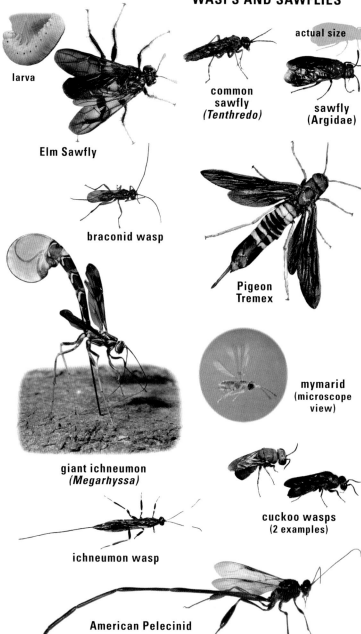

common sawfly *(Tenthredo)*

sawfly (Argidae)

braconid wasp

Pigeon Tremex

giant ichneumon *(Megarhyssa)*

mymarid (microscope view)

cuckoo wasps (2 examples)

ichneumon wasp

American Pelecinid

WASPS, BEES, AND ANTS

These belong to the order Hymenoptera, introduced on p. 354. A few of the insects below live in large, cooperative colonies and have remarkably advanced social systems.

Sphecid wasps (Sphecidae) are solitary stinging wasps. The **Black and Yellow Mud Dauber** *(Sceliphron caementarium)* makes mud nests under eaves and ledges, stocking them with paralyzed spiders as food for its larvae. The **Great Golden Digger** *(Sphex ichneumoneus)* hunts katydids, storing paralyzed victims in an underground burrow.

Wasps in the family **Crabronidae** were formerly included in Sphecidae. All are solitary, and females sting. Most dig burrows in soil or nest in preexisting cavities in wood or hollow twigs. Female **Eastern Cicada Killers** *(Sphecius speciosus)* may nest near each other in sandy areas. Males are territorial and aggressive but can't sting. Most crabronids are much smaller, like the fly-killing sand wasps in the genus ***Bembix.*** "Beewolves" of the genus ***Philanthus*** are also common.

The family **Megachilidae** includes mason bees and leafcutter bees. All are solitary, and females collect pollen on the underside of the abdomen rather than on their hind legs. **Leafcutters** (genus *Megachile*) snip pieces of leaves and roll them into barrel-like cells for their larval offspring. They stack the cells in a preexisting cavity in wood, rock, or other material. The **mason bees** *(Osmia)* use mud to partition preexisting tunnels into individual cells, each with a pollen and nectar ball for a larval bee.

Bees in the family **Apidae** include solitary species like the **Virginia Carpenter Bee** *(Xylocopa virginica)* and social species like the **Honeybee** *(Apis mellifera)*. Settlers brought honeybees to Jamestown in 1622. They are now so widespread, and so important in pollination and in honey production, that many people do not realize that these fascinating insects are not native here. **Bumblebees** (genus *Bombus*) are native and also social.

Velvet ants (Mutillidae) are actually solitary wasps, females of which are wingless. They pack a potent sting, though. They are parasitic in the nests of other stinging wasps and bees. Look for them in sandy areas.

Vespid wasps (Vespidae) include social yellowjackets and paper wasps, as well as solitary potter wasps and mason wasps. Yellowjackets (including the **Bald-faced "Hornet,"** *Dolichovespula maculata*) are fly-killers; paper, mason, and potter wasps hunt caterpillars. All fold their wings longitudinally at rest. Paper wasps chew up wood to make paper nests, often suspended under eaves. The **European Paper Wasp** *(Polistes dominulus)*, an import from Eurasia, was first identified near Boston in 1978, and it is now common throughout the northeast and elsewhere.

Ants (Formicidae) are all social, with at least one queen and usually hundreds or thousands of sterile female "workers" in each nest. Ants swarm at least once each year, liberating new, winged queens and males. Males die after mating, while queens shed their wings and set up housekeeping. **Carpenter ants** (genus *Camponotus*) are our largest ants. Ants of the genus ***Lasius*** are abundant in fields and lawns. Some ants defend themselves by excreting formic acid, but others have stingers.

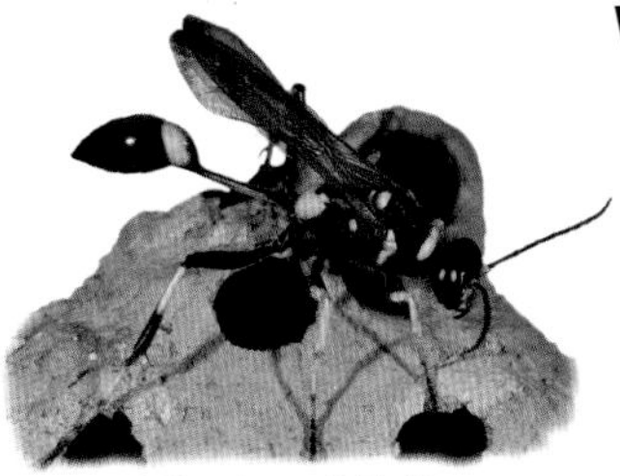

actual size

Black and Yellow Mud Dauber

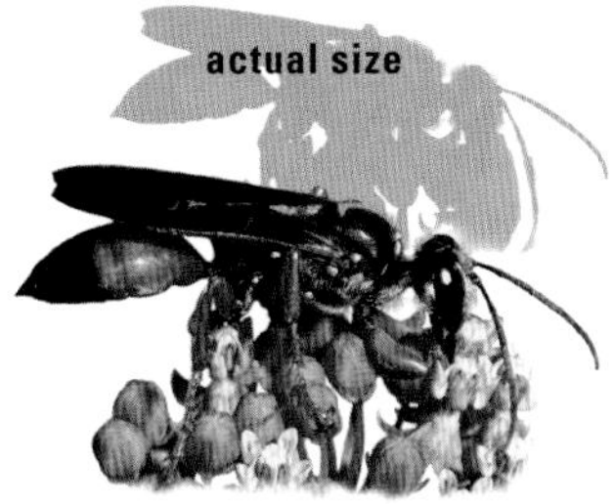

Great Golden Digger

sand wasp *(Bembix)*

Eastern Cicada Killer

Virginia Carpenter Bee

Honeybee

leafcutter bee

velvet ant

bumblebee

Bald-faced Hornet

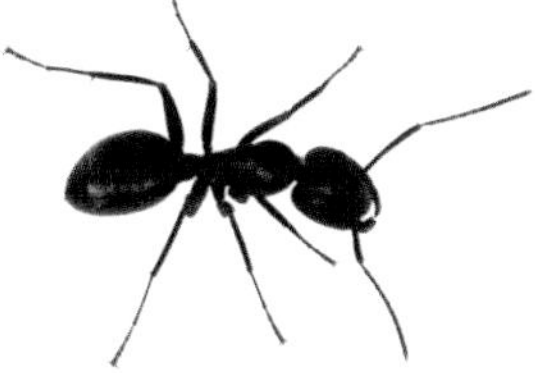

carpenter ant

ant *(Lasius)*

European Paper Wasp

OTHER INVERTEBRATES: SPIDERS

Spiders are not insects, but arachnids, literally in a separate class. Spiders have two body sections, eight legs, and spinnerets, but no wings or antennae. Most spiders have eight eyes, but web-builders see poorly. These are abundant animals that frequently cause fear and consternation owing to their venomous nature. The only species in New England with confirmed medical significance is the Northern Black Widow.

Text on noninsect land invertebrates contributed by Eric R. Eaton

The **Long-bodied Cellar Spider** *(Pholcus phalangioides)* is common indoors and outside. These members of the family **Pholcidae** spin sprawling, tangled webs in basements, cellars, crawlspaces, and similar niches. When disturbed, the lanky arachnids shake violently in place.

Orb weavers (family Araneidae) create the familiar wheel-like webs in yards, gardens, and fields. Females of the **Black-and-yellow Argiope** *(Argiope aurantia)*, also called Golden Garden Spider, are very large but surprisingly cryptic. Males are much smaller and seen less often. Look for the webs in tall grass, briars, and low shrubs. The snares usually sport a broad zigzag band of silk down the center, called a stabilimentum. The **Cross Spider** *(Araneus diadematus)* is native to Europe but is now widespread in the northeast U.S. It is probably the most common and conspicuous of New England orb weavers. Two specimens went up in Skylab in 1973 to research the effects of zero gravity on their web-spinning instincts. The **Barn Spider** *(Araneus cavaticus)* is the spider of *Charlotte's Web* fame. Look for it in rural areas, where it builds up high around barns and other outbuildings. The **Furrow Spider** *(Larinioides cornutus)* is seen most often at night. Look for its webs around outdoor lights.

Sheetweb weavers in the family **Linyphiidae** are easily recognized by their webs alone. The **Bowl-and-doily Spider** *(Frontinella communis)* lives among shrubs and trees, where it makes a bowl-shaped web with a flat sheet beneath it. The **Filmy Dome Spider** *(Neriene radiata)* makes a dome-like web closer to the ground.

Cobweb weavers (Theridiidae) make haphazard, three-dimensional webs indoors and outdoors. The **Common House Spider** *(Parasteatoda tepidariorum)* is a very common urban species. The **Boreal Cobweb Spider** *(Steatoda borealis)*, not shown, is often mistaken for a black widow but lacks the characteristic red markings. The genuine **Northern Black Widow** *(Latrodectus variolus)* has a broken red hourglass marking on the underside of the abdomen, as well as stripes and spots on top. It is the only spider in New England whose venom can cause severe injury to humans.

Jumping Spiders (family Salticidae) are about as "cute" as spiders get. They have the keenest vision of any land invertebrates. Two of their eight eyes are large and forward-facing, and these alert spiders will turn and look at you when you approach them. The **Zebra Jumper** *(Salticus scenicus)* is small but common. Look for it prowling the exterior walls of buildings. The larger **Bold Jumper** *(Phidippus audax)* hunts amid foliage of shrubs and trees.

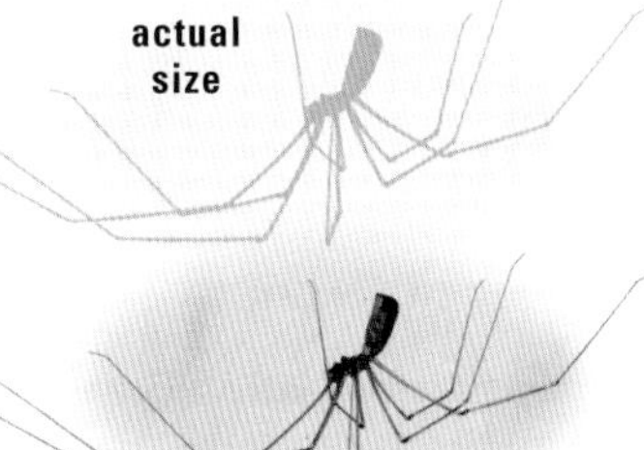

Long-bodied Cellar Spider

Black-and-yellow Argiope

Cross Spider

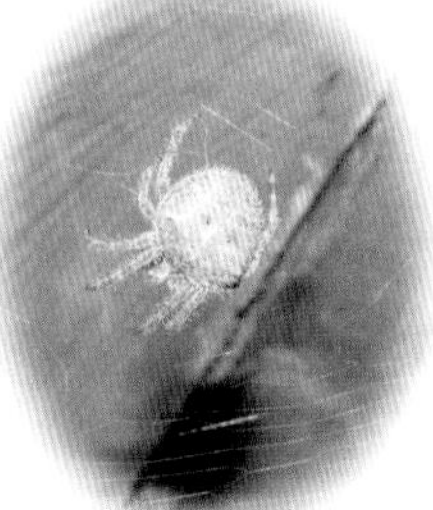

Barn Spider

Furrow Spider

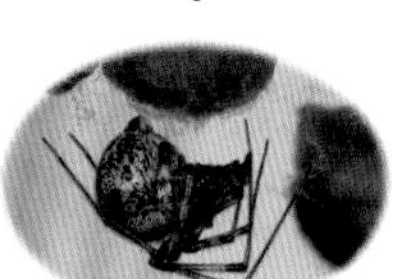

Common House Spider

Filmy Dome Spider

Northern Black Widow

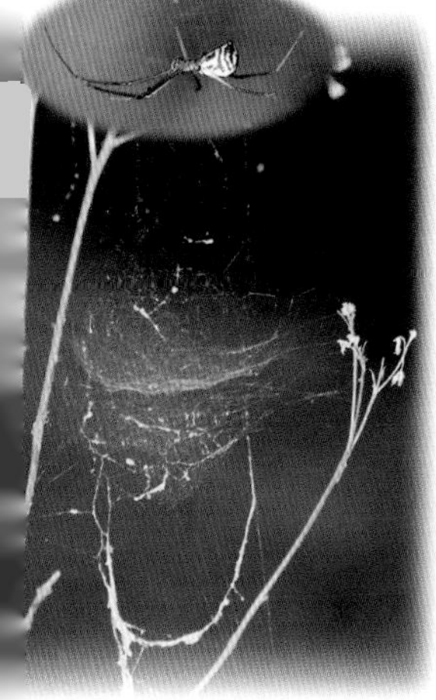

Bowl-and-doily Spider (with web)

Zebra Jumper

Bold Jumper

Crab spiders (family Thomisidae) have long front legs, short hind legs. Most sit and wait for potential prey insects to come to them. The **Flower Crab Spider** *(Misumena vatia)* lies in ambush on flowers, seizing bees, flies, and other pollinators that come looking for nectar. The female spiders can slowly change color from white to yellow or vice versa, the better to blend in with a given blossom. Crab spiders in the genus ***Xysticus*** are common on foliage and on tree trunks.

The family **Corinnidae** includes hunting spiders that do not spin webs. ***Trachelas tranquillus*** often strays indoors in autumn.

Members of the family **Gnaphosidae** are swift-running hunters. The **Eastern Parson Spider** *(Herpyllus ecclesiasticus)* sometimes enters homes but usually thrives outdoors in woodlands where it lives under rocks, boards, and other debris. Females lay egg sacs in the fall.

Funnelweb weavers (Agelenidae) weave thick, sheetlike webs with a funnel-like retreat where the spider lives. The webs are not sticky, but insects collide with the overhead foundation threads and fall to the sheet below. The spider then dashes out and quickly bites its victim, dragging it back into its lair to eat. Species in the genus ***Agelenopsis*** are the most commonly seen, especially in urban areas.

Prowling spiders of the family **Miturgidae** include the **Yellow Sac Spider** *(Cheiracanthium mildei)*. Native to Eurasia and northern Africa, this pale, nomadic spider spins a "sleeping bag" where walls meet the ceiling inside homes. It rests there during the day and prowls at night, spinning a new shelter after each foray. It has been mistakenly considered as venomous to people. The species is widespread in the U.S.

The **Nursery Web Spiders (Pisauridae)** include the **Six-spotted Fishing Spider** *(Dolomedes triton)*. Look for it near the edges of ponds and lakes where it waits for aquatic insects, tadpoles, and small fish to surface. ***Dolomedes tenebrosus*** is a huge, sprawling spider seen on fenceposts, tree trunks, and other vertical surfaces, especially at night. ***Pisaurina mira*** is abundant on foliage along forest edges. It varies in color pattern, most commonly with a broad, dark brown stripe down the back. Females in this family carry the egg sac in their jaws, eventually suspending it in a "nursery web" where the female guards it and the spiderlings that emerge.

Wolf Spiders (family Lycosidae) are powerful hunters most often seen on the ground or horizontal objects (in contrast to similar fishing spiders, which are usually seen in the vertical plane). Female wolf spiders carry the egg sac from their spinnerets at the tip of the abdomen. The spiderlings that hatch ride on mom's back until their next molt, after which they disperse. Wolf spiders such as the giants of the genus ***Hogna*** are mostly nocturnal. Try going out at night with a headlamp or flashlight: the eyes of wolf spiders sparkle in the darkness. ***Arctosa littoralis*** is common on beaches and in other sandy habitats, although it is most active at night, hiding under debris by day.

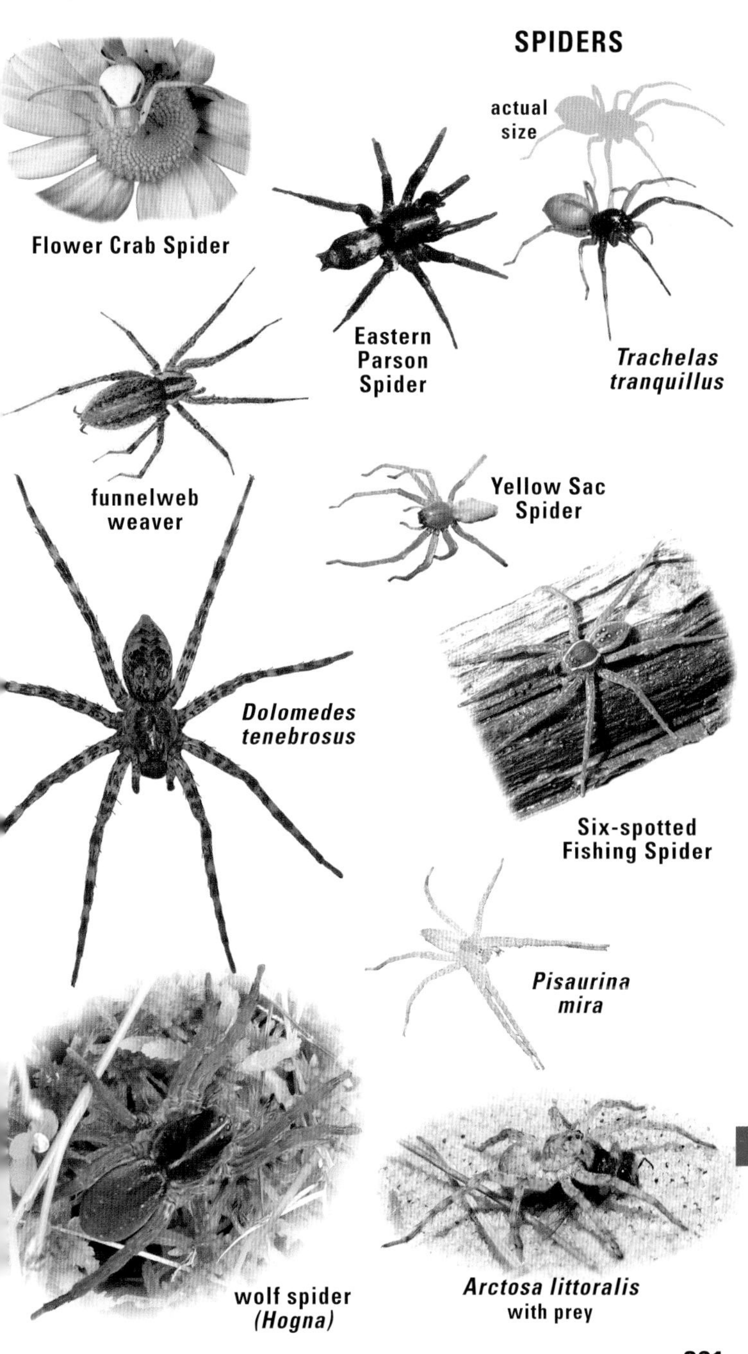

Flower Crab Spider

Eastern Parson Spider

Trachelas tranquillus

funnelweb weaver

Yellow Sac Spider

Dolomedes tenebrosus

Six-spotted Fishing Spider

Pisaurina mira

wolf spider *(Hogna)*

Arctosa littoralis with prey

OTHER ARACHNIDS

Spiders are not the only arachnids in New England. There is rich diversity among harvestmen, pseudoscorpions, and mites. Most of these are tiny organisms that one needs magnification to see with any detail.

Harvestmen (order Opiliones) are commonly known as "daddy-longlegs," but so are cellar spiders and even crane flies. Harvestmen are not venomous. They eat mostly decaying organic matter but also will kill small, weak, or injured invertebrates. Harvestmen secrete defensive chemicals from pores near the base of the second pair of legs and also practice "autotomy," willingly sacrificing legs when attacked. Most species have one pair of eyes, elevated on a tubercle. In the family **Sclerosomatidae,** the **Eastern Harvestman** *(Leiobunum vittatum)* is common on foliage and on outer walls of barns and buildings. A member of the family **Phalangiidae,** ***Phalangium opilio*** is the most studied of all harvestmen. Native to Eurasia, it is invasive here, frequenting disturbed habitats such as vacant lots.

The order **Ixodida** is the ticks. The family **Ixodidae** includes our common species. The **Black-legged Tick** *(Ixodes scapularis)* is the "deer tick" that vectors Lyme disease (named for Lyme, Connecticut, where it was first recognized in 1975). The larval stages in the two-year life cycle feed mostly on deermice *(Peromyscus)*. The second-year nymphs peak in summer when we are outdoors ourselves. Smaller than adults, they are difficult to detect before they latch on. Adult ticks feed on White-tailed Deer. The **American Dog Tick** *(Dermacentor variabilis)* is a larger tick. Rocky Mountain spotted fever and tularemia are transmitted by this species. Bites can also result in "tick paralysis." Larvae and nymphs feed mostly on rodents, while adults feed on larger mammals. Inspect yourself carefully after hiking in open woodlands and along forest edges.

Mites, in the same subclass **(Acari)** as ticks, are extraordinarily diverse. Their classification is complex and constantly changing. Most are microscopic. They occur everywhere, even in the pores of your eyelashes.

The order **Mesostigmata** includes members of the genus ***Pergamasus*** **(family Parasitidae),** predatory on other soil-inhabiting invertebrates such as springtails. ***Varroa destructor*** **(Varroidae)** plagues honeybees and contributes to the decline of colony health. The order **Actinedida** includes the **Erythraeidae,** one of several families of **velvet mites.** They are large and colorful for mites. Larval stages are parasitic on other arthropods, especially harvestmen. They go through an inactive stage and emerge as predatory adults. **Spider mites (Tetranychidae)** include notorious plant pests that spin silk. **Eriophyidae** are gall mites. Look for their work on leaves of cherry, maple, elm, even poison ivy. The order **Oribatida** includes abundant soil-inhabiting mites. The genus ***Euzetes*** **(family Euzetidae)** is abundant in leaf litter and humus. These "turtle mites" easily pass for tiny seeds.

Pseudoscorpions (order Pseudoscorpiones) are tick-sized predators normally found in soil, leaf litter, under bark, and in caves. They hitch rides on flying insects and so occasionally turn up in homes. Despite their odd appearance and formidable name, they are totally harmless to humans.

OTHER ARACHNIDS

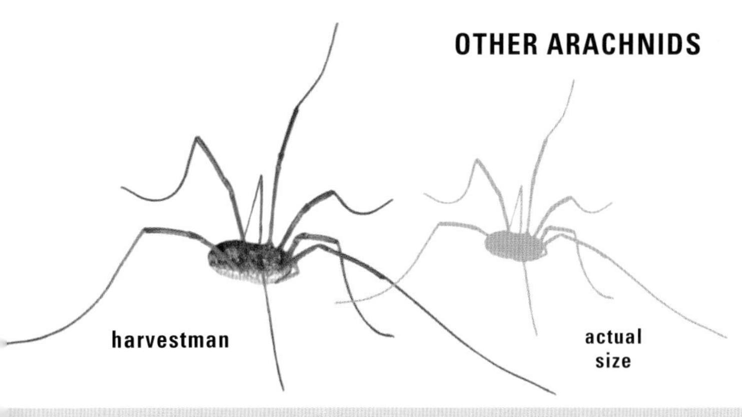

Most of the creatures below are truly tiny in life. Some are even microscopic. They are shown here much larger than life-size.

actual size

Black-legged Tick

American Dog Tick

Varroa mites

velvet mite

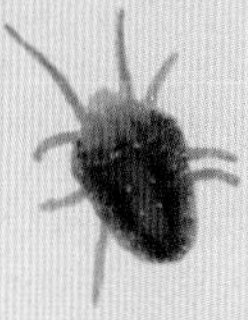

spider mite

pseudoscorpion

galls on maple leaf caused by gall mites (not to scale)

Pillbugs and Sowbugs (order Isopoda) are terrestrial crustaceans. They are decomposers of rotting wood and other organic debris. The **Woodlouse** or **Pillbug** *(Armadillidium vulgare)* can roll into a ball to protect itself, hence the nickname "roly-poly." This species and the **European Sowbug** *(Oniscus asellus)* are both native to Europe. Sowbugs are more flattened than pillbugs and cannot roll up.

Centipedes (class Chilopoda) are speedy, venomous predators with one pair of legs per body segment. The order **Scutigerimorpha** includes the **House Centipede** *(Scutigera coleoptrata)*, which can scale walls and dash across ceilings in its nightly forays for prey. Despite its startling appearance, it is harmless to humans. **Stone Centipedes (order Lithobiomorpha)** are common under rocks, boards, and in rotting logs. Females protect their eggs by coiling around them. **Soil Centipedes (Geophilomorpha)** are small but long, snakelike, and usually yellowish or whitish.

Millipedes (class Diplopoda) are slow, moisture-loving scavengers and vegetarians with two pairs of legs per body segment. Flat-backed millipedes **(order Polydesmida)** include the **Greenhouse Millipede** *(Oxidus gracilis)*, not shown, an Asian import now found in all states. ***Sigmoria trimaculata*** is a large, colorful species that secretes a cyanide compound in self-defense. The order **Spirobolida** includes our largest millipedes, up to 4" long.

Nonarthropod land invertebrates include **earthworms (phylum Annelida, class or subclass Oligochaeta)**. Native earthworms are essentially extinct in New England, wiped out in the last ice age. European and Asian species have replaced them. Many arrived in soil used for ships' ballast, or in root balls of imported plants. There are many species, and they are usually divided into three broad categories. **Anecic earthworms** live in deep vertical burrows but visit the soil surface. Large and heavily pigmented, they can burrow as deep as six feet. This group includes the **"night crawlers"** (genus *Lumbricus*) often seen on sidewalks and lawns. **Epigeic earthworms** do not tunnel, living and feeding in leaf litter. They are small and pigmented, like the **Red Wriggler** *(Eisenia foetida)*, widely sold for home composting and fishing bait. **Endogeic worms** make extensive horizontal burrows in the topsoil. They are small and pale.

Snails and slugs are gastropods **(phylum Mollusca, class Gastropoda)**. They eat mostly vegetation, using a toothed tonguelike organ called a radula to scrape up food. Their eyes are at the tips of tentacle-like stalks they can quickly retract. Each individual is both male and female, but they still must fertilize each other. A mating pair of gastropods is a surprisingly beautiful, albeit slimy, ballet. A study in the year 2000 revealed that Maine alone has 92 species. At least 4 snails and 11 slugs are nonnative. The family **Limacidae** includes the **Leopard Slug** *(Limax maximus)*, native to Europe. The **Whitelip Snail** *(Neohelix albolabris)*, family **Polygyridae,** is the largest native land snail in the northeast. It can reach more than an inch in diameter. It is mostly nocturnal; look for it beneath leaf litter or in rock crevices by day in second-growth forests. **Ambersnails** and their relatives in the family **Succineidae** are common on foliage, especially near water.

Woodlouse (Pillbug)

European Sowbug

actual size

House Centipede

Stone Centipede

Soil Centipede

Sigmoria trimaculata

night crawler earthworm

Leopard Slug

Whitelip Snail

ambersnail

INVERTEBRATES OF FRESH WATER

Many invertebrates in fresh water are insects, including larval stages of the species on pp. 334–336. Some other unrelated forms are treated here.

Crayfish are crustaceans, freshwater relatives of the lobster; our species belong to the family **Cambaridae.** They live in streams and ponds, walking on the bottom, feeding on a wide variety of living or dead plant material or small animals. If disturbed, they can swim backward with an explosive burst of speed. Most active at night, they often hide by day. North America has more than 300 species, most in the southeastern states; New England has at least a dozen species, although several of those are introduced. One of the most numerous natives is the **Eastern Crayfish** *(Cambarus bartonii).* It digs burrows underwater, often with a "chimney" of mud pellets sticking up above the ground near the water's edge. The **Rusty Crayfish** *(Orconectes rusticus),* native to the Ohio Valley, was accidentally introduced into New England — probably through the use of small ones as fish bait — and it has become a troublesome invasive in some areas.

Leeches make up the class **Hirudinea** of the segmented worm phylum **(Annelida).** North America has more than 60 species of freshwater leeches, many of which are found in streams or ponds of New England. One of the most numerous is ***Macrobdella decora.*** Olive brown with black and red spots, it swims well and uses its sucking mouthparts to attach to a frog, turtle, fish, or mammal to get a meal of blood. Once satiated, the leech drops off. Although they may cause squeamish reactions, leeches do little harm, and they are no reason to stay out of the water.

Freshwater mussels are among the least appreciated, most endangered, and most interesting creatures found in New England. These animals are mollusks, belonging to the bivalve group, which is introduced with other "seashells" on p. 370. These freshwater bivalves, however, belong to a separate order, **Unionoida.** They live partly buried at the bottoms of streams, rivers, and lakes. They feed by sucking water in and filtering it to remove food in the form of algae. This feeding behavior makes them valuable in keeping waters clean, but it also makes them vulnerable to the effects of pollution. More than half the species known for New England are now considered endangered, threatened, or of special concern.

After the female mussel is fertilized, she broods the tiny larval mussels (called glochidia) inside her shell for a period of weeks to months, then releases them into the water. These glochidia drift until they can grasp the gills or fins of a certain type of fish, and then they attach themselves and draw nutrients from the fish's blood for several weeks. At the end of that time, they drop off, sink to the bottom, and begin to develop into the adult form. Surprisingly, individuals of some species can live for decades.

In addition to these native mussels, the alien **Zebra Mussel** *(Dreissena polymorpha)* is abundant in Lake Champlain and has been found elsewhere in western Vermont, Massachusetts, and Connecticut. Through its sheer abundance, this small invader may take up most of the food available in its surroundings, thus causing further problems for our native species.

INVERTEBRATES OF FRESH WATER

Eastern Crayfish

Rusty Crayfish

freshwater leech

Eastern Elliptio

Eastern Lampmussel

some native freshwater mussels

Eastern Pondmussel

Zebra Mussel (invasive)

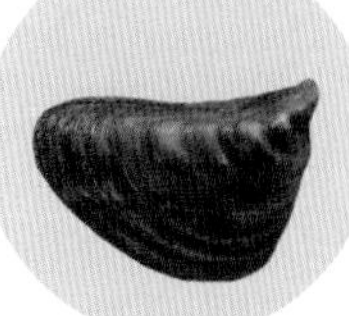

BEACH AND TIDEPOOL LIFE

The long coastline of New England, from southwestern Connecticut to down east in Maine, offers an abundance of opportunities for anyone interested in nature. This zone where the land meets the ocean is home to a unique set of living things that exist nowhere else.

The overall structure of the coastline varies from place to place. Sandy beaches are the rule in Connecticut, Rhode Island, and southeastern Massachusetts, culminating in the great sandy arm of Cape Cod. In northeastern Massachusetts, coastal New Hampshire, and southern Maine, sandy beaches alternate with rocky headlands and pebble or gravel beaches; moving up the Maine coast, more and more of the shoreline is rocky, with fewer sand beaches in protected coves.

Exploring tidepools along the Maine coast

One of the defining features of the coastline is the daily cycle of tides, the regular rise and fall of sea level relative to the land, with high tide and low tide each occurring roughly twice per day. Tides are caused mainly by the gravitational pull of the moon, and to a lesser extent that of the sun. As the earth rotates, water bulges out in the direction of the moon's gravity (and on the opposite side of the world as well). Because the moon is gradually revolving around the earth, with moonrise appearing to be roughly 45 to 50 minutes later each night, each cycle of tides takes more than 24 hours. The time between high tides at a given location is about 12 hours and 25 minutes.

The tidal effect is increased in narrow bays and estuaries. Here in New England, the difference between high and low tides is only about 3 feet in parts of Connecticut; in eastern Maine, in the lower stretches of the Bay of Fundy, the difference may be nearly 20 feet. (At the Bay of Fundy's upper end in Nova Scotia, the difference may be more than 50 feet!)

Tides have a profound effect on most things that live along the coast. Even birds, which may easily move from place to place as conditions change, may time their activities to the tides. Shorebirds such as sandpipers and plovers, for example, often forage actively on the tidal flats while the tide is going out, resting above the high-water mark at high tide, regardless of the time of day or night. Naturalists going out to the coast should get in the habit of checking the tide schedule ahead of time, because it will have a major impact on what we see and do there.

The area between the high tide and low tide marks, or intertidal zone, is a challenging environment for living things. It alternates between being exposed to air and being underwater, and in many places it is pounded by waves as well, so anything living there must be able to tolerate extremes.

Covered in this section. Of course, the birds along the coast, and many other things such as the wildflowers and insects, were treated in previous chapters of this book. We have used this section for things that did not fit well elsewhere.

Many of the living things along the water's edge are from groups that are not familiar elsewhere. For example, mollusks (see p. 370) are not a big part of our everyday experience elsewhere in New England, aside from snails and slugs, but they are omnipresent along the coast. Crustaceans play only minor roles on land and in fresh water (see pillbugs and crayfish, pp. 364–366), but crabs, lobsters, and other crustaceans are among the more conspicuous wildlife in areas near the ocean's edge.

Other groups of organisms along the coast may be even more unfamiliar. Urchins and sea stars (p. 384) belong to a distinct phylum and have no relatives on land. Sea anemones and jellyfish belong to yet another phylum with no members on land and only a few in fresh water. Seaweeds (p. 386) might look superficially like other "weeds" on land, but they are classified as forms of algae and essentially unrelated to any kind of land plants. Exploring nature along the edge of the sea gives us a chance to literally visit another world.

This young Frilled Anemone *(Metridium senile)*, growing on a rock underwater along the coast of Maine, looks rather like a plant (as its name suggests), but it is an animal in the phylum Cnidaria, related to the corals and jellyfish.

SEASHELLS

are familiar to anyone who has ever walked a beach, but many people never stop to think about the living creatures that created these shells. Practically everything that we would regard as a seashell is a structure made by a mollusk (phylum Mollusca). The mollusks are incredibly diverse, with close to 100,000 living species classified (and many others known only from fossil remains). Here in New England, several kinds of mollusks are common in shallow waters, and the shells of dozens of other species are regularly found washed up on beaches.

The characteristics that define the mollusks are the *mantle,* a fold in the body's surface that secretes the material that forms the shell, and the *radula,* a toothed, tonguelike organ used for feeding. Not all mollusks form shells; for example, slugs are shell-less members of this phylum, related to snails. Squids and octopus are mollusks also, without shells, living active lives underwater. But in this section, we focus on only those shells likely to be found along the shoreline in our region.

Mollusks found here mainly belong to three classes:

Chitons (class Polyplacophora) are small and oval-shaped, usually found clamped tightly to rocks. We illustrate one species on p. 379.

Snails and others (class Gastropoda) usually have a single shell, formed in a spiral; typical examples are shown on the next three pages, and some more unusual gastropods are on p. 379. On the typical gastropods, the living animal can extend its head and fleshy "foot" out through the opening, or aperture, in the shell, and it can withdraw inside. Many of the snails have a hardened surface, called the operculum, attached to the foot, and they can use this like a trapdoor to seal the opening when the animal has withdrawn inside the shell.

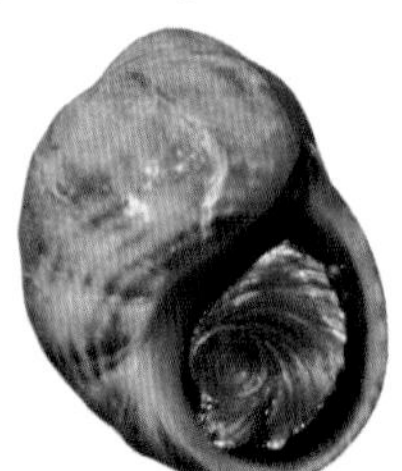

Common Periwinkle, with a silvery operculum blocking the aperture

Bivalves (class Bivalva) typically have two shell halves, or valves, joined by a hinge with a tough ligament and one or two strong adductor muscles. These elements of the hinge decompose after the animal dies, so the bivalve shells that we find washed up on the beach are usually only separated halves. On the living animal, the soft, fleshy body is protected between the shell halves. Some bivalves, such as the oysters, are quite sedentary after their youngest stages, spending their adult lives essentially in one spot. However, many bivalves get around to a surprising extent, burrowing into mud or sand with an extended fleshy "foot" or propelling themselves through the depths with quick spurts of water. Various bivalves, including clams, scallops, and oysters, are important elements in the cuisine of New England.

Northern Moon Snail in habitat

Northern Moon Snail
Lunatia heros 2"

Lobed Moon Snail
Polinices duplicatus 2"

SMALL SNAILS

Northern Yellow Periwinkle
Littorina obtusata
½"

Common Periwinkle
Littorina littorea 1"
abundant in tidepools on rocky shores

Spotted Moon Snail
Lunatia triseriata ½"

New England Nassa
Nassarius trivittatus ¾"

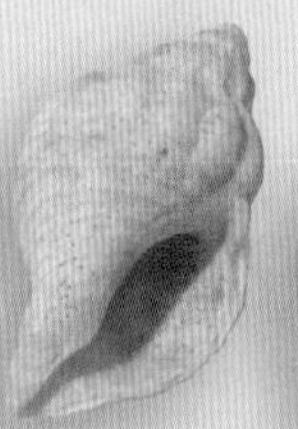

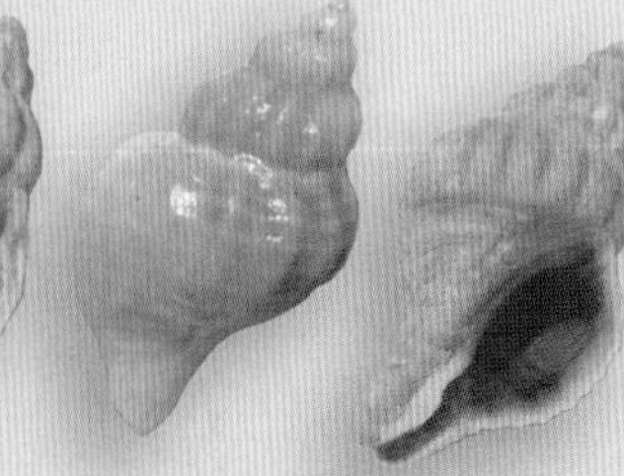

Dove Shell
Anachis sp. ½"

Oyster Drill *Urosalpinx cinerea* 1"
lives in shallow water, preys on oysters

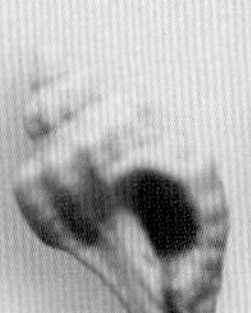

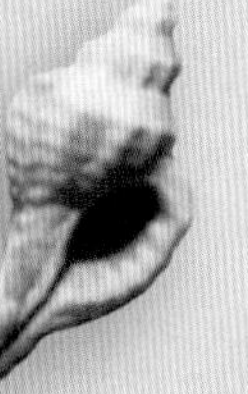

Thick-lipped Drill
Eupleura caudata ¾"

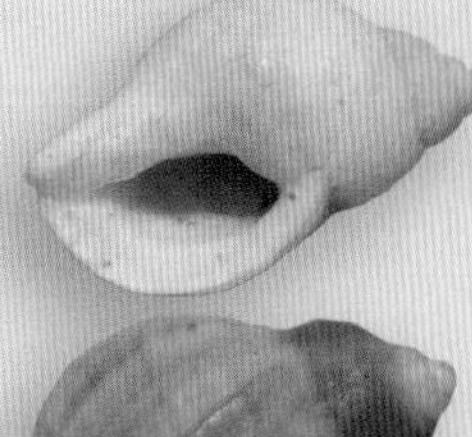

Atlantic Dogwinkle
Nucella lapillus 1"

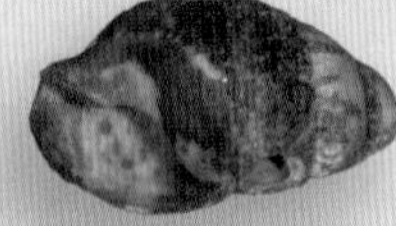

Eastern Mud Snail
Ilyanassa obsoleta ¾"
abundant on mudflats

Salt Marsh Snail
Melampus bidentatus
½" common in tidal marsh

Knobbed Whelk
Busycon carica
to 9″
largest shell on New England beaches

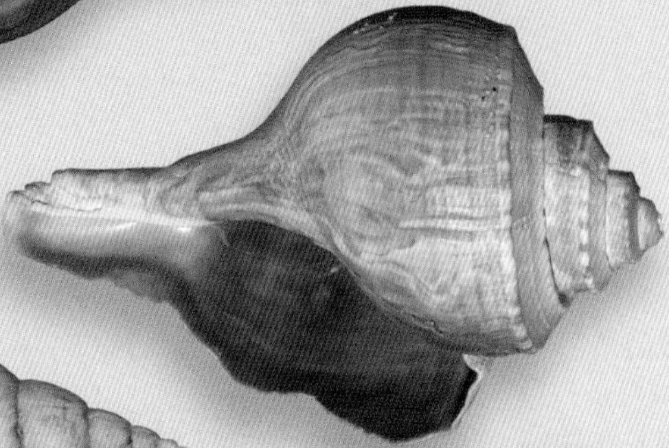

Channeled Whelk
Busycotypus canaliculatus
to 7″

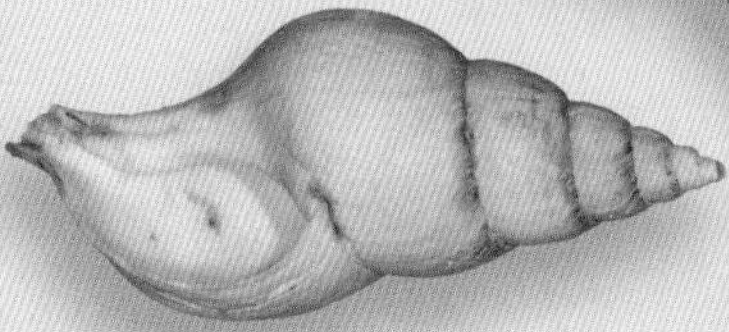

Stimpson's Whelk
Colus stimpsoni
to 4½″

Ten-ridged Whelk
(New England Neptune)
Neptunea decemcostata
to 4″
state shell of Massachusetts

Waved Whelk
Buccinum undatum
to 4″

young Quahogs
called "cherrystones" up to 2", "littlenecks" up to 3", but all are same species

Quahog
(pronounced "co-hog" or "kwa-hog")
Mercenaria mercenaria
adults to 4"
common just under surface of mudflats

False Quahog
Pitar morrhuanus **2"**

Mahogany Clam
(Black Clam, Ocean Quahog)
Artica islandica **to 4"**

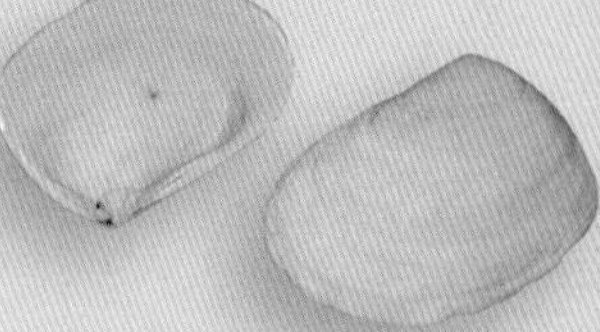

Wedge Clam
Mesodesma arctatum **1½"**

Soft-shelled Clam
Mya arenaria **3–6"**

Blood Ark *Anadara ovalis* 2″
one of the few mollusks
with red blood

Transverse Ark
Anadara transversa 1″
common in sandy shallows

False Angel Wing
Petricola pholadiformis 2″

Veiled Clam *Solemya velum* 1½″
stiff brown covering
extends beyond edge of shell

Propeller Clam
Cyrtodaria siliqua
3″

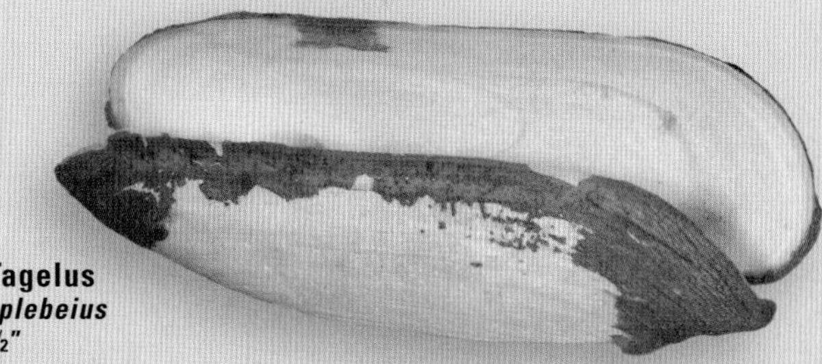

Stout Tagelus
Tagelus plebeius
3½″

Bay Scallop
Argopecten irradians
2½"
lives in shallow water, common in beds of eelgrass

living Bay Scallop showing small blue eyes

Iceland Scallop
Chlamys islandica
to 4"
lives in fairly deep water

Atlantic Deep-sea Scallop
Placopecten magellanicus
to 6–8"
lives in deep water, shells wash up on beaches

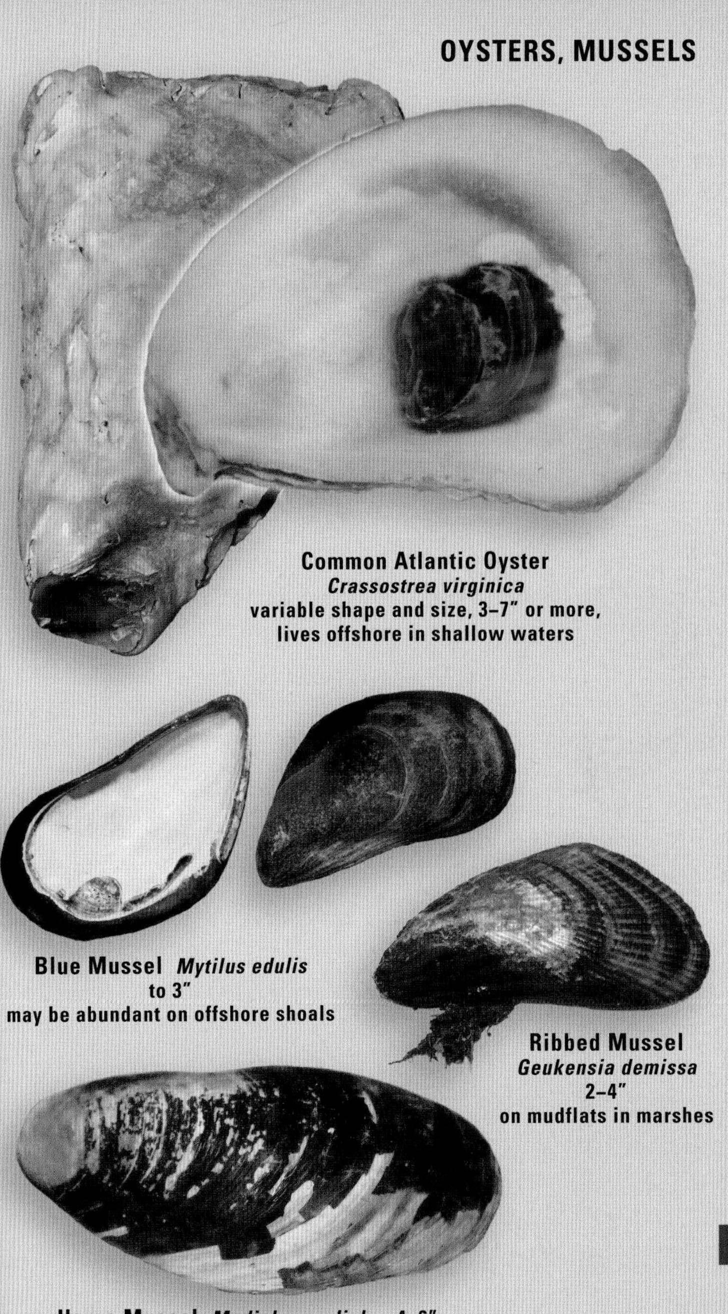

Common Atlantic Oyster
Crassostrea virginica
variable shape and size, 3–7″ or more, lives offshore in shallow waters

Blue Mussel *Mytilus edulis*
to 3″
may be abundant on offshore shoals

Ribbed Mussel
Geukensia demissa
2–4″
on mudflats in marshes

Horse Mussel *Modiolus modiolus* 4–6″
lives in deep water, shells wash up on beach

Jingle Shell *Anomia simplex* 1–2″
common; variable in color

Chestnut Astarte
Astarte castanea 1″

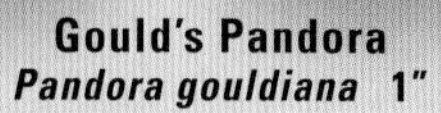

Gould's Pandora
Pandora gouldiana 1″

Northern Cardita
Cyclocardia borealis
1″

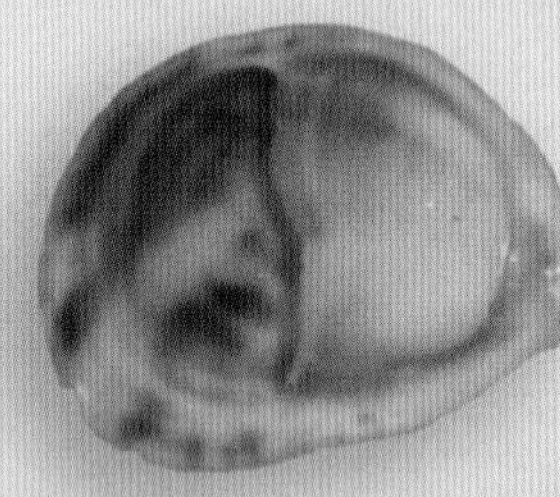

Common
Slipper Shell
(Boat Shell)
Crepidula fornicata
1½″
very common in shallow water

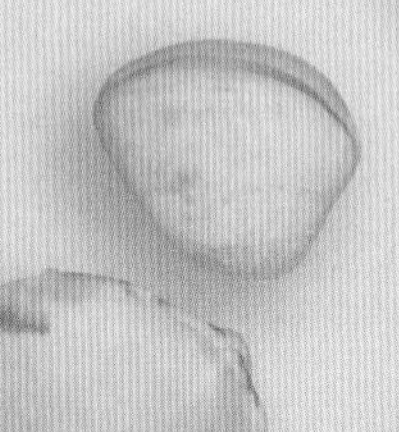

Morton's
Egg Cockle
Laevicardium mortoni
¾″

Convex Slipper Shell
Crepidula convexa ½″

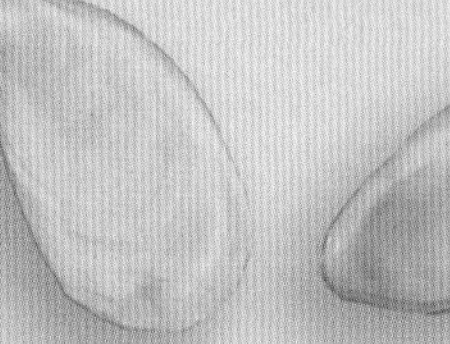

Eastern White Slipper Shell
Crepidula plana 1″

SOME ODD SHELLS

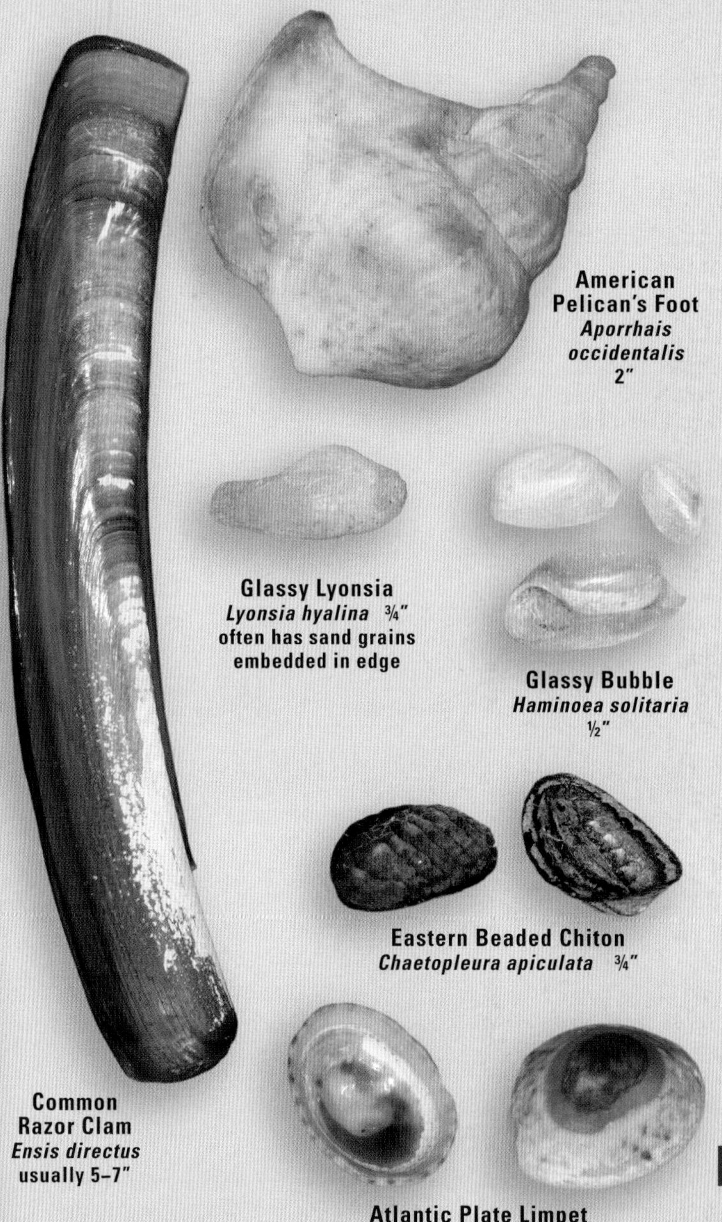

American Pelican's Foot
Aporrhais occidentalis
2"

Glassy Lyonsia
Lyonsia hyalina ¾"
often has sand grains embedded in edge

Glassy Bubble
Haminoea solitaria
½"

Eastern Beaded Chiton
Chaetopleura apiculata ¾"

Common Razor Clam
Ensis directus
usually 5–7"

Atlantic Plate Limpet
Testudinalia testudinalis
1"

MISCELLANEOUS FINDS ON THE BEACH

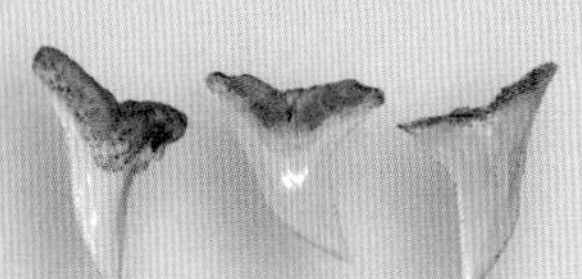

sharks' teeth
often found on beaches

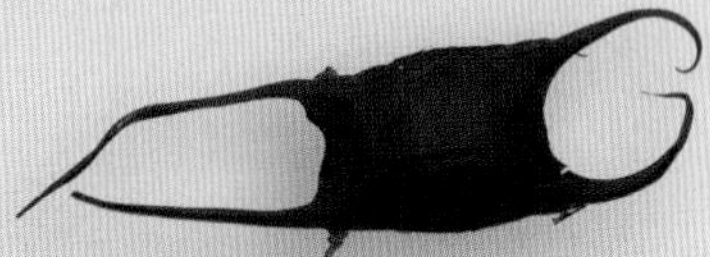

skate egg case
Skates are flat-bodied ocean fish (p. 274); their egg cases, sometimes called "mermaid purses," often wash up on beaches.

Sand Dollar
Echinarachnius parma
a flat creature of sandy ocean floor; brown to red in life, bleaches to white later

egg capsules of Channeled Whelk
(see p. 373) The egg capsules of these large snails are found in strings like this.

sea urchin external "skeleton"
(called the "test")
Live sea urchins are covered with spines (see p. 384).

worm shell
Vermicularia sp.

A Living Fossil: Horseshoe Crab

ATLANTIC HORSESHOE CRAB ***Limulus polyphemus***
One of the most distinctive animals on New England beaches. The name is misleading: not at all related to crabs or other crustaceans, horseshoe crabs belong to a class of their own, with a fossil history going back well over 300 million years. Living in deep water most of the year, adults come to the shallows in late spring, and females crawl up on sandy beaches to lay vast numbers of tiny greenish eggs. Despite their odd appearance, horseshoe crabs are completely harmless. ▶ Unmistakable — unlike anything else in the Atlantic. Adult females can be up to 2' long, counting the tail spike, while males average smaller. The youngest individuals look like very small versions of the adults but without the tail spike.

The Most Popular Crustacean: Lobster

NORTHERN LOBSTER ***Homarus americanus***
Famed for its role in New England cuisine and economy, this crustacean is common to abundant, especially toward the north. Lobsters feed as scavengers and predators on the ocean floor, often in shallow areas in summer, moving to deeper waters in winter. The youngest hatchlings are tiny and free-swimming, but after several molts of their outer shell (exoskeleton), they resemble very small versions of the adults. Old adults may live for decades and may be more than 2' long. ▶ Elongated body, flat tail, large front pincers. Nothing else in salt water in our area looks like it. (Crayfish, found in fresh water, are similar but smaller relatives of lobsters.)

CRABS

Most crabs are agile crustaceans of shallow waters or tidal flats. This heading includes creatures from several families, so they vary in their appearance and habits. All have five pairs of legs, with the front pair modified into claws and the hind pair sometimes paddle-shaped. Crabs can move in any direction, often with impressive speed, but they usually walk or run sideways. Most species feed mainly as scavengers, although some are more predatory, and fiddler crabs also feed on plant material.

ROCK CRAB ***Cancer irroratus***

Common all along the New England coast except for southwestern Connecticut. Regularly found in tidepools, under rocks in shallow water, and around piers and jetties. Family Cancridae. ▶ Up to 5" wide. Leading edge of shell between eye and outer corner has 9 "teeth" with smooth edges. Overall color dull yellowish, heavily mottled with reddish brown.

JONAH CRAB ***Cancer borealis***

Also common along New England coast, but not seen as often as Rock Crab, tending to occur in deeper water. Family Cancridae. ▶ Up to 6" wide. Similar to Rock Crab, but "teeth" on shell have *rough or jagged edges.*

GREEN CRAB ***Carcinus maenas***

Originally native to western Europe, this crab was first found in the New World in Massachusetts in the early 1800s. It is now one of New England's most numerous crabs. Because it is a predator on other creatures, including smaller crustaceans and mollusks, it may have a negative effect on some clams and other shellfish. Family Portunidae. ▶ Up to 3" wide. Leading edge of shell between eye and outer corner has 5 "teeth." Overall color is variable, from green to brown to dull reddish. Often mostly greenish above, yellowish below, but adult females are orange below.

LADY CRAB ***Ovalipes ocellatus***

Fairly common in summer north to Cape Cod, underwater in sandy areas. Fast-moving and aggressive, likely to pinch if disturbed. Family Portunidae. ▶ Up to 3" wide. Pale above, finely marked with clusters of tiny darker spots. Hindmost pair of legs flattened, paddle-shaped.

FIDDLER CRAB ***Uca* sp.**

Fiddlers (3 species) run about on tidal flats and beaches near salt marshes, retreating into their burrows if alarmed. Family Ocypodidae. ▶ Up to 1½" wide. Male has 1 front claw *greatly enlarged* and uses it mainly for gesturing in social displays. Female has both front claws small.

HERMIT CRAB ***Pagurus* sp.**

These small crabs (at least 5 species) are best known for their habit of living inside abandoned snail shells and carrying them as they scurry about the tidal flats. They will cling tenaciously to the inside of their shell, but they will also readily exchange it for another. Family Paguridae. ▶ Soft abdomen almost always hidden inside adopted shell; 2 long front pairs of legs and 2 claws exposed. Species identified mainly by details of claws.

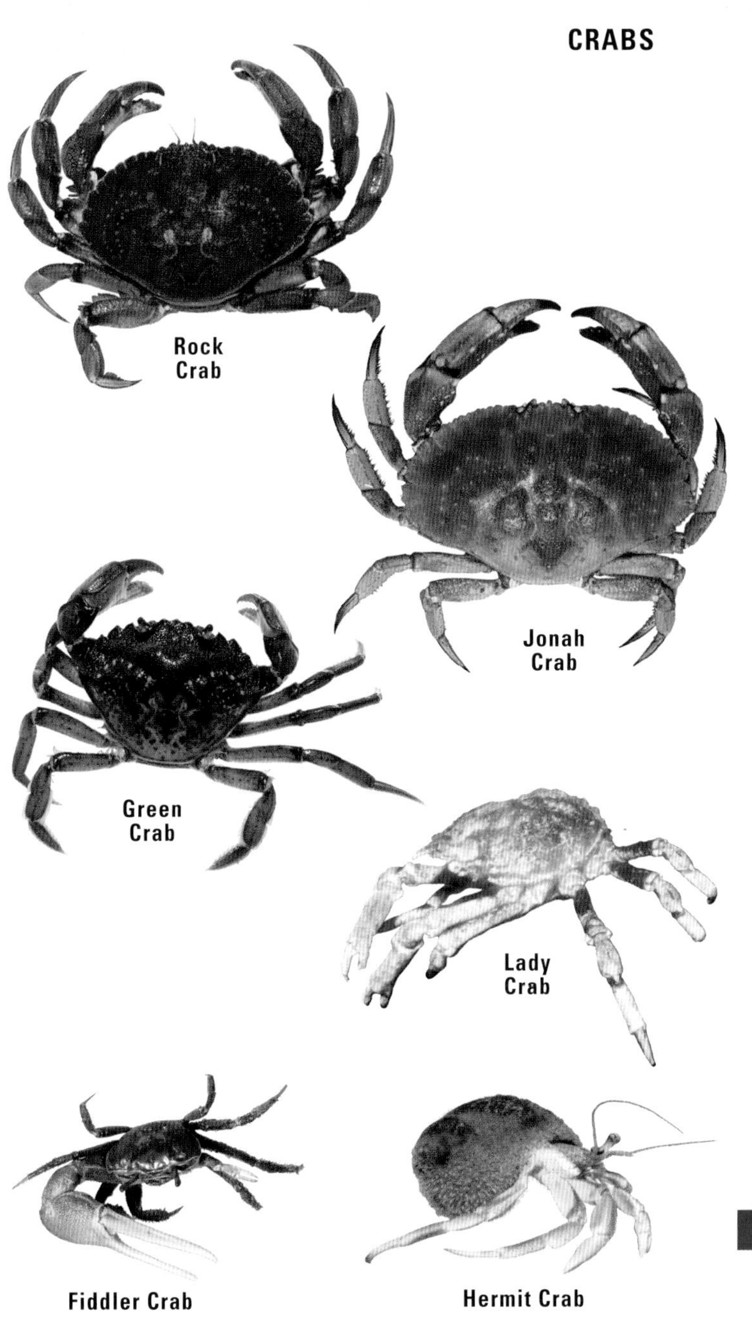
Rock
Crab
Jonah
Crab
Green
Crab
Lady
Crab
Fiddler Crab
Hermit Crab

VARIOUS SHORE AND TIDEPOOL CREATURES

Some small creatures of shallow water and of the water's edge are most easily observed at low tide, when the receding tide has left behind pools of water in rocks or on low spots in the mudflats.

Several of the animals represented in our pages of seashells can be found alive in tidepools. For example, periwinkles (p. 372) are often very numerous there, and chitons (p. 379) may be found regularly. On this page we discuss a few other creatures that may be found in tidepools, or on the rocks in the intertidal zone or just below the usual low-tide mark.

Barnacles are classified as crustaceans, although they bear scant resemblance to the crabs and lobster on previous pages. Thus they are in the phylum **Arthropoda,** along with insects. Urchins and sea stars are placed in the phylum **Echinodermata,** the spiny-skinned animals.

NORTHERN ROCK BARNACLE ***Balanus balanoides***

Barnacles are odd creatures that spend their adult lives glued in one spot, on rocks, pilings, or boats. Young barnacles hatch from eggs as tiny, free-swimming larvae; later they attach themselves to a solid surface, essentially gluing themselves down, and begin to secrete the hard outer shells in which they will spend the rest of their lives. Adult barnacles look like dead shells when exposed to air. When underwater, their shells open and close as they extend feathery appendages to sift microscopic bits of food from the water. Family Balanidae. ► Up to 1" across. Several barnacle species occur in New England, most quite similar, but this is usually the most common.

GREEN SEA URCHIN ***Strongylocentrotus droebachiensis***

Common in tidepools all along the New England coast, also extending out to deep water. Urchins can move about quite well with tube feet located on the underside. The mouth is also located on the underside, and urchins use it to feed on a wide variety of algae and small creatures. Family Strongylocentrotidae. ► The external "skeleton" (see p. 380) may be 3" across, but the animal is covered with long, thin spines, mostly green to yellow-green.

PURPLE SEA URCHIN ***Arbacia punctulata***

Generally less common than Green Sea Urchin, found from Cape Cod south. Family Arbaciidae. ► External "skeleton" up to 2" across, with spines often longer and fewer than those of Green Sea Urchin. Overall color is usually reddish brown to purple.

ASTERIID SEA STAR ***Asterias* sp.**

Often called "starfish," but not at all related to fish. Common offshore and in tidepools. Sea stars feed on mollusks and other creatures, using their powerful arms to pull open the shells of bivalves. Family Asteriidae. ► Up to 5–8" across. Has 5 stout arms, variable in color, with paler spines.

BLOOD STAR ***Henricia* sp.**

Small and colorful sea stars, fairly common toward the north. Family Echinasteridae. ► Up to 3" across. Has 5 relatively narrow arms, usually bright red, orange, or yellow.

Northern Rock Barnacle

Purple Sea Urchin

Green Sea Urchin

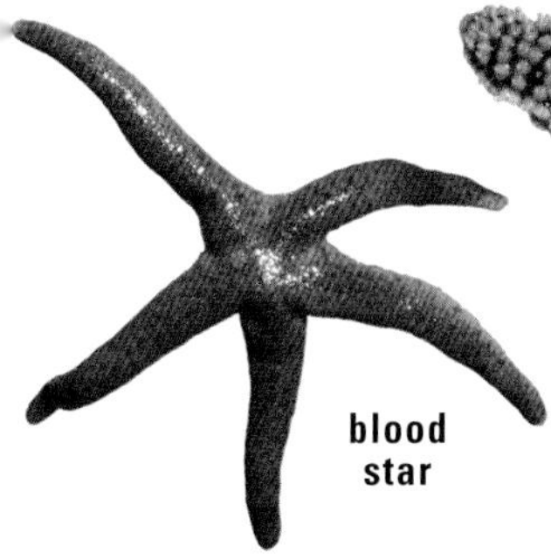

blood star

Asteriid sea star

SEAWEEDS

The general term "seaweed" is applied to a variety of things growing in the ocean and along its edge. They seem profoundly different from our familiar land plants, and indeed they are: most are classified as types of algae, so some scientists question whether they should be called plants at all. The classification of algae is complex and somewhat controversial; one approach that holds up well for seaweeds is to divide them broadly into green, brown, and red seaweed groups.

Seaweeds differ from more advanced land plants in lacking flowers, fruits, seeds, and even roots. In place of roots, those that grow on rocks have a structure called a holdfast; it holds the seaweed in place, but unlike an actual root system, it does not take up any moisture or nutrients.

SEA LETTUCE ***Ulva lactuca***

Very common in shallow water along the coast. From a perennial holdfast on rocks or other solid foundations, large sheets of slimy green Sea Lettuce grow each year, breaking loose and floating free later in the season. Able to tolerate some pollution of the water. Green seaweed group. ▶ Irregular flat or ruffled sheets of green, up to 2–3' long, thin and translucent, with a consistency of greasy waxed paper.

DULSE ***Palmaria palmata***

A common seaweed, attaching to rocks in the lower parts of the intertidal zone and in deeper water. An edible species, Dulse is still harvested and sold in Maine. Red seaweed group. ▶ Up to 1' long, broad and flat, forking into multiple lobes. Dull purplish red, almost opaque, with a tough and rubbery consistency.

KELP ***Laminaria* sp.**

The kelps are large, flat-bladed seaweeds that may grow anywhere from the lowest edge of the intertidal zone to deeper waters. Away from rocks where it grows, most often noticed when large specimens wash up on beaches. Brown seaweed group. ▶ Variable. Brown to yellowish brown, flat or with ruffled edges. May be up to 10–15' long, or longer in deep water.

ROCKWEED ***Fucus* sp.**

On rocky coastlines and around piers, great masses of rockweed and Knotted Wrack are exposed at low tide. Close inspection will reveal many tiny creatures sheltering in these masses, but be cautious about walking around them, because these seaweeds are incredibly slippery. Brown seaweed group. ▶ Long, limp stems (can be 3' long) with strong holdfast and with fleshy *midrib*. One common species has *paired* air bladders.

KNOTTED WRACK ***Ascophyllum nodosum***

Common on rocky shorelines, typically found in association with rockweeds. Brown seaweed group. ▶ Long, flat strands (can be 2' long or more), *without* raised midrib, but usually with oval air bladders.

SEAWEEDS
(not all shown at same scale)

Sea Lettuce

Dulse

Kelp

Washed up on rocks. May be more than 10' long.

rockweed

Knotted Wrack

CONSERVATION

New England's rich natural history plays a vital role in the quality of life here. Even those people who are not actively interested in nature can still appreciate the sight of spring blossoms or fall foliage, or the sounds of bird song. But the value of our natural heritage goes beyond its undeniable aesthetic appeal. Nature-related travel to the area, or ecotourism, plays a major role in the region's economy. Many other commercial activities, from fishing and clamming to the timber industry, depend on native wildlife and plants. Beyond that, there is the more basic fact that everything in nature is interconnected and interdependent. Conservation of natural resources should be of importance to everyone.

Autumn in the hills of Vermont

SUSTAINABILITY

When the Pilgrims landed, they found themselves surrounded by extraordinary natural riches. Forests of magnificent trees stood on every side; fish and wildlife were everywhere, in abundance beyond description. It seemed that nature's bounty in this new land would be inexhaustible.

Unfortunately, it proved to be all too exhaustible. Native American tribes had lived in a balance with their surroundings here for thousands of years, but the European colonists depleted the natural resources at an alarming rate. Over the following three centuries, most of the primeval forests were cut, most of the deer and other large animals disappeared, whales became scarce in the offshore waters, and some of the most abundant fish began declining in numbers. Formerly clear rivers were fouled with pollution and with excessive runoff from cleared land, and soil in some farming regions was depleted and degraded. It was becoming obvious that resources were being used at a level that could not be sustained for the long term.

What the colonists were learning, the hard way, was a series of lessons about sustainability. Just as New England had been one of the first regions of the U.S. to begin depleting its resources, it was among the first to begin practicing conservation. Massachusetts had a closed season on deer hunting as early as 1694, and Vermont, Connecticut, and New Hampshire all had enacted game laws of some kind by 1780. Forest management principles, regulations on fishing, and soil and water conservation all came into effect here earlier than in most parts of the country.

The movement toward sustainability is not just a matter of environmental issues — it has economic and social aspects as well — but in this section we are concerned with how it relates to the use of natural resources. The basic idea is that future generations should have access to the same resources that we enjoy today, or to even higher levels of these resources.

Of course, some resources are finite. Fossil fuels such as oil and coal may still be abundant in some areas, but they will eventually run out. Besides, burning of these fuels leads to an increase in the carbon dioxide in the atmosphere, which may be implicated in changing the overall climate of the planet. Ultimately we will have to switch to energy sources that are fully renewable, such as solar, wind, or tidal power; but all of these have potential negative effects on the environment as well. Creating true sustainability for future centuries will take a concerted effort, collective wisdom, and good science.

GRASS-ROOTS CONSERVATION

Never doubt that a small group of thoughtful, committed citizens can change the world. Indeed, it is the only thing that ever has.
— Margaret Mead

Most highly successful conservation efforts have begun with the efforts of individuals and small organizations, banding together to bring about major changes. Here are two examples with New England roots.

The Weeks Act and the protection of forests. Well before the dawn of the twentieth century, America had awakened to the importance of protecting forest land — not only to have continued sources for timber, but also for the forests' role in maintaining the health of watersheds. Indeed, a law passed in 1891 made it possible to set aside federally owned land as forest reserves. Many such reserves were soon established in the western states and territories. But in New England and elsewhere in the east, very little of the land was owned by the federal government. Under the existing laws, there was no good option for protecting large tracts of forest land.

With many private citizens and businesses dependent on healthy watersheds and stable waterways, pressure mounted for federal protection and

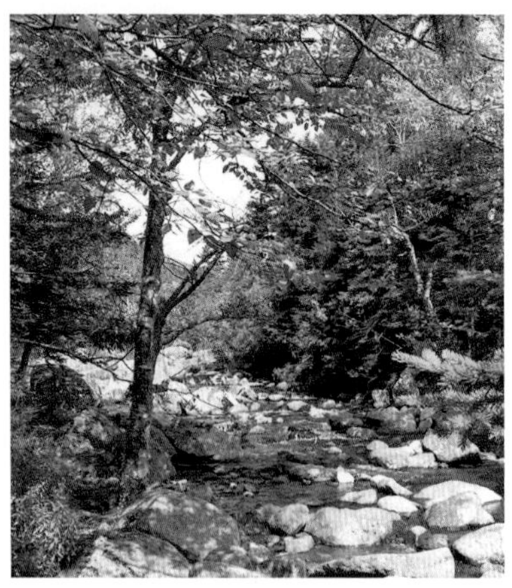

A stream in the White Mountains, New Hampshire

restoration of New England's forests. The White Mountains of New Hampshire became one area of focus, and concerned citizens formed the Society for the Protection of New Hampshire Forests in 1901. This group joined forces with other organizations such as the Appalachian Mountain Club and the National Forestry Association and began pressuring Congress to take action. Over the following decade, multiple bills were introduced, but none made it through to passage and signing.

Finally, in 1911, Congress passed the Weeks Act. Named for Representative John Weeks (R-MA), who guided it through the House, this bill authorized the use of federal funds to buy private lands to add to a national forest reserve system. John Weeks himself had grown up near the White Mountains, but he had had a successful career in banking, so he could argue that protecting forest made good business sense.

In the century since, this act has proven to be one of our most valuable pieces of environmental legislation, with tremendous benefits for conservation. Here in New England, the White Mountain National Forest (almost 800,000 acres in New Hampshire and western Maine) and the Green Mountain National Forest (more than 400,000 acres in Vermont) were protected as a result of this act.

The Audubon movement and the protection of birds. The egrets and other wading birds that we see along the New England coast were almost driven to extinction in the late 1800s. Their long plumes became incredibly popular in fashion, especially on hats. "Plume hunters" began raiding the nesting colonies of these birds throughout the eastern U.S., killing the adult birds for their feathers and leaving the young birds to starve.

Some ornithologists were aware of the slaughter. But the pressure to stop it came from some influential ladies in Boston, who read about the killing and decided to take action. In 1896 they formed the Massachusetts Audubon Society and began recruiting other women to boycott the use of feathers and birds on hats. The movement spread rapidly, with Audubon Societies springing up in one state after another, all of them lobbying their state legislatures to pass laws for bird protection. So persuasive were these groups that within four years, their efforts led to the passage of the federal Lacey Act, which prohibited the interstate shipment of feathers that had been taken in violation of state laws.

Still, the Lacey Act was only as strong as the weakest state laws, so the Audubon women (and the men that they recruited to help) continued to expand their efforts. Many of the state Audubon groups banded together in a national organization in 1901, formalized in 1905, as their influence grew. Finally, in 1911, New York passed the Audubon Plumage Bill, prohibiting the sale of the feathers of all native birds. Since New York City was the center of the plume trade, this law essentially shut it down. Ultimately, the Migratory Bird Treaty Act of 1918 would extend federal protections to almost all native birds.

But by this time, the Audubon groups were using their increasing level of organization to take aim at other threats to birds and the natural environment. Today, the National Audubon Society, the independent Massachusetts Audubon Society, and other Audubon groups are still working for conservation. And the egrets and other plume birds, reminders of their first success, are once again numerous in the marshes in summer.

Snowy Egret

BIODIVERSITY

They say variety is the spice of life. As naturalists, we certainly agree. A meadow filled with white asters might be attractive, but we prefer a meadow with dozens of different kinds of flowers. A morning chorus of robins may sound beautiful, but we prefer to hear the songs of many kinds of birds. But beyond these aesthetic issues, variety is important for scientific reasons.

For the natural world, variety is more than just spice; it's an essential ingredient. In nature, variety is often referred to as biodiversity. A simplified definition for this term would be "the variety of all life forms within a given habitat, ecosystem, or region, or an entire planet." New England is blessed with rich biodiversity, with thousands upon thousands of distinct species of living things finding their niches here.

A healthy habitat, or ecosystem, has many, many species interacting in countless ways. A single oak tree may be assailed by hundreds of species of insects that eat its leaves, acorns, wood, or roots, but those insects are kept in check by scores of other insects and dozens of birds, not to mention bats, toads, and other creatures. Some of the insects that attack the oak in some life stages may be pollinating its flowers in other stages of their lives. The acorns produced by the oak may be eaten by squirrels, jays, turkeys, or other creatures, but some of those animals will carry acorns away and bury them, thus unintentionally planting the next generation. When the oak dies, its fallen trunk will be broken down by many kinds of fungi, creating soil that will sustain future oaks and other plants. And so on. Every living thing is involved in this web of connections, all adding up to an intricate balance of nature.

Although every species has its own niche, a large amount of overlap is built into the system. Take away one species and it may not make a big difference: something else will pollinate that flower, bury that acorn, or eat that insect. But as we begin to take away more species, serious and unexpected consequences can result.

Imagine that you are building the wooden frame for a house. For it to be sturdy and durable, you'll probably use more nails than the absolute bare minimum necessary; and after it's built, you could probably pop out a nail here, a nail there, without it falling down. But how many nails can you remove before the frame becomes unstable? What happens if you remove one critical nail and the frame begins to collapse? A natural ecosystem is like that, on a much grander and more complicated scale: once we start removing species, we risk causing serious problems.

This is part of the reason why it's important to preserve biodiversity: not just so we can enjoy all that variety, but so the machinery of nature can continue to function. This is part of the reason why conservationists work to prevent extinction of species. Ironically, adding species to a habitat can cause as many problems as taking some away. In the next two sections we'll talk about two sides of this issue: endangered species and invasive species.

ENDANGERED SPECIES

The extinction of species is a natural thing, but it isn't inevitable, at least not on the time scales that we usually think about. Over long ages of time, some species may adapt and change radically as conditions change, while others may go extinct. But other kinds of living things may continue to exist, essentially unchanged, for millions of years, as long as their surroundings continue to satisfy their requirements for survival.

Within the last couple of centuries the world has seen an unnatural wave of extinctions, most of them caused (directly or indirectly) by humans. Before wildlife management was understood and before laws were in place, some species found here in New England were hunted to extinction. These included a coastal mammal, the Sea Mink, and an abundant bird, the Passenger Pigeon. Other species that no longer occur in New England but are still found elsewhere, such as Caribou and Cougar, are said to be extirpated from this region.

Endangered Species Act. An unnaturally rapid loss of species and loss of biodiversity is an alarming thing. Concern over this led to the passage in 1973 of a landmark piece of legislation, the U.S. Endangered Species Act (ESA). The stated purpose of the ESA was to protect and recover populations of imperiled species of animals and plants and the ecosystems upon which they depend. Under the ESA, after careful scientific review, a species in trouble could be listed as either Threatened or Endangered; once it was officially listed, a series of legal protections and other actions would come into effect. The ESA has had some notable successes: for example, Osprey, Bald Eagle, and Peregrine Falcon, all in serious trouble in the 1970s, have recovered extremely well.

State designations. In addition to the federal list, each New England state also maintains a list of species considered endangered or threatened within the state, sometimes adding other categories such as "Species of Special Concern." Species are often rare at the outer edges of their ranges, so animals or plants that are peripheral here are likely to show up on these state lists. For example, Eastern Hognose Snake, which reaches the limit of its range here, is listed as endangered in New Hampshire and as a species of concern in Rhode Island and Connecticut, but it is widespread and common over much of the southeastern U.S. Of course conservationists are interested in maintaining diversity at the state and local levels, but most effort goes into those species that are in danger of extinction throughout their ranges.

Here are some examples of species in need of protection every place that they occur.

Northern Right Whale. With approximately 300–400 individuals left in the Atlantic, the Northern Right Whale is among the rarest of all marine mammal species. Right Whales were so named for the gruesome reason that they are rich in blubbler and they float when dead, which made them an easy and profitable target for early whalers — so they were the "right" whales to kill. Despite protected status since 1949, their populations still have not recovered.

Northern Right Whales are migratory, spending the colder months off the southeastern U.S. and moving north in summer. Critical habitats that have been identified include Cape Cod Bay and the area over and just west of Georges Bank. These whales are no longer hunted, but continuing threats include collisions with ships and entanglement in fishing nets. An intensive, ongoing research and conservation program of the New England Aquarium is helping to shed light on ways to help the species.

Red Knot. This small sandpiper, not much bigger than a robin, is a champion of long-distance migration. It nests on Arctic tundra and winters on coastlines all over the world. The population that occurs in New England includes some individuals that may fly more than 18,000 miles round-trip between breeding grounds in the Canadian Arctic and wintering grounds at the southern tip of South America.

Since the 1990s, surveys on wintering grounds in South America and at stopover sites along the Atlantic Coast of the U.S. have shown alarming declines in numbers. One major factor apparently has been a decline in the food source that they need during their long spring migration. Red Knots, coming thousands of miles from South America, concentrate around Delaware Bay in spring to fatten up for the final leg of their journey to the Arctic. Historically their major food source here had been the eggs of Horseshoe Crabs, laid by the billions in May. Overfishing of Horseshoe Crabs during the 1990s led to a drastic decline in this food source, perhaps leading to reduced breeding success by Red Knots that arrived in the Arctic underfed. The Manomet Center for Conservation Science was among the first organizations to begin a serious program for conservation of the knots.

Red Knot

New England Blazing-star. This attractive late-summer wildflower is not federally listed as endangered or threatened, but it has been given some special designation in practically every state in which it occurs. The New England Blazing-star is listed as a species of special concern in Connecticut and Massachusetts, threatened in Maine (and New York), and endangered in New Hampshire and Rhode Island (and New Jersey). Therefore, although it has a fairly extensive range in the northeastern U.S., it clearly faces challenges and deserves protection.

The main issue for this flower is the fact that it is limited to scarce habitats, such as clearings or edges in open woodlands, meadows on sandy soil or dunes, and open scrublands near the coast. All of these habitats are subject to plant succession (or invasion by taller plants) or to development. Stands of this blazing-star are often small, and as local populations are wiped out, the species seems slow to spread into new areas.

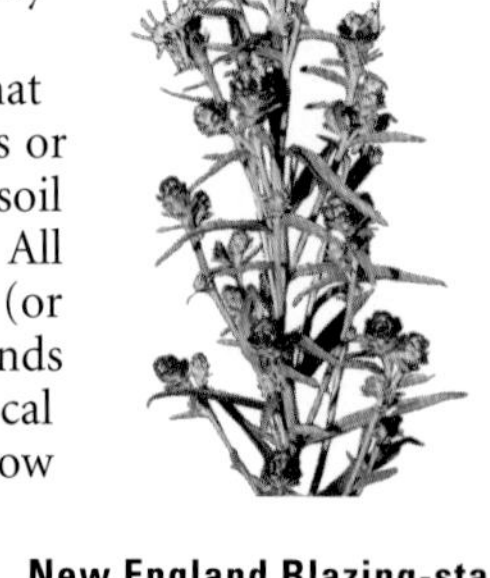

New England Blazing-star

INVASIVE SPECIES

Attractive and unusual plants have been transported outside their native ranges by humans from as far back as colonial times, right up to the modern day. Some are unknowingly introduced when seeds cling to shoes and clothing. Once established, without the normal natural balance of insects and diseases that would keep them in check within their native range, many exotic invasives spread aggressively, disrupting habitats and food sources for native species.

Most exotic species cause only minor damage. Often they are mostly confined to sites where the original habitat has been thoroughly altered and where the soil has been disturbed numerous times. For example, a high percentage of the plants growing in vacant city lots and along roadsides will be exotic species. A more serious issue involves those exotic species that spread aggressively beyond the disturbed sites and into native habitats. These plants may compete with and crowd out native plants, while reducing the value of the habitat for native animals.

An example of a troublesome invasive is Garlic Mustard, now very common in parts of southern New England and spreading farther north. A spring-blooming plant with tiny white flowers, Garlic Mustard grows well on open, disturbed sites with other weeds, but it also spreads aggressively into the shady understory of rich woods, forming solid stands and crowding out everything else. Many of our most distinctive native wildflowers also live in these moist woodland habitats, and they may be crowded out by this invader. Garlic Mustard also has a negative impact on a native butterfly, the Mustard White: females will lay eggs on this plant, because it is similar to native host plants, but the caterpillars generally do not survive and mature on it. This may be part of the reason why Mustard Whites are declining in numbers.

Garlic Mustard

Another invasive with a more obvious impact is Purple Loosestrife. A perennial with a strong, tough root system, this gaudy flower has taken over many wetland areas in the northeast, turning marshes and wet meadows into solid stands of this species. Because marshes and other wetlands are scarce and valuable habitats, hosting many rare native species, a takeover by Purple Loosestrife leads to an overall loss of biodiversity.

It is important to learn what plant species are invasive in the areas where we live and where we travel and to take precautions against inadvertently transporting them into other areas. In this guide we make note of a number of species of troublesome invasive plants. The New England Wild Flower Society is a good source of even more information on the issue.

However, it is not only the invasive plants that can wreak havoc on the natural balance. A number of invasive animals have made a significant impact in North America over the last 300 years. A small snail, the Common Periwinkle, was introduced to eastern Canada in the mid-1800s as a food source. But no one paused to consider the food source of the snail itself. Feeding primarily on plant rhizomes of marsh grasses and the algae that blanketed the rocky New England coast, they soon devoured nearly all of the plant matter in some areas, leaving nothing but the exposed rock.

Common Periwinkle

First introduced in New York City's Central Park in 1890, the European Starling spread slowly at first, but eventually it became one of North America's most widespread and abundant birds. Highly adaptable and aggressive, starlings compete with many of our native cavity-nesting birds, including Eastern Bluebirds, Purple Martins, and Red-headed Woodpeckers. In many areas, the starlings appear to have caused permanent reductions in the populations of these natives.

Invasive species are now believed to represent the number one habitat management problem facing wildlife agencies in this country. Clearly it is worth the effort to try to avoid introducing new, and potentially harmful, exotic species in the first place.

European Starling

WHAT CAN YOU DO FOR CONSERVATION?

Everyone can help with the conservation of our natural resources. The first step toward doing your part is to be well-informed.

Conservation Begins At Home. Some environmental challenges may seem so huge as to be insurmountable; however, there are small and simple steps that can make a significant difference. For example, supporting migratory bird habitat can be as simple as selecting the right kind of coffee.

Bird-friendly coffee. Coffee grown in the traditional way in the American tropics, shaded by the canopy of native trees, provides rich habitat for migratory birds. Unfortunately, since the 1970s, vast areas have been converted from shade coffee to sun coffee. The area is bulldozed, scraping away any remnants of native vegetation, and the coffee plants are doused with fertilizers, herbicides, and pesticides. Terrible for the soil, dangerous for the people who tend the plants, and disastrous for the migratory birds that depend on native forests for wintering habitat, the only payoff is higher yields in the short term.

With growing awareness of this issue, some companies attempt to cheat the system by planting a few nonnative trees and slapping a "shade-grown" label on their product. To ensure that the coffee you purchase actually comes from a farm that supports bird life, look for the Smithsonian Migratory Bird Center seal of Bird-Friendly coffee. This is the gold standard for coffee that is good for birds and good for people. It can still be a challenge to find; a good place to begin your search is with the New England company Birds & Beans. You can learn more at www.birdsandbeans.com.

The symbol of bird-friendly coffee, as certified by the Smithsonian Migratory Bird Center

The Three Rs: reduce, reuse, recycle. Introduced in the 1980s, the Three Rs campaign asks us to reduce what we use, reuse items as much as possible, and recycle products once they can no longer be used. Seems simple enough, and yet there are still too few who follow the Three Rs philosophy. In today's "throw away" society, it might seem hard to believe, but there was a time in our history when people had to be instructed on what a wastebasket was and how to use it, because the idea of throwing things away was mostly an alien concept. We have become a society overrun with our own refuse. Simple steps can make a difference. Live the Three Rs philosophy. Avoid purchasing water and other products in plastic bottles; reduce the amount of waste you produce by avoiding single-use products such as paper towels and napkins; and bring your own reusable grocery bags when you go shopping.

Reduce your energy consumption. There are so many simple ways to reduce the amount of energy we use that we have no legitimate excuse not to do so. Though a bit more expensive, replacing regular light bulbs with compact fluorescent bulbs saves money in the long run. They use one-quarter the energy of an ordinary light bulb and they last 8–12 times longer. Slight adjustments to your thermostat — even by just two degrees — can make a big difference throughout the course of one year. So can turning your computer off every night and hanging your clothes up to dry rather than using the dryer. Refrigerators account for up to 20 percent of household energy use; adjusting them to a reasonable temperature of 37° F (3° F for the freezer) will significantly reduce energy consumption. Put all of these things into practice, and together the energy savings really add up, both for you and for the health of the planet.

Your carbon footprint. Most forms of transportation burn fossil fuels. Riding a bike, walking when possible, carpooling, and using public transportation are ways to reduce your "carbon footprint" — that is, the amount of carbon dioxide that you put into the atmosphere. When you travel, especially long distances, try researching available programs that allow you to calculate and offset your carbon footprint through donations that support sustainable, responsible, renewable energy projects. These offset programs help to reduce the amount of energy produced from coal and oil or to compensate in other ways. Reforestation projects actually reduce the amount of carbon in the atmosphere by sequestering carbon dioxide emissions, providing health benefits for people and wildlife.

Support conservation organizations. One of the most effective ways to help with conservation is to add your support to organizations that are already doing good work. New England is blessed with many conservation groups. Some operate at the national or international level, some do their work at the state or regional level, while some are strictly local. All have their place in the big picture. We recommend researching the many groups out there, learning about how they carry out their missions and about how they will make use of the support that you give them. Your support might be in the form of financial donations or in donations of your time as a volunteer, but either way, you need to be confident that this organization will make the most effective use of what you are giving.

Support federal and state conservation agencies. This can be as easy as buying a stamp. The Federal Migratory Bird Hunting and Conservation Stamp, commonly known as the "Duck Stamp," is issued every year, and it is a vital tool for wetland conservation. About 98 cents out of every dollar generated by Duck Stamp sales goes directly to purchase or lease wetland habitat for protection in the National Wildlife Refuge (NWR) System. Here in New England, for example, more than 90 percent of the area of Missisquoi NWR in Vermont and more than 99 percent of Parker River NWR in Massachusetts were purchased with Duck Stamp dollars. The refuges are fabulous places for birds and other wildlife; like many other birders and naturalists, we are proud to buy our Duck Stamps every year.

The federal "Duck Stamp": it's a little gem of collectable art, and it saves habitat for migratory birds and other wildlife.

On a state level, there may be opportunities to support your state's wildlife agency by becoming a volunteer. Nearly every field-based project requires volunteers. Getting involved and donating your time not only supports wildlife research, but often allows citizens the opportunity to have some phenomenal experiences.

BE A VOICE FOR CONSERVATION

I went to the woods because I wished to live deliberately, to front only the essential facts of life, and see if I could not learn what it had to teach . . .
— Henry David Thoreau, in *Walden,* 1854

A replica of Thoreau's small and simple house still stands at Walden Pond.

One of America's most original and enduring voices, Henry David Thoreau went to the woods around Walden Pond near Concord, Massachusetts, to develop some of his most important ideas. He was a skilled naturalist and a keen observer, and his knowledge of the natural world illuminated his best writing. Concepts that he presented are still influential in conservation, sustainability, and the attempt to live in harmony with nature.

But you don't have to write a masterpiece to make an impact. If you love the outdoors, one of the best things you can do to encourage proper stewardship of our natural resources is to talk about it. The crucial first step in building support for conservation is to help connect people with nature. If you're a bird watcher, consider inviting a nonbirding friend, family member, or colleague along on your next walk or field trip. If you're a hiker, camper, or backpacker, invite a few new friends along on your next outing. You don't have to be an expert to foster an interest in nature. All it takes is a willingness to share the wonder and value of time spent outdoors.

Naturalists leading a group of children on an exploration at Massachusetts Audubon Society's Wellfleet Bay Wildlife Sanctuary

ACKNOWLEDGMENTS

In a way, we have been gathering material for this guide all our lives. But our active research for it began in 2004, and in the eight years since then, we have received help from many individuals and institutions. Compiling this guide truly was a team effort involving many players.

Our most obvious debt of gratitude is owed to the guest authors who wrote key sections of this guide. Eric R. Eaton, primary author of the *Kaufman Field Guide to Insects,* wrote almost all the text on insects and other invertebrates for the present volume as well, and his expertise and clarity of expression are evident on every page. Eric H. Snyder, a talented young naturalist with a special flair for earth sciences, wrote the section on geology and provided most of the photographs for it as well. Ken Keffer, currently education director at the Black Swamp Bird Observatory, put his knowledge and his awesome communication skills to work in writing the section on habitats.

Of course, the illustrations in a field guide are as essential as the text. Most of the illustrations in this guide are digital images based on photographs. More than 1,000 of the photos were our own, but that accounted for only about half of the images needed; for the rest, we received material from the 130 other photographers listed on pp. 402–404. Some of these images had been used previously in other volumes in the Kaufman Field Guides series, so we benefited once again from the photo research done by Nora Bowers and Rick Bowers for those earlier books. But most of the images are new, and we are grateful to John R. Sawvel for his painstaking work in tracking down hundreds of photos of plants and animals of all kinds to fill in the gaps. Thanks also to Mark Shieldcastle for helping us to locate some challenging photos.

In researching this guide, one of our primary resources was the Audubon Camp on Hog Island, Maine, where we have taught many sessions in summer and fall. During those sessions we learned a huge amount from our fellow instructors and from participants. Special thanks to Seth Benz, Stephen W. Kress, Scott Weidensaul, Tom Leckey, Sara Morris, Sue Schubel, and Pete Salmansohn.

We also made repeated visits to the Garden in the Woods, the showplace of the New England Wild Flower Society (NEWFS) in Framingham, Massachusetts, to observe and photograph plants. Bonnie Drexler and the rest of the staff were exceptionally helpful in answering our questions and directing us to specific plants and resources. NEWFS does good conservation work throughout the region and deserves broad public support.

Another major resource for us was the fine Cape Cod Museum of Natural History in Brewster, Massachusetts. Much of our information about coastal ecosystems and wildlife was gleaned from our repeated visits to this museum.

We cannot begin to list all the state parks, state forests, national forests, and other protected areas that we visited in all six states of the region.

Places like Groton State Forest, Vermont, and Great Swamp Management Area, Rhode Island, may not be well known to tourists, but they were treasure troves for traveling naturalists like us. A few sites owned or managed by private organizations deserve special mention. These include Eastern Egg Rock in Maine, where we were allowed to visit thanks to Stephen W. Kress and Project Puffin; the Wellfleet Bay and Drumlin Farm sanctuaries of Massachusetts Audubon Society; and the Audubon Center of Greenwich, Connecticut.

Some of our photos of elusive animals were taken at Back to the Wild, an animal rehabilitation center in Castalia, Ohio. Mona Rutger, who pours her heart and soul into running this facility, certainly qualifies for sainthood by now; she was generous in allowing us to observe and photograph some of the animals in her care. We studied and photographed some reptiles and amphibians at the Toledo Zoo, thanks to the generosity of Kent Bekker, R. Andrew Odum, and Andi Norman.

Preliminary photo editing — removing the images from their backgrounds — is a time-consuming and painstaking task, and much of that work for this guide was performed by Julie A. Shieldcastle, Barb Myers, Theresa Milak, and Dana Bollin. Some information on the text side was compiled by Ethan Kistler.

Once again it was a pleasure to work with the professionals at Houghton Mifflin Harcourt. Our editor, Lisa White, one of the world's finest young editors of natural history books, always found time to help with every challenging question. Others who helped us in essential ways included Beth Fuller, Brian Moore, Cheryl Rivard, Rolee Kumar, Taryn Roeder, Katrina Kruse, Laney Whitt, and Tim Mudie. In the earliest stages of discussion of the possibility of producing this guide, the late Harry Foster provided insightful and valuable advice.

Finally, special thanks to our friends Wendy Strothman and John Bishop, who hosted us both in Boston and in Maine, and who shared many adventures with us in the field. Wendy was formerly Kenn's publisher and is now our agent, but she goes far beyond the usual commitment of a literary agent in supporting books, authors, and ideas. Her belief in the value of nature study has been an inspiration throughout the long process of finishing this book.

PHOTOGRAPHER CREDITS

The majority of the illustrations used in this guide are digitally edited images based on photographs. We (Kenn and Kimberly) took more than 1,000 of these photos, but that amounted to only about half of the images needed, and for the rest we had to rely on the fine photographers acknowledged below. Photos are listed by page number (in bold), followed by a dash and the number of the image. Images on each page are numbered from top to bottom and from left to right.

The map of general bedrock types on p. 10 is based on material from G.R. Robinson, Jr., and K.E. Kapo, published online by the U.S. Geological Survey as USGS Open-File Report 03-225. The sky maps and constellation diagrams on pp. 22–35 and the marine mammal paintings on pp. 183 and 185 are by Kenn Kaufman.

John C. Abbott: **335**-1, 7; **351**-2
Dr. J. Scott Altenbach: **181**-2, 3, 7, 8
Jennifer Anderson @ USDA-NRCS PLANTS database: **71**-11
Matt Ashton: **367**-4, 5, 6
Ron Austing: **235**-4
Roger W. Barbour: **177**-6; **179**-5
Troy Bartlett: **343**-13; **359**-7, 10
Scott Bauer / USDA ARS: **343**-8; **363**-4
R. A. Behrstock / Naturewide Images: **337**-3
Steve Bentsen: **225**-9
Nic Bishop: **355**-2; **357**-5
Rick and Nora Bowers / BowersPhoto.com: **165**-3; **169**-1, 4, 6; **173**-4, 7; **175**-5; **181**-1, 5, 9, 10; **183**-2; **189**-3, 4, 5, 6, 9, 10; **191**-1, 2, 3, 14, 15, 18, 19; **193**-2, 3, 5, 6, 9; **199**-6, 12; **201**-4, 5; **203**-3; **207**-2, 4, 9, 12, 13; **209**-11; **211**-8, 9; **213**-4, 5, 8, 12, 13; **215**-4, 9; **217**-2, 8, 9; **219**-6, 8, 9, 10, 11; **221**-7; **223**-3, 8, 9, 12, 14; **225**-7, 8; **227**-2, 4; **229**-3, 5, 9, 14, 15; **231**-4, 7; **233**-8; **235**-5, 6, 8, 10; **237**-1; **239**-4, 6; **243**-2, 3, 12; **247**-1; **249**-5, 7; **251**-1, 8; **253**-3, 8; **301**-1, 7, 9; **303**-15, 23; **305**-1, 12; **307**-3; **309**-6; **311**-1, 2, 5, 11, 13, 15; **313**-8; **335**-3; **353**-7; **394**-1
Jim P. Brock: **301**-4; **311**-12; **315**-11
T. Travis Brown: **95**-2; **289**-6; **367**-2
Peter Bryant: **351**-6; **355**-11; **357**-1, 3
John Chisholm: **279**-1, 3, 6; **287**-3
Bent Christensen: **277**-4
William S. Clark: **205**-4, 5, 6, 8, 9, 10, 11; **209**-1, 3, 14
Tom Coates: **345**-2
James Cokendolpher: **333**-7, 8; **339**-12; **345**-14; **357**-10; **363**-5
Will Cook: **107**-7; **129**-2, 8; **139**-2, 3; **141**-3
Al Cornell: **213**-6, 9;
Gerald and Buff Corsi / Visuals Unlimited: **173**-3
Jay Cossey: **317**-8; **333**-10
Todd Crail: **289**-5
Alan Cressler: **155**-5; **161**-1, 5
Rob Curtis / The Early Birder: **327**-15; **333**-5; **337**-13; **339**-9; **341**-6; **343**-1, 4, 6, 7; **345**-1, 4, 5, 6, 7, 9; **347**-1, 10, 11; **349**-4, 6, 7; **351**-3; **353**-1, 2, 6, 8, 9; **355**-3, 4, 5, 9; **357**-2, 4, 6, 8; **359**-3; **361**-1; **363**-2; **365**-5
Mike Danzenbaker: **191**-9; **193**-15; **197**-12; **199**-9, 16; **203**-4, 6, 11; **229**-1, 2; **243**-9
Larry Ditto: **171**-5
Sidney W. Dunkle: **339**-4
Eric R. Eaton: **343**-3; **355**-8; **359**-1, 4, 8; **361**-2, 3, 4, 5, 6, 7, 8, 9, 10
Randy Emmitt: **313**-11; **315**-12
Arthur V. Evans: **347**-2
William Ferguson: **333**-4; **349**-11, 16; **353**-10; **365**-6
Evelyn Fitzgerald: **69**-6; **119**-7; **127**-5; **129**-1; **133**-7
Donald Flescher / Marine Biological Laboratory: **275**-3, 4; **279**-2; **281**-4, 5; **283**-1
Gerard Fuehrer / Visuals Unlimited: **171**-7
David H. Funk: **337**-9, 11, 12, 14, 15; **345**-3; **349**-14; **351**-7, 13; **353**-4; **355**-7

Lynden Gerdes @ USDA-NRCS PLANTS database: 117-7
Terry Goss: 277-1, 2, 5
Bob Gress: 165-5
Joyce Gross: 349-15
Scott Hanko: 297-6
Russell C. Hansen: 229-6
Charles Harrington / USDA Agricultural Research Service: 349-9
D. E. Herman @ USDA-NRCS PLANTS database: 123-3
R. E. Hibpshman: 275-5
Charlie Hickey: 51-3; 59-3, 4, 9; 63-7; 65-9; 81-6, 7; 93-5, 9; 109-12, 13; 119-8; 123-2; 127-2; 129-5; 133-5, 6
John Himmelman: 321-1; 327-12
Wyb Hoek / Marine Mammal Images: 183-3
Michael Huft: 143-1
Cathy and Gordon Illg: 175-2
David Illig: 339-17
Craig W. Jackson: 157-4
Courtnay Janiak: 387-2, 3
Bill Johnson: 347-5; 353-11; 357-9; 359-6
Kevin T. Karlson: 191-17; 193-17; 195-10; 197-11; 199-17; 203-2; 209-6, 9; 217-6; 225-4; 227-10; 231-1; 233-2, 5; 237-3; 245-10; 249-12; 251-7, 9, 10
Russ Kerr: 203-10; 209-10
George O. Krizek: 315-10
Greg W. Lasley: 189-8
Tom and Pat Leeson: 165-4, 6; 169-2, 3, 7; 171-1; 173-5, 8; 175-1, 3, 4
Stephen Luk: 285-2
Bruce Mactavish: 203-1
Malcolm M. Manners: 135-2
Steve Maslowski / Visuals Unlimited: 167-5; 171-3
Felicia McCaulley: 287-1
Joe McDonald / Visuals Unlimited: 167-4; 173-1
Robin McLeod: 345-8
Charles W. Melton: 191-8
Richard Migneault: 71-7, 8
Jeffrey Miller: 317-3, 4; 329-6
Robert H. Mohlenbrock @ USDA-NRCS PLANTS database: 55-5; 85-4, 8; 109-11; 115-5; 121-4, 6; 144-2
C. Allan Morgan: 183-1
Dan Mullen: 53-4; 69-8; 123-4; 125-8
Tom Murray: 159-1, 2; 333-12; 339-3, 13; 349-10; 353-5; 363-6; 365-7, 9, 10, 11; 367-3, 7
Phil Myers: 333-9
Dave Neely: 281-3; 283-5; 289-1, 4; 295-2
Alan G. Nelson: 169-5
Alan G. Nelson / Root Resources: 253-7
Blair Nikula: 337-2
North Dakota state office @ USDA-NRCS PLANTS database: 131-5
John Roger Palmour: 127-7
James F. Parnell: 165-2; 171-6
Herbert A. Pase III / ForestryImages.org: 355-1
Michael Patrikeev: 171-4; 179-4, 6
Amanda M. Pippen: 277-3
Jeffrey S. Pippen / www.duke.edu/~jspippen/nature.htm: 73-4, 5; 77-2, 4; 91-2, 3, 6; 117-1; 137-5; 157-5, 6; 359-9
Betty Randall: 171-8
Don Roberson: 203-7
Eda Rogers: 183-4
Fritz Rohde: 283-4; 287-7
Michael C. Rosenstein: 275-2
Edward S. Ross: 347-4
Jane Ruffin: 307-2, 8, 9; 315-15
Eli Sagor: 133-2, 3
Andrée Reno Sanborn: 63-5; 79-12; 81-3, 4; 121-13; 129-3; 157-1, 7, 8; 159-3, 5; 257-3, 8; 267-4, 5, 6
Nick Scobel: 257-1, 2; 259-2; 261-1, 2, 4; 263-8, 9; 265-5; 267-7; 271-5
Lynn Scott: 323-12; 329-7
Sealord Photography: 275-1; 285-4, 5; 287-5; 293-7
John Shaw: 303-9; 305-13; 307-6; 309-3; 311-7; 313-12, 13; 315-6, 7
Ann and Rob Simpson: 165-1; 333-3
Arnold Small: 229-10
Brian E. Small: 189-11; 191-5, 6, 10, 11, 16; 193-1, 11, 12, 14; 195-9; 197-7; 199-11; 201-10; 205-16; 207-1, 8; 209-12, 13; 211-1; 213-7; 217-7, 10; 219-4, 7; 221-5, 6, 11, 12; 223-6; 225-10; 227-1, 7, 9; 233-9; 235-2; 237-10; 243-11; 247-8, 13, 14, 17; 251-3, 5, 14; 253-12
Eric H. Snyder: 12-1; 13-1, 2; 14-1, 2, 3; 15-1, 2, 3; 16-1, 2; 17-1, 2, 3, 4, 5
John Sohlden / Visuals Unlimited: 179-1
John Sorensen: 203-5; 209-8
Bill Stark: 337-10

Kamal Al Sultan / AmericanLegacy-Fishing.com: 285-3
Pat and Clay Sutton: 307-12
William Tanneberger: 77-6, 7; 89-5; 113-6; 123-5, 6; 135-6, 7; 141-6; 155-6
Dave Taylor / Senses of Wildness Inc.: 287-8; 293-3
William C. Taylor @ USDA-NRCS PLANTS database: 93-2
Nate Tessler: 283-2, 3; 287-6; 289-2, 8; 291-2, 6; 293-1, 2; 297-5
Uland Thomas (NANFA): 291-1; 295-1; 297-2
Merlin D. Tuttle / Bat Conservation International: 181-6
John and Gloria Tveten: 167-1; 177-1, 2, 3, 5, 8; 181-4; 301-2; 303-1, 6; 305-4, 7; 307-11; 309-5, 7; 313-1, 2; 315-4; 317-2, 11, 12, 14, 17; 319-1, 2, 8, 14; 327-8; 329-10; 333-6; 339-11; 343-5, 9; 351-1, 8, 10; 355-6; 359-12
Tom J. Ulrich: 177-7
R. W. Van Devender: 177-4; 179-2, 3
Per Verdonk: 73-6; 75-8; 77-5; 83-2; 85-6; 89-9; 95-5; 131-6; 133-1; 137-4; 139-8
Tom Vezo: 167-2; 171-2; 175-6; 193-16, 18; 199-3; 201-6; 209-7; 213-10; 221-2; 223-2; 225-6; 229-7; 235-1, 3; 237-2; 239-8; 245-8, 12; 247-2, 7; 249-9; 251-13
Robyn Waayers: 339-1; 347-7
Matt Wallace and Lew Deitz: 343-10
Richard Walters / Visuals Unlimited: 347-3
Nancy M. Wells / Visuals Unlimited: 167-6
Michael Wigle: 337-5, 6, 7
Alex Wild: 355-10; 357-12
Bob Wilson / Visuals Unlimited: 319-15
Kenneth Paul Wray III: 44-1; 261-3; 263-6, 7; 265-1, 2, 3, 4; 267-1, 2; 269-3, 4, 6, 7; 271-3; 367-1
Brian J. Zimmerman: 291-3, 4, 5, 7; 293-4, 5, 6; 295-3, 5, 6, 7; 297-3
Dale and Marian Zimmerman: 193-13; 205-15, 17; 209-2, 4, 5, 15; 231-3; 253-10, 14

INDEX TO ENGLISH NAMES

While the one-page index on the last page will direct you to some of the most popular entries, this index includes all species and major subjects covered in the guide. In seeking entries here, look under group names. For example, to look up Paper Birch, start by looking under B (for "Birch, Paper"), not under P for Paper. With only a few exceptions, we have not indexed scientific names here, but we have tried to include alternate and "unofficial" English names that are in popular usage.

QUICK INDEX: KAUFMAN FIELD GUIDE TO NATURE OF NEW ENGLAND

(For complete listings, see the full index beginning on p. 405)